WHITE-COLLAR AND CORPORATE CRIME

WHITE-COLLAR AND CORPORATE CRIME

A Documentary and Reference Guide

GILBERT GEIS

Documentary and Reference Guides

GREENWOOD

AN IMPRINT OF ABC-CLIO, LLC
Santa Barbara, California • Denver, Colorado • Oxford, England

Library of Congress Cataloging-in-Publication Data

Geis, Gilbert.
   White-collar and corporate crime : a documentary and reference guide / Gilbert Geis.
      p. cm. — (Documentary and reference guides)
   Includes bibliographical references and index.
   ISBN 978–0–313–38054–9 (hard copy : alk. paper) — ISBN 978–0–313–38055–6 (ebook)
1. White collar crimes. 2. Commercial crimes. I. Title.
HV6768.G452   2011
364.16′8—dc23   2011019659

ISBN: 978–0–313–38054–9
EISBN: 978–0–313–38055–6

15 14 13 12 11   1 2 3 4 5

This book is also available on the World Wide Web as an eBook.
Visit www.abc-clio.com for details.

Greenwood
An Imprint of ABC-CLIO, LLC

ABC-CLIO, LLC
130 Cremona Drive, P.O. Box 1911
Santa Barbara, California 93116-1911

This book is printed on acid-free paper ∞

Manufactured in the United States of America

In loving memory of Robley Elizabeth Geis

CONTENTS

ACKNOWLEDGMENTS

Numerous persons in direct and indirect ways have been crucial to the work that went into the present book and much of my earlier work on the subject of white-collar and corporate crime and various other subjects.

Most importantly, there is my family which has made my life, personal and professional, quite gratifying. I mention only those members who were close in terms of this particular book or when I was writing it, but I remain deeply indebted to all of them.

I am grateful to Arnie Binder, John and Val Braithwaite, Craig Morris, Mickey Braswell, Chris and Nora Brown, Ivan and Lesley Bunn, Frank Cullen, Joe DiMento, Mary Dodge, David Friedrichs, Tina Fischer, Bill Frohlich, Ellen Geis and Andy Freeman, John Gill, Colin Goff, Trish Goforth, Peter Grabosky, Patrick Huston, Ted and Chris Huston, Paul Jesilow, Jeanette LaVie, Mike Levi, Don Managuale, Sanjoy Mazumdar, Claire McLean, Bob Meier, Shawn and Dea Movery, Jeanie Oliver and Dave Hudson, Don and Jo-Ellen Parker, Henry Pontell, Don Paolli, David Shichor, Janet Temko, Kathleen Tuttle, Joe Wells, Bobby and Renee Wolff, and Richard Wright. There are numerous others who, if not on the list, I hope realize that I appreciate them, and it is only space constraints and my carelessness which led to them not being mentioned by name.

The Selected References and Bibliography segment was the result of diligent work by Kitty Calavita, Mary Dodge, Rodney Huff, and Laura Valcore.

Samdy Towers was wonderful to work with as an editor at ABC-CLIO; thoughtful, innovative, meticulous, and intelligent: what more could a writer ask? Later two very competent persons—Sakthi Priyah and Arathi Pillai—supervised my copy editing and I am grateful for their good work. Pictures were diligently gathered up by Nina Gomez and permissions secured by Erin Ryan. I thank them both very much.

READER'S GUIDE TO RELATED DOCUMENTS AND SIDEBARS

PREFACE

Crimes, misdeeds, and self-serving actions by business executives and the corporate enterprises that employ them underlay the severe meltdown of the global economic marketplace that got under way in the last third of the first decade of the current century. Families were forced from their homes in the United States because they had been talked into so-called subprime loans by slick salesmen who were well aware that their customers would not be able to make the payments on the homes they had yearned for if the real estate bubble burst, as it most assuredly sooner or later would. Loan applications were faked—bus drivers were reported to be earning $200,000 a year. Down payments were no longer required, and low or nonexistent interest rates were offered without the offsetting information that in two or five or some other number of years down the road, the interest rate would zoom up to a level well beyond the ability of the purchaser to handle it.

The crisis metastasized. Unemployment rose steeply, further undercutting the possibility that recipients of subprime loans could meet their mortgage payments. Investment banks whose portfolios were stuffed with millions, sometimes trillions, of dollars' worth of risky subprime mortgages found themselves unable to raise enough capital to meet increasing customer demands to cash in on their stock holdings as they came to realize that the institutions were in serious financial trouble. The American crisis, the worst economic catastrophe since the Great Depression of 1929, quickly engulfed markets throughout the world. In many countries these foreign institutions had purchased huge amounts of the American housing debts, lured by incorrect assessments of the risk factors involved and the allure of high returns.

The economic catastrophe brought to the foreground a theme that has resonated throughout the whole of recorded history: that persons and business entities with power will at times take advantage of lax or nonexistent regulatory regimes to play fast and loose with ethical standards and with the demands of the criminal law. In ancient Greece, seven centuries before the beginning of the current calendar, Solon, a leading statesman and lawgiver, issued edicts that condemned middlemen, who were seen as siphoning off profits that should go entirely to the person who produced the product. Solon's philosophy on morality and the marketplace is reflected in a poem that he wrote:

> Often the wicked prosper, while the righteous starve;
> Yet I would never exchange my fate for theirs.
> My virtue for their gold. For mine endures,
> While riches change their owner every day.

Roman law decreed that *dardanarii*—those who engaged in conspiring to raise the price of grain, oil, bread, meat, or salt by the detention of cargo ships to keep their goods from reaching the marketplace; the hiding away of grain and other foods; and similar practices—were to be fined. Roman law also focused on the honesty of magistrates, who were charged with supervision of marketplace trading; women and slaves, who did the shopping, were encouraged to provide the authorities with evidence of wrongdoing by these officials.

Roman law foreshadowed today's suspicion of corporations. According to Edward Gibbon, in his time the foremost historian of the empire, Roman rulers "viewed with the utmost jealousy and distrust any association among their subjects, and the privileges of public corporations, though formed for the most harmless or beneficial purposes, were bestowed with a very sparing hand."

Warnings and actions against business exploitation of the public were common in ancient Judeo-Christian societies. As Herbert Kelman and V. Lee Hamilton observe, the Jewish prophets "bitterly attacked the luxurious lifestyles of the elite, their corruption, hypocrisy, immorality, injustice, and oppression of the poor." In the biblical Apocrypha, we hear the prophet Micah proclaim that "a merchant shall hardly keep himself from doing wrong; and an huckster shall not be freed from sin. . . . As a nail sticketh fast between the joinings of the stones, sin doth stick close between buying and selling." St. John Chrysostom, the Greek archbishop of Constantinople, echoed this view. "*Homo mercator vix aut nunquam potest Deo*" [A man who is a merchant can seldom please God], he wrote, and added: "Therefore, no Christian ought to be a merchant, or if he will be one, he should be cast from the church of God." The harsh judgment led one writer to observe that in those times men could hardly imagine the merchant's strongbox without picturing the devil squatting on its lid.

The same theme has been enunciated through the ages. Pope Pius XI in 1931 wrote: "The worst injustices and frauds take place beneath the common name of a corporate firm." Jewish theology sums up the importance of impeccable commercial ethics, declaring that the first question a person would be asked in the hereafter during judgment was: "Hast thou been honest in business?" A sixteenth-century rabbi compared money to fire in that one could not do without it, yet should not get too close to it.

Dante, perhaps the greatest literary figure of the Middle Ages, in his *Divine Comedy* declared fraud to be the worst vice. In Dante's blueprint of Hell, white-collar criminals occupy the nethermost position. He wrote:

Fraud more displeases God
And therefore the fraudulent
Are the lower, and more pain
Assails them

The behaviors being condemned received a verbal designation in 1939 when Edwin H. Sutherland, a sociology professor at Indiana University, labeled them as "white-collar crime." The term now has worldwide recognition although it no longer accurately characterizes the people that Sutherland was discussing. Business executives, professionals such as doctors and lawyers, and high-level politicians today often dress in informal outfits without white collars, and women, who increasingly are moving into the uppermost echelons of the world of work, can hardly be identified uniformly as individuals whose attire is marked by a white collar.

The idea of corporate crime as distinctive from wrongdoing by individuals also has a long history. The concept first was employed to distinguish harmful and irresponsible acts by monastic groups. In the American colonial times, municipalities and other entities were held responsible for failures to maintain bridges and roadways. For example, in 1834 the city of Albany, New York, was indicted criminally for failure to clean the basin of the Hudson River, which was alleged to have become choked with mud, rubbish, and the dead carcasses of animals.

Today, when they do not offer vivid pictures of war dead, the front pages of daily newspapers are likely to show photographs of corporate executives adorned in expensive business suits and state-of-the-art handcuffs, being taken into custody or led into a criminal court by government agents wearing orange jackets with large letters on the back that say POLICE. This development differs dramatically from earlier days when news that a business leader had been charged with a criminal act (unless it involved something scandalous like a sex murder) was buried in the business sections of newspapers.

Less attention, however, inevitably comes to be focused on wrongdoing that is charged against a corporate entity like Enron or Adelphia or WorldCom than against an individual culprit, because readers and listeners, the lifeblood of the media, are much less interested in the impersonal than the personal, and corporations cannot be displayed with any visual intensity on the evening television news broadcast, which typically will have to settle for a brief glimpse of the corporate headquarters with an identifying sign on its building.

On the other hand, if a corporation's glaring wrongdoing can be visually portrayed in television footage and newspaper photographs, the media can prove to be highly attentive. The recent explosion of an oil rig in the Gulf of Mexico resulted in vivid images of the fire blast and the oil pouring forth into the gulf. Pictures of oil-soaked animals, unable to navigate, added to the intensity of public condemnation of British Petroleum. The U.S. Department of Justice was moved to implement an investigation to determine if BP or other involved corporations should be prosecuted criminally, for negligence or other violations of penal statutes. Ultimately, the Department decided that there were no compelling grounds for a criminal prosecution.

Legally, in British and American law—and increasingly in world legal systems—a corporation may be tried for a criminal act committed on its behalf by people who work for it. Obviously, a corporation cannot be tried for crimes such as rape, but in recent years several companies have been charged with murder, most notably the Ford Motor Company for what the prosecutor alleged was its reckless negligence in the design of the Pinto automobile. In that case, the company, represented by a brigade of skilled attorneys, was acquitted on a legal technicality.

American law operates under the fictional notion that a corporation is the same as a human being in regard to its constitutional rights. This is true despite the often-repeated statement from an early English court ruling that a corporation has no soul to damn and no body to kick. Besides, a corporation, of course, unlike a human being, has no limited span of existence on this earth and no corporeal body that can be hauled into court. The only exception in American jurisprudence is that a corporation cannot use the Fifth Amendment defense that it will not supply information or respond to queries because to do so could incriminate it. This exception presumably arose because corporations do not run the risk of imprisonment or execution. Humans, for their part, can remain mute if they claim that answering questions might contribute to a finding of guilt. The prosecutor in a criminal case must prove his or her case beyond a reasonable doubt without the help of the defendant. In the United States "taking the fifth" cannot be discussed before the jury; in the United Kingdom, recent amendments have allowed prosecutors to call attention to this silence and to suggest that it ought to be considered when a verdict is debated.

The criminal liability of corporations largely grew out of a belief that they had become so powerful in the United States that it was necessary to employ the criminal law to try to restrain them. This view was echoed by many during the recent economic meltdown in the catchphrase "In America Wall Street rules Main Street." In a large organization, however, it may be difficult to pinpoint the particular culprits in the company who committed the illegal act. Besides, because of the doctrine of limited liability, shareholders in a corporation cannot lose anything beyond what they have invested in the entity. As the satirist Ambrose Bierce tellingly put it in his *The Devil's Dictionary*, the word "corporation" refers to "an ingenious device for obtaining individual profit without individual responsibility." A particular reason to go after corporations criminally is that they obviously have much greater resources than their executives and employees, and these can be commandeered by the courts to help to reimburse victims. Besides, a criminal conviction carries a strong element of shame that is not present in regard to civil proceedings. But this often insulates individual businesspeople from the consequences of their wrongdoing, because the fines levied against the business firm come out of the pockets of the firm's stockholders while the actual perpetrators escape penalties.

These and similar matters fall under the heading of white-collar and corporate crime, and their ingredients will be thoroughly documented and analyzed in the pages that follow. The subject matter often is mind-boggling in terms of the enormous sums involved, amounts that far overshadow the losses to victims of traditional street crimes such as burglary and robbery. White-collar and corporate crimes also carry in their wake subtle undesirable consequences. Street crimes may unite a society against the offenders, but white-collar and corporate crimes can undermine the social fabric and create a distrust of a nation's leaders. This is reflected in the political realm in the continuing stories of sexual and financial scandals committed by elected officials and the resultant low voter turnout at the polls. "I don't ever vote," says one cynic. "It only encourages them."

The aim of this book is to provide documentary material and leads to other writings that deal with the essential elements and notable instances of white-collar and corporate crime. This information is accompanied by interpretative and analytical commentary so that a reader can examine sources and evaluate analyses in order to come to an informed opinion on the issue being considered. Each document in this book will begin with a lead-in that sets the stage for the document itself and includes the following information: (1) a statement that places the document in the context that gave rise to it; (2) the date of its creation; (3) the source of the document; and (4) a statement of its significance. After that, there is the document itself. A section on relevant material bearing on the matter contained in the document invites the interested reader to plunge more deeply into the issue raised. Most sections also include sidebars that present vignettes or other information that adds human interest details to the matter under review.

The documents, sidebars, analyses, further readings, and other contents in each of the chapters contained in this collection are intended to convey the extreme importance of a subject that often is not given the attention that it deserves. The manner in which persons with power act often determines the tone of the moral and ethical behavior that pervades a social system. If the leaders are corrupt and crooked, those in lesser positions are very likely to conclude that that behavior is a model to be duplicated by those who want to get ahead, to obtain the golden goodies that wealth accumulated by criminal acts can purchase.

It is important for the reader to know the ideology that I have brought to the absorbing task of accumulating the more than 135,000 words that constitute this volume. I do not categorically condemn all lawbreaking—by either white-collar violators or street offenders. There are some laws that I believe ought not to be obeyed, at least if you are courageous enough to risk the consequences of your rebellion. The most obvious recent example concerns the sanctioned use of waterboarding and other forms of torture of captives incarcerated in the course of the war on terrorism. It was wrong, and arguably those who did it should have been prosecuted and those who were asked to do it should have refused. More immediately, in regard to white-collar crime I am suspicious of strict liability statutes, that is, laws that allow no defense to those deemed responsible for actions by others, such as a corporate executive who can be held criminally liable if one of his or her subordinates bribes a supplier or extorts a kickback. On the other hand, I have little sympathy with people in positions of power who knowingly and recklessly cheat and endanger others by their illegal actions. Nor do I necessarily overlook acts that are harmful but are not forbidden by criminal law, often because those who fashion the criminal law are the same persons who are engaging in the harmful acts. An obvious example can be found in the failure of the criminal law to forbid extravagant campaign contributions. Such contributions obviously are a form of bribery; that is, those who give them expect to get something back, and often do, from the politicians to whom they donated.

But those same politicians are the ones who decree how the statute books define the crime of bribery. Equally, whether a harmful act is dealt with by a criminal court or by a regulatory agency can, I believe, be ignored and instead attention be focused on the nature of the act itself, whether it is harmful behavior or merely a violation of a minor procedural stipulation.

The 13 chapters that constitute the body of this volume contain a mixture of various sources, including an occasional excerpt from a novel or a satirical newspaper column. Most, however, are official documents promulgated by legislative bodies or courts. I begin by looking at the origin of the designation "white-collar crime" and some of the considerations involved in various definitions of the term. Chapter 2 discusses the men who were called Robber Barons, unscrupulous buccaneers who largely made their fortune by corrupt actions associated with the building of railroads. The following chapter discusses the muckrakers who, like investigative reporters today, delved into the misdeeds of the early financiers.

These historical inquiries are followed by consideration of various forms of white-collar and corporate crime. Chapter 4 takes up antitrust violations, and is followed by a look at major scandals during the period from 1877 to 1993, including the Crédit Mobilier plot; the infamous scheme perpetrated by Charles Ponzi; the crimes of Ivar Kreuger, Richards Whitney, and Robert Vesco; and the looting that went on in the savings and loan industry. Insider trading and related crimes, including those committed by Ivan Boesky, Michael Milken, and Martha Stewart, make up chapter 6, while crimes by government officials and those by professionals, such as doctors and lawyers, are considered in chapters 7 and 8.

Environmental offenses, particularly the Love Canal disaster and the *Exxon Valdez* oil spill, constitute the subject matter in chapter 9, while the Enron and Arthur Andersen cases, among similar others, provide the material for chapter 10. Bernard Madoff and other operators of Ponzi schemes are reviewed in the following chapter. Then I discuss details of the 2008 economic meltdown, and end with a look at some suggested remedies and at details of the complex financial reform measure passed by the Congress in 2010.

NOTES

Quoted sources in this Preface are Plutarch, "Solon," in *The Rise and Fall of Athens: Nine Greek Lives*, translated by Ian Scott Kilver (Baltimore: Penguin, 1960), p. 45. The Gibbon quote appears in Lionel Trilling, *Matthew Arnold* (New York: Columbia University Press, 1949), p. 55. The views of the Jewish prophets are noted in Herbert C. Kelman and V. Lee Hamilton, *Crimes of Obedience: Toward a Social Psychology of Authority and Responsibility* (New Haven, CT: Yale University Press, 1989), p. 62. The statement of St John Chryostom is found in Reinhard Zimmermann, *The Law of Obligations: Roman Foundations of the Civilian Tradition* (Cape Town, South Africa: Juta, 1990, p. 170); and the comment about the devil perched on mercantile strongboxes is from Henri Pirenne, *A History of Europe*, translated by Bernard Miall (Garden City, NY: Doubleday, 1958), vol. III, p. 229. Pope Pius XI's statement appears in his *Quadragesisimo Anno* [After Forty Years] (Ann Arbor, MI: Pieran Press, 1931), para. 2. The question to be put to Jews on entering the hereafter is found in Edward Zipperstein, *Business Ethics in Jewish Law* (New York: KTAV, 1981), p. 73. The Dante quotation is from Dante Allighieri, *Inferno*, translated by Charles S. Singleton (London: Routledge & Kegan Paul, 1970), canto II, lines 25–28, p. 11.

1

WHAT IS WHITE-COLLAR AND CORPORATE CRIME?

INTRODUCTION

On first thought, it might appear that there need be little concern with establishing the precise nature of what is meant by white-collar and corporate crime, the subjects of this volume. But few, if any, terms in the realm of criminal activity have evoked more definitional disagreements than these concepts. Perhaps the most common view is that, if nothing else, white-collar and corporate crime involve events that are committed by a pen or computer rather than at the point of a revolver or knife.

Some have argued that white-collar crime is marked by the absence of violence. But on closer scrutiny, that distinction does not hold up. Doctors often maim patients by negligent acts—the wrong foot is amputated; a miscalculated drug dosage is administered—and miners are suffocated in a collapsed mine shaft when explosions that better foresight might have prevented take place.

The most controversial consideration in regard to the proper way to determine what is and what is not white-collar crime concerns the status of the perpetrator, the position he or she holds, and the relationship between these considerations and the behavior being considered. It is evident that a bank president who sells his large holding of stock in his company when he learns that it is going to take a severe financial hit during the following month—a matter not yet known to the public—is committing the white-collar crime of insider trading. But how about the elevator operator who overhears two indiscreet executives discussing an impending financial takeover and not only immediately buys shares in those companies but also tells a millionaire who subsequently rides the elevator about the forthcoming merger? Should the elevator operator be considered a white-collar criminal? How about the millionaire who invests heavily on the basis of this tip?

Persons studying and writing about white-collar crime have taken differing views on such definitional matters. One position is that the only reasonable way to label persons or entities as white-collar offenders is to await the verdict of a judge or jury.

But what about the person who by reasonable standards appears to be guilty but has hired an eminently talented lawyer who, in underworld language, is successful in enabling him or her to beat the rap.

Corporate crime by and large has avoided these semantic and definitional quagmires, although controversy persists regarding, first, whether a criminal offense ought to be charged against a nonhuman that is not capable of acting without the behavior of real persons. In Japan, a corporation cannot be held criminally liable unless a person also is convicted. Second, there is the question whether civil litigation ought to be grouped with criminal white-collar and corporate crime data since the civil approach often is primarily an expedient tactic for dealing with a situation that equally well could have been handled in a criminal court.

This chapter explores aspects of the definitional dilemma, setting the stage by reproducing parts of the speech by sociologist Edwin H. Sutherland that introduced the term "white-collar crime" to an academic and, ultimately, a public audience. Media reaction to Sutherland's talk is examined, as well as the views of those who favor reformulating Sutherland's approach, as exemplified in the work of a research team based at the Yale Law School.

Consideration is then accorded to the doctrine of corporate criminal liability, followed by a review of the Ford Pinto case in which a company was charged with manslaughter. The chapter concludes with an examination of the Supreme Court's 2010 decision in *Citizens United v. FEP*, which upheld the principle that corporations must be guaranteed constitutional protections given to humans.

White-Collar Crime Violates Trust and Therefore Creates Distrust

- **Document:** Excerpts from the address by 56-year-old Professor Edwin H. Sutherland of Indiana University to the joint meeting of the American Sociological Society and the American Economic Association. Sutherland was the president of the sociological organization.
- **Date:** December 29, 1939.
- **Where:** The two scholarly organizations were holding their annual meetings at the Benjamin Franklin Hotel at Ninth and Chestnut Streets in downtown Philadelphia. Room rates at the hotel ran from $3.50 to $6.00 for a night's lodging.
- **Significance:** The exploitative practices by persons with power had been documented and deplored throughout human history, but Sutherland's pioneering contribution was to place the subject front and center in the academic world and to highlight a term—"white-collar crime"—that would call public, legal, and academic attention to forms of behavior by powerful people that tore at the integrity of the society.

DOCUMENT 1.1

This paper is . . . a comparison of crime in the upper or white-collar class, composed of respectable or at least respected business and professional men, and crime in the lower class, composed of persons of low socioeconomic status.

The thesis of this paper is that . . . crime is not closely associated with poverty, and that an adequate explanation of crime must proceed along different lines. The conventional explanations are invalid principally because they are derived from biased samples. . . . that have not included vast areas of criminal behavior of persons not in the lower class. One of these neglected areas is the criminal behavior of business and professional men ...

White-collar criminality in business is expressed most frequently in the form of misrepresentation in financial statements of corporations, manipulation in the stock exchange, commercial bribery, bribery of public officials directly or indirectly in order to secure favorable contracts and legislation, misrepresentation in advertising, and salesmanship, embezzlement and misapplication of funds, short weights and measures, and dishonest grading of commodities, tax frauds, misapplication of funds in receiverships and bankruptcies. These and many others are found in abundance in the business world.

In the medical profession ... are found illegal sale of alcohol and narcotics, abortion [illegal at the time], illegal services to underworld criminals, fraudulent reports and testimony in accident cases, extreme cases of unnecessary treatment, fake specialists, restriction of competition, and fee-splitting. Fee-splitting is a violation of specific laws in many states and a violation of the conditions of admission to the practice of medicine in all ... It has been reported that two-thirds of the surgeons in New York City split fees. ...

These varied types of white-collar crime in business and the professions consist principally of violation of delegated or implied trust, and many of them can be reduced to two categories: misrepresentation of asset values and duplicity in the manipulation of power. The first is approximately the same as fraud or swindling and the second is similar to the double-cross.

The latter is illustrated by the corporation director who, acting on inside information, purchases land which the corporation will need and sells it at a fantastic profit to the corporation. The principle of this duplicity is that the offender holds two antagonistic positions; one of them is a position of trust which is violated, generally by misapplication of funds, in the interest of the other position. A football coach permitted to referee a game in which his own team was playing would illustrate this antagonism of positions ...

The financial cost of white-collar crime is probably several times as great as the financial cost of all crimes which are customarily included as the "crime problem." An officer of a chain grocery store in one year embezzled $600,000 which was six times as much as the annual losses from five hundred burglaries and robberies of the stores in the chain ...

The financial loss from white-collar crime, great as it is, is less important than the damage to social relations. White-collar crime violates trust and therefore creates distrust, which lowers social morale and produces social disorganization on a large scale. Other crimes have relatively little effect on social institutions or social organization ...

The Federal Trade Commission made several automobile companies to stop advertising their interest rate on installment purchases as 6 percent, since it was actually 11½ percent. Also, it filed complaints against *Good Housekeeping* ... charging that its seal led the public to believe that all products bearing those seals had been tested in their laboratories, which was contrary to fact. Each of these involves a charge of dishonesty which might have been tried in a criminal court as fraud ...

White-collar criminals are segregated administratively from other criminals, and largely as a consequence of this are not regarded as real criminals by themselves, by the general public, or by the criminologists.

The difference in the implementation of the criminal law is due chiefly to the disparity in the social position of the . . . offenders. Judge Woodward, in imposing sentence upon the officials of H. O. Stone and Company [a bankrupt real estate firm in Chicago], who had been convicted in 1933 of the use of the mails to defraud, said to them, "You are men of affairs, of experience, of refinement and culture, of excellent reputation in the business and social world." That statement might be used as a general characterization of white-collar criminals, for they are oriented basically to legitimate and respectable careers. Because of their social status they have a loud voice in determining what goes into the statutes and how the criminal law as it affects them is implemented . . .

A statement made by Daniel Drew [a speculator in railroad stocks] describes the criminal law with some accuracy: "Law is like a cobweb; it is made for flies and the smaller kinds of insects, so to speak, but lets the big bumblebees break through. When technicalities of the law stood in my way, I have always been able to brush them aside as easy as anything."

Source: Edwin H. Sutherland, "White-Collar Criminality," *American Sociological Review* 5, no. 1 (February 1940): 1–12.

ANALYSIS

Edwin Hardin Sutherland was a professor of sociology and chair of the department at Indiana University when he forcefully brought the concept of white-collar crime to the attention of his colleagues in 1939. He derided the then-popular explanations of crime—for example, poverty, immigration, Freudian complexes, mental retardation or illness, and broken homes—and insisted that white-collar and corporate crime were best understood as the result of what persons learned as they absorbed the values of their associates. Criminal behavior would result when indoctrination by learning experiences antagonistic to law-abiding behavior outweighed those favoring conformity to the law. A *New Yorker* cartoon years later would lampoon the values of some corporate entities when it depicted a business executive telling an underling, "Honesty is the best policy. It's just not our policy."

Sutherland was born in the Nebraska heartland, where he was exposed to the populist ideas that were current in the state, ideas that saw big business, especially the railroads, as enemies of the predominantly rural faming population. Sutherland's father was a prominent Baptist minister who became president of Grand Island College, where Sutherland received his bachelor's degree. Sutherland's doctorate was earned at the University of Chicago, which boasted the most prominent department of sociology in the country.

In his initial pronouncement, Sutherland indicated, as Document 1.1 shows, that white-collar crime was "crime in the upper or white-collar class, composed of respectable or at least respected business and professional men." Today's writers would most certainly add "and women" to the end of the sentence, and it is clear that the definition offered was not very precise in regard to exactly what kinds of behavior and acts should be considered as constituting white-collar crime. A close reading of this stab at a proper definition indicates the scorn Sutherland possessed for the well-to-do crooks he was writing about: the phrase "respectable or at least respected" has a strong note of sarcasm.

Nine years after his presidential address, Sutherland in a speech before students at DePauw University in Indiana sought to clarify somewhat his subject matter: "I have used the term white-collar criminal to refer to a person in the upper socioeconomic class who violates the law designed to regulate his occupation . . . The term is used more generally to refer to the wage-earning class which wears good clothes at work, such as clerks in stores." The disconnect between a store clerk and a person in the upper socioeconomic class illustrates the imprecision with which Sutherland portrayed the exact nature of his subject matter.

A year later in his classic monograph, *White Collar Crime*, the first portion of this earlier definition set out in the paragraph above was retained, but the sentence about the wage-earning class and its attire had been cut. Nonetheless, in the book's appendix Sutherland included anecdotal material that had been provided by his students about their sales experience in such enterprises as shoe stores. He also included reports of employee theft and watch and auto repair frauds. Illustrating his relative indifference to definitional nicety, Sutherland buried the characterization of his subject matter in a footnote in which he wrote that "white collar is used here to refer principally to business managers and executives." He did specifically exclude acts, such as murder, adultery, and intoxication, that typically were not associated with the occupational role of upper-class perpetrators, although recent, well-publicized sexual misadventures of prominent politicians often appear to involve the exercise of their power over employees that is associated with illegal sexual harassment.

A 1980 case adjudicated by the U.S. Supreme Court demonstrates one resolution of the dispute between a definition focusing consideration of white-collar crime only on persons of high socioeconomic status who violate laws associated with their work situation or one extending the concept to any person who commits a specified offense. That debate, as we shall point out in some detail later in this chapter, has preoccupied many students of white-collar crime. In the case of *Chiarella v. United States* (445 U.S. 222), Vincent Chiarella worked as a markup man for Pendrick Press, a financial printer. He was responsible for formatting the paperwork on proposed mergers and hostile corporate-takeover bids. Until very late in the process, the names of

---

DID YOU KNOW?

The Populist Platform

The foundation of Edwin Sutherland's campaign against white-collar crime lies in the platform of the populist movement. In an 1892 editorial in the party's Nebraska newspaper, the Populist Party set out what it believed were the two paramount issues facing the electorate:

1. Shall the corporations, who have so long dominated and corrupted our politics, and robbed our people through extortionist charges, be retired from power, and the people given freight rates no higher than those now in force in Iowa?
2. Shall our state offices be administered by selfish men who ignore the law, and violate their official oaths that they may enrich themselves at the expense of the taxpayers, and under whose past domination the most monstrous and shameful corruption has prevailed, or shall these offices be administered by honest men in the interest of the people?

the involved businesses were represented by either blanks or fictitious names. But Chiarella sometimes was able to figure out the actual parties, and in five instances he purchased stocks in them. When the deals came through, he profited by slightly more than $30,000 over a period of 14 months.

The Securities and Exchange Commission (SEC) charged Chiarella with insider trading, and he was sentenced to forfeit his profits and serve a one-year prison term. The Supreme Court, however, in a 6–3 decision, reversed the conviction on the ground that Chiarella was not a corporate insider and therefore was not obliged to restrain from using confidential information without publicly disclosing that information; as a result, the Court concluded that he had not breached a specific fiduciary duty. Presumably, Sutherland would have agreed and maintained that Chiarella should not be considered a white-collar criminal.

The best subsequent formulation that captures the essence of Sutherland's definition has been offered by Albert Reiss and Albert Biderman: "White-collar violations are those violations of the law to which penalties are attached that involve the use of a violator's position of significant power, influence, or trust in the legitimate economic or political institutional order for the purpose of illegal gain, or to commit an illegal act for personal or organizational gain." Readers should note the omission of the word "crime" in the definition, and some might balk at the uncertain word "significant," which inevitably raises the question of how significant must an act be in order to qualify as "significant."

DID YOU KNOW?

The Woodward Connection

Undoubtedly most, if not all, readers of Document 1.1 unsuspectingly passed over one obscure item in the Sutherland presidential address that in time would become associated with what likely is the most notorious white-collar crime in the history of the United States. The reference in Sutherland's talk is to Judge Woodward and his comments in a case involving the H. O. Stone real estate company, an Illinois business.

Judge Woodward was Alfred E. Woodward, a lawyer living in Wheaton, Illinois. He had attended Oberlin College on an athletic scholarship, and in his senior year was captain of the football team. After receiving a law degree at Northwestern, Woodward entered the Navy, rising to the rank of lieutenant junior grade. In 1970, he gained a seat as a judge in the state's eighteenth district, embracing DuPage County, which is part of the Chicago metropolitan area, and from 1973 to 1975 he was chief judge of the court, before beginning a 17-year term as a judge on the Illinois second district appellate court.

Judge Woodward's children included Robert Woodward, the *Washington Post* reporter who, with Carl Bernstein, was largely responsible for the revelations that implicated President Richard Nixon in the burglary of the Democratic National Committee headquarters in the Watergate building complex in Washington, D.C., on June 17, 1972. Five burglars were caught red-handed. The trail led back the president, who tried to cover up his involvement, a tactic that backfired when it was discovered that he had made incriminating tapes of Oval Office conversations. The work of Woodward and Bernstein was featured in the motion picture *All the President's Men*, starring Robert Redford and Dustin Hoffman. Several of Nixon's aides were given prison terms, including Attorney General John Mitchell, and the president resigned in 1974 while facing an imminent threat of impeachment.

FURTHER READINGS

Friedrichs, David. (1992). "White-Collar Crime and the Definitional Quagmire: Provisional Solution." *Journal of Human Justice* 32:5–21.

Geis, Gilbert. (1991). "White-Collar Crime: What Is It?" In Kip Schlegel and David Weisburd, (Eds.), *White-Collar Crime Reconsidered* (pp. 31–52). Boston: Northeastern University Press.

Geis, Gilbert, and Colin Goff. (1994). "Introduction." In Edwin H. Sutherland, *White Collar Crime: The Uncut Version* (pp. ix–xxxiii). New Haven, CT: Yale University Press.

Poveda, Tony G. (1994). *Rethinking White-Collar Crime*. Westport, CT: Praeger.

Rosoff, Stephen, Henry Pontell, and Robert Tillman. (2010). *Profit without Honor: White-Collar Crime and the Looting of America* (5th ed.). Upper Saddle River, NJ: Prentice Hall.

Savelsberg, Joachim J. (1994). *Constructing White-Collar Crime: Rationalities, Communication, Power*. Philadelphia: University of Pennsylvania Press.

Shapiro, Susan P. (1980, December). *Thinking about White Collar Crime: Matters of Conceptualization and Research*. Washington, DC: National Institute of Justice, U.S. Department of Justice.

Sutherland, Edwin H. (1941). "Crime and Business." *Annals of the American Academy of Political and Social Science* 117:112–18.

Sutherland, Edwin H. (1949). *White Collar Crime*. New York: Dryden.

The *New York Times* Reports Sutherland's Address

- **Document:** The *New York Times'* extensive coverage of Edwin H. Sutherland's presidential address appeared on the first page of what is regarded as the nation's most important newspaper. The 13-paragraph report, without the writer's byline (as was customary at the time), devoted 4 of those paragraphs at the end to other presentations at the conference with the first 9 paragraphs focusing on Sutherland's talk.
- **Date:** December 28, 1939.
- **Where:** The *New York Times* headquarters.
- **Significance:** The fact that the media accorded so much attention to the gathering of sociologists and economists is notable. Today, the media tend to ignore national meetings of scholarly groups except on occasion to caricature them as meat markets (sites where new PhDs rather frantically seek to find a job) or bastions marked by the reading of papers riddled with incomprehensible jargon or arcane statistics. The newspaper report regarding Sutherland's speech also represents a recognition of what was seen as an academic focus on an issue of great public importance.

DOCUMENT 1.2

HITS CRIMINALITY IN WHITE COLLARS

Dr. Sutherland Says the Cost Of Duplicity in High Places
Exceeds Burglary Losses

"ROBBER BARONS" OUTDONE

Special to the *New York Times*

PHILADELPHA, Dec. 27

"White-collar criminality" was sharply attacked by the retiring president of the American Sociological Society, Dr. Edwin H. Sutherland of Indiana University, in an address tonight which discarded accepted conceptions and explanations of crime . . .

Dr. Sutherland described present-day white collar criminals as "more suave and deceptive" than last century's "robber barons" and asserted that "in many periods more important crime news may be found on the financial pages of newspapers than on the front pages."

Using for his basis what he declared was the high incidence of crime in business and in the professions, Dr. Sutherland denied that crime was "closely correlated with poverty or with the psychopathic and sociopathic conditions associated with poverty."

"The conventional explanations are invalid principally because they are derived from biased samples," he said, "samples that have not included vast areas of criminal behavior of persons not in the lower class."

"Stealing Candy from a Baby"

Dr. Sutherland stated that white-collar criminality flourished at points "where powerful business and professional men come in contact with persons who are weak," and added:

"In this respect it is similar to stealing candy form a baby. Many of the crimes of the lower class, on the other hand, are committed against persons of wealth and power in the form of burglary and robbery. For that reason the laws which apply to the lower class have been implemented much more efficiently than those which apply to the upper class."

The speaker said that white-collar crime in business and the professions consisted chiefly in "violation of delegated or implied trust" and might be reduced to two categories, "misrepresentation of asset value and duplicity in the manipulation of money."

. . . "The better business bureaus and crime commissions, composed of business and professional men," he said, "attack burglary, robbery, and cheap swindles, but overlook the crimes of their own members."

Source: "HITS CRIMINALITY IN WHITE COLLARS; Dr. Sutherland Says the Cost of Duplicity in High Places Exceeds Burglary Losses 'ROBBER BARONS' OUTDONE Plan to Put Youthful Offenders Under New State Agencies Described to Economists ["]Stealing Candy From Baby" Offers Model Curb for Youth," *New York Times*, December 28, 1939, 12.

ANALYSIS

The *New York Times* report demonstrated the mass appeal of the theme that Sutherland enunciated. This usage of the term "white-collar crime" in the speech and in the newspapers foretold the very strong grasp the concept would have on the public mind. The term itself would be translated into a host of foreign languages, such as the French *crime en col blan*, the Italian *il crimine die colletti bianchi*, and the Spanish *el delito de cuello blanco*.

The *New York Times* coverage predictably has a formal tone to it. Other reports were more polemical. Under the headline, "Poverty Belittled as a Crime Factor," the *Public Ledger* in Philadelphia with much greater exuberance provided its readers with a colorful story regarding Sutherland's theme and, particularly interesting, took special note of the reaction of his audience.

The *Public-Ledger* said that Sutherland's speech was "a revolutionary approach" that offered a "withering denunciation" of acts of white-collar crime. This was a perfectly accurate portrayal that refutes Sutherland's remark early in his talk, perhaps intended to be self-protective in terms of the academic ethos of scientific neutrality, that his only aim was to reform criminology, not to lambaste businesses. The Philadelphia daily described the listeners as "an astonished audience" that heard Sutherland "figuratively heave scores of sociological textbooks into a waste basket." This too, however overstated, has a strong element of truth, at least in regard to studies of crime, because henceforward explanations seeking to be universal would have to account for the cause of lawbreaking by persons who on the face of it seemed to have no reasons to further enrich themselves by committing criminal acts. Nor were they likely to be impoverished, mentally ill, or suffering from Oedipal fixations.

FURTHER READINGS

Dershowitz, Alan M. (1961). "Increasing Community Control over Corporate Crime." *Yale Law Journal* 71:289–306.

Evans, Sandra S., and Richard J. Lundman. (1983). "Newspaper Coverage of Corporate Price-Fixing: A Replication." *Criminology* 29:529–41.

Gerber, Jurg, and James F. Short Jr. (1986). "Publicity and the Control of Corporate Behavior: The Case of Infant Formula." *Deviant Behavior* 13:325–47.

DID YOU KNOW?

Judges' Use of the Term "White-Collar Crime"

There is no offense on the statute books with the title of white-collar crime, but a host of behaviors that are outlawed by statute have come to be regarded by American judges as representative of what they believe constitutes white-collar crime. Since it is of no consequence in practice whether or not they formulate a precise definition of the behavior, judges often are fast and loose with the designation.

As one of innumerable examples of what is known as dicta—words and ideas that have no real bearing on the outcome of the case at hand—we can note the opinion of former Chief Justice Rose Bird of California in a case involving parents who sought the court's permission to have their developmentally disabled daughter sterilized. They argued that she tended to be sexually promiscuous and should not be exposed to the prospect of pregnancy. Besides, if she were sterilized, a process forbidden under California state law, she could be allowed much more freedom of movement and association that would enhance the quality of her life.

Justice Bird, in a dissenting opinion that called for prohibiting the sterilization on the ground that it undermined a woman's right to procreate, called attention to Oklahoma's Habitual Criminal Sterilization Act, which, before it was declared to be unconstitutional by the U.S. Supreme Court (*Skinner v. Oklahoma*, 316 U.S. 535, 1942), had called for the sterilization of persons convicted of three felonies involving "moral turpitude." But the statute specifically exempted revenue acts, embezzlement, and political offenses from the roster of felonies that would permit sterilization. Justice Bird, referring to the Oklahoma law, declared that it mandated sterilization "with exceptions for certain white collar crimes." The usage assumed a familiarity of readers with the term "white-collar crimes" and rather casually applied the term to behaviors that Sutherland and others arguably would not regard as belonging within its embrace. Bootlegging, for example, a revenue offense common in a dry state such as Oklahoma then was, would likely fall outside Sutherland's definition, and he varied in his position regarding embezzlement, since most white-collar crimes enriched the corporation while embezzlement was directed against the financial interest of the corporation.

Source: In the Conservatorship of Valerie N., 707 P.2d 760 (California 1985).

Mintz, Morton. (1985, November). "Why the Media Cover Up Corporate Crime." *Trial* 28, no. 11:72–75.

Randall, Donna M. (1987). "The Portrayal of Corporate Crime in Network Television Newscasts." *Journalism Quarterly* 64:150–53.

Rosoff, Stephen M. (2007). "The Role of the Mass Media in the Enron Fraud: Cause or Cure?" In Henry N. Pontell and Gilbert Geis (Eds.), *International Handbook of White-Collar and Corporate Crime* (pp. 513–22). New York: Springer.

Defining White-Collar Crime in Legal Terms

- *Document:* In the Foreword to this document, Henry S. Ruth Jr., director of the National Institute of Law Enforcement and Criminal Justice, an agency created in 1968 by the Omnibus Crime Control and Safe Streets Act following on the work of a presidential commission in 1966–67, notes that the Institute "had developed an intense concern that so-called 'white-collar crime' receives scant attention from law enforcement and the research community." Ruth added that "only recently has the public displayed an increased awareness of the vast economic and social harms caused by those who obtain money and property through illegal schemes and deceptive business practices."

  The Institute assigned Herbert Edelhertz, a University of Michigan Law School graduate, who headed the Fraud Section in the Criminal Division of the federal Department of Justice's criminal enforcement division, to examine the subject of white-collar crime and to recommend how it should be viewed and dealt with by the government agencies. The document excerpts parts of Edelhertz's report.

- *Date:* 1970.

- *Where:* The document was issued by the U.S. Government Printing Office.

- *Significance:* This document offered a counterdefinition of white-collar crime to that set forth by Edwin H. Sutherland. In particular, it advocated a focus on the violation of a considerable laundry list of statutes and advocated the abandonment of the idea that perpetrators fitting the category should be persons of high social status.

DOCUMENT 1.3

Our justified concern with common crime and organized crime should not be allowed to obscure our view of the totally destructive and costly, but less dramatic criminal activities, which are popularly called white-collar crime.

White-collar crime is covert, and not immediate in its impact. It is therefore difficult to move to the forefront of issues calling for public attention ... Yet white-collar crimes are serious, and must be investigated and prosecuted promptly. To ignore white-collar crime is to undercut the integrity of our society. To deny or postpone action is an abdication of law enforcement responsibility. . . .

Definitions of White-Collar Crime

The term "white-collar crime" is not subject to any one clear definition. Everyone believes he knows what the term means, but when definitions are compared there usually are sharp divergences as to whether one crime or another comes within the definition. It may well be that, as Humpty Dumpty said to Alice, "it means just what I choose it to mean—neither more nor less."

For the purpose of this paper, the term will be defined as *an illegal act or a series of illegal acts committed by nonphysical means and by concealment or guile, to obtain money or property, to avoid the payment or loss of money, or to obtain business or personal advantage.*

It is a definition that differs markedly from that advanced by Edwin H. Sutherland ... Sutherland's definition is far too restrictive. His view ... did not comprehend the many crimes committed outside one's occupation. Ready examples of crimes falling outside one's occupation would be personal and nonbusiness false income tax returns, fraudulent claims for social security benefits, concealing assets in personal bankruptcy, and use of large-scale buying on credit with no intention or capability to ever pay for purchases. His definition does not take into account crime as a business, such as a planned bankruptcy, or an old-fashioned "con game" operated in a business milieu. . . .

Sutherland was basically concerned with society's disparate approach to the crimes of the respectable and well-to-do on the one hand, and those of the poor and disadvantaged on the other. His definition of white-collar crime concentrated, therefore, on characterizing violators rather than violations. The definition on which this paper is based is, hopefully, a more inclusive one.

White-collar crime is democratic. It can be committed by a bank teller or the head of his institution. The offender can be a high government official with a conflict of interest. He can be a destitute beneficiary of a poverty program who is told to hire a work group and puts fictional workers on the payroll so that he can appropriate their wages. The character of the crime must be found in its modi operandi and its objectives rather than in the nature of the offenders.

It is important that in our definitions of crime we concentrate on the nature of the crime rather than on the personal characteristics or status of the criminal . . .

White-collar crime is a low visibility, high impact factor in our society. Because of the changes in the nature of our economic organization, particularly new developments in marketing, distribution, and investment, it is a fair assumption that white-collar crime has increased at a rate that exceeds population growth . . .

The social and economic costs of tax violations, self-dealing by corporate employees and bank officials, adulteration and watering of foods and drugs, charity frauds, insurance frauds, price fixing, frauds arising out of government procurement, and abuses of trust are clearly enormous even though not easily measured. . . .

The ideal scheme or plan, from the point of view of the perpetrator, is one in which the victim never learns the true nature of the blow struck. Charity frauds classically illustrate such a scheme. The takings are small for each individual, . . . and few victims have sufficient personal interest in their contributions to attempt to follow up. As a result charity frauds almost always are exposed through the curiosity of news media or the vigilance of public officials, rather than the result of investigations following victims' complaints. . . .

The following categories should serve as a helpful starting point:

(1) Crimes by persons operating on an individual, *ad hoc* basis, for personal gain in a nonbusiness context.

(2) Crimes in the course of their occupations by those operating inside business, Government, or other establishments, or in a professional capacity, in violation of their duty of loyalty and fidelity to employer or client.

(3) Crimes incidental to and in furtherance of business operations, but not the central purpose of such business operations.

(4) White-collar crime as a business, or the central activity of the business . . .

Source: Herbert Edelhertz, *The Nature, Impact and Prosecution of White-Collar Crime* (Washington, DC: National Institute of Law Enforcement and Criminal Justice, Law Enforcement Assistance Administration, U.S. Department of Justice, May 1970).

ANALYSIS

The position taken in this monograph about the proper way to define white-collar crime established the battle line between a social science and a legal approach to the subject matter. For social scientists, the law is the product of a legislative and judicial system that tends to be concerned with special interests, most notably favoring businesses and the wealthy, who contribute the money to politicians that is essential to their achievement or continuation in office. The late Senator Paul Simon of Illinois observed that the only reason that contributions by lobbyists to politicians are not regarded as criminal bribery is that politicians define what constitutes criminal bribery.

The eminent British political scientist Harold Laski wryly pinpointed the class bias in the criminal law. "The state lays down the ultimate rules of behavior," he wrote. "It lays them down, no doubt, in order that welfare may be achieved at the maximum deemed possible by those who effectively control its authority. But it is important to realize that this maximum as an end is rarely, if ever, an objective agreed upon as desirable by all members of society." As examples, Laski pointed out that slaves hardly subscribed to slave-holding laws and peasants to the roster of offenses that worked in favor of landlords.

It is obvious that Sutherland's formulation has a strong element of propaganda in terms of fingering activities of the powerful, and was rooted in the idea that public opinion and mainstream criminology represented at heart a crusade against powerless members of the underclass. Sutherland and those who followed in his footsteps saw no problem in working with a definition that focused on upper-class abuses of power. John Braithwaite, regarded by many as the most distinguished criminologist of current times, after a thorough review of the state of white-collar crime, concluded that "probably the most sensible way to proceed . . . is to stick with Sutherland's definition." Braithwaite points out that this definition at least excludes welfare cheats and credit card frauds.

Edelhertz's approach, nonetheless, offers a roster of offenders who can, if his definition is employed, self-evidently be regarded and studied as white-collar criminals. Sutherland's definition suffers from a certain degree of ambiguity—after all how high a status and how much respect need a person have to meet Sutherland's criteria? But Edelhertz's definition poses problems as well. For one thing, many persons he would regard as having committed a particular crime actually had done something else and often more serious, but a prosecutor deemed it the better strategy to try to convict them of an offense that was much easier to prove before a jury or much more likely to result in a plea negotiation. Martha Stewart, a household name in the world of elegant living, was suspected of insider trading on the stock market. But she was tried and found guilty of perjury for lying to a grand jury about her behavior with her stockbroker. Perjury was not the core offense, but it was the easiest charge by which to persuade the jury of her guilt.

Critics of Edelhertz's formulation have deemed it unnecessarily verbose with a tendency, not uncommon in legal writing, to throw in anything that might conceivably be relevant. Why, for instance, does he employ the phrase "a series of acts" when a single act is sufficient to meet the definition? Why focus on motive, which is not required to be demonstrated in an American criminal court? Why include con games? Nor is it clear where Edelhertz stood on the issue of formal criminal adjudication of an act before it should be regarded as a crime of the white-collar variety. Should a person who is apparently guilty of a specified white-collar crime but who goes free because of a technical violation by law enforcement personnel be regarded as a white-collar criminal or as an innocent party?

The fact that he excluded violent acts from his definition has been another point of contention. Offenses such as unnecessary surgery, the knowing manufacturing and marketing of unsafe pharmaceuticals and automobiles, and a failure to label poisonous materials in the workplace or to adequately protect dangerous machinery could be regarded as white-collar crimes with a strong component of violence. Miriam Saxon, for instance, in questioning the Edelhertz formulation pointed to the MER/29 case involving Richardson Merrell, a pharmaceutical corporation that knowingly sold a drug to reduce cholesterol that subjected an estimated 5,000 persons to side effects such as cataracts and, for some, permanent sight loss. The company, according to interoffice memoranda that surfaced during the pretrial discovery process, had known that the drug caused cataracts in test dogs and monkeys but concealed that information. For Saxon, the company had committed a violent white-collar crime. And lest there be any doubt that in the public imagination white-collar crime includes acts of violence, a recent full-page advertisement in the *New York Times* for Joseph Finder's novel *Company Man*, about the nefarious acts of a corporate CEO, proclaimed in one-inch-high letters: WHITE / COLLAR / CRIME ISN'T / ALWAYS BLOODLESS.

The American Bar Association largely adopted Edelhertz's definition, although it preferred the term "economic offenses" to "white-collar crimes." It modified the nonviolent element in the earlier definition in a footnote stating that nonviolence referred to the means by which the crime is committed, although granting that "the harm to the society can frequently be described as violent." It might be wondered why it was the harm to the society that interested the legal writers rather than the harm to the individual victim.

FURTHER READINGS

American Bar Association. (1971). *White Collar Crime*. Washington, DC: American Bar Association.

Braithwaite, John. (1985). "White-Collar Crime." In Ralph H. Turner and James F. Short Jr. (Eds.), *Annual Review of Sociology* (pp. 1–25). Palo Alto, CA: Annual Reviews.

Caldwell, Robert G. (1958, March). "A Reexamination of the Concept of White-Collar Crime." *Federal Probation* 22:30–36.

Finder, Joseph. (2005). *Company Man*. New York: St. Martin's Press.

Fine, Ralph Adam. (1972). *The Great Drug Deception: The Shocking Story of MER.29 and the Folks Who Gave You Thalidomide*. New York: Stein & Day.

Hill, Stuart. (Ed.). (1987). *Corporate Violence: Injury and Death for Profit*. Totowa, NJ: Rowman & Littlefield.

Saxon, Miriam. (1980). *White-Collar Crime: The Problem and the Federal Response*. Washington, DC: Congressional Research Office, Library of Congress.

Sutherland, Edwin H. (1945). "Is 'White-Collar Crime' Crime?" *American Sociological Review* 10:132–39.

Tappan, Paul W. (1947) "Who Is the Criminal?" *American Sociological Review* 12:96–102.

The Yale Law School Studies of White-Collar Crime

- *Document:* During the presidential administration of Jimmy Carter, the National Institute of Justice granted a large sum of research money to faculty members at the Yale Law School to conduct an investigation of white-collar crime, a topic that before and since has suffered from indifferent or nonexistent levels of federal research funding. The Yale group pondered a proper definition of their subject and concluded that reliance on laws offered the best prospect for productive research. They abandoned Sutherland's focus on status and the abuse of power, and embraced in their study sample violators who, they noted, largely came from the middle class of American society.
- *Date:* The research was conducted from 1982 until 1991.
- *Where:* The work was carried out by a consortium of scholars at the Yale Law School in New Haven, Connecticut.
- *Significance:* The focus on persons who had violated specific laws represented a dramatic departure from the traditional understanding of white-collar crime. It made for more feasible research work because a clear-cut group of persons to be studied could be readily identified, but it lacked the bite and ideological verve that Sutherland's definition offered.

DOCUMENT 1.4

The absence of a precise definition of white-collar crime has plagued white-collar crime scholars from the onset. The confusion began with Sutherland himself. Sometimes he stressed crimes committed by individuals of high status, while at other times he stressed crimes carried out in the course of one's occupation. In his major empirical contribution to the study of white-collar crime, he focused on crimes committed by organizations or by individuals acting in organizational capacities . . .

Sutherland's definition established status, occupation, and organization as central features of white-collar crime study. However, in the more than half century since he coined the term, it has come to have different meanings depending on the research problem encountered. . . .

[W]e believe that Sutherland's emphasis on elite status was in part a function of the different opportunity for white-collar criminality that existed in his day. It was natural for Sutherland to focus on businessmen in lofty positions . . . because relatively few Americans beyond these elite men had any opportunity for committing such illegalities. But changes in our society since then have placed the opportunity for white-collar crimes in the hands of a much broader class of Americans, most of them people who were excluded from these activities in the past. In part, the rapid growth of white-collar jobs in America in the last fifty years has spawned such changes. . . . The advent of the computer, for example, gives large numbers of people access to the documents and transactions that are so much a part of white-collar illegalities. The growth of modern state bureaucracies has placed millions of dollars in the hands of people who never would have had access to such sums in the past. The development of a credit economy has also expanded the opportunities for such crimes. . . .

White-collar crime was defined [in our studies] as "economic offenses committed through the use of some combination of fraud, deception, or collusion. . . . Eight specific offenses were chosen . . . for inclusion in the sample used in the Yale study. . . . These are securities fraud, antitrust violations, bribery, bank embezzlement, postal and wire fraud, false claims and statements, credit and lending institution fraud, and tax fraud.

Source: David Weisburd, Elin Waring, and Ellen E. Chayet, *White-Collar Crime and Criminal Careers* (New York: Cambridge University Press, 2001).

ANALYSIS

The general category of illegal behavior that commanded Sutherland's interest has in Europe most often been called "economic crime," while the United Nations hews much closer to Sutherland's approach by concentrating on what it labels "abuse of power." The Yale team obviously opted for the definition that deflected attention from prominent lawbreakers to a sample that included a much larger group of what can be regarded as run-of-the-mill offenders. Females in the Yale sample were characterized by "occupational marginality." Virtually all of the female bank embezzlers, for instance, were clerical workers, and as many as one-third of the women in some crime categories were unemployed, a far cry from a basic ingredient of Sutherland's focus. One writer, tongue in cheek, portrayed the women in the Yale study as "frayed-collar criminals."

Neil Shover of the University of Tennessee and Frank Cullen of the University of Cincinnati have suggested that the Yale team, themselves a group of elites, imposed its own ideological predilections by broadening the roster of white-collar criminals so that it no longer focused exclusively on powerful persons who had gone astray. They note that the definitional conflict is between what Shover and Cullen label the "populist" perspective, which situates white-collar crime in the struggle against economic inequality, and the "patrician" perspective, which, they maintain, takes a narrower, more technical, and less reform-oriented view of white-collar crime. The patrician view shows less interest in examining the significance of political and economic conditions as they bear upon white-collar crime. Rather, it is said to uncritically accept the status quo.

Source: Neal Shover and Francis T. Cullen, "Studying and Teaching White-Collar Crime: Populist and Patrician Perspectives," *Journal of Criminal Justice Education* 19 (2008): 155–74.

FURTHER READINGS

Johnson, David T., and Richard A. Leo. (1993). "The Yale White-Collar Crime Project: A Review and Critique." *Law & Social Inquiry* 18:63–99.

Weisburd, David, Elin Waring, and Ellen Chayet. (1995). "Specific Deterrence in a Sample of Offenders Convicted of White-Collar Crimes." *Criminology* 33:587–607.

Weisburd, David, Elin Waring, and Stanton Wheeler. (1990). "Class, Status, and the Punishment of White-Collar Criminals." *Law & Society Review* 15:233–43.

Weisburd, David, Stanton Wheeler, Elin Waring, and Nancy Bode. (1991). *Crimes of the Middle Class: White-Collar Offenders in the Federal Courts*. New Haven, CT: Yale University Press.

Wheeler, Stanton. (1993). "The Prospects for Large-Scale Collaborative Research: Revisiting the Yale White-Collar Crime Research." *Law & Social Inquiry* 18:103–13.

Wheeler, Stanton, Kenneth Mann, and Austin Sarat. (1988). *Sitting in Judgment: The Sentencing of White-Collar Offenders*. New Haven, CT: Yale University Press.

The Doctrine of Corporate Criminal Liability

- *Document:* Not until near the end of the first decade of the twentieth century did the U.S. Supreme Court, ruling in *New York Central & Hudson River Railroad Company v. United States*, certify that a corporation could be held liable for a crime involving intent. The motivating force behind this ruling was the court's belief that tougher measures were necessary to control powerful businesses that were profiting from wrongdoing.

- *Date:* 1909.

- *Where:* U.S. Supreme Court.

- *Significance:* The opinion, written by Associate Justice William Rufus Day, established firmly the principle that a corporation could be held criminally responsible for lawbreaking by its agents, whether or not the higher-ups had sanctioned or were aware of the illegal behavior. Had the court concluded otherwise, only civil penalties and injunctions and similar sanctions, often referred to mockingly as "slaps on the wrist" or "costs of doing business," could be imposed on corporations, who often could pass the penalties on to customers by raising their prices. These responses also lacked the moral stigma that characterized criminal actions. For corporations that depend upon the goodwill of customers, stigma has the potential to seriously impact earnings. It also is believed that criminal penalties are much more likely than fines to deter future offenses by the wrongdoer and by others who might contemplate committing such offenses. The assumption is that business executives are rational, calculating persons and that the higher the moral and social costs compared to financial penalties, the more likely they are to adhere to the law.

DOCUMENT 1.5

[T]he railroad company and Fred L. Pomeroy, the assistant traffic manager, were convicted for the payment of rebates to the American Sugar Refining Company and others upon shipments of sugar from the city of New York to the city of Detroit.... The sugar refining companies were engaged in selling and shipping their products in Brooklyn and Jersey City, and W. H. Edgar & Son were engaged in business in Detroit, Michigan where they were dealers in sugar.... [I]t was agreed that Edgar & Son should receive a rate of 18 cents per 100 pounds from New York City to Detroit.... [I]t is abundantly established that this concession was given to Edgar & Son to prevent them from resorting to transportation by the water route between New York and Detroit, thereby depriving the roads interested in the business, and to assist Edgar & Son in meeting the severe competition with other shippers and dealers. The shipments were made accordingly and claims of rebate made on the basis of five cents a hundred pounds from the published rates ...

That anything done or omitted to be done by a corporation common carrier subjects it to the act to regulate commerce, ... which, if done or omitted to be done by any director or officer therefore, or any receiver, trustee, lessee, agent or person acting for or employed by such corporation ... shall also be held to be a misdemeanor committed by such corporation and upon conviction thereof it shall be held to like penalties as are prescribed in such acts ...

It is contended that these provisions of the law are unconstitutional because Congress has no authority to impute to a corporation the commission of criminal offenses, or to subject a corporation to criminal prosecution by reason of the things charged. The argument is that to thus punish a corporation is in reality to punish the innocent stockholders, and to deprive them of their property without opportunity to be heard, consequently without due process of law. And it is further contended that these provisions of the statute deprive the corporation of the presumption of innocence ... It is further urged that as there is no authority shown by the board of directors or the stockholders for the criminal acts of the agents of the company, in contacting for and giving rebates, they could not be lawfully charged against the corporation. As no action of the board of directors could legally authorize a crime, and as indeed the stockholders could not do so, the arguments come to this: that owing to the nature and character of its organization and the extent of its power and authority, a corporation cannot commit a crime of the nature charged in this case....

[L]iability is not imputed because the principal [corporation] actually participates in the malice or fraud, but because the act is done for the benefit of the principal while the agent is acting within the scope of his employment, ... and justice requires that the latter shall be held responsible for damages to the individual who has suffered by such conduct....

[T]hese agents were bound to respect the regulation of interstate commerce enacted by Congress, requiring the filing and publication of rates and punishing departures therefrom.

It is true that there are some crimes, which in their nature cannot be committed by corporations. But there is a large class of offenses, of which rebating under the Federal statutes is one, where the crime consists in purposely doing the things prohibited by statute. In that class of crimes we see no good reason why corporations may not be held responsible for and charged with the knowledge and purposes of their agents, acting within the authority conferred upon them. If it were not so, many offenses might go unpunished, and acts be committed in violation of law ...

It is part of the public history of the times that statutes against rebates could not be effectually enforced so long as individuals only were subject to punishment for violation of the law, when the giving of rebates or concessions enured to the benefit of the corporation of which the individuals were but the instruments. . . .

We see no valid objection in law, and every reason in public policy, why the corporation which profits by the transaction, and can only act through its agents and officers, shall be held punishable by fine because of the knowledge and intent of its agents to whom it has intrusted the authority to act in the subject-matter of making and fixing rates of transportation, and whose knowledge and purposes may well be attributed to the corporation for which the agents work. While the law should have regard to the rights of all, and to those of corporations no less than to those of individuals, it cannot shut its eyes to the fact that the great majority of business transactions in modern times are conducted through these bodies, and particularly that interstate commerce is almost entirely in their hands, and to give them immunity from all punishment because of the old and exploded doctrine that a corporation cannot commit a crime would virtually take away the only means of effectually controlling the subject-matter and correcting the abuses aimed at.

Source: New York Central & Hudson River Railroad Company v. United States. 212 U.S. 481 (1909).

ANALYSIS

This case marked a sharp turn away from an earlier position on corporate crime. The Supreme Court opinion makes it clear that its approval of the concept of corporate criminality was based on its belief that there was no more effective way to limit the power of corporate bodies except to hold them criminally responsible for unacceptable business practices.

Under English common law, a corporation could not be held criminally responsible. In 1613 the Kings Bench in England, the country's highest court,

DID YOU KNOW?

Drowning from Corporate Negligence

The U.S. Supreme Court had the final word on whether corporations could be held criminally responsible, but before that essential ruling federal appellate courts had upheld fines for what was judged to be corporate negligence. In a major case, an appellate court ruled that a corporation that failed to provide adequate life preservers on its steamships as mandated by a law concerning vessels could be found guilty of manslaughter. The wooden sideboard steamboat *General Slocum* had caught fire in New York's East River and, according to court records, 900 persons—90 percent of the passengers—perished by burning or drowning. The court ruled that the absence in the law of an appropriate punishment that could be visited on the Knickerbocker Steamship Company, which owned the vessel, did not exempt it from criminal liability, since this was but an inadvertent oversight on the part of the Congress and not an attempt to make corporations immune. The captain of the ship was sentenced to 10 years in prison, but was pardoned by the president after serving 3 years. The company and is officers received nominal fines.

Source: United States v. Schaick, 134 F. 592 (Southern District, NY, 1904); Edward T. O'Donnell, *Ship Ablaze: The Tragedy of the Steamboat General Slocum* (New York: Broadway Books, 2002).

in the case *In re Sutton's Hospital* (77 English Reports 937) explained the basis for the doctrine of corporate immunity from criminal actions. In quoting the decision, I have put in brackets ancient usages that might not be readily understood by contemporary readers. The English court declared: "A corporate aggregate of many is invisible, immortal, and of an intendment and consideration of law [that is, the entity is created by law]. They cannot commit treason, nor be outlawed [that is, banished from the land], nor ex-communicated, for they have no souls, rather can they appear in person, but by attorney. A corporation aggregate of many cannot do fealty [that is, swear an oath of loyalty to their lord or country], for an invisible body can neither be in prison nor swear; it is not subject for imbecilities or death of the natural body or diverse other causes."

Given the economic meltdown of recent times and the gross miscalculations and deceits fostered by leading corporate bodies, some might argue that the court's contention that corporate bodies cannot manifest "imbecilities" misses the mark.

Almost a century after the *Sutton's Hospital* ruling, Sir John Holt, who is best remembered as the judge whose skepticism served to end the prosecution and hanging of witches in England, in *Anonymous Case (No. 935)* (88 English Reports 1518) in a single sentence put forth his interpretation of the law regarding corporate criminality: "A corporation is not indictable, but particular members of it are," Holt declared. These early declarations were echoed by William Blackstone, the outstanding eighteenth-century compiler and interpreter of English law in his four-volume *Commentaries*: "A corporation cannot commit treason, or felony, or other crime in its corporate capacity, though its member may in their distinctive individual capacities."

States had begun moving away from this age-old doctrine, but uncertainly prevailed as to whether the U.S. Supreme Court would allow this significant change in regard to organizations that engaged in interstate commerce over which the Congress and the court had jurisdiction. The *New York Center and Hudson River Railroad* case put an end to that uncertainty.

DID YOU KNOW?

Misleading and False Mislabeling

What sociologist Edwin Sutherland wrote three-quarters of a century ago about advertising by corporations is no less true today, albeit with greater subtlety. Sutherland proclaimed that some advertisements sought to sell products that were physically dangerous, with the perils denied, minimized, or unmentioned, and he pointed out that garments advertised as silk or wool were almost entirely cotton. Alligator shoes were not made from the hides of alligators; furniture said to be walnut was not constructed from walnut lumber; turtle-oil cream was not made from turtle oil; and rugs advertised as Oriental were not made in the Orient. Caskets advertised as rustproof had been found to rust; garments said to be moth-proof were not; garden hoses specified as three-ply were only two-ply. Storage eggs were sold as fresh eggs. Facial creams said to be skin foods and corrective of wrinkles neither fed the skin nor corrected wrinkles. Some corporations had been found to advertise their tea as made from tender leaves, specially picked for these companies, when in fact their tea was purchased from lots brought in by importers who sold the same tea to other firms.

Source: Edwin H. Sutherland, "Crimes of Corporations," in Sutherland, *On Analyzing Crime*, ed. Karl Schuessler (Chicago: University of Chicago Press, 1973), 83–84.

FURTHER READINGS

Bernard, Thomas J. (1984). "The Historical Development of Corporate Criminal Liability." *Criminology* 22:3–17.

Coffee, John C., Jr. (1981). " 'No Soul to Damn, No Body to Kick': An Unscandalized Inquiry into the Problem of Corporate Punishment." *Michigan Law Review* 79:386–459.

Coleman, Bruce. (1975). "Is Corporate Criminal Liability Really Necessary?" *Southwestern Law Journal* 28:908–27.

Geis, Gilbert, and Joseph F. C. DiMento. (2002). "Empirical Evidence and the Doctrine of Corporate Criminal Liability." *American Journal of Criminal Law* 29:341–75.

Khana, Victor S. (1996). "Corporate Criminal Liability: What Purpose Does It Serve?" *Harvard Law Review* 109:1477–534.

McClean, Joseph E. (1946). *William Rufus Day: Supreme Court Justice from Ohio*. Baltimore: Johns Hopkins Press.

Orland, Leonard. (1980). "Reflections on Corporate Crime: Law in Search of Theory and Scholarship." *American Criminal Law Review* 17:501–20.

Roberts, Vernon. (1950). "Justice William R. Day and Federal Regulation." *Mississippi Valley Historical Review* 37:39–60.

Wells, Celia. (1993). *Corporations and Criminal Responsibility*. Oxford: Clarendon Press.

The Ford Pinto Case

- *Document:* Mark Dowie, an investigative reporter, focused national attention on the alleged defects of the Ford Pinto automobile. The problem was located in what was said to be a misplaced gas tank that resulted in catastrophic consequences from collisions that involved the car's rear end.
- *Date:* September–October 1977.
- *Where:* *Mother Jones*, a liberal magazine (see Sidebar 1.6).
- *Significance:* The Ford Pinto case established in a well-publicized manner that corporations could be charged with crimes of violence, including murder and manslaughter.

DOCUMENT 1.6

One evening, in the mid-1960s, Arjay Miller was driving home from his office in Dearborn, Michigan, in the four-door Lincoln Continental that went with his job as president of the Ford Motor Company. On a crowded highway, another car struck him from the rear. The Continental spun around and burst into flames. Because he was wearing a shoulder-strap seat belt, Miller was unharmed by the crash, and because his doors did not jam he escaped the gasoline-drenched, flaming wreck. But the accident made a vivid impression on him. Several months later, on July 15, 1965, he recounted the incident to a U.S. Senate subcommittee that was hearing testimony on auto safety legislation. "I still have burning in my mind the image of that gas tank on fire," Miller said. He went on to express an almost passionate interest in controlling fuel-fed fires in cars that crash or roll over. He spoke with excitement about the fabric gas tank Ford was testing at that very moment. "If it proves out," he promised the senators, "it will be a feature you will see in our standard cars."

Almost seven years after Miller's testimony, a woman who for legal reasons we will call Sandra Gillespie, pulled onto a Minneapolis highway in her new Ford Pinto. Riding with her was a young boy, whom we'll call Robbie Carlton. As she entered the merger lane, Sandra Gillespie's car stalled. Another car rear-ended hers at an impact speed of 28 miles per hour. The Pinto's gas tank ruptured. Vapors from it mixed quickly with the air in the passenger compartment. A spark ignited the mixture and the car exploded in a ball of fire. Sandra died in agony a few hours later in an emergency hospital. Her passenger . . . is still alive; he has just come home from another futile operation aimed at grafting a new ear and nose from skin on the few unscarred potions of his body . . .

Why did Sandra Gillespie's Ford Pinto catch fire so easily seven years after Ford's Arjay Miller made his apparently sincere pronouncements? An extensive investigation by *Mother Jones* . . . has found these answers.

Fighting strong competition from Volkswagen for the lucrative small-car market, the Ford Motor Company rushed the Pinto into production in much less than the usual time. Ford engineers discovered in preproduction crash tests that rear-end collisions would rupture the Pinto's fuel system extremely easily. Because assembly-line machinery was already tooled when engineers found this defect, top Ford officials decided to manufacture the car anyway—exploding gas tank and all—*even though Ford owned the patent on a much safer gas tank.*

For more than eight years afterwards, Ford successfully lobbied, with extraordinary vigor and blatant lies, against a key government safety standard that would have forced the company to change the Pinto's fire-prone gas tank.

By conservative estimates Pinto crashes have caused 500 burn deaths to people who would not have been seriously injured if the car had not burst into flames. Burning cars have become such an embarrassment to Ford that its advertising agency, J. Walter Thompson, dropped a line from the end of a radio spot that read, "Pinto leaves you with that warm feeling."

Ford knew that Pinto is a firetrap, yet it had paid out millions to settle damage suits out of court, and is prepared to spend millions more lobbying against safety standards. . . . Pinto is the biggest-selling subcompact in America, and the company's operating profit on the car is fantastic . . .

Finally, in 1977, new Pinto models have incorporated a few minor alterations necessary to meet that federal standard Ford managed to hold off for eight years. Why did the company delay so long in making these minimal, inexpensive improvements?

Ford waited eight years because its internal "cost-benefit analysis," *which places a dollar value on human life*, said it wasn't profitable to make the changes sooner . . .

Although the particular story is about the Pinto, the way in which Ford made its decision is typical of the U.S. auto industry generally. There are plenty of similar stories about other cars made by other companies. But this case is the worst of them all.

Mother Jones had studied hundreds of reports and documents on rear-end collisions involving Pintos. These reports conclusively reveal that if you ram into that Pinto you were following at over 30 miles per hour, the rear end of the car would buckle like an accordion, right up to the back seat. The tube leading to the gas tank cap would be ripped away from the tank itself and gas would immediately begin sloshing onto the road around the car. The buckled gas tank would be jammed up against the differential housing . . . , which contains four sharp protruding bolts likely to gash holes in the tank and spill still more gas. The welded seam between the main body frame and the wheel well would split, allowing gas to enter the interior of the car.

Now all you need is a spark from a cigarette, ignition, or scraping metal, and both cars would be engulfed in flames. If you gave the Pinto a really good whack—say, at 40 mph—chances are excellent that that its doors would jam and you would have to stand by and watch its trapped passengers burn to death.

This scenario is no news to Ford. Internal company documents in our possession show that Ford had crash-tested the Pinto at top-secret sites more than 40 times and that *every* test made at over 25 mph without special structural alteration of the car has resulted in a ruptured fuel tank. Despite this, Ford officials denied having crash-tested the Pinto . . .

Dr. Leslie Ball, the retired chief for the NASA manned space program and a founder of the International Society of Reliability Engineers, recently made a careful study of the Pinto. "The release to production of the Pinto was the most reprehensible decision in the history of American engineering," he said.

Los Angeles safety expert Byron Bloch has made an in-depth study of the Pinto fuel system. "It's a catastrophic blunder," he says. "Ford made an extremely irresponsible decision when they placed such a weak tank in such a ridiculous location in such a soft rear end. It's simply designed to blow up—premeditated."

A Ford engineer, who doesn't want his name used, comments: "The company is run by salesmen, not engineers, so the priority is styling, not safety." . . .

So when J. C. Echold, Director of Automotive Safety (chief anti-safety lobbyist for Ford) wrote to the Department of Transportation . . . he felt secure attaching a memorandum that in effect says it is acceptable to kill 180 people and burn another 180 every year, *even though we have the technology that could save their lives for $11 a year.* . . .

When the Pinto liability suits began, Ford strategy was to go to a jury. Confident it could hide the Pinto auto tests, Ford thought jurors of solid American registered voters would buy into the industry doctrine that drivers, not cars, cause accidents. It didn't work. It seems that citizens are much quicker to see the truth than bureaucrats. Juries began ruling against the company, granting million-dollar awards to plaintiffs.

"We'll never go to a jury again," says Al Slechmir, in Ford's Washington office. "Not in fire cases, juries are just too sentimental. They see those charred remains and forget the evidence. No sir, we'll settle."
. . .

[T]he only government penalty meted out to auto companies for noncompliance to standards has been a miniscule fine, usually $5,000 to $10,000. One

---

DID YOU KNOW?

More on the *Mother Jones* Pinto Story

The periodical *Mother Jones*, in which Mark Dowie broke the story of the hazardous gas tank built into the Ford Pinto, is named after Mary Harris, a woman born in Cork, Ireland. She was married to George Jones and worked as a dressmaker and teacher. She moved to Chicago after her husband died and lost all her belongings in the 1871 Chicago fire. She turned her efforts to aiding the labor movement, served jail terms for her efforts, and was instrumental in the movement to abolish child labor. She got the name of Mother Jones for her efforts to improve the working conditions of miners. A member of Congress labeled her "the grandmother of all agitators." Her response was that she hoped to live long enough to become the great-grandmother of agitators for good causes. She is perhaps best remembered for the saying: "Pray for the dead, and fight like hell for the living."

wonders how long the Ford Motor Company would continue to market lethal cars were Henry Ford II and Lee Iacocca [the company president] serving 20-year prison terms in Leavenworth for consumer homicide.

Source: Mark Dowie, "Pinto Madness," *Mother Jones* 28 (September–October 1977): 18–32.

ANALYSIS

The damage suits against the Ford Motor Company reached staggering heights. In mid-February 1978 a jury awarded Richard Grimshaw, a Pinto burn victim, $12.5 million in punitive damages, an amount that at the time was said to be the largest ever decreed in a personal injury suit. This sum was added to the $2.8 million given to Grimshaw as compensatory damages. The total subsequently was reduced to $6 million by a California judge, but obviously the stakes for Ford were escalating significantly (*Grimshaw v. Ford Motor Company*, 119 California Appellate 3d. 757, 1981).

Then came a landmark criminal charge filed by a prosecutor in Indiana. The facts alleged were these: On August 10, 1978, three young women were incinerated as a consequences of a 30 mph rear-end collision of another car with their 1973 Ford Pinto. They had stopped for gas, left the gas tank cap on the car roof, and when it rolled off they had to make a U-turn and stopped the car with it slightly on the road because of a low wall bordering the highway. Meanwhile, a driver in a Chevy van had reached down for a cigarette—the pack had fallen to the car floor—and, when he looked up, he was too close to the Pinto to avoid a collision. The van's front bumper, a thick pine board, rammed into the Pinto's rear. An instant later the Pinto burst into flames and the three young women were dead, incinerated.

Michael Cosentino, a local Indiana prosecutor, who had been sickened by the awful deaths of Judy, Lyn, and Donna Ulrich, filed criminal charges against Ford. In a pathbreaking move, he charged Ford with reckless homicide for allowing such a vehicle to be on the road. At the heart of the prosecution's case were the company's calculations that balanced the dollar value that they assigned in

DID YOU KNOW?

Death by Corporate Negligence

An autopsy confirmed that death did not come immediately for Patrick M. Walter. On June 14, 2002, while working on a sewer pipe in a 10-foot-deep trench, he was buried alive under a rush of collapsing muck and mud. A plumber's apprentice, barely 22 years old, Walter had tried to claw his way to the surface of the pit. But sludge filled his throat and thousands of pounds of dirt pressed on his chest, until he could no longer draw a breath.

The regulations of the Occupational Health and Safety Administration mandate that persons doing the job that Patrick Walters was performing be trained so that they can recognize dangerous conditions and ensure that they are made safe. There also must be an inspection by a competent person before work begins, sloping walls must be constructed, and a ladder and metal box shield are required in excavations that are more than five feet deep. None of these precautions had been taken in the Walters case, nor had they been in place 13 years earlier when another person working for the same business, the Moeves Plumbing Company, located in Fairfield, Connecticut, was buried alive under nearly identical circumstances.

Efforts by his family to secure a criminal prosecution in recognition of Walters's death ran into endless roadblocks. Claiming that the government betrayed his son's memory, Walters's father vowed to fight the Occupational Safety and Health Administration for the remainder of his life. His son's body was interred in a mausoleum rather than buried. His mother said she would never allow his remains to be put into the ground again.

Source: David Barstow, "A Trench Caves In, a Young Worker Is Dead. Is it a Crime?" *New York Times*, December 23, 2003, 1.

regard to the consequences of rear-end collisions against the cost of recalling and repairing the unsafe fuel tanks. Ford chose not to fix the tanks because such an approach was deemed not to be cost effective.

Ford executives testified that they were unaware of the risks, and several told the jury that they had purchased Pintos for their driving-age children.

There were 29 days of testimony in the Ford Pinto trial that produced 6,000 pages of transcript, and 200 exhibits were introduced as evidence. It took the jury 25 ballots before they were able to render a unanimous verdict. Ford was acquitted of all three counts of reckless homicide. Among other explanations jurors would offer for their decision was the belief that a lack of adequate safety was inherent in small cars. But it also seemed plausible that the Ford Motor Company, given its resources and the very high caliber of the attorneys it was able to hire, had been able to outwit and outgun the Indiana prosecution team. Nonetheless, the fact that the case was heard in a criminal court conveyed a warning to corporate America that businesses no longer were exempt from criminal responsibility for decisions that could be tied to violent outcomes. If nothing else, the reputation (and, as a consequence, the sales) of a corporation would be jeopardized by the publicity associated with a criminal trial. The Pinto case represented a dramatic shift toward holding organizations responsible for institutional violence.

FURTHER READINGS

Birsch, Douglas, and John H. Fielder. (Eds.). (1994). *The Ford Pinto Case: A Study in Applied Ethics, Business, and Technology.* Albany: State University of New York Press.

Cullen, Francis T., Gray Cavender, William J. Maakestad, and Michael L. Benson. (2006). *Corporate Crime Under Attack: The Fight to Criminalize Business Violence* (2nd ed.). Newark, NJ: Lexis/Nexis.

Gates, Randall S. (1992). *White Collar Crime and the Ford Pinto Case.* Virginia Beach, VA: Regent University.

Gioia, Dennis A. (1992). "Pinto Fires and Personal Ethics: A Script Analysis of Missed Opportunities." *Journal of Business Ethics* 11:379–89.

Lee, Matthew T., and M. David Ermann. (1999). "Pinto 'Madness' as a Flawed Landmark Narrative: An Organizational and Network Analysis." *Social Problems* 46:30–47.

Ridley, Ann, and Louise Dunford. (1994). "Corporate Liability for Manslaughter: Reform and the Art of the Possible." *International Journal of the Sociology of Law* 22:309–28.

Strobel, Lee Patrick (1980). *Reckless Homicide?: Ford's Pinto Trial.* South Bend, IN: And Books.

Swigert, Victoria L., and Ronald A. Farrell (1980–81). "Corporate Homicide: Definitional Process in the Creation of Deviance." *Law and Society Review* 15:170–83.

Corporations and the Constitution

- *Document:* On January 20, 2010, in *Citizens United v. the Federal Election Commission*, the U.S. Supreme Court by a 5–4 vote declared unconstitutional an Act of Congress that made it a felony for a corporation to use its general funds to engage in "electioneering campaigning" if there were fewer than 30 days remaining before the primary election in question or 60 days before the general election. The Supreme Court majority ruled that the law was unconstitutional as a violation of the protection enunciated in the First Amendment guaranteeing free speech.

  The dissent focused on the fact that a corporation is not a person and should not be granted the legal privileges accorded human beings. The document offers excerpts from both the majority opinion and Justice John Paul Stevens's dissent since they bear most directly on the question of corporate criminal liability

- *Date:* January 20, 2010.
- *Where:* U.S. Supreme Court.
- *Significance:* The decision in *Citizens United v. Federal Election Commission* invigorated the doctrine that corporations as collections of human beings may themselves be charged and convicted for criminal actions. Often what happens is that those who made or endorsed illegal decisions escape punishment by bargaining to have the corporation, which means primarily its stockholders, face the criminal charges. But the dissent in *Citizens United* reemphasized that corporations are not human, and as creations by the state need not necessarily receive all the guarantees accorded living persons.

DOCUMENT 1.7

Citizens United v. Federal Election Commission

JUSTICE [ANTHONY] KENNEDY delivered the opinion of the Court [joined by Chief Justice Roberts, Justices Antonin Scalia, Clarence Thomas, and Samuel Alito] . . . :

When government seeks to use its full power, including the criminal law, to command whether a person may get his or her information or what distrusted source he or she may not hear, it uses censorship to control thought. This is unlawful. The First Amendment confirm the freedom to think for ourselves . . .

CHIEF JUSTICE ROBERTS, with whom JUSTICE SCALIA JOINS, concurring . . .

Despite the corporation-hating quotations the dissent has dredged up, it is far from clear that by the end of the eighteenth century [when the Constitution was written] corporations were despised. If so, how come there were so many of them? . . . There were approximately 335 charters issued to corporations in the United States by the end of the eighteenth century . . . Moreover, what seems like a small number by today's standards surely does not indicate the relative importance of corporations when the Nation was considerably smaller . . .

Even if we thought it proper to apply the dissent's approach of excluding from First Amendment coverage what the Founders disliked, and even if we agreed that the Founders disliked founding-era corporations; modern corporations might not qualify for exclusion. Most of the Founders' resentment towards corporations was directed at state-granted monopoly privileges that individually chartered corporations enjoyed. Modern corporations do not have such privileges, and probably would have been favored by most of our enterprising Founders . . .

The dissent says that when the Founders "constitutionalized the right to speak in the First Amendment, it was free speech of individual Americans that they had in mind." This is no doubt true. All the provisions of the Bill of Rights set forth the rights of individual men and women—not, for example, of trees or polar bears. But the individual person's right to speak includes the right to speak *in association with other individual persons.*

DISSENT BY [JUSTICE JOHN PAUL] STEVENS . . .

The conceit that corporations must be treated identically to natural persons in the political sphere is not only inaccurate but also inadequate to justify the Court's disposition of this case.

In the context of election to public office, the distinction between corporate and human speakers is significant. Although they make enormous contributions to our society, corporations are not actually members of it. They cannot vote or run for office. Because they may be managed and controlled by nonresidents their interests may conflict in fundamental respects with the interests of eligible voters . . .

Citizens United . . . never sought a declaration that [BCRA] was fatally unconstitutional as to all corporations and unions;; instead it argued only that the statute could not be applied to it because it was "funded overwhelmingly" by individuals. . . .

[T]he authority of legislatures to enact viewpoint-neutral regulations based on content is well settled. We have upheld statutes that have, for example, allowed state-run broadcasters to exclude independent candidates from televised debates. We have upheld statutes that prohibit the display or distribution of campaign materials near a polling place . . . And we have consistently approved laws that bar Government employees, but not others, from contributing to or participating in political activities . . .

Under the majority's view, I suppose it may be a First Amendment problem that corporations are not permitted to vote, giving that voting is, among other things, a form of speech . . .

Thomas Jefferson famously fretted that corporations would subvert the Republic. See Letter from Thomas Jefferson to Tom Logan (Nov. 13, 1816 . . . : "I hope we shall . . . crush in [its] birth the aristocracy of our monied corporations which dare already to challenge our government to a show of strength and bid defiance to the laws of our country." . . .

It might also be added that corporations have no consciences, no being, no feelings, no thoughts, no desires. Corporations help structure and facilitate the activities of human beings, to be sure, and their "personhood" often serves as a useful legal fiction. But they are not "We the People" by whom and for whom our Constitution was established.

Source: Citizens United v. the Federal Election Commission, 130 U.S. 876 (2010).

ANALYSIS

Citizens United is a wealthy, conservative nonprofit corporation with a yearly budget of about $12 million. It raises and spends money to attempt to elect or defeat persons seeking political positions and legislative proposals that it supports or opposes. Citizens United's identifying mantra is "Dedicated to the Restoring Our Government to Citizen's Control," presumably meaning citizens who agree with the ideological positions of Citizens United.

During the primary season before the 2008 presidential election, Citizens United sought to circulate a 90-minute documentary film titled *Hillary: The Movie* that depicted then-Senator Hillary Clinton, who was seeking the Democratic Party's nomination, in extremely unflattering terms. It was not allowed to do so because of the Bipartisan Campaign Reform Act of 2002 (BCRA). Citizens United sued the Federal Election Commission, lost in the federal district court, but prevailed in the Supreme Court.

Justice Anthony M. Kennedy declared that the BCRA, otherwise known as the McCain-Feingold Act for campaign reform, was unconstitutional and built his case on the argument that First Amendment rights could not be curtailed in the case of corporations if the behavior in question was permissible for individuals. He made much of the fact that the media were corporations, and yet they clearly were beyond the boundaries of any congressional ban on free expression. Kennedy was not impressed with the idea that shareholders in a corporation might not approve of the causes and the persons to whom they were providing financial support, again relying on an analogy to the media as corporations who do not solicit the views of their shareholders when they advance partisan editorial electoral recommendations.

The *Citizen United* case bears directly upon questions of corporate crime because it reinforces the position that corporations must be granted all the constitutional guarantees accorded to accused individuals. It is noteworthy that Citizens United had not asked for a ruling on the constitutionality of checks on corporate speech; the Court took it upon itself to raise and deal with that issue. Its action provoked critics on the opposite side of the political spectrum to adopt a stance previously employed by conservatives who rallied against left-of-center judges they labeled "activists." The term "conservative activist judges" came into use in the wake of the *Citizens United* decision.

In 1957 in a labor union case, *United States v. Auto Workers* (352 U.S. 567), Justice Felix Frankfurter had indicated the root of the restraints imposed on corporate bodies. He noted that in the late nineteenth century there had been "a popular feeling that aggregated capital unduly influenced politics, an influence not stopping short of corruption." To support his position Frankfurter turned to comments by two eminent historians: "The nation was fabulously rich," Samuel Eliot Morris and Henry Steele Commager had written about this time period in the fourth edition of their book, *The Growth of the American Republic* (1950), "but its wealth was gravitating rapidly into the hands of a small portion of the population, and the power of wealth threatened to undermine the political integrity of the country."

DID YOU KNOW?

Fallout from the *Citizens United* Supreme Court Decision

The most dramatic moment in President Barack Obama's 2010 State of the Union address was when he caustically criticized the Supreme Court's *Citizens United* decision on national television and before an audience in which, sitting directly in front of him, were six members of the Court, three of whom had supported the decision and three who had opposed it. It was a most unusual happening. Presidents typically air their disagreements with Court rulings under less public conditions, such as press conferences. Justice Samuel Alito, a member of the majority in *Citizens United*, was seen to shake his head and, press reports uniformly agreed, to mutter the words "Not true."

Judgments on the episode were mixed. Republicans were likely to call the president's comments "rude." Columnist Frank Rich of the *New York Times*, on the other hand, thought that "the president was right to blast the 5–4 decision giving corporate interests an even greater stranglehold over a government they already regard as a partially owned on-shore subsidiary." More pointedly, Rich's media employer in an editorial blasted the Court decision. "The majority is deeply wrong," it maintained. "Most wrongheaded of all is its insistence that corporations are just like people. It is an odd claim since corporations are a creation of the state that exist to make money. It was a fundamental misreading of the Constitution to say that these artificial legal constructs have the same right to spend money on politics as ordinary Americans have to speak out in support of a candidate."

FURTHER READINGS

Chemerinsky, Erwsin. (2010). *The Conservative Assault on the Constitution*. New York: Simonn & Schuster.

Garland, Norman M. (1996). "The Unavailability to Corporations of the Privilege against Self-Incrimination: A Comparative Examination." *New York Law School Journal of International and Comparative Law* 16:55–77.

Hartmann, Thom. (2010), *Unequaal Protection: How Corporations Became "People" and How You Can Fight Back*. San Francisco, CA: Bernert-Kochleve.

Smolla, Rodney A. (2004). "The Debate over Corporate Speech and the First Amendment." *Case Western Reserve Law Review* 54:1277–89.

Von Spakovsky, Hans A. (2010). *Citizens United and the Restoration of the First Amendment*. Washington, DC: Heritage Foundation.

2

THE ROBBER BARONS

INTRODUCTION

A swashbuckling gallery of ruthless, self-serving business magnates appeared on the American scene in the early 1900s with the development of railroad transportation. Unchecked by regulators or by any but the most primitive oversight, they developed an array of hardball tactics that gave rise to their designation as "robber barons." They plundered the national treasury, bribing politicians to award lucrative contracts for the construction of a cross-national railroad system. They overcharged mercilessly for the work they performed and manipulated corporate arrangements so that the extravagant financial gains could go directly into their own pockets rather than into the pockets of their shareholders or as reduced prices for their customers.

Most of the robber barons found that they had accumulated so much wealth that they could allow some of it to be employed in philanthropic enterprises that would perpetuate their names and, hopefully, erase some of the blemish that attached to their reckless financial marauding.

The chapter concentrates on the most notorious figures of the era of financial piracy. In California, the foursome of Collis Huntington, Charles Crocker, Leland Stanford, and Mark Hopkins rapaciously plotted against rivals, always intent upon securing monopoly rights so that they could charge outrageous prices. When they had the upper hand they would demand that potential customers submit their profit-and-loss statements so that they could calculate the highest fee they could charge. Each of the four lived in majestic style in mansions that dazzled their San Francisco neighbors.

Jay Gould bought and then looted the Erie Railroad that operated between New York City and Buffalo. He flagrantly bribed legislators to pass laws that would enable him to line his pockets. Cornelius Vanderbilt was described by his biographer as having a "near legendary status as a self-absorbed bore and braggart, intent upon self-glorification and devoid of generosity." Daniel Drew, who made and lost fortunes speculating on railroads rather than tending to their operation, would finally be double-crossed by his associates, a victim of the dog-eat-dog tactics that characterized the robber barons.

J. P. Morgan was the robber baron whose legacy most lingers on. His heritage is preserved in the J. P. Morgan Chase company, a powerhouse that figured prominently in the maneuvers associated with the bailouts during the economic meltdown that is discussed in Chapter 13.

Who Were The Robber Barons?

- **Document:** A 22-page essay by J. Brad DeLong puts into perspective the virtues and vices of the so-called "robber barons." DeLong, who has written collaboratively with *New York Times* columnist Paul Krugman, a Nobel Prize winner in economics, and with Lawrence Summers, briefly director of the National Economic Council in the Obama administration, is a professor of economics at the University of California–Berkeley, and an associate of the National Bureau of Economic Research in Cambridge, Massachusetts.
- **Date:** January 1, 1998.
- **Where:** Online from Berkeley, California.
- **Significance:** The essay details and judges the role of the men who were labeled robber barons in regard to their economic activities and the distribution of wealth in their time as well as in earlier and later times. The document has been described as the "ultimate statement" on the subject of the robber barons.

DOCUMENT 2.1

In approximately 1919, nine of the twenty-one fortunes were *railroad* fortunes: fortunes made constructing and operating the 200,000 miles of railroad track that were built to cover the United States in the nineteenth century. Three of the fortunes were inherited. Five were in finance—and in 1990 finance meant almost exclusively *railroad* finance.

There were a few non-railroad fortunes: one ironmaster (Andrew Carnegie), a couple of department store owners, and stray fortunes derived from other industries.

But you do not go too wrong if you remember that the first wave of American fortunes were *railroad* fortunes.

First, we think that they were very different people. James J. Hill was a super engineer and manager, E. H. Harriman had extraordinary abilities to pick engineers to improve the operations of the Union Pacific Railroad . . .

There is a second thing about the robber barons: they *all* were ruthless . . .

And this is the third thing to note about the turn of the century robber barons: even though the base of their fortunes was the railroad industry, they were for the most part more manipulators of finance than builders of new track. Fortune came from the ability to acquire ownership of a profitable railroad and then to capitalize those profits by selling securities to the public. Fortune came from profiting from a shift— either upward or downward—in investors' perceptions of the railroad's future profit.

The fourth thing that stands out about the robber barons is how completely, totally corrupt they *all* were—or, if we allow them to defend themselves, how completely and totally corrupt was the system in which they were embedded.

Source: J. Bradford DeLong, "Robber Barons." Available at: http://www .j-bradford-delong.net/Econ_Articles/Carnegie/DeLong. Accessed March 29, 2011.

ANALYSIS

The term "robber barons" gained prominence in the United States with the publication in 1933, at the height of the country's words economic depression, of *Robber Barons* by Matthew Josephson. The term had its origin in medieval times when it was applied to unscrupulous English feudal lords who engaged in illegal and immoral practices, such as levying unauthorized fees as tolls for passageway through areas that they controlled.

In the United States, the epithet was directed at persons operating in a corporate context. The first corporation in the United States was not organized until 1786, and by 1801 there were only 8 manufacturing companies in the country and only 317 corporations of all types. Then came the railroads, swashbuckling across the country, killing unwary bystanders, setting fire to fields adjacent to their tracks, and using their extraordinary power to establish discriminatory and exorbitant rates. As muckraker Frank Norris described them, the railroad was "a battering monster, the terror of steel and steam, with its single eye . . . shooting from horizon to horizon . . . the symbol of a vast power, huge, terrible, flinging the echo of its thunder over all

---

DID YOU KNOW?

Sutherland on Robber Barons

In the course of his presidential address that ballyhooed the term "white-collar crime," Edwin H. Sutherland included robber barons in the embrace of his subject matter, saying:

> The robber barons of the last half of the nineteenth century were white-collar criminals, as practically everyone now agrees. Their attitudes are illustrated by these statements: Colonel Vanderbilt asked: "You don't think you can run a railroad in accordance with the statutes, do you?" A. B. Stickney, a railroad president, said to sixteen other railroad presidents in the home of J. P. Morgan in 1890, "I have the utmost respect for you gentlemen, individually, but as railroad presidents I wouldn't trust you with my watch out of sight." Charles Francis Adams [a member of the Massachusetts Railroad Commission] said, "The difficulty in railroad management . . . lies in the covetousness, want of good faith, and low moral tone of railroad managers, in the complete absence of any high standard of commercial honesty."

Source: Edwin H. Sutherland, "White-Collar Criminality," *American Sociological Review* 5 (1940): 1–12, at 2.

reaches . . ., leaving blood and destruction in its path . . . the soulless Force, the iron-hearted Power, the monster, the Colossus, the Octopus."

The railroads were America's first big business, and they made other businesses possible and necessary. The railroad industry in time was run by a group of ruthless entrepreneurs, the robber barons who were described by author Fon Boardman as "cold-hearted, selfish, sordid men," or as another writer put it, they were persons who were "scrupulously dishonest." President Theodore Roosevelt, for his part, castigated the robber barons as "malefactors of great wealth."

FURTHER READINGS

Boardman, Fon W., Jr. (1979). *America and the Robber Barons, 1865 to 1913.* New York: Henry Z. Walck.

Brewer, Thomas B. (1970). *The Robber Barons: Saints or Sinners?* New York: Holt, Rinehart, and Winston.

Jones, Peter D'Alroy. (1968), *The Robber Barons Revisited.* Boston: Health.

Josephson, Matthew. (1933). *The Robber Baron: The Great American Capitalists, 1861–1901.* New York: Harcourt and Brace.

McNeese, Tim. (2009). *The Robber Barons and the Sherman Anti-Trust Act: Reshaping American Business.* New York: Chelsea House.

Stiles, T. J. (1997). *Robber Barons and Railroads.* New York: Berkley.

The California Culprits

- **Document:** In 1948, Oscar Lewis published a 424-page book, *The Big Four*, that traced the unsavory activities of four California businessmen, each a distinctively different personality, who came together to make vast amounts of money in railroad deals. The extensive review of the book in *Time*, excerpted in Document 2.2, provides the basic details of the Big Four who brought the railroad to California.
- **Date:** August 15, 1938.
- **Where:** *Time* magazine.
- **Significance:** The information provided in the extract captures the essence of the tactics that characterized the robber barons of the post–Civil War period as well as the rapaciousness that underlay the effort to connect California and the West with the more settled eastern regions of the United States by providing railroad transportation across the imposing barrier of the Sierra Nevada mountains.

DOCUMENT 2.2

Readers of recent muckraking history . . . are likely to feel they have heard all they want to about early U.S. railroad building. In monotonous procession the great figures of the post-Civil War period follow each other—all up to their ears in political intrigues, angling for Federal land grants, corrupting legislatures, double-crossing the public, their stockholders and each other so consistently that it seems remarkable the railroads ever got built.

The Big Four of California (Charles Crocker, Leland Stanford, Mark Hopkins, and Collis P. Huntington), organizers of the Central Pacific, the Southern Pacific and innumerable West Coast companies, seem the most arrogant, most shameless of them all . . .

Crocker, [who] was in charge of the actual construction of the Central Pacific, boasted that he found fault with everything and that everybody was afraid of him . . . Because he admired the endurance of his Chinese cook, he favored Chinese crews over his partners' objections. . . . [T]he rival Union Pacific was pushing rapidly across level plaints, making fortunes for its owners. The partners were frantic but Crocker only added more Chinese, had them digging through rock so hard that four crews advanced only eight inches a day. When Stanford sent some drilling equipment, Crocker refused to let it be tried.

Stanford and Hopkins built huge houses on San Francisco's Nob Hill; Crocker spent $1,250,000 to rival them with a gaudy, towering architectural monstrosity. An undertaker who owned a small house in the same block refused to sell it; Crocker built a wooden spite fence 40-feet high, completely enclosing his neighbor's home. The undertaker retaliated by placing a coffin on his roof with a flagpole embedded in it that featured a skull and bones at its top. Dennis Kearney led a mob to tear down the fence and hang Crocker from the flagpole atop his 76-foot tower, but the mob decided to burn Chinese laundries and beat up laundrymen instead. . . .

Admirers compared Leland Stanford to Napoleon, Caesar, Alexander the Great and John Stuart Mill, but Partner Collis Huntington described him tersely as "a damned old fool." His profound thought before he answered a question made people look upon him as a thinker, until they discovered that it took him as long to answer a simple question as a difficult one.

Source: "California Quartet," *Time*, August 15, 1938.

ANALYSIS

By 1868, Californians Colis Huntington (1821–1900) (the Huntington Library in Pasadena bears his name), Leland Stanford (1824–93) (for whose deceased young son Stanford University in Palo Alto is named), Charles Crocker (1822–88) (who gave his name and money to found the Crocker Bank, later taken over by Wells Fargo), and Mark Hopkins (1813–78) (a renowned San Francisco hotel bears his name) were well on their way to controlling both the economic and the political destiny of California by means of their joint ownership of railroads.

The four men, three of whom were some six feet tall and weighed in the range of 250 pounds (Hopkins was the exception), were westward migrants from the East Coast. Huntington, for instance, had been born in oddly named Poverty Hollow in Harwinton, a Connecticut town with the first six letters of its named derived from Hartford and Windsor, from where its first settlers haled. Stanford

DID YOU KNOW?

On Collis Huntington

Late in his life Collis Huntington, the leader of the California cabal, lobbied Congress to try to get it to rescind or postpone the huge debt now due from the railroads for the 30-year bonds that had been issued in the 1860s. William Randolph Hearst, the proprietor of the *San Francisco Examiner*, seeking to thwart Huntington, dispatched his ace reporter, the sardonic Ambrose Bierce, to cover the story. "The spectacle of this old man standing on the brink of eternity, his pockets lined with dishonest gold which he knows neither how to enjoy nor to whom to bequeath, swearing it is the fruit of wholesome labor and homely thrift, and beseeching an opportunity to multiply the store, was one of the most pitiable it has been my lot to observe. He knows himself an outmate of every penal institution in the world; he deserves to hang from every branch of every tree of every State and Territory penetrated by the railroads, with the exception of Nevada, which has no trees."

Source: Richard Rayner, *The Associates: Four Capitalists Who Created California* (New York: Norton, 2008), 188.

DID YOU KNOW?

Stanford's Widow Gets Revenge

Edward A. Ross, a sociologist and friend of President Theodore Roosevelt, coined the term "criminaloid" in the first major effort by a social scientist to call attention to what later would be labeled "white-collar crime." In a memorable paragraph Ross described his subject in these words:

> The criminaloid counterfeits the good citizen. He takes care to meet all the conventional tests—flag worship, old-soldier sentiment, observance of all the national holidays, perfervid patriotism, party regularity and support. Full well he knows that giving a fountain or a park or establishing a chair on the Neolithic drama or the elegiac poetry of the Chaldeans will more than outweigh the dodging of taxes . . . and corrupting of city councils.

Ross would be fired from Stanford University, founded by robber baron Leland Stanford and his wife, in one of the most notorious academic freedom cases. Ross had angered Jane Lathrop Stanford, the university's surviving cofounder. Mrs. Stanford objected to Ross's political activism, his strongly stated criticism of the manner in which her husband had secured his fortune, and the exploitation of Chinese laborers working on the Union Pacific Railroad. "The Firing of E. A. Ross from Stanford University: Injustice Compounded by Deception." *Journal of Economic Education* 22 (1990): 183–90.

was from Watervliet (now Colonie) and Crocker from Troy, two upstate New York towns not far apart, while Stanford had been born in Richmond county in Virginia.

All four became California merchants. They had met in rooms over the dry goods store jointly owned by Huntington and Hopkins in Sacramento to plot building a railroad in the western part of the country. Huntington, later the leader of the quartet, was notorious for tactics such as sailing out to meet boats in San Francisco Bay, buying up their cargo, and then withholding the goods from the market until he could obtain a scarcity-dictated price—an age-old practice called forestalling in medieval England. Later Huntington would set railroad carrying rates at virtually extortionate levels, calibrated exquisitely to a point where the shipper could realize only enough profit to sustain himself. Huntington was aptly described as having a cash register for a heart.

A governmental body investigating the Pacific railroads exposed rampant fraud in the management of the lines, including the expenditure of $2.25 million to influence legislation. The magnates sought to retaliate by buying a Sacramento newspaper to use its pages to counteract the attacks.

FURTHER READINGS

Ambrose, Stephen. (2000). *Nothing Like It in the World: The Men Who Built the Transcontinental Railroad, 1863–1869*. New York: Simon & Schuster.

Bancroft, Hubert Howe. (1952). *History of the Life of Leland Stanford*. Oakland, CA: Biobooks.

Carter, Franklin. (1892). *Mark Hopkins*. Boston: Houghton Mifflin.

Clark, George. (1931). *Leland Stanford*. London: Oxford University Press.

Denison, John H. (1935). *Mark Hopkins: A Biography*. New York: Scribner's.

Latta, Estelle. (1963). *Controversial Mark Hopkins: The Great Swindle of American History*. Durham, NC: Colton Historical and Research Foundation.

Lewis, Oscar. (1938). *The Big Four: The Story of Huntington, Stanford, Hopkins, and Crocker, and the Building of the Central Pacific*. New York: Knopf.

Rayner, Richard. (2008). *The Associates: Four Capitalists Who Created California*. New York: Norton.

Williams, John Hoyt. (1988). *A Great and Shining Railroad: The Epic Story of the Transcontinental Railroad*. New York: Times Books.

Jay Gould and the Erie Railroad

- *Document:* The self-serving tactics of the robber barons were thoroughly documented in Gustavus Myers's classic multivolume *The History of American Fortunes*, which devoted one book to the men who had amassed massive wealth by crooked operations associated with the building of the railroads. Jay Gould is regarded as one of the prime examples of the robber baron breed. Document 2.3 offers Myers's portrayal of some of the activities of Gould and his robber baron associates.
- *Date:* 1911.
- *Where:* Published in Chicago by C. H. Kerr.
- *Significance:* The exposure of the infamous acts of men such as Gould led President Theodore Roosevelt to crusade against the more heinous acts of big business and to support the passage of the Sherman Antitrust Act of 1890 that outlawed business combinations in restraint of trade.

DOCUMENT 2.3

The first medium by which Jay Gould transferred many millions of dollars to his ownership was by his looting and wrecking of the Erie Railroad. . . .

The Erie Railroad, running from New York City to Buffalo and thence westward to Chicago, was started in 1832. In New York State alone, irrespective of gifts in other States, it received what was virtually a gift of $3,000,000 of State funds, and $3,217,000 interest . . . Counties, municipalities and towns through which it passed were prevailed upon to contribute freely donations of money, lands and rights. From private proprietors in New York State it obtained presents of land then valued at from $400,000 to $500,000, but now worth tens of millions of dollars. In addition, an extraordinary series of special privileges and franchises were given to it. The

In this 1870 Currier & Ives print, Cornelius Vanderbilt and James Fisk race for control of New York's rails. Fisk, along with co-conspiritor, James Gould, tricked Vanderbilt out of millions of dollars using the Erie Railroad as a cover. (Library of Congress)

process was manifold in every State through which the railroad passed. The cost of construction and equipment came almost wholly from the grant of public funds . . .

The people credulously supposed that their interests would be safeguarded. But from time to time, Legislature after Legislature was corrupted or induced to enact stealthy acts by which the railroad was permitted to pass without restriction into the possession of a small clique of exploiters and speculators. Not only were people cheated out of funds raised by public taxation and advanced to build the road . . . but this very money was claimed by the capitalist owners as private capital, large amounts of bonds and stocks were issued against it, and the producers were assessed in the form of high freight and passenger rates to pay the necessary interest and dividends of the spurious issues . . .

So little attention was given to efficient management that shocking catastrophes resulted at frequent intervals . . . Old Cornelius Vanderbilt . . . secretly began buying stock; by 1866 he had obtained enough to get control . . . To carry out Vanderbilt's plans, Jay Gould, demure and ingratiating, and James Fisk, Jr., a portly, tawdry, pompous voluptuary were hired as directors [by Daniel Drew, another railroad speculator]. They gave every appearance of responding obediently to Vanderbilt's directions. However, they quietly banded to mature a plot by which they would wrest away Vanderbilt's control.

Apparently to provide funds for improving the railroad, they voted to issue a mass of bonds. Large quantities of these they turned over to themselves as securities for pretended advances of money. These bonds were secretly converted into shares of stock . . . Vanderbilt . . . bought the stock unsuspectingly. [Soon after], amazed and furious, he realized that he had been gouged out of $7,000,0000. . . . The very next morning warrants were sworn out against Drew, Fisk and Gould. A hint quickly reached them; they thereupon fled to Jersey City, taking their loot with them. One of them bore away in a hackney coach bales containing $6,000,000 in greenbacks. The other two fugitives were loaded down with valises crammed with bonds and stocks.

Stuffing $500,000 into his satchel, Gould surreptitiously hurried to Albany. Detected there and arrested, he was released under heavy bail a confederate supplied … In the face of sinister charges of corruption, a bill legalizing the fraudulent stock issues was passed. Ineffectually did Vanderbilt bribe the legislators to defeat it; as fast as they took and kept his money, Gould debauched them with greater sums. One Senator in particular … accepted $75,000 from Vanderbilt and $100,000 from Gould, and pocketed both amounts …

From 1868 to 1872 Gould, abetted by subservient directors, issued two hundred and thirty five [sic] thousand more shares of stock. Fisk was murdered by a rival in 1872 in a feud over Fisk's mistress. His death did not interrupt Gould's plans.

[To a legislative investigative committee] Gould cynically gave … information. He could distinctly recall, he said, "that he had been in the habit of sending money into the various districts throughout the state," either to control nominations or elections for Senators or members of the Assembly. He considered "that as a rule, such investments paid better than to wait until the man got to Albany …" "In a Republican district I was a Republican, in a Democratic district, a Democrat, in a doubtful district I was doubtful, but I was always for Erie …" The funds that he thus used in widespread corruption came obviously from the proceeds of his grand thefts, and he might have added with equal truth, that with this stolen money he was able to employ some of the most eminent lawyers of the day, and purchase judges.

As for the small stockholders of the Erie Railroad, Gould easily pacified them by holding out the bait of a larger dividend than they had been getting under the former regime. This he managed by the common and fraudulent expedient of issuing bonds, and paying dividends out of proceeds. So long as the profits of these small stockholders was slightly better than they had been getting before, they were complacently satisfied to let Gould continue his frauds. This acquiescence in theft has been one of the most pronounced characteristics of the capitalistic investors, both large and small. Numberless instances have shown that they raise no objections to plundering management provided that under it their money returns are increased.

Source: Gustavus Myers, *A History of American Fortunes—Volume 2: Great Fortunes from Railroads* (Chicago: C. H. Kerr, 1909): chap. 10.

ANALYSIS

Jay Gould (1836–92), one of the men who earned the reputation of robber baron, has often been regarded as the worst of the group, or as children are wont to say "the baddest." Historian Alexander Noyes wrote that "few properties on which this man laid his hand escaped ruin in the end. He was not a builder, he was a destroyer." James R. Keene, a contemporary, denounced Gould as "the worst man on earth since the beginning of the Christian era. He is treacherous, false, cowardly, and a despicable worm incapable of a generous nature." It is said that Gould considered himself to be the most hated man in the United States in the nineteenth century, a quite likely conjecture. One of his more cynical remarks about human beings beneath him on the social scale was: "I can hire half of the working class to kill the other half."

Born Jason Gould to a poor farming family in Roxbury in upstate New York, he rose to become what was said to be the ninth richest man in American history. Gould first worked as a surveyor's assistant, preparing maps of some of the state counties, and at age 21 he entered business as a partner in a leather tannery in Stroudsburg, Pennsylvania. He soon relocated to New York City where he worked as a stockbroker and, most importantly, as a speculator, taking advantage of the unregulated business conditions prevailing at the time. From 1868 onward, he was a power in the financial world, manipulating companies, bribing judges, and exploiting customers. By 1880, Gould had virtual control of 10,000 miles of the American railroads, one-ninth of the national total.

As part of the Erie Railroad's westward move, Gould gained control of Wabash, a wheat-carrying railroad line. He devised a plan to push up the price of gold, thereby weakening the dollar, and to encourage foreign purchases of wheat from the United States, a move that led to a business panic on September 24, 1869, called "Black Friday," when the price of Double Eagle gold fell to almost half its previous face value. Later Gould came to own Western Union, the country's leading telegraph company, and the newspaper, the *New York World*.

Gould died of tuberculosis and is buried in Woodlawn Cemetery in the Bronx, a site made infamous when it was designated as the place where the kidnapper of Charles Lindbergh's son would claim the ransom money for the return of the child, who already was dead. The verdict on Gould as a human being is unsparing. One source sums it up by observing: "He remained ruthless, unscrupulous, and friendless."

DID YOU KNOW?

One Robber Baron Assesses a Colleague

Collis Huntington, primarily concerned with lobbying federal officials on behalf of the interests of the Big Four railroad magnates, kept up a running correspondence with David Colton, who came to handle many of their company's financial affairs. In one letter, Huntington passed along comments about a meeting with Jay Gould:

New York, March 24, 1875
Friend Colton . . .
    Gould has just left my office. He said he came in to talk coal. He said he wanted to get up a company and put in say 10,000 acres of coal land in Evanston [Wyoming], have the capital stock say $5,000,000, then supply the road at a fixed price, then supply the coal at a fixed price, the balance of the coal mined to be put on the cars at say, cost. The two railroads to transport the coal at cost, say three fourth cent per mile. Then after the coal is sold, divide the profits pro rata between the several interests. He thought there would be large amounts of money made out of it . . . Now I think that Gould was very much in earnest about this, or was when he was talking about it, and I wish you would write to me, giving me your views about it in detail, for it seems to me that much could be made of such an arrangement, if we could some way keep control, but I do not like to be mixed up with Gould in anything where it is possible for him to get control.
    Yours, etc.
    C. H. Huntington

Source: Salvador A. Ramirez, *The Octopus Speaks: The Colton Letters.* (Carlsbad, CA: Tentacled Press, 1982), 90.

FURTHER READINGS

Gordon, John Steele. (1988). *The Scarlet Woman of Wall Street: Jay Gould, Jim Fisk, Cornelius Vanderbilt, the Erie Railroad Wars, and the Birth of Wall Street.* New York: Weidenfeld & Nicolson.

Grodinsky, Julius. (1957). *Jay Gould: His Business Career, 1867–1892.* Philadelphia: University of Pennsylvania Press.

Hoyt, Edwin P. (1980). *The Goulds: A Social History*. New York: Weybright and Talley.

Klein, Maury. (1986). *The Life and Legend of Jay Gould*. Baltimore: Johns Hopkins University Press.

Lavender, David S. (1970). *The Great Persuader*. Garden City, NY: Doubleday.

O'Connor, Richard. (1947). *Gould's Millions*. Westport, CT: Greenwood.

Renehan, Edward J., Jr. (2005). *The Dark Genius of Wall Street: The Misunderstood Life of Jay Gould, King of the Robber Barons*. New York: Basic Books.

Cornelius Vanderbilt

- **Document:** Mark Twain is regarded by many as the greatest American writer of all time. In a tribute to Twain, the Norwegian novelist Knut Hamsun, a Nobel laureate in literature (a prize Twain fully deserved but never received), wrote of Twain: "He was not only a humorist, his humor had weight, he was a teacher and an educationalist. He offered people the deeper and worthier truths in the form of wit." In Document 2.4, "An Open Letter to Com. Vanderbilt," Twain attacks Cornelius Vanderbilt for his stingy hoarding of the ill-gotten wealth he had accumulated.
- **Date:** March, 1869.
- **Where:** *Packard's Monthly.*
- **Significance:** Twain sarcastically sets out the unattractive traits of a leading robber baron in a way that expresses the widespread contempt that Americans had for Vanderbilt's ruthless predations.

DOCUMENT 2.4

How my heart goes out in sympathy to you! how I do pity you Commodore Vanderbilt! Most men have at least a few friends, whose devotion is a comfort and solace to them. But you seem to be the idol of only a crawling swarm of small souls, who love to glorify your most flagrant unworthiness in print; or praise your vast possession worshipingly; or sing of your unimportant private habits and sayings and doings, as if your millions gave them dignity; friends who applaud your superhuman stinginess with the same gusto that they do your most magnificent displays of commercial genius and daring, and likewise your most lawless violations of commercial honor— for those infatuated worshiper of dollars not their own seem to make no distinctions, but swing their hats and shout hallelujah every time you do *anything*, no matter what it is. I do pity you. I would pity any man with such friends as these. I should think that you would hate the sight of a newspaper. I should think that you would not dare to glance at one, for fear you would find in it one of these distressing eulogies of something you had been doing, which was either infinitely trivial or else a matter you ought to be ashamed of....

One day one of your subjects comes out with a column or two detailing your rise from penury to affluence, and praising you as if you were last and noblest work of God, but unconsciously telling how exquisitely mean a man has to be in order to achieve what you have achieved . . . Next, a subject of yours prints a long article to show how in some shrewd, underhanded way . . . you have added another million or so to your greasy greenbacks; and behold, *he* praises you, and never hints that immoral practices . . . are a damning example to the rising commercial generation—more, a damning thing to the whole nation, while there are insects like your subjects to make virtue of them in print....

And next, a subject tells how when you owned the California line of steamers you used to have your pursers make out false lists of passengers, and thus carry some hundreds more than the law allowed—in this way breaking the law of your country and jeopardizing the lives of your passengers by overcrowding them during a long, sweltering voyage over tropical seas, and through a disease-poisoned atmosphere. And this shrewdness was duly glorified too. But I remember how those misused passengers used to revile you and curse you when they got to the Isthmus [of Panama] . . .

Three are other anecdotes . . . They only show how unfortunate and how narrowing it is for a man to have wealth who makes a god of it instead of a servant . . . All I wish to urge upon you now is, that you crush out your naïve instincts and go and do something *worthy* of praise—go and do something you need not blush to see in print—do something that may rouse one solitary good example . . . to the thousands of young men who emulate your energy and your industry; shine as one solitary grain of pure gold upon the heaped rubbish of your life. Do this, I beseech you, else through your example we shall shortly have in our midst five hundred Vanderbilts, which God forbid! Go, now please go, and do one worthy act. Go boldly, grandly, nobly, and give four dollars to some great public charity. It will break your heart, no doubt . . .

Don't misunderstand me, Vanderbilt. I know you own seventy millions; but then you know and I know that it isn't what a man has that constitutes wealth. No—it is to be *satisfied* with what one has, that is wealth. As long as one sorely *needs* a certain additional amount, that man isn't rich. Seventy times seventy millions can't make him rich as long as his poor heart is breaking for more.

Source: Mark Twain, "An Open Letter to Com. Vanderbilt," *Packard's Monthly: The Young Men's Magazine*, March 1869, 89–91. The periodical, which had begun publication in May 1868, declared that it was dedicated to fighting "the evils of the day . . . pursuing them as they are, without mitigation nor remorse." The "open letter" is reprinted in Mark Twain, *Collected Tales, Sketches, Speeches and Essays, 1852–1890* (New York: Library of America,1992), 285–90.

ANALYSIS

Cornelius Vanderbilt (1794–1877), the man who fought Jay Gould for control of the Erie Railroad, is believed to have been the person to whom the term "robber baron" first was applied. His life and achievements are chronicled in a 721-page biography by T. J. Stiles, published in 2009, and it is not without a certain irony that Stiles's previous book told the story of the life of frontier bandit Jesse James.

The Vanderbilts were early settlers in the American colonies. Cornelius's ancestors had migrated from Holland to New York in the 1650s. Cornelius was born 18 years after the American Revolution, while George Washington was still alive, and he would live long enough to play a role in the Civil War. He is credited with being the moving force in the creation of the modern corporation through his purchase and consolidation of New York's railroads. His biographer notes that Vanderbilt's admirers saw him as the ultimate example of the wonders of opportunity in America, of a man of common origins rising to the top through hard work and ability. His critics, as biographer Stiles observes, "called him grasping and ruthless, an unelected king who never pretended to rule for his people." He was regarded as niggardly, parsimonious, and vindictive, a man with a ravenous hunger for wealth. In the words of a biographer, Vanderbilt had a "near-legendary status as a self-absorbed bore and braggart, intent upon self-glorification, and devoid of generosity."

Vanderbilt grew up on Staten Island, the smallest of New York's five boroughs. Like Jay Gould, he came from a farming family of modest means; his father supplemented his meager agricultural income by operating a ferry between the island and Manhattan. Cornelius left school at the age of 11 and later would claim: "If I had learned education, I would not have the time to learn anything else." He remained only semiliterate throughout his life. Nearly 30, he would demonstrate the absence of schooling in the spelling and grammar of a letter he dispatched concerning a business deal: "I haeve this day impld a lawyer to bring an action . . . I no we cannot recovir but it will give them troble . . . This day [they] brought a suit against all my men even the kook. . . . these litiltle suites will cost nothing much."

As a young man, Vanderbilt worked on ferries and schooners and then, when they came into fashion, steamboats. He style was marked, in Stiles's term, by "elbows-out aggressiveness." It was when he began to build his own fleet of ships that Vanderbilt took on the title of Commodore, and his vanity extended to wearing full naval regalia. Vanderbilt's ruthlessness was characterized by either buying out competitors or waging all-out price wars in which he would cut fares until he had forced the other companies out of business, allowing him to sharply escalate his prices. Vanderbilt developed a chokehold on the commerce he was involved in. He would utter his own epitaph in an interview in 1878: "I have been insane on the subject of money making all my life," Vanderbilt told the newspaper's reporter. In another observation he set out his no-holds-barred philosophy: "You have undertaken to cheat me," he told a man with whom he had done business. "I won't sue you for the law is too slow. I'll ruin you." And he did exactly that to his competitor.

Vanderbilt moved from the world of steamships into that of railroads when he shrewdly came to appreciate that waterways were always susceptible to ruinous competition but railroad tracks were the monopoly of their possessor.

Vanderbilt became the richest man in America. By the time of his death he had accumulated assets of $105 million that today would be equivalent to more than $160 billion. By contrast, the fortune of Bill Gates, the founder of Microsoft and the richest American today, is listed at about $55 billion. Vanderbilt left virtually his entire estate to one son, William Henry, in an effort to keep it from being diluted by distribution among his 13 children, 12 of whom survived to adulthood. His favorite, George Washington Vanderbilt, a graduate of West Point, had contracted a fatal tuberculosis illness when serving with the Union Army during the Civil War. William Henry would become infamous for his remark in the face of criticism: "The public be damned."

In line with the actions of the corps of robber barons, Cornelius Vanderbilt left behind a structural monument to his memory. He endowed the newborn Capital University in Nashville, Tennessee, with what then was the munificent sum of $1 million. In gratitude it changed its name to Vanderbilt University, and is today regarded as one of the leading institutions of higher learning in the South. He also financed the construction in 1871 of Grand Central Station, the railroad terminus on 42nd Street and Park Avenue in midtown in New York City, adorned with a five-acre glass dome, and dubbed "the gateway to the nation."

DID YOU KNOW?

Vanderbilt's Power Plays

"In the mid-nineteenth century, Cornelius Vanderbilt built a vast economic empire in the United States. He built political and military ones as well. In the Civil War, he offered to use some of his ships to combat Confederate submarines. He organized a company of militia to deal with his competitors and, in a famous rejection of the law, said about it: 'Taint I got the power?' Vanderbilt believed that an important way to secure business success was to physically ensure it himself. A war-making capability was, in fact, an aspect of his business strategy. He operated at a time when the nation-state was just being born, and his corporate actions were more of an expansion of his entire entrepreneurial personality than an institutional sense of corporate foreign policy. In some ways, however, his aggressive militarism foreshadows the power of a corporation vis-à-vis a nation-state today."

Source: Thomas L. Fort, "The Time and Sense of Corporate Responsibility," *American Business Law Journal* 44 (2007): 289–329, at 291.

FURTHER READINGS

Croffut, William A. (1975). *The Vanderbilts and the Story of Their Fortune*. New York: Arno.

Hoyt, Edwin P. (1962). *Commodore Vanderbilt*. Chicago: Reilly and Lee.

Lane, Wheaton J. (1942). *Commodore Vanderbilt: An Epic of the Steam Age*. New York: Knopf.

Parker, Lewis. (2003). *Cornelius Vanderbilt and the Railroad Industry*. New York: Powerkids Press.

Renehan, Edward J., Jr. (2007). *Commodore: The Life of Cornelius Vanderbilt*. New York: Basic Books.

Smith, Arthur H. (1937). *Commodore Vanderbilt: An Epic of American Achievement*. New York: McBride.

Stiles, T. J. (2005). *The First Tycoon: The Epic Life of Cornelius Vanderbilt*. New York: Knopf.

Daniel Drew

- *Document:* It is uncommon to come into possession of a document alleged to be written by a robber baron who describes the malevolent pleasure he derives from outwitting and cheating others. Daniel Drew, deeply involved in the steamboat and, later, railroad financial manipulations, was said to have left behind a trunk full of notes that he intended to employ for the writing of his autobiography. Bouck White fashioned what he called these "jumbled" and "helter-skelter" materials into a revelatory book. Other writers, however, say that White, a Harvard-educated Congregational minister, and a socialist, a man who was said to be notably eccentric, improvised Drew's state of mind and wrapped his speculation around known facts. Either way, Document 2.5 offers a vivid portrait of how the mind of a robber baron might well work.
- *Date:* White's book was published in 1913.
- *Where:* Garden City, New York.
- *Significance:* Document 2.5 offers unusual and very rare insight, be it fact or fiction, into the thought process of a man intent on taking advantage of others in order to feather his own financial nest. The appeal of the book is indicated by the fact that it remains in print today, a century after its initial publication.

DOCUMENT 2.5

. . . I had other irons in the anvil. I didn't feel called upon to keep myself back, just in order to provide better transportation [on the Hudson River steamboat] for Putnam County farmers. I had my own fortune to make—my own career to carve out. Any fellow except he's a natural-born fool, will look out for number one first.

There were bigger prizes to be had in the Hudson River steamboat business than the Peekskill route. The Hudson River Association was running a line of boats from New York to Albany. Captain Vanderbilt had had a falling out with one of the directors of that association, and had put two rival boats on that route so successfully that he had compelled them to buy him out; he agreeing to withdraw from the boat business on that route for ten years. This left the coast clear. If Vanderbilt, by running competition boats, could scare them into buying him out at a good figure, I didn't see why I couldn't do the same. So I bought two boats, put them on the line to Albany, and ran them in competition with the River Association. This lasted for a year. At the end of that time it turned out as I had expected. The Association took me in with them on a pooling arrangement, my boats sharing the total earnings of the partnership.

This lasted a little while, and I was feeling big to be in with the company that was running so big a line of water transportation. By and by I wanted to make still more money. So I hit upon a scheme. While I was still in the Hudson River Association, I put another boat on the route as a competitor. Only, I ran it under the name of another fellow, giving out that he was the owner, so as to keep my own part in the matter hid. Then I cut prices on that independent boat in such a way as hurt the Association like sixty. Whenever we would hold a directors' meeting of the Association, if they were not already talking about it, I would steer the conversation around to the subject of the rival boat, and ask if something couldn't be done about it. Because, as I showed them, if we allowed that boat to run against us so freely, other fellows would be encouraged also to put boats on, and we would soon be nowheres. Finally, I got the directors to pass a resolution to buy up this troublesome rival. And I got them to appoint me as the agent to go and see her owner with our proposition.

"I think I can find him right away," said I. "His office is only a spit and a stride from here, so to speak." They said they would hold the meeting until I got back. So I left the room, went out, walked around the block, and came back with my report.

"A bit more buys the whistle," said I. "I've seen the owner and he is willing to sell. Only our figure isn't quite high enough. He says he is making money hand over fist. Pretty soon he thinks he will be able to get another boat on. But he doesn't want to be mean. He is willing to sell if we do what he thinks is reasonable. If we tack $8,000 more onto the offer, he'll close with us."

The directors debated. The boat was hurting us. Anybody could see that. I got a word in now and then, hinting how this pestersome was probably in a position to hurt us still more, unless we got him out of the way right off. Finally we voted to give the $8,000 more which the man had asked. I left them there in the meeting, went out, walked around the block again, came back and said the man had accepted; and if they would make out the papers, then and there, I would take them over to him and get the deed of sale.

I saw from this incident that I could match my wits against most anybody. Besides, this $8,000 which I had turned into my pocket out of the company's funds was not only so much clear gain to me, but was so much clear loss to them.

Source: Bouck White, *The Book of Daniel Drew: A Glimpse of the Fisk-Gould-Tweed Régime from the Inside* (Garden City, NY: Doubleday/Page, 1913), 98–100.

DID YOU KNOW?

Spider Webs and White-Collar Crime

During his presidential address, Edwin H. Sutherland, quoting Bouck White's biography of Daniel Drew, reported that Drew had once observed: "The law is like a cobweb; it's made for flies and the similar kinds of insects, so to speak, but lets the big bumblebees break through. When technicalities of the law stood in my way, I have always been able to brush them aside as easy as anything."

As a onetime college teacher of Greek, Sutherland perhaps knew that Drew (or White) had stolen this maxim, as Drew stole so much else, from an earlier—some 2,000 years earlier—source. In 1166, John of Salisbury had conveyed his cynicism in a letter to an English bishop. "Civil laws," he wrote, "as Anacharsis the Scythian said, are like spiders' webs, catching flies and letting greater flying things through." Anacharsis had made that statement in the late fifth or early sixth century before the Christian era, and it was widely circulated by the Roman writer Valerius Maximus, among several others. In 1790, satirist Jonathan Swift, author of *Gulliver's Travels*, also cribbed the epigram, noting that "laws are like cobwebs, which may catch small flies but let wasps and hornets break through." John Adams, the second president of the United States, tied the saying more directly to the fact that white-collar criminals avoid the penal consequences of their illegal acts. Referring to the ancient Greek constitution, Adams wrote that it "was but a cobweb, to bind the poor, while the rich would easily break through."

ANALYSIS

Whether literally accurate or not, the recital of Daniel Drew's thoughts and activities captures the essential mind-set of the men who were dubbed robber barons. Drew (1797–1879) was a key figure in the looting and pillage of the public that characterized the swashbuckling capitalists of his time.

Daniel Drew was born in the township of Carmel, New York, a dairy region north of New York City. He was poorly educated, and at the age of 15, when his father died, he served briefly in the War of 1812 as a paid volunteer, but did not see any action. After demobilization, he worked as a cattle drover and trader. In that occupation, Drew transported cattle from the countryside into New York City. The business was so successful that he expanded his operations to areas west of the Allegheny Mountains. To increase his profits, Drew had the cattle drink large quantities of water so that their weight and their price increased. The term "stock-watering," later applied to cheating Wall Street transactions, had its origin in this practice. Of his own activities and those of fellow robber barons, Drew is claimed by White to have said: "Business slobbers a fellow up. It's like teaching a calf to drink out of a pail—you're sure to get splashed and dirty. Business is a scramble for cash."

Document 2.5 offers a sketch of some of Drew's activities when he entered the steamboat business. Following that, he speculated in railroads. In his most notorious enterprise he was betrayed by Jim Fisk and Jay Gould in what has been called the "Erie Wars," a financial battle in 1870 marked by blatant dishonesty and corrupt practices by all parties. The Panic of 1873 further erased Drew's fortune, and three years later he declared bankruptcy and lived the remainder of his life on the generosity of his son.

A devout Methodist, Drew's memory is marked by his founding of Drew Theological Seminary, now Drew University, in Madison, New Jersey.

FURTHER READINGS

Adams, Charles F., and Henry Adams. (1871/1960). *Chapters of Erie and Other Essays.* Ithaca, NY: Seal Books.

Browder, Clifford. (1986). *The Money Game in Old New York: Daniel Drew and His Times.* Lexington: University of Kentucky.

Minnigerode, Maude. (1970). *Certain Rich Men: Stephen Girard, John Jacob Astor, Jay Cooke, Daniel Drew, Cornelius Vanderbilt, Jim Fisk.* Freeport, NY: Books for Libraries.

Sitterly, Charles F. (1938). *The Building of Drew University.* New York: Methodist Book Concern.

J. Pierpont Morgan—Part I

- *Document:* This first of the pair of documents dealing with the activities of J. Pierpont Morgan serves a dual purpose. First, it offers a contemporary view of Morgan that appeared in a prestigious magazine. Second, it provides a preview of the work of one of the prominent writers who would as a group be labeled "muckrakers," and whose position in the history of white-collar and corporate crime will be taken up in Chapter 4. Ray Stannard Baker, the author of the document, subsequently became the press secretary for President Woodrow Wilson and published 15 books on Wilson's correspondence, his life, and his ideas.
- *Date:* October 1901.
- *Where:* McClure's Magazine.
- *Significance:* Ray Stannard Baker's portrayal of J. Pierpont Morgan fed into the public antagonism toward the self-interested and self-serving tactics of the business tycoons whose designation as "robber barons" indicated first, their thievery, and second, their elite, seemingly impregnable social standing much like that of the nobility of the England aristocracy from whom American colonists had sought to separate themselves.

DOCUMENT 2.6

A few months ago an American citizen without title or office landed in England and so apprehensive was Threadneedle Street [location of the Bank of England and until 2004 of the London Stock Exchange] of his power in the financial world, and of the effect which his sudden death might have on the markets, that certain brokers, to protect themselves in their American investments, immediately took the extraordinary measure of applying to Lloyd's for insurance on his life, paying premiums at the rate of thirty pounds on the thousand for three months.

The citizen was J. Pierpont Morgan, who had just organized the most powerful industrial and financial institution the world has ever known. It matters not whether he was a large owner of the United States Steel Corporation; as its recognized and actual dictator, he controlled a yearly income and expenditure nearly as great as that of imperial Germany . . . and by employing two hundred and fifty thousand men, supported a population of over one million souls, almost a nation in itself. . . .

While in England, Mr. Morgan bought—whether for himself or for American clients, it matters not—one of the greatest of English steamship companies, the Leyland line, operating thirty-eight vessels between Europe and America. This move, following closely on the organization of the Steel Trust, was interpreted first as a blow to England's supremacy on the seas. It was natural and inevitable that Europe should anxiously inquire as to the further intentions of this man, to whom the purchase of a great steamship line seemed only the incident of a holiday . . .

No one could follow the accounts of his doings in England and of the deep concern which his presence caused, without realizing the meaning of power. Mr. Morgan, no doubt, controls and influences more money and money interests to-day than any other man in the world . . .

Significant of the changing centers of the world's money power is the fact that J. S. Morgan, the father, directed his banks from London, while J. Pierpont Morgan, the son, directs the larger system from New York. It was characteristic also that Morgan should have finally dominated every man and every firm with whom he came in contact; he must by nature be absolute dictator or nothing . . .

Besides his own private banking house here and its branches abroad, Mr. Morgan largely controls a powerful national bank in New York City—the National Bank of Commerce, of which he is the vice-president. It is known in Wall Street as "Morgan's Bank." He is a dominating influence in other banks and financial institutions, and a director . . . in twenty-one railroad companies, great and small . . . He is a director in the Western Union Telegraph Company, the Pullman Palace Car Company, the Aetna Fire Insurance Company, the General Electric Company, the greatest electric company in the world . . . He is a potent, and in times of trouble the controlling, factor in several of what are known as the "coal roads" of Pennsylvania—the Erie, the Lehigh Valley, the Central of New Jersey, and the Reading, together with their tributary coal fields . . . [H]e is at present practically director of the vast steel interests of the country, through the United States Steel Company, and he controls at least one Atlantic steamship line . . .

For a man of his age and size he seems unusually active, moving about with almost nervous alertness. He is a man of few words, always sharply and shortly spoken. When a man comes to him Mr. Morgan looks at him keenly, waiting for him to speak first, and his decision follows quickly.

Mr. Morgan knows to the last degree the psychology of meeting and dealing with men. The man who sits in his office, a citadel of silent and reserve force, and makes his visitor uncover his batteries is impregnable. This is Mr. Morgan's way—the way he dealt with a certain owner of coal mines in Pennsylvania, who knew that Mr. Morgan must have his property, and so had come down prepared to exact a good price, to "thresh it out with Morgan." Mr. Morgan kept him waiting a long time, and then he came out, bulky, cold, impressive, looked the coalman in the eye, and only broke the silence to say, "I'll give you \$——for your property." And there the bargain was closed. His way is to deal brusquely in ultimatums; he says "I'll do this" or "I'll do that," and that settles it . . .

DID YOU KNOW?

Morgan Airs His Views

In 1913, a U.S. House of Representatives Banking and Commerce subcommittee chaired by Arsène Pujo of Louisiana sought to establish that illegal monopolies controlled the railroads, banks, and other major commercial enterprises in the United States. J. P. Morgan, who would die soon after, seemed to be enjoying the opportunity to air his views before a congressional committee and by proxy a national audience. Finally, in what writer Jean Strouse notes "was to become the most famous dialogue in the hearings' thousands of pages of testimony," an interchange between the committee attorney, Samuel Untermeyer, and Morgan went like this:

Untermeyer: The basis of banking is credit, is it not?
   Morgan: Not always. That is an evidence of banking, but it is not the money itself. Money is gold and nothing else.

Untermeyer then asked whether it was not true that banks loan money to people because they believe that the borrowers have money behind them.

   Morgan: No, sir. It is because the people believe in the man.
Untermeyer: And he might not be worth anything?
   Morgan: He might not have anything. I have known a man to come into my office and I have given him a check for a million dollars when I knew that he had not a cent in the world. . . .
Untermeyer: Is not commercial credit based primarily upon money and property?
   Morgan: No, sir, the first thing is character.
Untermeyer: Before money and property?
   Morgan: Before money or property or anything else. Money cannot buy it . . . because a man I do not trust could not get money from me on all the bonds in Christendom.

Source: U.S. House of Representatives, Subcommittee on Housing and Banking, *Hearings,* 1912.

Economy in production, economy in management, economy in interest charges are what he has always sought. That is why he never misses an opportunity to strike a blow at competition in whatever form it may appear. Rival companies compete and lose money; Mr. Morgan steps in and combines them, thus saving not only the losses due to the competition, but economizing also in administrative expenses . . .

Mr. Morgan has been such a reorganizer and reconstructor of bankrupt corporations, especially railroads, that Wall Street has come to call the process re-Morganizing. . . .

Source: Ray Stannard Baker, "J. Pierpont Morgan," *McClure's Magazine* 17 (October 1901): 507–18.

ANALYSIS

Of Morgan personally, British writer Harold Nicholson, who knew him well, wrote in his diary: "There was about him a touch of madness or something immoral and abnormal. He had the mind of a super-criminal and the character of a saint." The writer E. L. Doctorow in *Ragtime* portrays Morgan as "a burly six-footer with a large head of sparse white hair, a white moustache and fierce intolerant eyes set just close enough to suggest the psychopathology of his will."

Junius Pierpont Morgan (1837–1913)—Pierpont, the name he preferred, was his mother's maiden name—was born in Hartford, Connecticut. Unlike virtually all of the roster of robber barons, he came from a long line of successful ancestors. Miles Morgan had brought the family to the New World in 1656 and helped found the city of Springfield, Massachusetts. Morgan's grandfather left his son property in Hartford, and the son parlayed his talents and inheritance into a partnership with Levi P. Morton, who later would become the vice president of the United States.

J. P. Morgan was well educated, a graduate of the highly regarded English High School in Boston, where the family had relocated, and he subsequently studied in German universities in Stutigen and Göttingen. He then entered banking, and paid a $300 fee to buy his way out of service during the Civil War, as had robber barons Andrew Carnegie and John D. Rockefeller.

After the war, Morgan made huge sums by lending money to an impoverished national government at high interest rates. Subsequently, he created a string of monopolies that used their stranglehold on the services they provided to reap gigantic profits. In 190, Morgan put together U.S. Steel, the world's first billion-dollar corporation. At the height of his success, Morgan and people he controlled held 341 directorships in 112 corporations, worth $22.2 billion, twice the value of all property in 13 U.S. southern states.

In Morgan's eyes, monopoly power was desirable if it was exercised by well-meaning persons, namely himself and those like him. A newspaper editorial of the time disagreed: "It will never do," the New York *Evening Post* declared, "to say that unchecked power is a good thing because it is in the hands of good men."

FURTHER READINGS

Allen, Frederick Lewis. (1949). *The Great Pierpont Morgan*. New York: Harper.

Canfield, Cass (1983). *Outrageous Fortunes: The Story of the Medicis, the Rothschilds, and J. Pierpont Morgan*. New York: Harper Bruce Jovanovich.

Carosso, Vincent (1987). *The Morgans, Private Investment Bankers, 1854–1913*. Cambridge, MA: Harvard University Press.

Chernow, Ron. (1990). *The House of Morgan, and American Banking Dynasty and the Rise of Modern Finance*. New York: Atlantic Monthly Press.

Jackson, Stanley. (1983). *J. P. Morgan, a Biography*. New York: Stein and Day.

Satterlee, Herbert L. (1939). *J. Pierpont Morgan: An Intimate Portrait*. New York: Macmillan.

Sinclair, Andrew. (1981). *Corsair: The Life of J. P. Morgan*. Boston: Little, Brown.

Strouse, Jean. (1999). *Morgan: American Financier*. New York: Random House.

Winkler, John. (1930). *Morgan the Magnificent: A Life of J. Pierpont Morgan*. New York: Vanguard.

Morgan and the Hall Carbine Scandal

- *Document:* A report concerning the alleged nefarious act of J. P. Morgan in a deal that involved selling defective arms to Major General John C. Frémont of the Union Army.
- *When:* The sales occurred in the 1861 at the onset of the Civil War.
- *Where:* U.S. Army.
- *Significance:* Document 2.7 illustrates one of the numerous shady deals conducted by a robber baron that involved self-serving actions causing harm to the well-being of his country.

DOCUMENT 2.7

Among the profiteering arms merchants of the Civil War was John Pierpont Morgan. Morgan was in his middle 20s when the war broke out, but he did not shoulder a gun during the entire conflict. He had heard of the great lack of rifles in the army, and he decided to do his share in bringing relief.

A few years earlier the army had considered as obsolete and dangerous some rifles then in use, known as Hall's carbines. These rifles were ordered to be sold at auction, and they were disposed of at prices ranging between $1 and $2, probably as curios. In 1861, there still remained 5,000 of the condemned arms. Suddenly, on May 28, 1861, one Arthur M. Eastman appeared and offered $3 apiece for them. This high price should have made the officials suspicious but apparently it did not. Behind Eastman was a certain Simon Sevens, who was furnishing the cash for the transaction, but the real broker of the enterprise was J. P. Morgan.

After the condemned guns had been contracted for, Stevens sent a wire to General Frémont informing him that he had 5,000 new carbines in perfect condition. Did Frémont want them? Immediately, an order (amounting to a contract) arrived from

Frémont urging that the rifles be sent at once. They were bought from the government, and Morgan paid $3.50 apiece for them, a total of $17,486. These condemned carbines were now moved out of the government arsenal and sent to Frémont, and the bill presented was $22 apiece—that is, $109,912, a profit of $92,426.

When Frémont's soldiers tried to fire these "new carbines in perfect condition," they shot off their own thumbs. Great indignation was raised by this transaction, when it became known, and the government refused to pay Morgan's bill. Morgan promptly sued the government, and his claim was referred to a special commission that was examining disputed claims and settling them.

The commission, curiously enough, did not reject the Morgan claim entirely, but denounced him for his unscrupulous dealings. It allowed half of the claim, and proposed to pay $13.31 a carbine, that is, $66,500 for the lot. This would have netted Morgan a profit of $49,000. But Morgan was not satisfied. He maintained that he had a "contract" from Frémont and that he was determined to collect in full.

Accordingly, he sued in Stevens's name in the Court of Claims and the court promptly awarded him the full sum because "a contract is sacred"—a decision that was the opening wedge of other "dead horse claims" that Congress had tried to forestall.

Source: Carol H. Englelbrecht and Frank C. Hanighen, *Merchants of Death: A Study of the International Armament Industry* (New York: Garland, 1972): Chap. 2, "Second Hand Death."

ANALYSIS

The carbine scam established a public view of J. Pierpont Morgan that stuck to him throughout his life, but the story told by his critics needs additional perspective. At least it can be said that the carbine deal was not of his construction; rather, it was Morgan who put up the money for the men who concocted it, and there were some, including a congressional committee, that placed the blame on the initiators of the scheme rather than on Morgan for the purchase and sale of the rifles to General Frémont. Frémont, who later would serve as one of the first U.S. Senators from California and subsequently make an unsuccessful run for the presidency, also had to assume some responsibility for not being more diligent in pinning down details regarding the out-of-date breach-loading rifles he was purchasing, carbines that last had been used in the Mexican war. In fact, in a letter to a friend several years before the Civil War, J. M. Imboden, the president of the Virginia Military Institute, had written of the Hall carbines: "They are very unsafe & I would not recommend them for your service." At the same time, it was apparent that Frémont, commander of the Army's Department of the West, was in desperate straits in regard to arms and needed a morale boost after the Union's staggering defeat at the Battle of Bull Run, the first major land battle of the war, fought at Manassas, Virginia, as Union forces sought to move on the Confederate capital at Richmond.

It could be readily be argued Morgan was but another of a ruthless gang of robber barons who fleeced the national treasury whenever they could find an opening, but his situation offers a particularly intriguing illustration of the problem of locating guilt and blame in what often are shady deals with a façade of regular business. R. Gordon Wasson, an employee of the Morgan interests, later traced with meticulous care the story of the Hall carbine business and concluded that Morgan, then but 24 years old, was innocent of any wrongdoing, that he merely lent Stevens $20,000 at 9 percent interest (a common rate at the time, though the 25% commission Morgan negotiated was not usual) so that he could pay for the weapons. Stevens's sister had been a high school teacher of Morgan's, although the two men had not met before the loan request was made. Wasson accuses earlier historians of unprincipled exaggerations of Morgan's activity in the effort to smear a capitalist and to locate a scapegoat for the weapons fiasco.

The underlying question, however, is not readily resolved. Did Morgan have a responsibility to determine the purpose to which his loan was being put? Did his failure to do so—or worse, his indifference to the answer to that question—make him something of an accomplice to the unscrupulous situation? It would be very difficult and perhaps not fair to penalize Morgan, most particularly in terms of a criminal charge, but whether he carried a moral responsibility that he did not meet in the Hall carbine affair is a matter that often perplexes those analyzing white-collar and corporate crimes, which frequently are considerably more complex than the Hall carbine scandal.

FURTHER READINGS

Godwin, Cardinal. (1930). *John Charles Fremont, an Explanation of His Career*. Stanford, CA: Stanford University Press.

Wasson, R. Gordon. (1941). *The Hall Carbine Affair: A Study of Contemporary Folklore*. New York: Pandick Press.

Wasson, R. Gordon. (1972). *The Hall Carbine Affair: An Essay in Historiography* (3rd ed.). Privately printed.

3

THE MUCKRAKERS

INTRODUCTION

The appearance of mass-produced periodicals that were affordable to the general population in contrast to the high-toned reading material tailored for the elite and well educated was a major contributor to the vitality and zest of the muckraking years in American reformist history. These magazines provided an outlet for what now is known as investigative journalism, the probing into the seamier sides of business and political activity. The muckraking material resonated with the desire of recently arrived immigrant families to challenge the ugly conditions under which they were forced to live and the exploitation of their labor. The U.S. population had grown almost exponentially, but government control of business practices, not to mention politicians' control of their own criminal excesses, had failed to keep pace with the needs of ordinary people.

The chapter first discusses *McClure's*, the major outlet for muckraking material, and then examines the lives and work of five of the most prominent figures in the muckraking movement: Ida M. Tarbell, Lincoln Steffens, Frank Norris, Upton Sinclair, and Jacob Riis.

The Mission of *McClure's Magazine*

- *Document:* *McClure's Magazine* was the major outlet for the investigative writers who came to be known as muckrakers. In one issue, the magazine featured revelatory contributions by such to-be-famous writing sleuths as Ida Tarbell, Ray Stannard Baker, and Lincoln Steffens on the exploitative oil monopoly fashioned by John D. Rockefeller (Tarbell), the wrongful acts of labor unions (Baker), and the rampant corruption in Minneapolis (Steffens). The magazine's publisher, S. S. McClure, took the occasion to comment more generally on the aims of the muckraking movement.
- *Date:* January 1903.
- *Where:* *McClure's Magazine.*
- *Significance:* The muckraking movement, which had the support of President Theodore Roosevelt, was vital for alerting the public to the unchecked and unrestrained tactics of power conglomerates in business and politics that victimized ordinary citizens. Muckraking revelations produced a legislative and judicial response that sought to rein in the worst offenders. One commentator has written that "the January 1903 issue of *McClure's Magazine* stunned its readers with its extraordinary content and came to be recognized as the most important single issue of a magazine in its era, if not in the history of American journalism."

DOCUMENT 3.1

Miss Tarbell has our capitalists conspiring among themselves, deliberately, shrewdly, upon legal advice, to break the law so far as it restrained them, and to misuse it to restrain others who were in the way. Mr. Baker shows labor, the ancient enemy of capital and the chief complaint of the trusts' unlawful acts, itself committing and excusing crimes. And in "The Shame of Minneapolis" we see the administration of a city employing criminals to commit crimes for the profit of the elected officials, while the citizens . . . stood by compliant and not alarmed.

Capitalists, working men, politicians, citizens—all breaking the law, or letting it be broken. Who is left to uphold it? The lawyers? Some of the best lawyers in the country are hired, not to go to court to defend cases, but to advise corporations and business firms how they can get around the law without too great a risk of punishment. The judges? Too many of them so respect the laws that for some "error" or quibble they restore to office and liberty men convicted on evidence overwhelmingly convincing to common sense. The churches? We know of one, an ancient and wealthy establishment, which had to be compelled by a . . . health officer to put its tenements in sanitary condition. The colleges? They do not understand.

There is no one left; none but all of us . . . The public is the people. We forget that we are all the people; that while each of us in his group can shove off on the rest the bill of today, the debt is only postponed. The rest of us are passing it back to us. We have to pay in the end, every one of us. And in the end the sum total of our debt will be our liberty.

Source: S. S. McClure, "Editorial," *McClure's Magazine* 20 (January 1903): 336.

ANALYSIS

The muckrakers, predecessors to investigative reporters and academics who study white-collar and corporate crime, were a group of men and women whose exposés were featured in books and the mass-circulation magazines of the time, most notably *McClure's*. As one writer noted: "The muckrakers mounted a concentrated attack against the citadel they believed dominated the landscape." The period of muckraking lasted from about 1903 to 1912 and captured the American imagination because of its daring, shock value, and consonance with public understanding of the way it was being injured and ripped off by those in positions of political and corporate power. Muckraking writers are credited with having published some 90 books and more than 2,000 articles.

Samuel Sidney McClure (1867–1949) was born into a hardscrabble family in County Antrim in Ireland. The McClures migrated to Indiana to avoid the dire poverty that marked Ireland's famine, the consequence of the failure of the potato crop. McClure graduated from Knox College in Galesburg, Illinois, and later bought a near-defunct magazine, gave it his name, and drove it up to a circulation of half a million. Restless, spewing forth ideas like a shotgun discharging pellets, McClure prodded his magazine into striking prominence. His stable of staff writers, as Lincoln Steffens, one of its members, said, "served as four-wheel brakes on the madness of McClure's genius." Ultimately, the superstar writers deserted McClure in 1906 to start their own, ultimately short-lived, magazine.

The decline of the muckraking movement was in part the result of pressures exerted by attacks from those they had fought against. But more significant was

> ### *DID YOU KNOW?*
>
> #### On the Word "Muckraker"
>
> The term "muckrake" was coined by Arthur Dent, an English Puritan clergyman, in his devotional guide, *The Plain Man's Pathway to Heaven*, published in 1610, which by 1704 had gone through 35 editions. Dent's book was one of the pitifully few possessions brought by John Bunyan's wife to their marriage. Bunyan later wrote *Pilgrim's Progress* while serving a jail term for his religious beliefs. In England, only the Bible outsold Bunyan's allegorical story during the seventeenth century. In it, Bunyan told of a man so preoccupied with his muckrake, gathering up the world's filth, that he failed to look upward to observe God's glories. Centuries later, President Theodore Roosevelt, who was sympathetic to the muckraking cause, would adopt the term to scold a particular writer who had lambasted some of Roosevelt's political allies. The crusading writers in turn adopted the word to describe their efforts.

the growing tendency of the muckrakers to descend into sensationalism and shrillness as each sought to outdo competitors to capture public attention. Muckraking had virtually disappeared when the First World War fostered perfervid patriotism and turned citizens' attention toward international affairs.

FURTHER READINGS

Chalmers, David M. (1974). *The Muckrake Years*. New York: Van Nostrand.

Filler, Louis. (1996). *Muckraking and Progressivism in the American Tradition*. New Brunswick, NJ: Transaction.

Fitzpatrick, Ellen F. (Ed.) (1994). *Muckraking: Three Landmark Articles*. Boston: Bedford Press of St. Martin's.

Lyon, Peter. (1963). *Success Story: Life and Times of S. S. McClure*. New York: Scribner's.

McClure, S. S. (1914). My *Autobiography*. New York: Frederick A. Stokes.

Miraldi, Robert. (Ed.) (2000). *The Muckrakers: Evangelical Crusaders*. Westport, CT: Praeger.

Muelder, Hermann R. (1984). *Missionaries and Muckrakers: The First Hundred Years of Knox College*. Urbana: University of Illinois Press.

Wilson, Harold S. (1970). McClure's Magazine *and the Muckrakers*. Princeton, NJ: Princeton University Press.

Ida Tarbell

- *Document:* Ida Tarbell's disclosure of the vicious business practices of Standard Oil pointed out that John D. Rockefeller had formed a low-profile entity named the South Improvement Company to buy competing oil refineries at below book value while simultaneously negotiating secret anticompetitive shipping rates with the railroads. Document 3.2 is Tarbell's presentation of the facts of that situation.
- *Date:* 1904.
- *Where:* In Tarbell's *The History of the Standard Oil Company.*
- **Significance:** Tarbell's report was instrumental in the passage of several remedial measures by the U.S. Congress, including in 1890 the Sherman Anti-Trust Act.

DOCUMENT 3.2

A little more time and [Rockefeller's] great scheme would be an accomplished fact. And then there fell in its path two of those never-to-be-foreseen human elements which so often block great maneuvers. The first was born of a man's anger. The man had learned of the [railroad rebate] scheme. He wanted to go into it, but the directors [of Rockefeller's enterprises] were suspicious of him . . . They didn't want him to have any of the advantages of their great enterprise. When convinced that he could not share in the deal, he took his revenge by telling people in the Oil Region [the independents who competed with Rockefeller] what was going on.

At first the Oil Region refused to believe, but in a few days another slip born of human weakness came to prove the rumor true. The schedule of rates agreed upon by the South Improvement Company and the railroads had been sent to the freight agent of the Lake Shore Railroad, but no order had been given to put them in force.

The freight agent had a son on his death bed. Distracted by sorrow, he left his office in charge of subordinates, but neglected to tell them that the new schedules on his desk were a secret. compact, whose effectiveness depended on their being held until all was complete.

The subordinates, failing to appreciate the situation, entered the rates and the Oil Region refiners found that their charges were to be increased 100 percent.

Source: Ida Tarbell, *The History of the Standard Oil Company* (New York: McClure Phillips, 1904).

Ida Tarbell used investigative journalism to expose John D. Rockefeller's plan to monopolize the oil industry in the Southern United States. (Library of Congress)

ANALYSIS

Ida Minerva Tarbell (1857–1944) was the superstar in a star-studded group of writers who brilliantly exposed the seamy side of political and social conditions in their time. She held a powerful and prominent journalistic position in a period when women rarely ventured into the workplace. Her fame was built upon a dedication to fact finding, digging assiduously through old documents, interviewing people who had pertinent information on her subject, and courageously telling the story as she found it, meticulously doling out praise for those admirable things accomplished by the people she wrote about in various books—Napoleon, Lincoln, and John D. Rockefeller most notably—and sternly holding them to account for their errors

Tarbell is something of a puzzle for feminists. She never married, in part apparently because it would interfere with her consuming dedication to research and writing, and she was opposed to giving women the right to vote, seemingly because she believed that they could dedicate themselves to advancing more worthy causes than the careers of politicians. She was the lone woman in her freshman class of 32 people at Allegheny College in Meadville, Pennsylvania. When she graduated she took a job for two years teaching school in Poland, Ohio, where she was responsible for classes in botany, geology, arithmetic, geometry, trigonometry, English grammar, Greek, Latin, French, and German. This background would prove useful when she moved into the wider realm of investigative reporting, often as the only woman in what overwhelmingly was a man's world.

Tarbell's monumental 815-page *The History of the Standard Oil Company* remains a readable classic, fact-filled, clear-eyed, and unremitting in its documentation and condemnation of the tactics employed by John D. Rockefeller in securing railroad rebates and crushing business opponents. One recent commentator declared that Tarbell's study of Standard Oil "is arguably the greatest work of investigative journalism ever written." Journalism professor Steve Weinberg has noted that had Tarbell not researched scrupulously and written about Standard Oil, John D. Rockefeller "might be revered today rather than reviled by so many." Weinberg adds that Tarbell's work consigned Rockefeller, the most admired and feared individual in America during his lifetime, to the roster of an infamous group of business villains. For her part, during her later years Tarbell was asked by a young history professor, "If you could rewrite your book [on Standard Oil] what would you change?" "Not one word, young man," she answered. "Not one word."

FURTHER READINGS

Brady, Kathleen. (1984). *Ida Tarbell: Portrait of a Muckraker*. New York: Seaview/Putnam.

Kochbesberger, Robert C., Jr. (1994). *More than a Muckraker: Ida Tarbell's Lifetime in Journalism*. Knoxville: University of Tennessee Press.

Tarbell, Ida. (1939). *All in a Day's Work: An Autobiography*. New York: Macmillan.

Tomkins, Mary E. (1974). *Ida M. Tarbell*. New York: Twayne.

Tarbell, Ida. (1904). *The History of the Standard Oil Company*. New York: McClure, Phillips.

Weinberg, Steve. (2008). *Taking on the Trusts: The Epic Battle of Ida Tarbell and John D. Rockefeller*. New York: Norton.

DID YOU KNOW?

Honoring Ida Tarbel

Almost a century and a half after her death, Ida Tarbell continues to be the recipient of an array of honors. In 1999, the *New York Times* rated her work on Standard Oil as the fifth most important piece of journalism for the entire century. In 2000, the Pennsylvania state legislature declared November 4 "Ida Tarbell Day," noting that her "passion for truth and knowledge are an enduring legacy for citizens of the Commonwealth and deserve special recognition." The following year, the U.S. Postal Service announced that Tarbell would be portrayed on one of a series of stamps. In 2002, Tarbell was one of 18 women inducted into the National Women's Hall of Fame. The ceremony was held in Seneca Falls, New York, where the first women's human rights convention took place in 1842.

Lincoln Steffens

- **Document:** In his monumental report, *The Shame of Our Cities*, Lincoln Steffens exposed the rampant bribery, extortion, buying of votes, and other nefarious activities that characterized boss rule in America's metropolitan cities. The document presents observations made by Steffens and Claude Wetmore in *McClure's* regarding conditions in St. Louis, then the fourth-largest city in the United States. Wetmore, at one time the city editor of the St. Louis *Post-Dispatch*, had written a timid first draft of the article, fearful that he might offend those who could ruin his career. Steffens rewrote the draft to make it a hard-hitting indictment of corruption and decrepitude in St. Louis.
- **Date:** October 1902.
- **Where:** *McClure's Magazine.*
- **Significance:** Document 3.3 provides a taste of the tone and content of muckraking criticism of conditions in American cities by the leading exponent of the genre.

DOCUMENT 3.3

Go to St. Louis and you will find the habit of civic pride in them; they will still boast. The visitor is told of the wealth of the residents, the financial strength of the banks, and of the growing importance of the industries; yet he sees poorly paved, refuse-burdened streets, and dusty and mud-covered alleys; he passes a ramshackle firetrap crowded with the sick and learns that it is the City Hospital; he enters the Four Courts [a building constructed in 1877 and razed in 1903 that housed courts, the police station, the jail, and the morgue] and his nostrils are greeted with the odor of formaldehyde used as a disinfectant and insect powder to destroy vermin; he calls at the new City Hall and finds half the entrance bordered with pine planks to cover up the unfinished interior. Finally he turns a tap in the hotel to see liquid mud flow in the wash basis or bathtub.

Source: Lincoln Steffens and Claude Wetmore, "Tweed Days in St. Louis." *McClure's Magazine* 19 (October 1902).

ANALYSIS

Lincoln Steffens had learned that it usually took identifying one key person on the scene to help him discover and report the inside story of corruption in an American city, an approach that served Bob Woodward and Carl Bernstein well when they dealt secretly with an assistant director of the Federal Bureau of Investigation, whom they dubbed Deep Throat, to learn the details of the Watergate scandal that brought down the presidency of Richard Nixon (see Chapter 8).

In St. Louis, Steffens had worked with Joseph W. Folk, the 32-year-old circuit attorney, a former corporation lawyer who had been elected to office as the city's chief law enforcement officer by an unusual collaboration of reformers and the St. Louis political machine. Steffens and Folk's work together would bring further fame to both men. Folk would be elected governor of Missouri, and Steffens would be recognized as the leading crusader in the United States for good government. As governor, Folk was responsible for laws restricting child labor, tightening up the control of race track betting, and inaugurating a direct primary, taking the right of selecting candidates away from the corrupt political bosses. His ardent Baptist faith led him to establish Sunday-closing laws for businesses and earned him the nickname "Holy Joe."

As Justin Kaplan, Steffens's leading biographer, wrote in 1974, St. Louis at the turn of the century represented "the worst that could happen to a city." Its population had soared since the beginning of the Civil War from 160,000 to 600,000 when Falk took office in 1901. "Revenues floated not into but past the city treasury," Kaplan notes, "just as the Mississippi, flowing past the city, yielded the citizens for drinking water only a trickle famously opaque and malodorous." In an interview with *Publishers Weekly* when his study of Steffens appeared, Kaplan compared the zest of the muckrakers to uncover white-collar crime to conditions today: "There was such a high level of crusading fervor and moral outrage then," he noted. "Now there's not the same passion." Kaplan thought the difference could be traced to the fact that "the crimes are much bigger today, but they are committed without that flamboyance or indiscretion that makes the crookedness of those days almost charming. Now it's the quiet, self-righteous but much more deadly crime done in a smooth, big business manner."

DID YOU KNOW?

Steffens and the Soviet Union

Lincoln Steffens's immersion in the squalid ingredients of urban America turned him into a cynic about democratic rule and the rampant greed and graft in the political realm. Regarding a trip in 1921 to the Soviet Union, he wrote glowingly: "I have been over into the future, and it works," an observation that often is shortened to "I've seen the future and it works." Steffens may have been right on target when he described the squalor and ugly boss rule of American cities, but he proved to be well off target in his judgment of the Soviet Union, based on his limited exposure to its system. As it turned out, it did not work, and in his later years Steffens backed away from his earlier enthusiasm for Communism.

For Steffens, conditions in St. Louis were eye-openers. "When I set out to describe the corrupt systems of certain typical cities," Steffens wrote in 1903, "I meant to show simply how people were deceived and betrayed. But in the very first study—St. Louis—the startling truth lay bare that corruption was not merely political; it was financial, commercial, social; the ramifications of boodles were so complex, various and far-reaching that one mind could hardly grasp them, and not even Joseph W. Folk, the tireless prosecutor, could follow them all."

Joseph Lincoln Steffens (1866–1936) was born in San Francisco. His father was a well-to-do conservative businessman who dealt in the import and export of paints, oils, and glass. Steffens grew up in Sacramento, the seat of the California state government, where he had his first contact with the cronyism and corruption that dominated local politics. Steffens, always a mediocre student at best, was sent to a military academy to try to instill a sense of discipline in him. He subsequently graduated from the University of California at Berkeley, then and now a site of rebellious ideas. He studied abroad in France and Germany for three years before taking a job as a police reporter in New York City, a position that exposed him to the seamier side of urban existence.

Steffens's classic report, *The Shame of Our Cities*, published in 1904, remains a significant and enduring commentary on American politics. Steffens's work still resonates in today's world. A check on the News segment of Lexis in February 2010 indicated that Steffens had been mentioned in newspapers 27 times during the previous year and 149 times during the past five years. The most general reference was to the similarity between what was going on today and what Steffens had found in his time. In an obituary tribute to Howard Zinn, a crusading reformer, for instance, historian Doris Kearns Goodwin noted: "I'm writing about Theodore Roosevelt, and the prominent force of the muckraking journalism will be a big part of what I'm writing about—Ida Tarbell and Lincoln Steffens and Ray Baker—because they created the climate of reform that Roosevelt gave voice to." There also was some play on Steffens's remark about the Soviet Union (see Sidebar 3.3). A discussion of current health care measures before Congress noted: "I have seen it and it doesn't work." Similarly, the San Bernardino (California) *County Sun* harked back to the creation of a crime wave by Steffens in its analysis of its local crime statistics (see Sidebar 3.4). Honoring the hundredth anniversary of the appearance of *The Shame of Our Cities*, a *New York Times* editorial saluted Steffens's pioneering investigative journalism:

"The Shame of Our Cities," one of the great works of American muckraking, turns 100 this spring, but it speaks uncannily to our times. In this age of Enron and Halliburton, of huge

DID YOU KNOW?

Creating a Crime Wave

The competition between the large number of daily newspapers in New York when Steffens was a police reporter for the *Evening Post* led to intense efforts by each to gain additional readers. Typically, stories of crime and gore pumped up circulation. Steffens, in collaboration with Jacob Riis, a man who later gained fame as a social reformer, decided to foster a crime wave in the city. When they sat around in the basement of the police headquarters where they could escape the summer heat outside and intermingle with the detectives and prisoners, gossiping and playing cards, they plotted that they would print the details of all burglaries in the city rather than only a choice few. Soon other daily papers began to fault their reporters for missing these stories. They imitated Steffens and Riis and by doing so created "a crime wave" and accompanying public panic. It was left to the reporters to cure the outbreak simply by not reporting so many offenses.

campaign contributions and reckless deregulation its arguments about the corrosive effects of business on government feel up to the minute. Every bit as timely is its call to arms.

Equally notable is the recent inclusion of Steffens in Carl Jensen's *Stories That Changed America* (2004). Jensen notes that *The Shame of Our Cities* was a national sensation and helped America take a hard look at itself. It showed that corruption in America was not a local problem but a national one. The book demonstrated, according to Jensen, that "the real villains were the supposedly upstanding corporate executives who believed they should do anything to make business succeed and that bribery was all right."

FURTHER READINGS

Bausum, Ann. (2007). *Muckrakers: How Ida Tarbell, Upton Sinclair, and Lincoln Steffens Helped to Expose Scandal, Inspire Reform, and Invent Investigative Journalism.* Washington, DC: National Geographic.

Kaplan, Justin. (1974). *Lincoln Steffens: A Biography.* New York: Simon & Schuster.

Palumbo, Patrick F. (1978). *Lincoln Steffens.* Boston: Twayne.

Piott, Steven L. (1997). *Holy Joe: Joseph W. Folk and the Missouri Idea.* Columbia: University of Missouri Press.

Steffens, Lincoln. (1931). *The Autobiography of Lincoln Steffens.* New York: Harcourt, Brace.

Stinson, Robert. (1979). *Lincoln Steffens.* New York: Ungar.

Winters, Ella, and Granville Hicks. (Eds.) (1938). *The Letters of Lincoln Steffens.* New York: Harcourt, Brace.

Frank Norris

- **Document:** Frank Norris's novel *The Octopus* captured in fictional form—and thereby in a manner more palatable to ordinary readers—the seething discontent of farmers and ranchers with the high-handed pricing tactics that the railroads could employ because of their monopoly status. Document 3.4, concerning a letter written by a wheat grower to his son, portrays the anger and disgust of California farmers with the latest exercise of blatant power by the railroad magnates.
- *Date:* 1903.
- **Where:** California's San Joaquin Valley.
- *Significance:* Norris's writing, illustrated in Document 3.4, served two purposes. Most directly, it dramatized and spread the discontent of the public with rapacious railroad practices, and second, it set an example for later writers about how to effectively convey their reformist message, most notably for Upton Sinclair, who followed closely on Norris's pioneering path.

DOCUMENT 3.4

"Ulsteen gave his decision yesterday," he continued, reading from his father's letter. "He holds, Ulsteen does," that grain rates as low as the new figure would amount to confiscation of property and that, on such a basis, the railroad could not be operated at a legitimate profit. As he is powerless to legislate in the matter, he can only put the rates back to where they originally were before the commissioners made the original cut, and it is so ordered ... Ulsteen and the Railroad Commissioners were thick as thieves. . . . " 'Legitimate profit, legitimate profit,' " [the grower's son] broke out. "Can we raise wheat at a legitimate profit with a tariff of four dollars a ton for moving it two hundred miles to a tide-water, with wheat at eighty-seven cents. Why not hold us up with a gun in our face, and say, 'hands up' and be done with it."

Source: Frank Norris, *The Octopus, A California Story* (New York: Doubleday, Page, 1903), 13.

ANALYSIS

Unsure from the text who Ulsteen, mentioned in the document might be, I e-mailed Donald Pizer, an emeritus professor at Tulane University, who had meticulously edited the collected writings of Norris. He answered: "I take it from the context that Ulsteen is a judge (or perhaps an arbitration quasi-judicial figure) who had heard the case brought against the Railroad Commission and decided against the ranchers. [The letter] goes on to imply that Ulsteen had been bribed by the Railroad to reach the decision."

The key words in the foregoing document and at the core of Frank Norris's muckraking novel are "legitimate profit." They are used as a debating point by the railroad forces and echoed by the wheat growers in regard to their own situation. In the previous chapter, dealing with the robber barons, we learned that, while they assuredly took initial risks, they harvested a profit that no reasonable person could describe as "legitimate," living luxuriously on the enormous fortunes they reaped at the expense of the taxpayers who had underwritten the construction of the railroads and the traders for whose benefit the lines allegedly had been built.

Frank Norris (1870–1902), christened Benjamin Franklin Norris after his birth in Chicago, was one of the stars of the muckraking movement during his brief lifetime. His father was a wealthy merchant dealing in jewelry, his mother an actress. The family moved to San Francisco when Frank was 14, and he was educated abroad before attending but not graduating from the University of California at Berkeley. He covered the Boer War in South Africa, and then, as a writer for *McClure's Magazine*, wrote from Cuba about the Spanish-American war.

The Octopus encapsulated in dramatic form the major ingredients of the conflict between the fictional Pacific and Southwestern Railroad and those it was gouging. It began with conflicts about rates, involved the killing by a railroad train of sheep that had wandered onto the tracks, moved into concerns over land ownership, and ended with armed conflict in which many were slaughtered, some of whom had figured prominently in Norris's novel.

Only 32 years old, Norris died of peritonitis as a result of a ruptured appendix and his book, *The Pit*, exposing corruption in trading in wheat futures on the Chicago Board of Trade, was published after his death.

> ### DID YOU KNOW?
>
> **The Railroad: The Colossus, the Octopus**
>
> The title of the book from which Document 3.4 was drawn comes from the final word of Frank Norris's compelling and chilling description of the railroads: "The leviathan with tentacles of steel clutching into the soil, the soulless Force, the iron-hearted Power, the monster, the Colossus, the Octopus."

FURTHER READINGS

Graham, Don. (1978). *The Fiction of Frank Norris: The Aesthetic Content*. Columbia: University of Missouri Press.

Graham, Don. (Ed.) (1980). *Critical Essays on Frank Norris*. Boston: Hall.

Hochman, Barbara. (1988). *The Art of Frank Norris, Story Teller*. Columbia: University of Missouri Press.

Husman, Lawrence E. (1999). *Harbinger of a Century: The Novels of Frank Norris*. New York: Peter Lang.

Macelrath, Joseph R., Jr., and Jesse S. Crisler (2006). *Frank Norris, a Life*. Urbana: University of Illinois Press.

Norris, Frank. (1901). *The Octopus: A Story of California*. New York: Doubleday, Page.

Norris, Frank. (1903). *The Pit: A Story of Chicago*. New York: Doubleday, Page.

Upton Sinclair

- *Document:* It is debatable whether Ida Tarbell's *The History of the Standard Oil Company* or Upton Sinclair's *The Jungle* was the most significant contribution to the muckraking movement. *The Jungle*, a novel, was a best-seller and aroused the American people to demand government action to remedy the conditions in the meatpacking industry that Upton Sinclair so vividly portrayed. Document 3.5, an excerpt from *The Jungle*, provides a taste of the information that Upton Sinclair embedded in his story of an immigrant working in a filthy, mind-numbing, unhealthy, and corrupt industry.
- *Date:* 1906.
- *Where:* Chicago, Illinois.
- *Significance:* The impact of *The Jungle* was swift and powerful. President Theodore Roosevelt read the book, sent two of his trusted representatives to Chicago to verify the conditions that Sinclair portrayed, and then invited Sinclair to the White House to discuss the situation he had depicted. The result was two pieces of pioneering and powerful legislation: the Pure Food and Drug Act of 1906 and the Meat Inspection Act of the same year.

DOCUMENT 3.5

On top of these were the rooms where they dried the "tankage," the mass of brown stringy stuff that was left after the waste portions of the carcasses had had the lard and tallow dried out of them. This dried material they would then grind to a fine powder, and after they had mixed it well with a mysterious but inoffensive brown rock which they brought in and ground up by the hundreds of carloads for that purpose, the substance was ready to be put into bags and sent out to the world as one of a hundred different brands of bone-phosphate. And then the farmer in Maine or California or Texas would buy this ... and plant it with his corn; and for several days after the operation the fields would have a strong odor, and the farmer and his wagon and the very horses that hauled it would all have it too.

Source: Upton Sinclair, *The Jungle* (New York: Doubleday, 1906).

ANALYSIS

Upton Sinclair (1878–1968) was a prolific writer of fiction and nonfiction, producing more than 50 books during his lifetime. He was born in Baltimore and educated and radicalized at City College of New York. Later, he twice ran unsuccessfully for Congress on the Socialist Party ticket, and then as a candidate of the Democrat Party for governor of California in 1933, getting 870,000 votes, not nearly enough to win.

The document indicates the duplicity of the owners of meatpacking businesses in selling as fertilizer a mixture that was largely made of rock and that offered no benefit to the purchaser. What particularly angered the public were additional portrayals by Sinclair of deceits that threatened their health and well-being. Diseased cows slaughtered for beef were ignored by government inspectors who had been bribed into inattention; tainted remnants of the guts and offal from cattle were swept up with debris lying on filthy floors of the packing house and sold as pulled ham. Dead rats were put into sausage-grinding machines. Workers were exploited mercilessly and paid miserably.

Sinclair, 28 years old, had been assigned the task of preparing a book about the meatpacking industry by a socialist organization. He spent nine weeks in disguise, working undercover as a packinghouse employee to gather material for the book. He then took refuge in a hand-built 18-foot-by-16-foot tar shack in Princeton Township in New Jersey to isolate himself and write the novel.

In *The Jungle* Sinclair tells the story of Jurgis Rudkus, an immigrant from Lithuania, who comes to the United States with his family with high hopes for the opportunity to live a decent life. The optimism is knocked out of him while working in the packinghouse, and he is fired when he beats up his boss, who had been harassing Jurgis's wife. Not long after, she dies in childbirth because they cannot afford medical care; then his young son is drowned in a muddy street. Five publishers turned the book down as too hot to handle until Doubleday took a gamble in

DID YOU KNOW?

The Prolific Pundit

Upton Sinclair is by far best remembered for his muckraking portray of the wretched conditions in the Chicago stockyards. But he was an astonishingly prolific writer, turning out 90 books during his lifetime. Among those, though long since forgotten, were a series of 11 volumes, covering 7,424 pages, describing the exploits of Lansing Budd, known more familiarly as Lanny Budd. The third of the series, *Dragon's Teeth*, won a Pulitzer Prize in 1947, and the volumes, best-sellers all, were translated into 21 languages. Sinclair portrayed Budd, the son of an arms merchant, as involved in virtually every major event in the first half of the twentieth century and as a trusted friend of all the world's leaders.

publishing it and won big. *The Jungle* remains a classic, and today is required reading in many high schools and colleges.

The book was instrumental in compelling Congress to enact the Meat Inspection Act of 1906. The major requirements of the act were:

- Antimortem and postmortem inspection of each carcass.
- Prevent diseased and unwholesome meat from entering food channels.
- Branding the labels "U.S. Inspected and Pass" and "U.S. Inspected and Contaminated."
- Disposal of the condemned in the presence of the inspector.
- Qualified reinspection during processing.
- Control over ingredients, dyes, chemicals, and other additives.
- Truthful, informative labels.
- Rigid sanitary standards.
- Plant construction standards.
- Stiff penalties for violations.

FURTHER READINGS

Arthur, Anthony. (2006). *Radical Innocent: Upton Sinclair*. New York: Random House.

Bloodworth, William A., Jr. (1977). *Upton Sinclair*. Boston: Twayne.

Mastoon, Kevin. (2006). *Upton Sinclair and the Other American Century*. Hoboken, NJ: Wiley.

Mookerjee, Rabindra N. (1988). *Art for Social Justice: The Major Novels of Upton Sinclair*. Metuchen, NJ: Scarecrow Press.

Sinclair, Upton. (1906). *The Jungle*. New York: Doubleday, Page.

Wiener, Gary. (Ed.) (2008). *Women's Rights in the United States:* Detroit, MI: Greenhaven.

Yoder, Jon A. (1975). *Upton Sinclair*. New York: F. Ungar.

Jacob Riis

- **Document:** Document 3.6 reproduces two tributes to Jacob Riis by President Theodore Roosevelt. The two men had first met when Roosevelt was the New York City police commissioner and Riis, as we noted earlier, was a police reporter working with Lincoln Steffens.
- **Date:** The first letter of praise appeared in 1901; the second in 1913.
- **Where:** The first appeared in *McClure's Magazine*; the second in Roosevelt's autobiography.
- **Significance:** Document 3.6 not only indicates the high regard in which Riis personally was held, but it also makes clear that the work of the muckrakers was attended to in high places and resulted in very important reforms.

DOCUMENT 3.6

"Recently a man, well qualified to pass judgment, alluded to Mr. Jacob A. Riis as 'the most useful citizen of New York.' Those fellow citizens of Mr. Riis who best know his work will be most apt to agree with this statement. The countless evils which lurk in the dark corners of our civic institutions, and have their permanent abode in the crowded tenement houses, have met in Mr. Riis the most formidable opponent ever encountered by them in New York City."

Source: Theodore Roosevelt, "Reform through Social Work: Some Forces That Tell for Decent in New York City," *McClure's Magazine* 16 (March 1901): 448.

"Jacob Riis, whom I am tempted to call the best American I ever knew, although he was already a young man when he came here from Denmark."

Source: Theodore Roosevelt, *An Autobiography* (New York: Macmillan, 1913), 66.

A Jacob Riis portrait of an Italian immigrant mother and her child in a New York City tenement in 1890. (Library of Congress)

ANALYSIS

Jacob August Riis (1849–1914) was the third of 15 children born into a farming family in the village of Ribe in Denmark. He migrated to the United States when he was 21 but found it very difficult to sustain himself. He worked intermittently as a carpenter but scrambled for the most menial jobs when times got tough, often living on little food and sleeping in the streets. In time, he began to obtain employment as a writer, and we have seen earlier in this chapter how, when he was a police reporter for the *New York Tribune*, Riis and Lincoln Steffens collaborated to bring to the attention of the public the seamier side of city living—the desperate and squalid details of human existence in the slums. He also exposed the negligent, uncaring landlords who exploited the largely immigrant population. In the 1880son the Lower East Side in New York City, for instance, 354,000 people crowded into a single square mile to make it the most densely populated place in the world.

Riis, uniquely for the time, became a skilled photographer and graphically illustrated the ugliness of slum life with vivid visual evidence. He was a pioneer in the use of flash powder, which allowed images to be taken of indoor and exterior settings in the night.

The grim portrayals of slum life by Riis were instrumental in passage in 1901 of the Tenement House Act, which mandated improved lighting and ventilation and upgraded toilet facilities in newly constructed apartment houses. Landlords, predictably, were enraged at the legislation that cut into their profits, calling it "a thunderbolt from a clear sky" and claiming that it would inhibit the construction of new housing and create demands for lower rents by tenants living in quarters lacking the improvements demanded by the act.

Neither of these consequences ensued, but the lax standards so well depicted by Riis were in evidence in the tragic Triangle Shirtwaist fire in lower Manhattan on March 25, 1911, the worst mass slaughter in the city's history until the September 11, 2001, destruction by jihadi hijackers who flew two airplanes into the World Trade Center. In the fire, 145 workers, almost all young immigrant women, were killed, either by the blaze itself or by jumping from the building. A number of them huddled on a fire escape, but all died when it collapsed and they plunged 100 feet to the sidewalk below.

The owners of the building were charged criminally, but, as proves so true in white-collar offenses, they hired an astute attorney who insisted that they were not aware of the hazards from the building's shoddy construction or that exit doors had been locked in violation of the law. In a civil case, the owners were made to pay $75 to the survivors of each of the victims.

FURTHER READINGS

Allard, Alexander. (1933). *Jacob A. Riis: Photographer and Citizen*. Millerton, NY: Aperture.

Buk-Swienty, Tom. (2008). *The Other Half: The Life of Jacob Riis and the World of Immigrant America* (Annette Buk-Swienty, Trans.). New York: Norton.

Fried, Lewis, and John Fierst. (1977). *Jacob A. Riis: A Reference Guide*. Boston: Hall.

Lane, James B. (1974). *Jacob A. Riis and the American City*. Port Washington, NY: Kennikat Press.

Riis, Jacob A. (1890). *How the Other Half Lives: Studies among the Tenements of New York*. New York: Scribner's.

Von Drehle, David. (2003). *Triangle: The Fire That Changed America*. New York: Atlantic Monthly Press.

Yochelson, Bonnie, and Daniel J. Czitrom. (2007). *Rediscovering Jacob Riis: Exposure Journalism and Photography in Turn-of-the-Century New York*. New York: New Press.

4

ANTITRUST CRIMES

INTRODUCTION

Some people say that they prefer competition because it pushes them toward a better performance. But where money is concerned, most notably in the world of business and high finance, competition tends to reduce prices and earnings, and it is deplored, at least in private, by those who have to live with it. The tension between "pure" capitalism, with the government staying quietly on the sidelines, and the interests of consumers is palpable. Efforts to thwart the development of monopolies trace back to early English common law with the counterefforts to create monopolies lying at the heart of those early attempts to break them up.

The current chapter considers the passage of the Sherman Antitrust Act in 1890, the hallmark of the initial efforts in the United States to prevent and penalize monopolistic practices. It then considers the major court case that laid out the (ever-controversial) ground rules to determine the existence of a monopoly. The predatory career of John D. Rockefeller is presented to put a face on financiers who ruthlessly sought to eliminate competition. The chapter then takes up the infamous heavy electric antitrust conspiracy of 1961 before closing with an examination of the antitrust case brought by the government against Microsoft.

The Sherman Antitrust Act (1890)

- *Document:* Document 4.1 sets forth the provisions of the Sherman Antitrust Act, the pioneering American attempt by the federal government to control cartels and monopolistic practices
- *When:* Enacted on December 2, 1889, to be effective July 2, 1890.
- *Where:* Passed by the Senate and the House of Representatives and signed into law by President Benjamin Harrison.
- *Significance:* The Sherman Act was a consequence of a massive public hostility to what people saw as the gouging and economic exploitation carried on by powerful corporate interests. They saw the capitalistic system's emphasis on free competition and its advantages for consumers being undercut by monopolies and a small group of ruthless entrepreneurs who had grown extravagantly rich by cornering the market in different products. The Sherman Act sought to put brakes on the creation of cartels and monopolies. By highlighting criminal penalties, the act reinforced the growing public mood that sought to punish white-collar and corporate offenders with something more stringent—and, hopefully, more effective—than injunctions and civil fines.

DOCUMENT 4.1

An act to protect trade and commerce against unlawful restraints and monopolies.

Sec. 1. Every contract, combination in the form of trust or otherwise, or conspiracy, in restraint of trade or commerce among the several States, or with foreign nations, is hereby declared to be illegal. Every person who shall make such contract or engage in any such combination or conspiracy shall be deemed guilty of a misdemeanor, and, on conviction thereof, shall be punished by fine not exceeding five thousand dollars, or by imprisonment not exceeding one year, or by both such punishments, at the discretion of the court.

Sec. 2. Every person who shall monopolize, or attempt to monopolize, or contract or conspire with any other person or persons, to monopolize any part of the trade or commerce among the several States, or with foreign nations, shall be deemed guilty of a misdemeanor, and, on conviction thereof, shall be punished by fine not exceeding five thousand dollars, or by imprisonment not exceeding one year, in the discretion of the court.

Sec. 3. Every contract, or combination in the form of trust or otherwise, or conspiracy, in restraint of trade or commerce in any Territory of the United States or of the District of Columbia, or in restraint of trade or commerce between any such Territory and another, or between any such Territory or Territories and any State or States or the District of Columbia, or with foreign nations, or with the District of Columbia and any State or States or foreign nations, is hereby declared illegal. Every person who shall make any such contract or engage in any such combination or conspiracy, shall be deemed guilty of a misdemeanor, and, on conviction thereof, shall be punished by a fine not exceeding five thousand dollars, or by imprisonment not exceeding one year, or by both such punishments, in the discretion of the court.

Sec. 4. The several circuit courts of the United States are hereby invested with jurisdiction to prevent and restrain violations of this act, and it shall be the duty of the several district attorneys of the United States, in their respective districts, under the direction of the Attorney-General, to institute proceedings in equity to prevent and restrain such violations. Such proceedings may be by way of petition setting forth the case and praying that such violation shall be enjoined or otherwise prohibited. When the parties complained of shall have been duly notified of such petition the court shall proceed, as soon as may be, to the hearing and determination of the case: and pending such petition and before final decree, the court may at any time make such restraining order or prohibition as shall be deemed just in the premises.

Sec. 5. Whenever it shall appear to the court before which any proceeding under section four of this act may be pending, that the ends of justice require that other parties should be brought before the court, the court may cause them to be summoned, whether they reside in the district in which the court is held or not, and subpoenas to that end may be served in any district by the marshal thereof.

Sec. 6. Any property owned under any contract or by any combination, or pursuant to any conspiracy (and being the subject thereof) mentioned in section one of this act, and being in the course of transportation from one State to another, or to a foreign country, shall be forfeited to the United States, and may be seized and condemned by like proceedings as those provided by law for the forfeiture, seizure and condemnation of property imported into the United States contrary to law.

Sec. 7. Any person who shall be injured in his business or property by another person or corporation by reason of anything forbidden or declared to be unlawful by this act, may sue thereof in any circuit court of the United States in the district in which the defendant resides or is found, without respect to the amount in controversy, and shall receive three fold the damages by him sustained, and the cost of suit, including a reasonable attorney's fee.

Sec. 8. That the word "person" or "persons," whenever used in this act shall be deemed to include corporations and associations existing under or authorized by the laws of either the United States, the laws of any of the Territories, the laws of any State, or the laws of any foreign country.

Source: Sherman Antitrust Act, *U.S. Statutes at Large* 26 (1890): 209, Chap. 647.

ANALYSIS

The Sherman Antitrust Act of 1890 is the keystone of American antitrust policy. It was based largely on a measure passed in Ohio two years earlier (Act of April 19, 1898; 1898 Ohio Laws 93, part 143) titled "An act to define trusts and provide for criminal penalties and civil damages, and punishment of corporations, persons, firms, and associations or persons connected with them, and to promote free competition in commerce and all classes of business in the State." The federal law was, under the Constitution, restricted to entities engaged in interstate commerce, a term increasingly given broader meaning, leaving the states to deal with violations occurring within their borders. The considerably greater resources of the federal government would dictate that the major antitrust cases would largely be adjudicated in federal courts.

For a law so famous and so important, the Sherman Act, as the eminent legal historian Lawrence Friedman has pointed out, is surprisingly brief: it took up fewer than two pages of text in the statute book. The Sherman Act, Friedman observes, is "terse," "vague," and "ambiguous." Notably absent in it are definitions of such key terms as "monopoly" and "restraint of trade." Note might be made that the health insurance measure introduced by Senate Democrats during the first year of the Obama administration ran to more than 2,000 pages. The reason for the briefness and the gaps in the antitrust measure likely lie in the fact that while Congress was responding to public pressure to do something about the stranglehold enjoyed by the ever-increasing number of rapacious monopolistic businesses, it did not want to do too much, thereby running the risk of cutting off campaign contributions from these very sources. The tightrope dance between pleasing competing constituencies was a given that legislators had to learn to walk carefully or otherwise risk having to find other work. Certainly the fact that an antitrust offense was declared to be a misdemeanor with the most severe penalty being a year in a county jail indicates that Congress was not ready to impose significant penalties that might much more effectively control the outlawed behavior.

DID YOU KNOW?

Senator John Sherman, the Sponsor of the Antitrust Law

John Sherman, the man for whom the Sherman Antitrust Act was named, was born in Lancaster, Ohio. He was the younger brother of William Tecumseh Sherman, the Civil War general responsible for the scorched-earth policy in Atlanta that contributed significantly to the end of the war and the reelection of Abraham Lincoln as president. Sherman's father was a successful lawyer who became a member of the Ohio Supreme Court. He had died young, leaving his widow with 11 children to raise.

Sherman, a Republican, was head of the Senate Finance Committee when he sponsored the antitrust law. It passed the Senate by a vote of 51–1 and the House by 242–0, a very far cry from the divisive party line situations that have characterized congressional actions in the present century. Subsequently, Sherman served as Secretary of the Treasury under President Benjamin Hayes.

During the first several decades of the life of the Sherman Act, enforcement of the law was virtually nonexistent. The Department of Justice filed only 9 cases in the 5 years following passage of the Act, only 16 in the first 12 years, and merely 22 during the first 15 years of the act's existence. And these few early cases often met with judicial disapproval. In 1892, for instance, a federal district judge in Minnesota in the case of *U.S. v. Nelson* (52 Fed. 246) put aside an indictment against Benjamin Nelson and a group of lumber dealers who were alleged to have conspired to raise the price of pine lumber by five cents a thousand feet (the allegation was "too indefinite and uncertain," the court ruled), and an attack on the cash register industry also fizzled out in the courts in 1893 in *U.S. v. Patterson* (205 Federal Reporter 292). The government's 1895 lawsuit in *U.S. v. E. C. Knight Co.* (156 U.S. 1) also fell to the ground when the Supreme Court declared that the company, which controlled 98 percent of the country's sugar-refining capacity, was a monopoly of "manufacture," not of "commerce," and that only the latter was prohibited by the Sherman Act.

In addition, the Sherman Act in its early days tended to be used against labor organizations rather than, as seemingly was its original intent, business operations.

FURTHER READINGS

Burton, John, Jr. (1966). "An Economic Analysis of Sherman Act Indictments." In James M. Clabault and John F. Burton, Jr. (Eds.), *Sherman Act Indictments, 1955–1965*, 103–44. New York: Federal Legal Publications.

Dewey, Donald J. (1990). *The Antitrust Experiment in America.* New York: Columbia University Press.

Elzinga, Kenneth G., and William Breit. (1976). *The Antitrust Penalties: A Study in Law and Economics.* New Haven, CT: Yale University Press.

Letwin, William (1965). *Law and Economic Policy in America: The Evolution of the Sherman Antitrust Act.* New York: Random House.

Page, William H. (1991). Ideological Conflict and the Origins of Antitrust Policy. *Tulane Law Review* 66:1–67.

Sigler, George. (1985). The Origin of the Sherman Act. *Journal of Legal Studies* 14:1–12.

Torelli, Hans B. (1955). *The Federal Antitrust Policy: Organization of an American Tradition.* Baltimore: Johns Hopkins University Press.

Walker, Albert H. (1910). *History of the Sherman Law of the United States of America.* New York: Equity Press.

Clipping the Wings of Standard Oil

- **Document:** The failure to take tough and effective actions against restraints of trade, in part because of the failure of the Sherman Act to specify with greater precision those behaviors that it sought to prevent, came to an end with the Supreme Court ruling in *Standard Oil of New Jersey*.
- **When:** May 15, 1911.
- **Where:** U.S. Supreme Court.
- **Significance:** The *Standard Oil* decision opened the legal door to validate forceful actions against corporations that sought to gain a stranglehold on an industry that would allow them to set prices and regulations as they pleased without fear of losing customers to competitors.

DOCUMENT 4.2

Case Summary

Procedural Posture

Defendant oil companies sought review of an order from the Circuit Court of the United States for the Eastern District of Missouri, which held that the combining of the defendants' stock constituted a restraint of trade and an attempt to monopolize the oil industry.

Overirew

Plaintiff United States filed an action alleging that the defendants, an oil corporation and 37 other corporations, were engaged in conspiring to restrain the trade and commerce in petroleum and monopolize the petroleum industry. The trial court

Title page of Ida Tarbell's exposé *History of the Standard Oil Company,* accompanied on facing page by a sketch of Standard founder John D. Rockefeller. (Library of Congress)

awarded judgment to the plaintiff, finding that the combining of defendants' stock constituted a restraint of trade and an attempt to monopolize. The Supreme Court affirmed, holding that the plaintiff established prime facie intent and purpose on the part of defendants . . . was not a result of normal response methods of industrial development, . . . The Court found that defendants sought to exclude others from the trade and to control the movement of petroleum in the channels of interstate commerce.

Opinion

MR. CHIEF JUSTICE [EDWARD DOUGLASS] WHITE delivered the opinion of the court.

The Standard Oil Company of New Jersey and 33 other corporations, John D. Rockefeller, William Rockefeller and five other individual defendants prosecute this appeal to reverse a decree of the court below, . . . [T]he bill alleged that the combination and its members obtained large preferential rates and rebates in many and devious ways over their competitors from various railroad companies, and that by means of the advantage thus obtained many, if not virtually all, competitors were forced either to become members of the combination or were driven out of business . . .

Without attempting to follow the elaborate averments [claims] on these subjects spread over fifty-seven pages of the printed record, it suffices to say that such averments may properly be grouped under the following heads: Rebates, preferences and other discriminatory practices in favor of the combination by railroad companies, restraint and monopolization by control of pipe lines, and unfair practices against competing pipe lines; contracts with competitors in restraint of trade; unfair methods of competition, such as local price cutting at points where necessary to suppress competition; espionage of the business of competitors, the operation of bogus independent companies, and payment of rebates on oil, with the like intent; the division of the United States into districts and the limiting of the operations of the various subsidiary corporations as to such districts so that competition in the sale of petroleum products between such corporations had been entirely eliminated and destroyed; and, finally reference was made to what was alleged to be the "enormous and unreasonable profits" earned by the Standard Oil Trust . . . as a result of the alleged monopoly; which presumably was averred to as a means of reflexively inferring the scope and power acquired by the alleged combination. . . .

Both as to the law and as to the facts the opposing contentions pressed in the argument are numerous and in all their aspects are so irreconcilable that it is difficult to reduce them to some fundamental generalization, which by being disposed would decide them all. For instance, as to the law. While both sides agree that the determination of the controversy rests upon the correct construction and application of the first and second segments of the Anti-trust Act, yet the views as to the meaning of the Act are as wide apart as the poles . . . And this also is the case as to the scope and effect of authorities [earlier cases] relied upon, even although in some instances one and the same authority is asserted to be controlling.

So also as to the facts. Thus, on the one hand, with relentless particularity and minuteness of analysis, it is insisted that the facts establish that the assailed combination took its birth in a purpose to unlawfully acquire wealth by oppressing the public and destroying the just rights of others, and that its entire career exemplifies an inexorable carrying out of such wrongful intent, since, it is asserted, the pathway of the combination . . . is marked with constant proof of wrong inflicted up the public and is strewn with the wrecks resulting from crushing out, without regard to law, the individual rights of others. . . . On the other hand, in a powerful analysis of the facts, it is insisted that they demonstrate that the origin and development of the vast business which the defendants control was but the result of lawful competitive methods, guided by economic genius of the highest order, sustained by courage, by a keen insight into commercial situations, resulting in the acquisition of great wealth, but at the same time serving to stimulate and increase production, to widely extend the distribution of the products of petroleum at a cost largely below that which would have otherwise prevailed, thus proving at one and the same time a benefaction to the general public as well as of enormous advantage to individuals. . . .

Source: Standard Oil Company of New Jersey v. United States, 221 U.S. 1 (1911).

ANALYSIS

The Supreme Court justices, faced with the issues set forth in Document 4.2, decided that Standard Oil was in violation of the Sherman Antitrust Act. They defended their finding with the following justification: "We see no cause to doubt the correctness of these conclusions considering the subject from every aspect, that is, both in view of the facts established by the record and the necessary operation and effect of the laws we have," the court concluded. The justices decreed that the Standard Oil had to be broken up into 34 independent companies. Among these would be Exxon, Mobil, Marathon, and Conoco.

The decision was a seminal move that put flesh on the ribs of the bare-bones Sherman Act. Most importantly, it applied what might be called a rule of reason to the determination of monopolies: that is, the decision enunciated the view that a court is charged with looking at all the evidence and deciding whether the arrangement being adjudicated inhibits a reasonable degree of free trade. In his dissent to this element of the court's opinion, Justice John Marshall Harlan maintained that the statute outlawed all restraints of trade per se and that judges should not seek to determine the consequences of

---

DID YOU KNOW?

The $350,000 Cost of Failure to File

An illustrative case of the working of the Hart-Scott-Rodino Act arose in 2003 when Scott R. Sacane, the owner of a hedge fund company, was slapped with a $350,000 fine for failure to notify the Federal Trade Commission of the acquisition of two companies by his Cayman Islands-based Master Fund subsidiary. The regulatory agency found that the amount of money involved mandated prior filing and that since Sacane would receive voting rights on more than half of the acquired companies' stock, he also had to file under the "ultimate parent" provision of the law.

Congress is required to reset the filing conditions every year, and in 2010 for the first time it decreased the amount involved that necessitated notification. The figure dropped from $65.2 million to $63.4 million.

---

the mergers but rather break them up when they are found to exist. Later, a new interpretative wave would employ a rule-of-reason approach to determine whether a monopoly might have redeeming virtues, such as superior service or lower prices for customers because of such considerations as a larger amount of business or reduced overhead achieved by consolidation and elimination of duplication.

In response to the *Standard Oil* decision, Congress in 1914 added the Clayton Act and the Federal Trade Commission Act to the antitrust crusade in order to strengthen the original antitrust legislation. The Clayton Act, which supplied some specificity and extended the reach of antitrust, represented a turn away from the criminal law toward administrative regulations to deal with unfair competition. The Clayton Act aroused considerable disquiet among both its supporters and antagonists in regard to its scope and how it should be employed.

The Clayton Act enumerated four practices to be regulated—price discrimination, tying and exclusive-dealing contracts, mergers, and interlocking directorships. Illustrative of tying contracts was the practice of motion picture distributors to make theaters purchase an "oater," that is, a second-rate western film, in order to obtain access to a blockbuster that would attract large audiences. Some motion picture distributors, until they were forbidden by the Clayton Act, had insisted that theaters show only their films and not those of competitors, and in some instances the companies that produced the motion pictures themselves owned the theaters and boycotted the products of other film producers.

Other amendments and additions followed, including the Robinson-Patman Act in 1936, which buttressed the price discrimination ban, and the Celler-Kefauver Act of 1950, which toughened the antimerger rules. At the end of 1975, as part of a program to combat inflation, Congress enacted the Antitrust Procedures and Penalties Act that changed violations of the Sherman Act from misdemeanors to felonies and increased the maximum fines from $50,000 to $1 million for corporations and from $50,000 to $100,000 for individuals. The Hart-Scott-Rodino Antitrust Amendment Act of 1976 required prior filings with the government regarding proposed mergers. Its aim was to head off undesirable combinations before they took place rather than having to go through the cumbersome process of undoing them subsequent to their occurrence.

FURTHER READINGS

Blaisdell, Thomas C. (1932). *The Federal Trade Commission: An Experiment in the Control of Business*. New York: Columbia University Press.

Bringhurst, Bruce. (1979). *Antitrust and the Oil Monopoly: The Standard Oil Cases, 1890–1911*. Westport, CT: Greenwood.

Cox, Edward F., Robert C. Fellmerth, and John F. Schultz. (1969). *The Nader Report on the Federal Trade Commission*. New York: Baron.

Katzman, Robert A. (1980). *Regulatory Bureaucracy: The Federal Trade Commission and American Policy*. Cambridge, MA: MIT Press.

Martin, David Dale. (1959). *Mergers and the Clayton Act*. Berkeley: University of California Press.

Walker, Albert H. (1911). *The "Unreasonable" Obiter Dicta of Chief Justice White in the Standard Oil Case: A Critical Review*. New York: Privately printed.

John D. Rockefeller

- *Document:* The first part of Document 4.3 offers an excellent summary of the key elements of the Standard Oil monopoly case. Following that are excerpts from the testimony of J. D. Archbold, a key member of the Standard Oil Trust established by John D. Rockefeller.
- *Date:* The summary statement is undated; Archbold's testimony took place in 1888.
- *Where:* The hearing was held in a committee room of the U.S. House of Representatives.
- *Significance:* Taken together, the two segments of Document 4.3 provide, first, a factual view of the way Standard Oil developed and exploited its monopoly power and, second, in the brief excerpts from Archbold's hearing, how the oil moguls saw or, at least, claimed to see the situation.

DOCUMENT 4.3

John D. Rockefeller entered the oil-refining business in Cleveland in 1863, just four years after oil had been discovered in northwestern Pennsylvania. Profits were large as demand for kerosene and other petroleum-based products grew rapidly. Cleveland was a great transport hub, and Rockefeller became adept at playing off the major railroads against each other to win preferential rates for his oil. By the time Rockefeller established the Standard Oil Company of Ohio in 1870, he already controlled 10 percent of United States petroleum refining. In January 1872 a secret deal was struck . . . between Standard Oil and the major United States railroads led by the Pennsylvania, to set up a front organization, the South Improvement

Company (SIC). The railroads would raise the rates for all refiners, but members of SIC, notably Standard Oil, would receive rebates of 50 percent on oil shipments. In addition, SIC members would receive "drawbacks" of 40 cents on every barrel shipped by rival refiners. Each railroad was to receive a fixed share of the oil shipped by SIC members.

The response in the oil district was violent when it was announced that freight rates had doubled overnight for everyone except a few privileged refiners. Public pressure soon forced the railroads to abrogate the SIC contract. In the few months of its existence, however, Rockefeller managed to buy out twenty-two of his twenty-six Cleveland competitors, many of whom, fearing that they would be crushed by the SIC, sold out for a pittance. This marked the beginning of Standard Oil's reputation for ruthlessness. Having acquired a monopoly in Cleveland, Rockefeller moved on to other cities, adopting similar tactics to crush the competition. By the 1880s his empire—the Standard Oil Trust had been created in 1882—controlled some 85 percent of oil shipped in the United States. Rebates and drawbacks remained among his main weapons. Good relations with banks allowed him to buy out his rivals with cash, sometimes in secret deals . . .

After the "Cleveland massacre" of 1872, Standard Oil was increasingly dogged by lawsuits and investigations accusing it of unfair practices. Apart from rebates, these included reports of intimidation of agents of rival companies, accounts of sabotage of rival pipelines, and even a charge, later dismissed by a state court, that Rockefeller had ordered a rival refinery in Buffalo to be blown up. By the end of the 1880s there was a crescendo of protests against all trusts, especially Standard Oil . . . The extract reproduced here gives the testimony of John D. Archbold, Rockefeller's right-hand man . . . Like most of the Standard Oil executives, Archbold proved an infuriatingly evasive witness, persistently refusing to answer questions about internal finances, failing to remember relevant data, denying knowledge of drawbacks, dismissing rebates and denying that rate discrimination had forced a large number of refiners into bankruptcy.

Despite the Sherman Anti-Trust Law of 1890, the authorities remained largely impotent in the face of the Standard Oil monopoly for a long time. They began to move in during the 1900s, boosted by the investigative journalism of Ida Tarbell and others. In 1907, Standard Oil received the largest fine in United States corporate history—$29m—for accepting rebates, although it was thrown out on appeal.

Testimony of J. D. Archbold [1888]

QUESTION: What is your business? ANSWER: I am in the petroleum business.

Q: In what capacity? A: I am the president of the Acme Oil Company.

Q: That is one of the companies that is in the Standard Trust? A: Yes, sir. . . .

Q: You got the very best terms you could out of the railroads? A: Yes, sir.

Q: No matter what other people got? A: I was not attending to business for other people.

Q: But you were at all times willing to do the best you could for yourself? A: To make the best arrangement I could for the concern to which I was dealing.

Q: Irrespective of any considerations of whether the obligations of the railroads as common carriers authorized them to do so or not? A: That was a matter for them to consider and not me.

Q: You did not intend to keep their consciences? A: I would have had a hard job, I am afraid. . . .

Q: Now, am I to accept your answer made [earlier] that you cannot now recall any particular rate of freight or drawback which you had, as true? A: No, sir. I would not undertake to state from memory the record of any rate at any time.

Q: You do not know how it was, then, $10 or 10 cents a barrel at any one time? A: That's a very wide range.

Q: Yes; because I think it takes a very wide range to bring you to any knowledge of anything you do not want to answer. A: I shall not testify to anything I do not know

Q: I desire to know whether there exists anything in the natural formation of the country[,] in the supply of the oil [,] in the laws of the States which you traverse, or in the business combinations which you have formed that would prevent capital entering into the same field and competing with you, and if there be any-thing whatever of that sort I desire to know it. A: There is nothing of the kind. Our hold on this trade and our position in it is, we believe . . . the result of the application of better methods and of better business principles . . . and on that basis only can we hold it or survive . . . The people who come to tell you differ-ently tell you that which is false . . . They are people who have failed through their lack of ability to succeed, and who would not succeed under any circum-stances. They are soreheads and strikers.

Source: The segment prior to the transcript of the interrogation of J. D. Archbold by a congressional committee was prepared by the Hamilton College Library, Clin-ton, New York. It is based largely on material in books by Chernow, Tarbell, and Chandler that are listed in the Further Readings below. The Archbold testimony is from *Proceedings of the Committee on Manufactures in Relation to Trusts*, U.S. House of Representatives, 50th Congress, 1st Session, Report No. 312 (1888).

ANALYSIS

John D. Archbold, the man who confronted the congressional investigating com-mittee, would assume the presidency of Standard Oil of New Jersey after the parent company was divided up by order of the Supreme Court in 1911. He is best known today as a heavy donor to Syracuse University, whose athletic stadium once bore his name. When he died in 1916, Archbold's probated will showed a total wealth of more than $412 million.

John Davison Rockefeller, the driving force of Standard Oil, was in his time the richest man in America. He lived for 97 years, from 1839 to 1937. In the last years before his death, it is said that a version of the daily *New York Times* was delivered to him that had been reworked to contain only the good news so as not to upset or unnerve the elderly man.

Rockefeller was born on a farm in Richford, in upstate New York, the second of six children. His father traveled extensively away from home, calling himself a "botanic physician" and selling, among other elixirs, a quack medicine proclaimed to cure cancer. When John was 16, the family moved to a suburb of Cleveland. His brother Frank fought in the Union Army during the Civil War, but John took advantage of the program that allowed draft-eligible men to purchase a substitute to replace them. By the time he entered his early 30s, John Rockefeller, with four others including his brother William, had founded the Standard Oil Company, an Oho corporation. Rockefeller, as he expressed it, believed that "competition is a sin." It took only eight years before the *New York World* would castigate Standard Oil as "the most cruel, impudent, pitiless and grasping monopoly that ever fastened on a society."

FURTHER READINGS

Chandler, Albert. D., Jr. (1977). *Visible Hand: The Managerial Revolution in American Business.* Cambridge, MA: Belknap Press.

Chernow, Ron. (1998). *Titan: The Life of John D. Rockefeller.* New York: Random House.

Flynn, John T. (1932). *God's Gold: The Story of Rockefeller and His Times.* New York: Harcourt, Brace.

Goulder, Grace. (1972). *John D. Rockefeller: The Cleveland Years.* Cleveland, OH: Western Reserve Historical Society.

Hawke, David F. (1980). *John D.: The Founding Father of the Rockefellers.* New York: Harper & Row.

Latham, Earl. (1949). *John D. Rockefeller: Robber Baron or Industrial Statesman?* Boston: Heath.

Nevins, Allan. (1940). *John D. Rockefeller: The Heroic Age of American Enterprise.* New York: Scribner's.

Tarbell, Ida M. (1904). *The History of the Standard Oil Company.* New York: McClure, Philips.

The Heavy Electrical Equipment Antitrust Case

- *Document:* The government had been alerted to the possibility of collaboration on bids by a group of companies involved in the sale of heavy electrical equipment when authorities at the Tennessee Valley Authority pointed out that they had received identical bids from several companies in regard to heavy electrical equipment, a situation inexplicable in regard to so complex a product, unless the companies had themselves established the figures and each had routinely submitted them without bothering to alter the numbers. Document 4.4 represents the observations of the judge before whom the *United States v. General Electric* case was tried and who imposed sentence on the defendants.
- *Date:* February 6, 1961.
- *Where:* The case was heard in the federal trial court of the Eastern District of Pennsylvania.
- *Significance:* The antitrust conspiracy case had at least two major consequences. First, it captured the attention of the public because it involved prominent, name-recognizable companies and garnered heavy media attention for a considerable period of time, particularly when the U.S. Senate conducted its own investigation of the affair. Second, the jail sentences, however indulgent, represented a much tougher approach than had been common in white-collar crime cases.

DOCUMENT 4.4

Before imposing sentence, I want to make certain observations concerning the bills of indictment here involved. They cover some forty-eight individual defendants and thirty-two corporations which comprise virtually every large manufacturer of electrical equipment in the industry. This is a shocking indictment of a vast section of our economy, for what is really at stake here is the survival of the kind of economy under which America has grown to greatness, the free enterprise system.

The conduct of the corporate and the individual defendants alike, in the words of the distinguished assistant attorney general who headed the Antitrust Division of the Department of Justice, have flagrantly mocked the image of that economic system of free enterprise which we project to the country and have destroyed the model which we offer today as a free world alternative to state control and eventual dictatorship. Some extent of the vastness of the schemes for price fixing, bid rigging and job allocation can be gleaned from the fact that the annual corporate sales covered by these bills of indictment represent a billion and three quarters dollars.

Pervasiveness likewise may be judged by the fact that the sales herewith are concerned with a wide variety of products and were made not only to private utilities throughout the country, but by sealed bid to the Federal, state and municipal governments.

This court has spent long hours in what it hopes is a fair appraisal of a most difficult task. In reaching that judgment, it is not at all unmindful that the real blame is to be laid at the doorstep of the corporate defendants and those who guide and direct their policy. While the Department of Justice has acknowledged that they were unable to uncover probative evidence which could secure a conviction beyond a reasonable doubt, of those in the highest echelons of the corporations here involved, in a broader sense they bear a great responsibility for the present situation, for one would be most naïve indeed to believe that these violations of the law, so long persisted in, affecting so large a segment of the industry and finally, involving so many millions upon millions of dollars were facts unknown to those responsible for e conduct of the corporation and, accordingly, under their various pleas, heavy fines will be imposed.

Source: New York Times, February 7, 1961, 26.

ANALYSIS

The obvious indignation of Judge J. Cullen Ganey as he pronounced sentence upon the defendants in the General Electric case reflected the fact that matters in regard to tolerance of white-collar crime had changed considerably. Franklin Roosevelt's presidency in the 1930s and 1940s ushered in a vigorous period of antitrust enforcement. In the years 1930 to 1939, the Justice Department concluded 85 cases, winning 78. Thurman Arnold, the head of the antitrust division, filed 65 cases in 1940 and 71 in 1941. Many of the case were related to the Second World War and directed against companies that allegedly supported the German cause. From 1940 to 1949, the antitrust division concluded 382 cases, winning 304 of them. In 1959, in a hand tools industry case, the first prison sentence for price-fixing was imposed. In recent times, the level of government activity against mergers, bid rigging, and price-fixing has fluctuated, seemingly reflecting the political and economic views of the political party in power.

The General Electric heavy electrical equipment case in 1961 was regarded, in the words of the judge, as "the most serious violations of the antitrust laws since the time of their passage of the Sherman Act at the turn of the century." The most notable characteristic of the conspiracy was its willful and blatant nature. The antitrust violators did not anticipate being apprehended. "I didn't expect to get caught and I went to great length to conceal my activities so that I wouldn't get caught," said one. They used plain envelopes when mailing information to each other, and were meticulous in cleaning up any wastepaper lying around after their meetings. They adopted fictitious names and conspiratorial codes. The attendance roster for their meetings was known as the "Christmas card list" and the gatherings as "choir practice." They used public telephones for much of their communication, and they met either at trade association conventions or at sites selected for their likely anonymity. Some would later file false travel expense claims, so as to mislead their superiors about what they were up to and where they had been, but they did not ask for more money than they had laid out: apparently, whatever else was going on, it would not do to cheat their employers.

At the meetings, negotiations centered about the establishment of a "reasonable" division of the market for various products. Sometimes the conspirators would draw lots to determine who would submit the lowest bid; at other times, the appropriate arrangement would be determined by a rotating system that was referred to as "the phase of the moon."

During later congressional hearings, one of the conspirators indicated his mindset in regard to what he was doing:

> One faces a decision, I guess, at such times about how far to go with company instructions, and since the spirit of such meetings only appeared to be correcting a horrible price level, that there was no attempt to actually damage customers, charge excessive prices, there was no personal gain in it for me, the company did not seem actually to be defrauding. . . . So I guess morally it did not seem quite so bad as might be inferred by the definition of the activity itself.

Exception might be taken to every one of the executive's statements. Consumers assuredly were harmed by the phony bids because they had to pay more for the product than likely would have been the case in a truly competitive situation.

Almost all of the corporate entities charged in the heavy electrical equipment conspiracy pleaded guilty. The company officials tended to plead *nolo contendere*, which typically means: "I did it but I don't want to admit it in public." That plea also can make civil suits more difficult for those who pursue that route, since they do not have a guilty plea by the defendant to introduce as evidence of wrongdoing but must prove the harmful behavior.

The pleas resulted in fines and jail terms of 30 days imposed on seven defendants, four of whom were vice presidents, two, division managers, and one a sales manager. The warden at the Montgomery County Jail would call them "model prisoners." All indicated a desire that their families not visit them while they were incarcerated.

A number of the defendants adopted the position that by fixing prices they had served a worthy purpose by stabilizing prices. This altruistic stance almost invariably was combined with an attempted distinction among illegal, immoral, and criminal acts, with the defendant expressing the view that what he had done might have been designated by the statutes as criminal, but either he was unaware of such a designation or he thought it unreasonable that acts with admirable consequences should be considered criminal. The testimony of one executive during a congressional hearing by the Senate Subcommittee on Antitrust and Monopoly illustrates this view:

COMMITTEE ATTORNEY: Did you know the meetings with competitors were illegal?

WITNESS: Illegal? Yes, but not criminal. I didn't find that out until I read the indictment . . . I assumed that criminal action meant damaging someone, and we did not do that . . . I thought that we were more or less working on a survival basis in order to make enough to keep our plant and employees.

For the most part personal explanations for the conspiracy were located in corporate pressures rather than in avarice or lack of law-abiding character. The defendants almost invariably testified that they came new to the job, found price-fixing an established way of life, and simply entered into it as they did into other aspects of their work.

In 1946, General Electric had issued a directive that spelled out the company's policy against price-fixing in terms stronger than those found in the antitrust laws. Most executives believed that the directive was merely for public consumption and not to be taken seriously. One man, however, refused to engage in price-fixing after he had initialed the document forbidding it. A witness explained to the Senate subcommittee what followed:

[My superior] told me: "This fellow is a fine fellow . . . except he was not broad enough for his job, that he was so religious he thought that having signed that he should not do any of this and he was getting us in trouble with competitors." The man was merely transferred laterally because of his objections to price-fixing. As the sentencing judge had indicated, those who went along were careerists, focused on comfort, security, and their income.

The General Electric antitrust case illustrated the dire warning of Adam Smith, the economist most associated with advocacy of the glory of capitalistic markets, which, he maintained, will self-correct any errant ways. But Smith also was well aware of the intense desire of profit-seeking organizations to avoid cutthroat competition, indeed, if possible, to

---

DID YOU KNOW?

Portrait of an Antitrust Offender

The highest executive to be given a jail sentence was William Ginn, a General Electric vice president. He had been born in Atlanta and was 46 years old at the time he was convicted of violating the antitrust law. He held a degree in mechanical engineering from Georgia Tech, was married, and had three children. Ginn had served as a lieutenant commander in the Navy during the Second World War and, not without some irony, was a member of the New York Governor's Temporary State Committee on Economic Expansion.

Shortly after his sentencing, Ginn issued a statement to the media, noting that he was to serve a jail term "for conduct which has been interpreted as being in conflict with the complex antitrust laws." Some wondered how it would have sounded if a burglar characterized his conviction as being "interpreted as being in conflict with the complex laws of theft." The GE officer also had some unkind words for his company when he testified before a Senate committee: "When I got out of being a guest of the government for thirty days, I had found out that we were not to be paid when we were there and I got, frankly, madder than hell."

Employed by General Electric shortly after graduation from college, he previously had been mentioned as a possible president of the company. He complained bitterly about the way he had been portrayed by the media. He maintained, for instance, that they "don't use the term 'price fixing.' It's always 'price rigging' or trying to make it as sensational as possible." After his release from jail, the former GE vice president was named assistant to the president and shortly thereafter president of the Baldwin-Lima-Hamilton Corporation in Philadelphia with a salary about one-half of what he had been making at General Electric.

avoid any competition that might reduce their profits. In his classic *The Wealth of Nations* (1776) Smith had written: "People of the same trade seldom meet together, even for merriment and diversion, but that convention ends in a conspiracy against the public or in some contrivance to raise prices."

FURTHER READINGS

Baker, Wayne E., and Robert R. Faulkner. (1993). "The Social Organization of Conspiracy: Illegal Networks in the Heavy Electrical Equipment Industry." *American Sociological Review* 58:837–60.

Conklin, John E. (1977). *"Illegal but Not Criminal": Business Crime in America*. Englewood Cliffs, NJ: Prentice Hall.

Fuller, John G. (1962). *The Gentleman Conspirators: The Story of Price-Fixing in the Electrical Industry*. New York: Grove.

Geis, Gilbert. (1967). "The Heavy Electric Equipment Antitrust Cases of 1961." In Marshall B. Clinard and Richard Quinney (Eds.), *Criminal Behavior Systems*, (pp. 139–50). New York: Holt, Rinehart & Winston.

Herling, John. (1962). *The Great Price Conspiracy: The Story of Antitrust Violations in the Electrical Industry*. Washington, DC: Robert B. Luce.

Sonnenfeld, Jeffrey, and Paul R. Lawrence. (1978). "Why Do Companies Succumb to Price Fixing?" *Harvard Business Review* 56 (July–August): 141–57.

Walton, Clarence C., and Frederick W. Cleveland, Jr. (1966). *Corporations on Trial: The Electrical Cases*. Belmont, CA: Wadsworth.

Microsoft Charged with Sherman Act Violations

- **Document:** Excepts from the 149-page Findings of Fact by Judge Thomas Penfield Jackson relating to charges that Microsoft had illegally stifled competition by a range of pricing and marketing tactics that violated the stipulations of the Sherman Antitrust Act of 1890.
- **Date:** November 5, 1999.
- **Where:** The federal district court in Washington, DC.
- **Significance:** The findings by Judge Jackson gave renewed life to the antitrust law that had been largely bypassed during the business-sympathetic presidential administration of George H. W. Bush. By targeting Microsoft, a company well known to most Americans, the case called attention to alleged rip-offs that imposed financial losses upon a large number of American consumers who had come to rely upon Internet communication.

DOCUMENT 4.5

Finding of Fact

The consolidate civil antitrust actions alleging violations of the Sherman Act §§ 1 and 2, and various state statutes by defendant Microsoft Corporation, were tried by the Court, sitting without a jury, between October 19, 1998, and June 4, 1999. The Court has considered the record evidence submitted by the parties, made determinations as to its relevancy, and materiality, assessed the credibility of witnesses both written and oral, and ascertained for its purposes the probative significance of the documentary and visual evidence presented. . . .

The Relevant Market

Currently there are no products, nor are there likely to be any in the near future, that a significant percentage of consumers world-wide could substitute for Intel-compatible PC operating systems without incurring substantial costs. Furthermore, no firm that does not currently market Intel-compatible PC operating systems could start doing so in a way that would, within a reasonably short period of time, present a significant percentage of customers with a viable alternative to existing Intel-compatible PC operating systems. It follows that, if one firm controlled the licensing of all Intel-compatible PC operating systems worldwide, it could set the price of a license substantially above that which would be charged in a competitive market and leave the price there for a significant period of time without losing so many customers as to make the action unprofitable. Therefore, in determining the level of Microsoft's market power, the relevant market is the licensing of all Intel-compatible PC operating systems world-wide. . . .

Microsoft Power in the Relevant Market

Microsoft enjoys so much power in the market for Intel-compatible PC operating systems that if it wishes to exercise this power solely in terms of price, it could charge a price for Windows substantially above that which would be charged in a competitive market. . . . Microsoft enjoys monopoly power in the relevant market.

Viewed together, three main facts indicate that Microsoft enjoys monopoly power. First. Microsoft's share of the market for Intel-compatible PC operating systems is extremely large and stable. Second, Microsoft's dominant market share is protected by a high barrier to entry. Third, and largely as result of that barrier, Microsoft customers lack a commercially viable alternative to Windows.

Market Share

Microsoft possesses a dominant, persistent, and increasing share of the world-wide market for Intel-compatible PC operating systems. Every year for the last decade, Microsoft's share of the market for Intel-compatible PC operating systems has stood above ninety percent. For the last couple of years the figure has been at least ninety-five percent and analysts predict that the share will climb even higher over the next few years. Even if Apple's Mac OS were included in the relevant market, Microsoft's share would still stand well above eighty percent.

The Applicants' Barrier to Entry

What for Microsoft is a positive feedback loop is for would-be competitors a vicious cycle. For just as Microsoft's large market share creates incentives for ISVs [Independent Software Vendors] to develop applications first and foremost for Windows, the sale or non-existent market share of an aspiring competitor makes it prohibitively expensive for the aspirant to develop its PC operating system into an acceptable substitute for Windows . . .

IBM's inability to gain widespread developer support for the OS/2 Warp operating system illustrates how the massive Windows installed base makes it prohibitively costly for a rival operating system to attract enough developer support to challenge Windows ... IBM ... spent tens of millions of dollars in an effort to attract ISVs to develop or "clone" part of the Windows API set. Despite these efforts, IBM could obtain neither a significant market share nor ISV support for OS/2 Warp ... IBM ultimately determined that the applications barrier prevented effective competition against Windows 9.5. . . . IBM now targets the product at a market niche, namely enterprise customers (mainly banks) that are interested in particular types of application that are run on OS/2 Warp.

Price Restraints Posed by Piracy

Although there is no legal secondary market for Microsoft PC operating systems, there is a thriving illegal one. Software pirates illegally copy software products such as Windows, selling each copy for a fraction of the vendor's usual price. One of the ways Microsoft combats piracy is by advising OEMs [original equipment manufacturers] that they will be charged a higher price for Windows unless they drastically limit the number of PCs that they sell without an operating system pre-installed. In 1999, all major OEMs agreed to this restriction. Naturally, it is hard to sell a pirated copy of Windows to a customer who has already received a legal copy included in the price of his new PC system.

Microsoft's Pricing Behavior

Microsoft's actual pricing behavior is consistent with the proposition that the firm enjoys monopoly power in the market for Intel-compatible PC operating system. The company's decision not to consider the prices of other vendors' Intel-compatible operating system when setting the price of Windows 98, for example, is probative of monopoly power. One would expect a firm in a competitive market to pay much closer attention to the prices charged by other firms in the market. Another indication of monopoly power is the fact that Microsoft raised the price that it charged OEMs for Windows 95 just prior to releasing the new product. In a competitive market, one would expect the price of an older operating system to stay the same or decrease upon the release of a newer, more attractive version. Microsoft, however, was only concerned with inducing OEMs to ship Windows 98 in favor of the older version. It is unlikely that Microsoft would have imposed this price increase if it were genuinely concerned that the OEMs might shift their business to another vendor of operating systems or hasten the development of viable alternatives to Windows.

An aspect of Microsoft's pricing behavior that while not tending to prove monopoly power, is consistent with it is the fact that the firm charges different OEMs different prices for Windows, depending on the degree to which the individual OEMs comply with Microsoft's wishes. Among the five largest OEMs, Gateway and IBM which in various ways have resisted Microsoft's efforts to enlist them in its efforts to preserve the applications barrier to entry, pay higher prices than Compaq, Dell, and Hewlett Packard, which have pursued less contentious relationships with Microsoft ...

Similar Experiences of Other Firms in Dealing with Microsoft

... [I]t is Microsoft's corporate practice to pressure other firms to halt software development that either shows the potential to weaken the applications barrier to entry or competes directly with Microsoft's most cherished software products. ...

When IBM refused to abate the promotion of those of its own products that competed with Widows and Office, Microsoft punished the IBM PC Company with higher prices, a late license for Windows 9.5, and the withholding of technical and marketing support ...

Microsoft has harmed even those customers who desire to use Internet Explorer, and no other browser, with Windows 98 ... Specifically, it has increased the likelihood that a browser crash will cause the entire system to crash and made it easier for malicious viruses that penetrate the system via Internet Explorer to infect non-browsing parties of the system ...

[There is] no technical reason for Microsoft's refusal to supply Windows 95 without Internet Explorer 1.0 and 2.0 ...

[I]t is significant that, while all vendors of PC operating systems undoubtedly share Microsoft's stated interest in maximizing consumer satisfaction, the prohibitions that Microsoft imposes on OEMs are considerably more restrictive than those imposed by other operating system vendors. For example, Apple allows its retailers to remove applications that Apple has pre-installed and to reconfigure the Mac OS desktop. For its part, IBM allows its OEM licensees to override the entire OS/2 desktop in favor of a customized shelf or to set an application to start automatically the first time the PC is turned on. The reason is that these firms do not share Microsoft's interest in protecting applicants barrier to entry ...

Microsoft's effort to maximize Internet Explorer's share of browser usage at Navigator's expense has done just that ... The period since 1996 has witnessed a large increase in the usage of Microsoft's browsing technologies and a concomitant decline in Navigator's use ... The relative shares would not have changed nearly as much as they did ... had Microsoft not devoted its monopoly power and monopoly profits to precisely that end ...

By constraining the freedom of OEMs to implement certain software programs in the Windows boot sequence, Microsoft foreclosed an opportunity for OEMs to make Windows PC systems less confusing, and more user-friendly, as customers desired. By taking the actions listed above, and by enticing firms into exclusivity arrangements with valuable inducements that only Microsoft could offer and that the firms reasonably believed they could not do without, Microsoft forces those consumers who otherwise would have elected Navigator as their browser, to either pay a substantial price (in the form of downloading, installation, confusion, degraded system performance, and diminished memory capacity) or content themselves with Internet Explorer ...

Most harmful of all is the message that Microsoft's actions have conveyed to every enterprise with the potential to innovate in the computer industry. Through its conduct toward Netscape, IBM, Compaq, Intel, and others, Microsoft has demonstrated that it will use its prodigious market power and immense profits to harm any firm that insists on pursuing initiatives that could intensify competition against one of Microsoft's core products. Microsoft's past success in hurting such companies and stifling innovation deters investment in technologies and businesses that exhibit the potential to threaten Microsoft. The ultimate result is that some innovations that would truly benefit consumers never occur for the sole reason that they do not coincide with Microsoft's self-interest.

Source: United States v. Microsoft and *New York v. Microsoft*, Civil Action No. 1322; U.S. District Court for the District of Columbia (1999).

ANALYSIS

The Microsoft case got under way on May 18, 1998, when the federal Department of Justice and 22 states filed a suit against the company on the ground the personal computers marketed by Microsoft bundled its flagship Internet Explorer browser software with the Microsoft Windows operating system, providing unfair competition with browsers such as Netscape Navigator, and Opera. The allegation was that such a tactic by Microsoft was an illegal thwarting of competition so that Microsoft could protect and extend its software monopoly. Microsoft claimed that Internet Explorer was not a product but a feature, a claim rejected by the district court.

The findings of fact set out by Judge Thomas Penfield Jackson in the Microsoft case, excerpted in Document 4.5, were accepted by the appellate court (after the Supreme Court declined to hear the case). Judge Jackson, a graduate of Dartmouth and Harvard Law School, had been appointed to the bench in 1992 (he retired in 2004). His most widely quoted remark on the case was that the Microsoft executives were "stubborn mules who should be whipped by a two-by-four."

The appellate court ruled that Judge Jackson should have recused himself from hearing the case because of media comments he had made. It overruled his decision that Microsoft should be broken up into two separate companies, one to produce the operating system and one to produce other software components.

Thereafter the Department of Justice dropped its push to divide up Microsoft. The company and the government reached an agreement in 2001 under which Microsoft agreed to share its application program initiatives with other companies and to appoint a three-person panel that would be given full access to Microsoft systems, records, and source codes for five years. When this arrangement expired in 2007, Microsoft agreed to a two-year extension.

DID YOU KNOW?

The Disconcerting Dark Figure of Antitrust Crime

"We would like to know, but cannot find, firm answers to issues such as whether organizations increasingly resort to criminal conspiracies to control prices when enforcement is more lax than previously, either because of ideological political influences or because, say, a watchdog agency's operating budget has been eviscerated. Such inquiry is frustrated by the fact that the extent of the events of basic and vital importance to us—the antitrust offenses themselves—is unknown and undoubtedly unknowable. The absence of essential data often makes interpretation of antitrust activities much like the work of the Roman haruspex, those diviners who pretended to discover the meaning of natural prodigies by 'reading' the entrails of sacrificial animals."

Source: Gilbert Geis and Lawrence Salinger, "Antitrust and Organizational Deviance," in Peter A. Bamberger and William J. Sonnenstuhl, eds., *Research in the Sociology of Organizations (Deviance in and of Organizations)* (Stamford, CT: JAI Press, 1998), 74–75.

The case drew considerable criticism from those who believed that the courts had focused on structural considerations to the neglect of consumer interests; that is, it had failed to explore satisfactorily the question of whether patrons were best served by the way Microsoft did business or whether the company's actions harmed buyers.

At the same time, Microsoft found itself under fire from the European Union. Novell charged Microsoft with illegally blocking its competitors from participating in the computer market. Microsoft was said to charge royalties for products sold by a supplier of the company's operating system whether or not the unit contained Windows. A settlement saw Microsoft relax some of its demands, and at the same time pay a fine of $799 million as a penalty for its former actions. The European Commission in 2004 smacked Microsoft with a fine of 497 euros, about $600 million.

DID YOU KNOW?

Judge Jackson Blasts Microsoft

After being rebuked by the District of Columbia Appeals Court for not having stepped down from hearing the Microsoft case because he had earlier expressed controversial views to the media, Judge Thomas Penfield Jackson made no bones about his feeling in regard to Microsoft personnel and the company itself as he examined their courtroom performance. Microsoft executives, Jackson proclaimed, had "proven time and again to be inaccurate, misleading, evasive, and transparently false . . . Microsoft is a company with an institutional disdain for both the truth and the rule of law that lesser entities must respect. It also is a company whose senior management is not adverse to offering specious testimony to claims of its wrongdoing."

A spokesperson for Microsoft refrained from rising to the bait. "We respectfully dissent," was the company's response, with the added observation that since the case had not yet been settled, the company believed that it would not be proper to argue in public with Judge Jackson's comments.

FURTHER READINGS

Elzinga, Kenneth, David Evans, and Albert Nichols. (2009). "*United States v. Microsoft*: Remedy or Malady?" *George Mason Law Review* 9:633–90.

Evans, David S. (Ed.) (2002). *Microsoft: Antitrust and the New Economy: Selected Essays.* New York: Kluwer Academic.

Evans, David S. (Ed.) (2001). *Did Microsoft Harm America? Two Opposing Views.* Washington, DC: American Enterprise Institute/Brookings Joint Center for Regulatory Studies.

Liebowitz, Stan, and Stephen E. Margolis. (1999). *Winners, Losers and Microsoft: Competition and Antitrust in High Technology.* Oakland, CA: Independent Institute.

Page, William H., and John E. Lopatka. (2007). *The Microsoft Case: Antitrust, High Technology, and Consumer Welfare.* Chicago: University of Chicago Press.

Reynolds, Alan. (2001). *The Microsoft Antitrust Appeal: Judge Jackson's "Findings of Fact" Revisited.* Westfield, IN: Hudson Institute.

5

MAJOR SCANDALS AND SCAMS: 1864–1993

INTRODUCTION

The annals of American history are replete with memorable instances of white-collar and corporate crimes. Some involve a considerable cast of characters, both individual and organizational. Others, like several to be examined in this chapter, focus on a single person who carried out a lawbreaking financial scam of such enormity and ingenuity that it stands out among the many sordid episodes that constitute the historical record of white-collar and corporate crime.

The chapter first considers the Crédit Mobilier scandal in the late 1800s that intertwined railroad moguls and high-level politicians. It then discusses four of the better-known white-collar criminals: Charles Ponzi, the Italian-born swindler who gave his name to schemes that pay old investors with the money of new investors; Ivar Kreuger, the Swedish match king, who duplicated Ponzi's tactics on a much larger, worldwide stage; Richard Whitney, a member of the American elite, the president of the New York Stock Exchange, who embezzled huge sums to cover his investment losses; and Robert Vesco, who robbed $200 million from a company he had purchased, fled the United States, and lived out the remainder of his life in various Central and South American countries. The chapter also discusses the scam perpetrated on the pharmaceutical company McKesson and Robbins by Donald Coster (aka Philip Musica) and the savings and loan debacle that cost taxpayers billions of dollars to cover the lootings perpetrated by crooks operating in the deregulated industry.

The Crédit Mobilier

- **Document:** The Crédit Mobilier outrage was a railroad scandal that reached to the upper echelons of the federal government. In 1864, a director of the Union Pacific had established a trust company, the Crédit Mobilier of America, that was totally owned by a small group of the directors of the Union Pacific, headed by Thomas C. Durrant (see Sidebar 5.1), the Union Pacific's vice president. The defunct Pennsylvania Fiscal Agency had been given a charter that allowed it to deal in investments securities. The Union Pacific, responsible for the midwest to far west railroad development, bought the agency cheaply and rechristened it as the Crédit Mobilier of America. Because they controlled the Union Pacific, the insiders were able to award building contracts to Crédit Mobilier, providing wildly favorable terms and paying exorbitant prices for the assigned work. By this ruse they siphoned money, primarily allocated by the federal government, from the Union Pacific books into their own pockets. They were robbing not only the government but also shareholders in the railroad. Document 5.1 presents the results of a subsequent congressional investigation of the Crédit Mobilier.
- **Date:** 1873.
- **Where:** United States House of Representatives.
- **Significance:** The report not only outlines the underhanded acts of the Crédit Mobilier but also calls for strong remedial actions, including retrieval of much of the ill-gained profits realized by the conspirators.

DOCUMENT 5.1

By statutes of July 1, 1862 and July 2, 1864 . . . Congress created a corporation to be known as the Union Pacific Railroad Company, with authority to construct and maintain a railroad and telegraph from a point on the one hundredth meridian of longitude west from Greenwich to the western boundary of Nevada Territory, upon a route and on the terms specified, there to connect with another road largely endowed by the Government, so as to form a continuous line of railroad from the Missouri river to the navigable waters of the Sacramento river in California, and thereby to unite the railroad system of the eastern States with that of California, strengthen the bond of union between the Atlantic and Pacific coast, develop the immense resources of that great central portion of the North American continent and create a new route for commerce from the Atlantic to Europe and Asia. . . .

To aid in accomplishing this vast result, the corporation was clothed by the Government with a proportionately vast endowment . . .

Your committee found themselves constrained to report that the moneys borrowed by the corporation . . . only to meet the necessities of construction . . . have been distributed as dividends among the corporation; that the stock was issued, not to men who paid for it at par in money, but who paid for it not more than thirty cents on the dollar . . . ; that of the Government directors [on the Union Pacific board] some of them have neglected their duties, and others have been interested in the transactions by which the provisions of the organic law have been evaded; that at least one of the commissioners appointed by the President has been directly bribed to betray his trust by the gift of $25,000; . . . and that there has been an attempt to prevent the exercise of the reserved power in Congress by inducing influential members of Congress to become interested in the profits of the transaction . . .

The results of these proceedings were . . .

1. While the charter of the Crédit Mobilier required its affairs to be managed by a board of directors and its principal business office to be in Philadelphia, the actual conduct of its affairs was wholly by the men acting as a board of trustees and in the city of New York so that this unlawful arrangement attempted to disguise and did in fact disguise these persons by means of a fictitious and pretended and not a real use of the corporate powers of the Crédit Mobilier.
2. While the charter of the Union Pacific Railroad Company required its corporate powers to be wielded by a board of fifteen directors, ten of whom should be *bona fide* holders of stock and should be elected by stockholders representing capital which had been actually paid in full and in money, this contrivance placed virtually all the power and control of said railroad corporation, its property and franchises, in the hands of the same person, and beyond the management provided by law, thereby disguising and intending to disguise an unlawful seizure of the powers of the company, an unlawful . . . issue of stock, bonds, and scrip, and an unlawful distribution of its property among the parties.

3. While the United States subordinated its own lien to secure reimbursement of the loan of its bonds . . . for the purpose of constructing the road, moneys have been borrowed under the privilege so conferred and distributed as dividend. . . .

4. Instead of securing a solvent, powerful well-endowed company, able to perform the important public functions without interruption in times of commercial disaster and in times of war, and able to maintain its impartiality and neutrality in dealing with all connecting lines, it is now weak and poor, kept from bankruptcy only by the voluntary aid of a few capitalists who are interested to maintain it, and liable to fall into the control of shrewd and adroit managers, and to become an appendage to some of the railroad lines of the East. . . .

Before proceeding to discuss the question of remedy, your committee take occasion to say that, in making this investigation they have labored under great disadvantages. The books containing the records of these transactions are voluminous and complicated. The estimates of engineers made before the letting of various contracts cannot be found. The presence, as a witness, of General Granville M. Dodge, the chief engineer, under whose supervision the principal part of the work was done could not be procured, although diligent efforts were made to that end. Telegrams were sent to him, inviting his attendance as a witness, and a deputy sergeant-at-arms was sent for him, who diligently sought him for weeks, but he has been unable to find him. Your committee have information from which they feel warranted in saying that they believe that he has been purposely avoiding the service of the summons.

Source: U.S. House of Representatives, Select Committee to Investigate the Alleged Crédit Mobilier Bribery, 42nd Congress, 3rd Session, *Report*, Washington, DC: U.S. Government Printing Office, February 20, 1873.

ANALYSIS

The elusive General Grenwille Dodge [the congressional report misspells his first name] was hiding out in a remote hill area of Texas when the sergeant-at-arms so diligently tried to track him down. Dodge was a native of Massachusetts, but lived most of his life in Iowa. He was a Union Army general during the Civil War and served in Congress for a term lobbying on behalf of the Union Pacific. Trained as a civil engineer, he worked for four years supervising the railroad's construction, and was a major stockholder in the Crédit Mobilier.

When it was uncovered, the Credit Mobilier scheme became the leading symbol of corruption, greed, and the abuse of power in the business world. The initial discovery of underhanded actions appeared in a New York newspaper, the *Sun*, on September 4, 1872, when it was reported that the Crédit Mobilier had distributed shares to Congressmen Oakes Ames, who in turn prodded members in the retinue of President Ulysses S. Grant to come aboard at bargain prices. The news story blasted what it called "the most damaging exhibition of official and private villainy and corruption ever laid bare to the gaze of the world," noting that "the public had long known in a vague sort of way that the Union Pacific was a gigantic steal." The bombshell *Sun* report, as is true of so many white-collar scandals, was fueled by a disagreement between two of the perpetrators of the scheme, one of whom turned whistleblower to expose the other.

Abraham Lincoln had made it a major goal of his administration to foster the linkage of America by a network of railways, and members of Congress, heavily lobbied and bribed by gifts of money and stocks, allocated huge sums to aid in the construction of railroad roadbeds. Many of these allocations by the terms of the Railroad Act of 1862 required repayment with 6 percent interest some 30 years following the completion of the rods, a moment glorified by the meeting of the eastern and western railroads at Promontory Point in Utah on May 10, 1869. The moguls who received the government money sought to evade the obligations attached to their debt. It had been specified, for

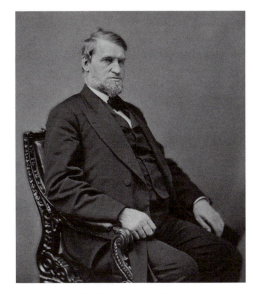

Congressman Oakes Ames of Massachussettes, ca. 1860. Ames was censured by Congress after pursuing his interests with Credit Mobilier among his fellow congressmen. (Library of Congress)

instance, that the cost of carrying troops would be deducted from the loan; the railroad people worked hard to reduce that repayment sum by half and then to eliminate it altogether.

Besides the self-serving skimming of Union Pacific funds by the Crédit Mobilier and the exorbitantly inflated bills presented to the American treasury, a major ingredient of the Crédit Mobilier scandal was the work of Congressman Ames of Massachusetts, who, in his role as a Crédit Mobilier investor, as he phrased it had "placed the stock where it would produce the most good for us." In all, 30 representatives and senators were given stock in the company at prices far below its market value. Some had to pay out no money at all; the dividends from the stock proved to be sufficient to pay for their purchase.

Although an investigating committee had recommended expulsion for Ames and a colleague, James Brooks of New York, who was also involved in the scandal, the full house chose only to censure the two men. No criminal charges were brought. The censure said it was for Ames's "seeking to secure congressional attention to the affairs of a corporation in which he was interested, and whose interest directly depended upon the legislation of Congress, by inducing members of Congress to invest in stocks of said corporation."

Jay Boyd Crawford in the melodramatic language of the time portrayed the congressional session that voted censure in the following terms:

[Ames] sat there silent, immutable, a deathly pallor on his countenance, calmly waiting for the awful decision. Mr. Brooks [was] looking more like a corpse than a human being. Those were awful moments for these men, as name after name was called [to vote] and recorded on the everlasting pages of history, where generations yet unborn might come, and reading, point the finger of scorn at those names thus shrouded in eternal history. A whole life was lost, all honor gone.

Matters did not quite eventuate as Crawford presumed they would. Ames, who died not long afterward, gave his name to the city in Iowa where Iowa State University is located, and in time the legislature of Massachusetts, prompted by an Ames descendant who was lieutenant governor of the state, passed a measure vindicating Ames of any wrongdoing.

The investigating committee also looked into the dealings of other legislators and government officials, including James A. Garfield of Ohio, who later would be elected president of the United States. Schuyler Colfax, then the country's 17th vice president, was forced to pass up the chance for reelection and retired under a cloud to a life of lecturing. His place on the Republican national ticket was taken by Henry Wilson, who also had been under investigation for having profiled from Crédit Mobilier bribery. Wilson would die in office in 1875.

The case against the vice president typifies the way that public figures when trapped seek to extricate themselves from a situation that stands to end what had been a successful political career. Under oath, Colfax declared: "I state explicitly that no one ever gave, or offered to give me any shares of stock in the Crédit Mobilier or the Union Pacific Railroad. I have never received, nor had tended to me any dividends in cash, stock, or bonds accruing on any stock in either of said organizations."

For his part, Oakes Ames testified before the same investigative committee that he had given 20 shares of Union Pacific and Crédit Mobilier stock to Colfax at the vice president's request. Ames advanced the purchase money since Colfax said that he could not afford to pay for the stock at the time. Soon after, the Union Pacific declared an 80 percent dividend, and Ames said that he had applied that sum toward Colfax's account. A while later, the Crédit Mobilier paid a dividend that gave Colfax $1,200.

As Edward Winslow Martin (a pseudonym used by James Dabney McCabe) notes in reporting these events in *Behind the Scenes in Washington, Being a Complete and Graphic Account of the Crédit Mobilier Investigation* (1873): "M. Colfax emphatically denied Mr. Ames's statement." But a check of Colfax's bank account indicated a cash deposit of $1,200 shortly after the payment of the dividend. "The production of this account," Martin observes, "placed Mr. Colfax in a terrible position . . . The

---

DID YOU KNOW?

The Union Pacific's Evil Genius

" 'Tall, lean, slightly stooped, and with sharp features and penetrating eyes, his mouth covered by a drooping moustache and straggly goatee, [Thomas] Durant looked the part of a riverboat gambler some thought he was,' wrote Union Pacific historian Maury Klein. Durant was devious and secretive; hot-tempered and flamboyant; prickly and power hungry. He was a lover of luxury and a reckless spender. He trusted nobody and nobody trusted him. People called him 'the Doctor' because he'd graduated from medical college in Albany [New York]. He was never cut out to be a medical man . . . He was . . . decadent . . . and self-tormenting, simultaneously tense and languid. In the fiction of Herman Melville [*The Confidence Man: His Masquerade*, 1857] he was embodied in that other archetype of the time, the confidence man, the angry and irate genius, intent on putting things over. In the real, turbulent America of the day, he found his destiny in the art of manipulation, and business . . . He seized control of the Union Pacific in 1862 and in time became known as the 'first dictator of the railroad world.' But for Durant, trains were from the start only an instrument, a means. The end lay elsewhere, in power, in control."

Source: Richard Rayner, *The Associates: Four Capitalists Who Changed California* (New York: Norton, 2008), 56.

circumstantial evidence against him was appalling. His best friends stood aghast and pitied him from their very souls." Colfax's story was said to be greeted by the public and the press with "mockery and ridicule."

FURTHER READINGS

Crawford, Jay Boyd. (1880/1969). *The Crédit Mobilier of America: Its Origin and History, Its Works of Constructing the Union Pacific Railroad and the Relation to Members of Congress Therewith*. New York: Greenwood.

Green, Fletcher. (1957). *Origin of Crédit Mobilier of America*. Indianapolis, IN: Bobbs-Merrill.

Kens, Paul. (2009). "The Crédit Mobilier Scandal and the Supreme Court: Corporate Power, Corporate Person, and Government Control in the Mid-Nineteenth Century." *Journal of Supreme Court History* 34:170–82.

Poulet, Elisabeth. (1999). *The Role of Banks in Monitoring Firms: The Case of the Crédit Mobilier*. London: Routledge.

Trent, Logan D. (1981). *The Crédit Mobilier of America*. New York: Arno Press.

Charles Ponzi

- *Document:* Charles Ponzi promised investors in his scheme a 50 percent return in 45 days, but also stipulated that they could withdraw the exact amount of the money they gave him if they desired to do so before the expiration of the 45-day period. Six persons who took advantage of that provision were sued by the trustee appointed to deal with Ponzi's assets after his company was placed in bankruptcy. The trustee sought successfully to get back the money they had withdrawn. He had lost his case in the district court and the circuit court of appeals but won in the U.S. Supreme Court. The case was tried as *Cunningham v. Brown*.
- *Date:* The decision was handed down on April 28, 1924.
- *Where:* The Supreme Court of the United States.
- *Significance:* The decision, written by Chief Justice William Howard Taft, established the important rule that in a scam such as the Ponzi scheme no investor should be preferred to another in the distribution of what remained as booty collected by the person or group that operated the scam.

DOCUMENT 5.2

Mr. Chief Justice Taft delivered the opinion of the Court . . .

The litigation grew out of the remarkable criminal financial career of Charles Ponzi. In December, 1919, with a capital of $150, he began borrowing money on his promissory notes. . . . He spread the false tale that on his own account he was engaged in buying international postal coupons in foreign countries and selling them in other countries at 100 per cent profit, and that this was made possible by the excessive differences in the rates of exchange following the war. He was willing, he said, to give others the opportunity to share with him this profit. By a written promise to pay them $150 for every $100 loaned, he induced thousands to lend him. He stimulated their avidity by paying his ninety-day notes in full in forty-five days, and by circulating the notice that he would pay any unmatured note presented in less than forty-five days at 100% of the loan. Within eight months he took in $9,582,000, for which he issued his notes for $14,374,000. He paid his agents a commission of 10 per cent. With the 50 per cent. promised to lenders, every loan paid in full with the profit would cost him 60 per cent. He was always insolvent and became daily more so, the more his business succeeded. He made no investments of any kind, so that all the money he had at any time was solely the result of loans by his dupes.

The defendants made payment to Ponzi as follows:

Benjamin Brown—July 20th—$600
Benjamin Brown—July 24th—600
H. T. Crockford—July 24th—1,000
Patrick W. Horan—July 24th—1,600
Frank W. Murphy—July 22nd—$600
Thomas Powers—July 24th—500
H. P. Holbrook—July 24th—1,000

By July 1st, Ponzi was taking in about one million dollars a week. Because of an investigation by public authority Ponzi ceased selling notes on July 26th, but offered and continued to pay all unmatured notes for the amount originally paid in, and all matured notes which had run forty-five days, in full. The report of the investigation caused a run on Ponzi's Boston office by investors seeking payment and this developed into a wild scramble when, on August 2nd, a Boston newspaper, most widely circulated, declared Ponzi to be hopelessly insolvent, with a full description of his situation written by one of his recent employees. To meet this emergency, Ponzi concentrated all his available money from other banks in Boston and New England in the Hanover Trust Company, a banking concern in Boston that had been his chief depository. . . .

At the opening of business on July 19th, the balance of Ponzi's deposit accounts at the Hanover Trust Company was $334,000. At the close of business on July 24th it was $871,000. That sum was exhausted by withdrawals of July 26th of $572,000, of July 27th of $280,000, and as of July 28th of $905,000, a total of more than $1,765,000. In spite of this, the account continued to show a credit balance because new deposits from other banks were made by Ponzi. It was finally ended by an overdraft on August 9th of $331,000. The petition in bankruptcy was then filed . . . The claims that have been filed [in this case] are for the money lent and not for the 150 per cent. promised. . . .

The outstanding facts are not in doubt. It is only in the interpretation of these facts that our difference of view [with the lower court] arises . . .

Certainly Ponzi was not returning their [lenders'] money on any admission of fraud. The lenders merely took advantage of his agreement to pay his unmatured notes at par of the actual loan . . . The real transaction between him and those who were seeking him is shown by the fact that there were five hundred to whom he gave checks in compliance with his promise and who were defeated merely because there were no more funds . . .

[The defendants] had one of two remedies to make them whole. They could have followed the money wherever they could trace it and have asserted possession of it on the ground that there was a resulting trust in their favor, or they could have established a lien for what was due them in any particular fund of which he had made it a part. These things they could do without violating any rule against preference in bankruptcy [that is, that they were being given advantages over others in the same position as they were], because then they would have been endeavoring to get their own money, and money in the estate of the bankrupt. But to succeed they must trace the money and therein they have failed. It is clear that all the money deposited by these defendants was withdrawn from deposit some days before they applied for and received payment of the unmatured notes . . . [I]t is impossible to trace into the Hanover deposit of Ponzi after August 1st, from which defendants' checks were paid, the money which they paid him into that account before July 26th. There was, therefore, no money coming from them upon which a constructive trust, or an equitable lien could be fastened.

The decrees [of the lower courts] are reversed.

Source: Cunningham v. Brown, 265 U.S. 1 (1924).

ANALYSIS

Charles Ponzi (1882–1949) gave his name to a form of white-collar crime—the Ponzi scheme—that resurfaced during the recent economic meltdown when the nefarious swindles of Bernard Madoff (see Chapter 11) grabbed headlines in the American press and received extensive television coverage. The basic elements of a Ponzi scheme are very simple. You have to convince enough people to put money into an investment that you are promoting by promising them very attractive profits. Then you pay the investors with the funds that keep coming in from people who are dazzled by what the initial investors have "earned." Very often those original investors reinvest their accrued "profits," so that the scheme does not falter by having to pay out more than it is taking in. Until—and there always is an until, and it typically comes when the scheme is suspected and investors scramble to salvage whatever they can. Usually the promoter of the Ponzi scheme has used a large part of the money he or she received for extraordinarily extravagant indulgences. Ponzi schemes demonstrate the wisdom of one of the oldest adages of the marketplace: if something is offered that flagrantly flies in the face of common sense, it probably is nonsensical—and likely crooked.

The difference between a Ponzi scheme and a pyramid fraud is that the latter depends upon entrants themselves recruiting subsequent participants in the deception. A pyramid scheme will involve a communication that indicates that the recipient should send a certain amount of money to the person at the head of a list (often the originator or an ally of the originator of the scheme) and, by doing so, add your own name to the end of the list, presumably putting you in line to receive a very considerable sum from many others when you rise to the top of the list—an eventuality that very rarely will come to pass.

Charles Ponzi was born Carlo K. Ponzi in the town of Lugo in the duchy of Parma, Italy, and emigrated to Boston when he was 20 years old. He spent the following 14 years going from city to city, working as a dishwasher, waiter, store clerk, and interpreter. An improvement in his fortunes saw him as a bank clerk in Montreal, but that period ended with a criminal charge of forgery and a three-year prison sentence. In 1907, back in Boston, he obtained a job answering foreign mail for a business firm. A letter from Spain included an international postage reply coupon. For Ponzi the coupon became a revelation. It had cost but one cent in Spain but could be traded in for six cents worth of postage in the United States. The coupons were about the size of a dollar bill but nearly square, with intricate watermarks, and a drawing of a woman dressed in flowing robes and delivering a letter from one part of the globe to another. The coupons were the result of an agreement among 63 countries arranged at the International Postal Congress in Rome in 1907. To facilitate correspondence between richer relatives abroad and poorer families in their home countries, the Congress had established a system of international reply coupons that could be purchased in one country and redeemed for postage stamps in another.

Ponzi failed to appreciate that there was only a very limited market for the coupons in the United States and that his scheme would be impossible to carry out. He established the Securities Exchange Company toward the end of 1919 with $150 of his own money. The "dividends" that he paid in 45 days were at a rate that would have come to 2,400 percent annually.

Huge lines formed outside Ponzi's office as people clamored to invest in his scheme. The average investor purchased $300 worth of the elegant yellow certificates that Ponzi offered. Soon branch offices were opened. All told, some 40,000 people put money into Ponzi's scheme. He could have purchased almost 200,000 postal coupons with the money he collected; the records indicate that he bought but two coupons.

Ponzi believed that an appearance of success was vital to the promotion of his plan. He dressed elegantly, owned numerous trademark gold-handled canes, and bought a 22-room mansion in a Boston suburb. He refused to discuss the details of his investment program. Were he to do so, he claimed, the Astors, Vanderbilts, and DuPonts would begin to compete with him.

The beginning of the end began for Ponzi when the *Boston Post* spread details of his scheme on a front-page story with this blaring two-inch-high headline: "DECLARES PONZI NOW HOPELESSLY INSOLVENT." The material had been purchased by the newspaper for $5,000 from William

---

DID YOU KNOW?

Get-Rich-Quick Schemes

"Before Ponzi began his scam, residents of New England had had a good deal of experience with Get Rich Quick 'opportunities.' Fast-talking salesmen had promised fortunes from silver fox-fur farms and from engines that that supposedly used water for fuel. Some had claimed divine intervention or inspiration. Many had caricatured high finance—offering stocks, bonds, insurance, and complicated fraudulent loan deals. Some combined elements of several approaches to portray themselves as money managers. What they all had in common was a three-step playbook: splash, cash, and dash: Make a big impression, grab as much money as possible, and disappear before being discovered."

Source: Mitchell Zuckoff, *Ponzi's Scheme: The True Story of a Financial Legend* (New York: Random House, 2006), 101.

McMaster, whom Ponzi had hired as his press agent. McMaster, who earlier had worked for the *Post* as a reporter, would get an additional $1,000 if his story held up. He justified his whistle-blowing with a memorable observation, an observation that public relations people undoubtedly would find at least mildly hilarious today: "As a publicity man my first duty is to the public." Crowds stormed Ponzi's office, demanding their money back. State officials suspended trading in Ponzi stock and declared his company to be bankrupt. Two days later Ponzi admitted that he had served prison time in Canada on a forgery charge and later had been incarcerated in the Atlanta federal penitentiary for trying to smuggle five Italians from Canada into the United States.

Ponzi was sentenced to five years in a federal prison for his coupon scheme, and the *Post* became the first (and still the only) Boston newspaper to win a Pulitzer Prize. When Ponzi was released on bail to appeal a charge against him in Massachusetts, he ran off to Florida, changed his name, and began to market worthless swampland that he proclaimed to be prime property. When he finally was located, he got a seven-year prison term in Massachusetts, and then was deported to Italy.

In Rome, he worked as a translator for Benito Mussolini, the country's fascist dictator, who appointed him to head the Brazilian office of the Italian airline in Rio de Janeiro. The airline closed during the Second World War, and Ponzi died in the charity ward of a Rio hospital. His name has achieved a certain kind of immortality that he undoubtedly never dreamed possible. Among his memorials is an entry in the illustrious *Oxford Dictionary of the English Language* under the heading of "Ponzi scheme," with the definition "a form of fraud in which belief in the success of a fictive enterprise is fostered by payment of quick returns to first investors from money invested by others."

When the dust had cleared and the state of Massachusetts had recovered all the Ponzi assets it could locate, it offered to pay 30 cents on the dollar to persons who would turn in the Ponzi certificates that they held. Many refused to do so. As Donald Dunn notes, they were "holding onto the belief that Ponzi somehow would make good on his promise of fifty percent interest." There also was a reluctance among those who had been swindled to admit to themselves that they had been foolish. Today, as collectors' items, those notes are worth a great deal more than their cost plus the unfulfilled interest promise.

DID YOU KNOW?

On J. Rufus Wallingford

As noted in Sidebar 5.2, the fascination inherent in get-rich-quick schemes did not originate with Ponzi's bizarre doings. Two decades before Ponzi launched his financial melodrama, George Randolph Chester had published a series of sketches abut a fictitious conman, J. Rufus Wallington, in the widely circulated magazine, the *Saturday Evening Post*, and then collected them into a novel titled *Get-Rich-Quick Wallingford: A Cheerful Account of the Rise and Fall of an American Business Buccaneer*. Wallingford, in Chester's portrayal, was one of "a select circle of gentlemen who make it their business to rescue and put carefully hoarded money back into circulation."

The novel formed the basis for a long-running Broadway play at the Gaiety Theatre, written by George M. Cohan, one of the theater's superstars. Wallingford is portrayed as fleecing investors with a scheme based on carpet tacks. Exposed and jailed, he is saved by his devoted wife and a businessman he had swindled. The businessman declares that Wallington is no more than "the logical development of the American tendency to 'get there' no matter how." He hires Wallingford as an executive in his company. The novel and stage adaptation indicate the tendency of Americans to pay a grudging respect to those who outwit the system in a grandiose way, even if they harm many others while doing so.

The Wallingford persona also so intrigued readers and theater audiences that it inspired a silent serial firm with 14 two-reel episodes, released in 1915 under the title of *The New Adventures of J. Rufus Wallingford*.

FURTHER READINGS

Charles K. Ponzi website. http://www.mark-knutson.com.

Dunn, Donald H. (1975/1993). *The Incredible Story of the King of Financial Cons*. New York: Broadway Books.

Ponzi, Charles. (1937/2001). *The Rise of Mr. Ponzi*. Naples, FL: Inkwell.

Wells, Joseph T. (2000). "Meet Mr. Ponzi: Charles Ponzi." In *Frankensteins of Fraud: The 20th Century's Top Ten White-Collar Criminals*, 23–68. Austin, TX: Obsidian Press.

Zuckoff, Michael. (2005). *Ponzi's Scheme: The True Story of a Financial Legend*. New York: Random House.

Ivar Kreuger

- *Document:* Document 5.3 presents the roster of loans to foreign countries that were made by Kreuger's company as of 1930, at the height of the Great Depression. The total is believed to reach $387 million in U.S. dollars, an amount that would be in the vicinity of $70 billion today.
- *Date:* 1995.
- *Where:* Data compiled in Stockholm, Sweden.
- *Significance:* The tabulation provides a vivid portrait of the reach of Kreuger's financial empire before its collapse.

DOCUMENT 5.3

- Poland I, 1925: $6 million; and Poland II, 1930: 32.4 million
- Free State Danzig, 1930: $1 million
- Greece I, 1926: £1million; and Greece II, 1931: £1 million
- Ecuador I, 1927: $2 million; and Ecuador II, 1929, $1 million
- France, 1927: $75 million
- Yugoslavia, 1928, $22 million
- Hungary, 1928: $36 million
- Germany I, 1929: $125 million; and Germany II, 1930: $1.5 million
- Latvia, 1928: $6 million
- Romania, 1930: 30 million
- Lithuania, 1930: 6 million
- Bolivia, 1930: $2 million
- Estonia, 1928: SEK [Swedish krona] 7.6 million
- Guatemala, 1930: $2.5 million
- Turkey, 1930: $2.5 million

Kreuger also had planned to issue a loan of $75 million to Italy in 1930, but the deal was never completed.

Source: Lars-Erik Thunholm, *Ivar Kreuger* (Stockholm: T. Fischer & Co.,1995).

ANALYSIS

Swedish-born Ivar Kreuger (1880–1932), trained as a civil engineer, by 1930 had gained control of two-thirds of the world's production of matches and, on the basis of that monopoly, amassed a fortune. Operating on a scale that made Charles Ponzi appear to be a rank amateur, Kreuger recklessly used his profits for personal extravagances .The stocks and bonds in his company paid stunning annual interest rates of 16 to 20 percent, but the money was the result of paying off one group of investors with money entrusted to him by another group.

At the time Krueger committed suicide, he owned factories, forests, mines, and real estate that included a posh penthouse on New York's Park Avenue. His company was one of the earliest enterprises with a global reach. Krueger had loaned more than $300 million to financially strapped countries throughout the world in exchange for exclusive privileges in the production of matches. Ultimately, he overextended himself and began to employ crooked accounting practices, hiding losses in the more than 400 subsidiaries that his Swedish trust controlled.

The tightening worldwide money market during the post-1929 economic depression forced Krueger to seek to sell a telecom venture to the International Telegraph and Telephone (ITT) company. ITT auditors were shocked to discover the glaring disparity between what Kreuger claimed and the reality. With his empire collapsing, Krueger committed suicide in his Paris apartment. He left a note saying: "I am too tired to continue." When a financial writer was recently asked to explain the subsequent regulation of the New York Stock Exchange, he said the answer could be stated in two words: "Ivan Kreuger."

FURTHER READINGS

Allen, Trevor. (1932). *Ivar Kreuger, Match King, Croesus, and Crook.* London: J. Long.

Churchill, Allen. (1967). *The Incredible Ivar Kreuger.* London: Weidenfeld and Nicholson.

Kreuger, Torsten. (1968). *The Truth about Ivar Kreuger: Eye-Witness Accounts, Secret Files, Documents.* Revised and enlarged translation by Barrows Mussey. Stuttgart, German: Seewald.

Partnoy, Frank. (2009). *The Match King: Ivar Kreuger, the Financial Genius behind a Century of Wall Street Scandal.* New York: Public Affairs.

Shaplen, Robert. (1960). *Kreuger: Genius and Swindler.* New York: Knopf.

Sparling, Earl. (1939). *Kreuger's Billion Dollar Bubble.* New York: Greenberg.

Stoneham, William H. (1932). *The Life and Death of Ivar Kreuger.* Indianapolis: Bobbs-Merrill.

Thunholm, Lars-Erik. (1995). *Ivar Kreuger.* Stockholm, Sweden: T. Fischer.

Wells, Joseph T. (2000). "Keeper of the Flame: Ivar Kreuger." In *Frankensteins of Fraud: The 20th Century's Top Ten White-Collar Criminals* (pp. 71–112). Austin, TX: Obsedian.

Richard Whitney

- *Document:* Richard Whitney, a former president of the New York Stock Exchange, was investigated by an Exchange committee that announced its findings after the Exchange had opened. A gong sounded, trading was halted, and the statement that constitutes Document 5.4 was read.
- *Date:* March 8, 1938.
- *Where:* On the floor of the New York Stock Exchange.
- *Significance:* The public was shocked by exposure of the crookedness of a man who had for five years (1930–35) been president of the New York Stock Exchange and a fervent speaker calling for honesty in business. Whitney's downfall was instrumental in tighter controls on securities trading, and, equally as important, it created a sense of distrust among the public of people in prominent financial positions

---

DOCUMENT 5.4

"In the course of examination of the affairs of Richard Whitney and Company, the Committee on Business Conduct discovered on March 1, 1938, conduct apparently contrary to just and equitable principles of trade, and on Monday, March 3, 1938, at 1:30 p.m. presented to a special meeting of the Governing Committee charges and specifications. Hearings on the charges were set for March 17. This morning the firm of Richard Whitney and Company advised the Exchange that it was unable to meet its obligations and its suspension for insolvency was announced from the rostrum of the Exchange shortly after 10 a.m."

Source: Richard Whitney, "Opening Statement," New York Stock Exchange, March 3, 1938.

ANALYSIS

To the elite insiders who dominated Wall Street trading and the powerful investment houses, the most shocking aspect of the scandal involving Richard Skinner Whitney Jr. (1888–1974) was that he was one of them, not an upstart from the Midwest or a middle-class entrepreneur who had made it big. It was this background that led Whitney to try to get the Stock Exchange committee to cover up his misdeeds. "After all I'm Richard Whitney," he is reported to have told them. "I mean the Stock Exchange to millions of people."

Whitney was born in Barnstable, Massachusetts, into a very prominent Boston banking family and educated at the exclusive Groton private school and at Harvard University, where he was a member of the best clubs. He married Gertrude Sheldon Sands, who stood by him throughout his travails. She previously had been wed to the grandson of Cornelius Vanderbilt, a robber baron whose life and deeds are examined in a previous chapter.

Whitney located in New York City and formed his own firm, which worked closely with J. P. Morgan Company, where his older brother was a top executive. Black Thursday struck on October 24, 1928, when prices on the New York Stock Exchange plunged precipitously. The Dow average had tumbled from 381 in September to 272 on Black Thursday. A group of bankers raised $130 million to try to prop up the faltering market, and Whitney was appointed to carry out the task. He paraded on the Exchange floor, loudly making purchases of blue chip stocks, such as U.S. Steel, Anaconda Copper, and General Electric, at premium prices. It was a valiant if unsuccessful effort to stave off the Depression, and Whitney afterward became highly regarded as the businessman who had used what people thought was his own money to avert the economic disaster.

Not long after, Whitney was elevated from vice president to president of the New York Stock Exchange and served in that position from 1930 to 1935. Meanwhile, he consistently made poor investments of his own, losing huge sums, and cadging loans in the millions from his family and friends and doubling down (that is, betting twice as much as before on a losing investment in the hope of retrieving his money). When that only made matters worse he embezzled money, including $150,000 from the Yacht Club, where he was treasurer, and $667,000 from the New York Stock Exchange Gratuity Fund that had been established to aid the widows and orphans from families of deceased stock brokers. When Whitney finally declared bankruptcy, he listed debts of $36 million, including $30 million he had borrowed.

Whitney pled guilty to grand larceny, the only charge leveled against him—stealing money from the estate of his father-in-law. The judge, William Allen, berated Whitney before sentencing him. "To cover up your debts and insolvency," Allen said, "you resorted to larceny, fraud, misrepresentation, and falsification of books." Whitney was given a 5- to 10-year term, and when he was transported to Sing Sing prison, some 6,000 people appeared at Grand Central station (constructed with Vanderbilt money) to see him being led off in handcuffs. A model prisoner, Whitney was released after serving three years and four months. His brother paid off all his debts, and Richard went to work managing a dairy farm owned by his family and later started his own small textile firm.

The hypocrisy that characterized Richard Whitney's crimes is evident in a much-quoted speech that he had given before the Chamber of Commerce in Philadelphia on April 24, 1931, titled "Honesty in Business," in which he granted that unsavory acts of dishonesty were still rampant on the New York Stock Exchange but indicated that he was diligently rooting out the wrongdoers. This from a man whom reporter Peter Carlson, writing in the *Washington Post* years later, would characterize as being "as crooked as a pretzel."

The core element of Richard Whitney's white-collar offense, the criminal violation of financial trust, would become the topic of a classic book by Donald Cressey, who had studied under Edwin H. Sutherland. To be included in the study, trust violators had to meet two conditions: (1) they had accepted an occupational position in good faith; and (2) they had violated the expectation of trust attached to that position. The first condition was verified by statements from the men such as: "I had no idea I was going to do this until the day it happened."

Study subjects were 133 male inmates from three prisons (Illinois State penitentiary at Joliet, the California Institution for Men at Chino, and the United States Penitentiary at Terre Haute, Indiana). The men were interviewed for an average of 15 hours each over a period of five months to determine the roots of their violation. Cressey finally concluded that he had unearthed an explanatory schema that fit every one of the men he had talked with. He maintained that whenever all three characteristics were present, a trust violation would occur, while the absence of any one would result in the absence of a trust violation:

> Trusted persons become trust violators when they conceive of themselves as having a financial problem which is non-shareable, are aware the problem can be secretly resolved by violation of the position of financial trust, and are able to adjust their conceptions of themselves as trusted persons with their conceptions of themselves as users of the entrusted funds or property.

A nonshareable problem, Cressey maintained, comes to exist when people conceive of themselves as being in financial trouble but feel unable or unwilling to seek help from another person due to fear that they will lose status and/or forgo the respect of others. The problems the men faced typically involved status-seeking or status-maintaining situations; they had, for instance, purchased homes that that they could not afford because they felt they had to put on a flashy front to impress their boss and fellow employees. It was noteworthy that not one of the married men in Cressey's sample felt able to share his dilemma with his wife.

The men already possessed the knowledge that they could, at least for the moment, resolve their problem by stealing funds entrusted to them or to their employer. They would explain to Cressey the onset of their awareness of this possibility with phrases such as: "It dawned on me," or "I realized I could."

The final and most important element necessary for a trust violation to occur lay in the ability of the potential crook to rationalize the behavior as acceptable in regard to his image of himself. The process became necessary to avoid having to confront the reality that what the person was going to do constituted theft and harmed other people. For independent businessmen and long-term violators, these rationalizations took the form of a belief that they were only "borrowing" money and would return it in due time. Another justification was that the funds really belonged to them because they had been underpaid for what they were doing and how much they were earning for the company. Cressey also found that a number of the trust violators sought to justify their acts by observing that some of the most respected businessmen—people we have dealt with in previous chapters—got their start by using other people's money.

Cressey's formulation later drew criticism from criminologist Gwynn Nettler, who maintained that the folk wisdom regarding trust violators was correct, that the offenders were likely to have been prodded by overspending on reckless activities—the "wine, women, and song" theme—rather than by the conditions that Cressey postulated. Nettler found the idea of a nonshareable problem far from persuasive. "The concept is sufficiently vague that any condition may, after the criminal fact, be denominated as a non-shareable problem that triggered the breach of trust," Nettler insisted, adding, "Such looseness is unsatisfying."

In regard to the particular case of Richard Whitney, neither the interpretative approach taken by Cressey nor the critique by Nettler seems altogether on target. Whitney shared his financial problems at least implicitly with an endless array of friends and relatives whom he fleeced with exorbitant loans. He enjoyed an extravagant lifestyle but, as far as we know, it was very poor investments rather than lifestyle self-indulgence that brought him to ruin.

FURTHER READINGS

Brooks, John. (1969). *Once in Golconda: A True Drama of Wall Street*. New York: Harper & Row.

Cressey, Donald R. (1953). *Other People's Money: A Study in the Social Psychology of Embezzlement*. Glencoe, IL: Free Press.

Green, Gary. (1993). "White-Collar Crime and the Study of Embezzlement." *Annals of the American Academy of Political and Social Science* 525: 95–106.

Lundberg, Ferdinand. (1938). *Who Controls Industry? And Other Questions Raised by Critics of America's 60 Families, with a Note on the Crimes of Richard Whitney*. New York: Viking Press.

Nettler, Gwynn. (1974). "Embezzlement without Problems." *British Journal of Criminology* 14:70–77.

Zietz, Dorothy. (1981). *Women Who Embezzle or Defraud: A Study of Convicted Felons*. New York: Praeger.

DID YOU KNOW?

Women Embezzlers

The factors said by Cressey to be behind the abuse of trust and those depicted by Nettler proved to be off the mark when the study subjects were women who had stolen money from their employers. Dorothy Zietz found that overwhelmingly the women that she interviewed in a California prison had broken the law in order to provide money to help those close to them—husband, children, or friends, and not for their own use. Zietz rather dramatically noted of the women offenders: "Their behavior seemed to have a Joan of Arc quality, a willingness to be burned at the stake to obtain for a loved one the medical care or some service needed and essential for his welfare." This interpretation might be regarded as a bit overdramatic. Joan of Arc, for instance, was a single woman who led the French Army, because, she said, God had commandeered her to do so in order to keep the king on the throne. A reader cannot be certain that the inmates Zietz interviewed were attempting to put an altruistic face on what might have been a selfish act.

In a later study, Kathleen Daly reported that only 29 percent of her female sample of offenders similar to Zietz's could be said to have been motivated by the reasons put forward by Zietz, but she stressed that the number who stole for altruistic reasons was much higher for women than for men. Mary Dodge, writing somewhat later about women and white-collar crime, speculated that it was likely that more and more women, as they succeeded in smashing the glass ceiling that restricted them to low-level business positions, would be found to duplicate the behavior of male white-collar criminals who embezzle funds or commit similar business frauds. Statistics indicate the accuracy of this prediction: women constituted 16 percent of persons arrested for embezzlement in 1965, a figure that had soared to 64 percent by 2010.

Sources: Dorothy Zietz. (1981). *Women who embezzle and Defraud: A Study of Convicted Felons*. New York: Praeger, and Kathleen Daly. (1989). "Gender and Varieties of white–collar crime," *Criminology* 27: 769–94.

McKesson & Robbins, Inc.

- **Document:** Before the advent of the Internet and the explosion of available biographical information, some accurate, some less so, *Who's Who in America* was the standard source for details about the background and achievements of several thousand of the country's and some of the world's leaders. Document 5.5 presents the *Who's Who* entry (these are self-written after a solicitation by the publisher) for Frank Donald Coster, who would be the leading figure in the McKesson & Robbins scandal that rocked the business world in the later 1930s. Coster was, as *Time* magazine observed, "one of the most incredible characters that ever left a fingerprint in the sands of time."
- **Date:** 1938–39.
- **Where:** *Who's Who in America.*
- **Significance:** The material in Document 5.5 holds the key to an understanding of the core elements of one of the most notorious white-collar crimes of the last century.

DOCUMENT 5.5

Costa, Frank Donald. corp. official; b. Washington, D.C., May 12, 1884; s. Frank Donald and Marie Girard C.; Ph.D., U. Heidelberg, 1909, M.D., Univ. of Heidelberg, 1911; married Carol Jenkins Scheffin of Jamaica, N.Y., May 1, 1921. Practicing physician, N.Y. City 1912–14; pres. Girard & Co., Inc. (successor to Girard Chem. Co., 1914–26; pres. McKesson & Robbins, drug mfr., since 1926; also pres. McKesson & Robbins, Ltd., dir. Bridgeport City Trust Co. Fairfield (Conn.) Trust Co., Methodist. *Clubs:* New York Yacht, Bankers, Lotus, Advertising (New York);

University; Black Yacht Rock (Bridgeport); Brooklawn County. *Home:* Fairfield, Conn. Office: McKesson & Robbins, Inc., Bridgeport, Conn.

Source: Albert Nelson Marquis, *Who's Who in America, 1938–1939.* (Chicago: A. N. Marquis & Company, 1938).

ANALYSIS

There is one startling problem with the biographical information in Document 5.5 that Coster supplied for publication in *Who's Who*. Most of it is a blatant lie. After a decade of tossing aside the request from the biographical directory for information, Coster had finally succumbed to the grand illusion he had created and fobbed it off on the widely used reference book. Had they been the least suspicious the editors might have noticed the absence of any indication of where Coster received his undergraduate training.

Coster's real name was Philip Mariano Fausto Musica, and he lived from 1897 to 1938. He had not been born in Washington, DC, but rather in New York City, into a family that ultimately would include eight children, four sons and four daughters. The family had settled in what was known as "Little Italy." His father, Antonio, first ran a barbershop and then opened a store that sold cheeses imported from Italy. Philip quit school when he was 14 to work in his father's business.

In 1909, Philip was convicted of bribing a customs officer to lower the reported weight of the cheese the Musicas were bringing into the country in order to reduce the excise tax on it. He was fined $5,000 and sentenced to serve a year in the Elmira Reformatory. On release, he formed the United States Hair Company, which sold human hair, sometimes for $80 a pound, to women who favored the towering coiffures that were fashionable at the time. Musica's next scam was to borrow nearly a million dollars, using invoices from nonexistent branches in London, Paris, and Naples as security. He had forged inventories to qualify for loans. When that scheme blew up, he tried to escape the country, but he was apprehended just as the *S. S. Heridia* was set to weigh anchor and depart New Orleans for Panama. Musica pled guilty to grand larceny after negotiating an agreement that none of his family would be prosecuted. He gained early release from prison after serving three years in New York City's Tombs by agreeing to serve as a stool pigeon, under the alias of William Johnson, to try to locate German spies at work in the United States during the First World War.

In 1920 Musica turned up in Mount Vernon, New York, just north of New York City, with $2,000, and began making what he declared to be hair tonic as Girard and Company and the Adelphi Pharmaceutical Company. It seems unquestionable that he actually was dealing in bootleg liquor during this period of Prohibition in the United States and prospering mightily. He also was involved in selling arms illegally to forces fighting in the Spanish civil war. Musica made enough money to be able, with the help of a bank loan, to purchase McKesson & Robbins, a pharmaceutical company founded by John McKesson in 1833 that to the present day continues to trade on the New York Stock Exchange.

Musica had changed his name, first to Frank Costa and then to F. Donald Coster, and falsified his background, including giving himself a PhD and a medical degree from Heidelberg University in Germany, and he employed several of his kin in his newly acquired company. They began draining off funds for their personal use by establishing a fictitious Canadian warehouse that stored equally fictitious merchandise that had allegedly been paid for by the funds that they themselves had taken. More than 20 percent of the company's assets were false. Essential to the scheme was the involvement of three of Philip Musica's younger brothers. Arthur Musica, now known as George Vernard, operated a fictitious sales agency, W. W. Small & Co., that pretended to store McKesson inventory. The deceit involved a battery of seven typewriters, each with a different typeface, and a collection of phony business stationery; Robert Musica, operating as Robert Dietrich, was in charge of shipping; and George Musica, now George Dietrich, served as an assistant treasurer of McKesson & Robbins.

To keep a former partner, Joseph Brandino, a Sicilian gangster, from revealing Coster's true identify, Musica was paying blackmail to him, an offense for which Brandino was subsequently convicted.

Musica learned from a morning radio news report that his 13-year reign under false colors of the McKesson ruse had been exposed and that he was accused of stealing some $3.2 million. Federal marshals were on the way to his Connecticut home to arrest him. His wife had been troubled by Musica's severe depression, and she and one of the staff had hidden the three guns that were kept in the house. But Musica had located the cache. He took a .38 police revolver, locked himself in a bathroom, and, standing in front of the washbasin mirror, put a bullet into his right ear, blowing his head to pieces and falling back into the bathtub. He left a four-page suicide note that blamed the incompetence of others for his thefts from McKesson. There also was a note that said, "I am a Catholic, please notify a priest in case of an accident." Catholic doctrine does not permit suicides to receive the last rites, but a priest nonetheless was summoned and apparently offered final rites.

McKesson & Robbins would outlive Coster's depredations. In 2009, having taken back its original name and relocated in San Francisco, McKesson and Company won acclaim from *Fortune* magazine as the "world's most admired company" in the health care industry. Musica fits Sutherland's definition of a white-collar criminal as a person who, if not respectable, was at least respected. He had even once been

---

DID YOU KNOW?

Who's Who's Lament

Almost 60 years after *Who's Who* promulgated the phony information that it had received from Philip Musica, it issued a volume including biographies of those listed earlier who had since died. But it felt obligated to explain why it did not reproduce the entry for Coster/Musica:

> Coster, Frank Donald. The sketch of the president of McKesson & Robbins, Inc.... is the only instance ... during nearly five decades of continuous publication involving over 77,000 biographies—of a fictitious biographer forcing himself on the editors of *Who's Who* ... This imposter had for years successfully fooled banks, boards of directors, famous clubs' admission committees, trade organizations, stock exchanges and some of the leading businessmen and officials. It later developed that he had falsified birth certificates filed which apparently substantiated his biographical data, to which he added fraudulent educational information. Although buried as Coster he was actually Phillip [*sic*] Musica, an ex-convict.

The obvious outrage of the editors at having been tricked is a bit disingenuous. Many people have invented details of their birthplace and birth dates, and the newspapers regularly feature stores of academics, government officials, and others who have lied about their origins and qualifications. It was because Coster/Musica had done so with such blatant daring and, for a time, with dramatic results that compelled *Who's Who* to castigate him when it came to publishing *Who Was Who*.

approached by a contingent of prominent businessmen who sought to persuade him to run for president of the United States.

FURTHER READINGS

Keats, Charles. (1964). *Magnificent Masquerade: The Strange Case of Dr. Coster and Mr. Musica*. New York: Funk & Wagnalls.

Shaplen, Robert. (1955). The Metamorphosis of Philip Musica. *New Yorker*, October 22, 49–81; October 29, 39–79.

Staunton, John J. (1977). *The Case of the Crude Drug Wizard: Mr. Musica of McKesson and Robbins*. Annandale, N.S.W., Australia: University of New England.

Robert Vesco

- *Document:* After fleeing from the United States before the authorities could arrest him, Robert Vesco found himself embroiled in a myriad number of lawsuits. As the judge quoted in Document 5.6 observed, Vesco was the hovering spirit in the proceedings although he was not present in person. In this document the issue concerns the attempt by the International Controls Corporation to gain possession of various things that Vesco was alleged to have acquired with company funds, many held by different entities.
- *Date:* January 15, 1974.
- *Where:* U.S. Court of Appeals for the Second Circuit, New York City.
- *Significance:* The judge provides details of some of activities engaged in by Vesco that saw him charged with criminal conduct by the SEC.

DOCUMENT 5.6

OPINION

[Irving] Kaufman, Chief Judge

A mere glance into the multifarious financial manipulations of Robert Vesco reveals a web of corporate and financial transactions of astonishing intricacy. Although the applicants before us do not include Mr. Vesco himself, who we note parenthetically has refused to return to the Southern District of New York and seems to be safely ensconced in Nassau, the Bahamian capital, beyond the reach of the United States, we cannot ignore his pervasive presence in the litigation which prompted these appeals. Having allegedly utilized appellee International Controls Corp (ICC), as a financial source and vehicle for his purported securities manipulations, Vesco, and his individual and corporate associates have now become the objects of ICC's efforts to recover whatever assets remain.—assets ranging from, (1) a Boeing 707 aircraft, owned by the appellant Skyways Leasing Corp., a wholly owned subsidiary of appellant Fairfield Aviation Corp., in turn wholly owned by appellant Fairfield General Corp. . . . to (2) 84,380 shares of ICC common stock transferred by Vesco and his children to appellant Vesco & Co. Inc., to (3) a pleasure yacht the Patricia III, which although used exclusively by Vesco and his family, is claimed by intervenor-appellant Andean Credit S.A. Thus, we are asked by appellants . . . in three separate appeals, to review the propriety of preliminary injunctions . . . restraining the disposition of these various assets claimed by ICC, injunctions which, with some modifications, we affirm.

I. INTRODUCTION

On November 27, 1972, the Securities and Exchange Commission (SEC) filed a complaint in the Southern District of New York . . . alleging a scheme of extraordinary magnitude, deviousness, and ingenuity in violation primarily of the anti-fraud provision of the Securities and Exchange Act of 1934. In brief, the SEC charged that Robert Vesco masterminded, and, with his cohorts, implemented a plan involving the manipulation of the assets and securities controlled by Vesco . . . The SEC asserted that as a result of this elaborate shell game, clothed in the garb of securities transactions, Vesco and others had seized control of over $200 million, deposited in banks ranging geographically from Luxembourg to Costa Rica . . .

II. THE FAIRFIELD GROUP APPEAL . . .

On June 15, 1971, Skyways, then a wholly-owned subsidiary of Fairfield Aviation, which, in turn, was a wholly-owned subsidiary of ICC, purchased an aircraft from Pan American World Airlines, Inc., for $3,375,000. Thereafter, on October 1, 1971, Skyways leased the plane to ICC for a five-year period for an approximate gross rental of $3,500,000 . . . This lease was not submitted to the ICC board of directors for approval until December 8, 1971 . . .

ICC spent $600,000 to $700,000 to refurbish the plane. These improvements, however, were not of the sort generally associated with business purposes but rather, suited the personal comforts, conveniences and zest for living of the primary user of the 707, Vesco.

III. THE VESCO & CO. APPEAL

The circumstances surrounding applicant Vesco & Co.'s alleged role in the purported scheme to defraud ICC are, in the context of this sprawling and labyrinthine lawsuit, remarkably straightforward. Indeed, our knowledge of the details relating to Vesco & Co. derives principally from an affidavit submitted by Milton Stern, counsel for Vesco & Co., in support of his unsuccessful motion to dismiss the complaint. Vesco & Co., it appears, was incorporated in Delaware on July 12, 1972 as an estate planning device for Robert Vesco. At that time, Vesco exchanged 800,000 shares of ICC common stock for all of the preferred stock of Vesco & Co. The common stock of Vesco & Co. is owned by Patricia Vesco, Vesco's wife, as custodian for Vesco's children. The sole asset of Vesco & Co. is the block of ICC common stock which, through the additional contributions of the Vesco children, totals 846,380 shares.

Furthermore, we have been advised that the officers of Vesco & Co. are Mrs. Vesco and Shirley Bailey, Vesco's personal secretary.

On facts such as these, which hardly can be characterized as common, routine or without the semblance of taint, ICC moved for and was granted a preliminary injunction enjoining Vesco & Co. from disposing of the 846,380 of ICC common stock.

Source: International Controls Corp. v. Vesco, 490 Federal Reporter 2d 1334 (2nd Circuit, 1974).

ANALYSIS

The career of Robert Vesco, a consummate wheeler-dealer who seemed incapable of abiding by the law even when the risks escalated to a very high level, illustrates some of the advantages that white-collar criminals enjoy over more traditional types of criminals. The huge amounts of money they often steal allow them to hire very talented defenders, to bribe their way out of trouble, and to live luxurious lives.

Robert Lee Vesco was born in Detroit in 1935 and died in Cuba shortly before his 72nd birthday in 2007. A *New York Times* reporter would describe Vesco as looking like a "tough guy out of Hollywood central casting—tall, craggy-faced with a mustache, long sideburns and sunglasses."

Vesco had dropped out of high school after deciding that the time involved in classes and studying was keeping him from getting rich more rapidly; his sister, by contrast, would earn a PhD and work as a psychology professor at Michigan State University. By 1965, Vesco had created the International Controls Corporation and kept acquiring companies to form a flourishing conglomerate. Five years later he purchased Investor Overseas Services, Ltd., a Swiss-based company that was being run into the ground by Bernie Cornfeld, another notorious white-collar crook (see Sidebar 5.7). Vesco looted the Investor Overseas Services' treasury to the tune of $224 million. He also contributed through an intermediary an illegal payment of $200,000, delivered in cash to Maurice Stans, the treasurer of Richard Nixon's reelection campaign. It is presumed that the money represented an offering to have the president call off the SEC's investigation of Vesco's crimes. At his peak, Vesco was named by *Forbes* magazine as one of the richest men in America. The article noted as Vesco's occupation—"thief."

Facing arrest, in 1973 Vesco boarded a corporate jet and fled to Costa Rica. It is not clear whether the jet was another of his air fleet or its queen, the Boeing 707 named the *Silver Phyllis* because Vesco said its male passengers all were going to catch syphilis from the playgirls who performed in the disco cabin built into the aircraft.

Vesco bribed Costa Rica president José Figueres Ferrer to have the government enact the "Vesco Law," a statute that allowed Ferrer to unilaterally grant political asylum to anyone he chose so that Vesco could remain in Costa Rica free from the threat of extradition to the United States to face criminal charges for securities fraud, drug trafficking, and political bribery. Sarcastically, the media labeled Vesco "the undisputed king of fugitive financiers."

In 1977, a new government repealed the sanctuary law, and Vesco moved first to the Bahamas where he did business with a cocaine kingpin. The next stop was Antigua. In that Caribbean retreat, Vesco tried to purchase Barbuda, an island that is part of Antigua, and turn it into a sovereign state. That plan fell through, and Vesco moved on to Cuba on the basis of a promise that he could assist the Cubans in dodging the trade embargo that blocked American goods from coming into their country. He got involved with Fidel Castro and Castro's brother, as well as Donald Nixon Jr., a nephew of Richard Nixon and a longtime Vesco confederate in a scheme to market Trioxidal or TX, said to be a miracle drug that could cure arthritis and cancer as well as a mélange of other ills. Vesco also became active in the smuggling of illegal drugs. Tests failed to support the therapeutic claims for Trioxidal, and Castro became disenchanted with the wealthy and crooked expatriate and had Vesco arrested and tried by a three-judge panel in Havana. He was sentenced to 13 years in prison on the charge of "fraud and illicit economic activity," but he was quietly released in 2005 and moved to a Havana suburb, grew a beard, and took the name Tom Adams. He reportedly died of lung cancer two years later, but, as in the case of Ivar Kreuger, there were those who believe that his death was faked so that he could continue to carry on his schemes under cover. But pictures of Vesco on his release from prison show a very haggard, obviously very ill man.

DID YOU KNOW?

Bernie Cornfeld's Caper

Bernard Cornfeld established the Investor Overseas Services company in Europe, outside the reach of American regulatory rules and taxes. People had begun pouring money into mutual funds in lieu of direct investments in this or that particular stock. Mutual fund managers, who worked full-time at tracking Wall Street doings, presumably would be able to make better stock picks than the normal investor. Besides, the funds offered the protection of diversification. What Cornfeld did went a step further: his company was a mutual fund that invested not in stocks but in other mutual funds. He called the venture "The Fund of Funds" and employed some 25,000 people to push its sales. At first, he targeted Americans living overseas and the large American military contingent in Europe, and later he began to sell to German and Italian citizens who had no other access to the American stock market.

In a Paris conclave with potential investors, Cornfeld demonstrated his sales pitch. "Do you sincerely want to be rich?," he challenged the largely American expatriate audience. "Does it mean everything to you? Do you want to be used by the capitalist system or do you want to use it?"

When Investor Overseas Services collapsed, Cornfeld was imprisoned in Switzerland for 11 months before being released because a judge ruled that there had been insufficient evidence to keep him locked up. He went back to America and died on a trip to London in 1957 at the age of 67.

FURTHER READINGS

Dorman, Michael. (1975). *Vesco: The Infernal Money Making Machine*. New York: Berkley.

Herzog, Arthur. (1987). *Vesco: From Wall Street to Castro's Cuba: The Rise, Fall, and Exile of the King of White Collar Crime*. New York: Doubleday.

Hutchinson, Robert A. (1974). *Vesco*. New York: Praeger.

Wells, Joseph T. (2000). "The Outlaw: Robert Vesco." In *Frankensteins of Fraud*, 170–213). Austin, TX: Obsidian Press.

The Savings and Loan Debacle

- *Document:* As the savings and loan crash turned from an annoyance to a catastrophe, efforts got under way to determine the cause and to fashion a cure for the problem. A congressionally appointed committee cochaired by John Snow, a former secretary of the Treasury, spearheaded one of the major investigations. Document 5.7 reproduces some of its findings in its report to the president and to Congress.
- *Date:* 1993.
- *Where:* Washington, DC.
- *Significance:* The committee's report was influential in the passage of the Financial Institutions Recovery and Reform Act of 1989 that sought to put an end to the orgy of self-serving transactions that bled the savings and loan industry to death and cost the taxpayers hundreds of millions of dollars.

DOCUMENT 5.7

The S&L Crisis

The recession . . . significantly worsened a crisis in the savings and loan industry.

In 1990, there were approximately 4,590 state- and federally-chartered savings and loan institutions with total assets of $616 billion. Beginning in 1979, S&Ls began losing money due to spiraling interest rates. Net S&L income, which totaled $781 million in 1980, fell to a loss of $4.6 billion in 1981 and a loss of $4.1 billion in 1982. Tangible net worth for the entire S&L industry was virtually zero.

The Federal Home Loan Bank Board (FHLIB) regulated and inspected S&Ls, and administered the Federal Savings and Loan Insurance Commission (FSLIC), which insured deposits at S&Ls. But the FSLIC's enforcement practices were significantly weaker than those of other federal banking agencies. Until the 1980s, savings and loan had limited lending powers. The FHLIB was, therefore, a relatively small agency overseeing a quiet, stable industry. Accordingly, the FHLIB's procedures and staff were inadequate to supervise S&Ls after deregulation gave the financial institutions a broad array of new lending powers. Additionally, the FHLIB was unable to add to its staff because of stringent limits on the number of personnel it could hire and the level of compensation it could offer. These limitations were placed on the agency by the Office of Management and Budget, and were routinely subject to the political whims of that agency and political appointees in the Executive Office of the President . . .

Because of its weak enforcement powers, the FHLIB and FSLIC rarely forced S&Ls to correct poor financial practices. The FHLIB relied heavily on its persuasive powers and the states to enforce banking regulations. With only five enforcement lawyers, the FHLIB was in a poor position to enforce the law even had it wanted to.

One consequence of the FHLIB's lack of enforcement ability was the promotion of deregulation and aggressive, expanded lending to forestall insolvency. In November 1980, the FHLIB lowered net worth requirements for federally-insured S&Ls from 5% of deposits to 4%. The FHLIB further lowered net worth requirements to 3% in January 1982. Additionally, the agency only required S&Ls to meet these requirements over a 20-year period. The phase-in rule meant that S&Ls less than 20 years old had practically no capital reserve requirements. This encouraged extensive chartering of new S&Ls, because a $2 million investment could be leveraged into $1.3 billion in lending.

Congressional deregulation worsened the S&L crisis . . . These changes allowed S&Ls to make high risk loans to developers. Beginning in 1982, S&Ls rapidly shifted away from traditional financing into new, high-risk investment activities such as casinos, fast-food franchises, ski resorts, junk bonds, arbitrage schemes, and derivative investments.

As the risk exposure of S&Ls expanded, the economy slid into recession. Soon, hundreds of S&Ls were insolvent . . . The FSLIC pushed mergers as a way to avoid insolvency. From 1980 to 1982, there were 493 voluntary mergers and 259 forced mergers of savings and loans overseen by the agency. . . .

Federal inaction worsened the industry's problems . . . [T]he Reagan administration did not want to alarm the public by closing a large number of S&Ls.

The S&L crisis triggered by the recession lasted well beyond the end of the economic downtown. The crisis was finally quelled by passage of the "Financial Institutions Recovery and Reform Act of 1989."

Source: National Commission on Financial Institutions Reform, Recovery and Effectiveness, *Origins and Causes of the S&L Debacle: A Blueprint for Reform: A Report to the President and Congress of the United States*, 1993.

ANALYSIS

The collapse in the 1980s and 1990s of savings and loan institutions—nearly a thousand of them went under—would cost taxpayers between $150 million and

$175 million. This bill does not count payments on government bonds sold to finance the bailout costs. The S&Ls had become time bombs waiting to explode—to be exploited—as a result of the government deregulation of the industry, a development prompted by intense lobbying of legislators and big-money campaign contributions. The deregulation rationale grew in considerable part out of flawed logic. It was said that since the S&Ls were operating so effectively, it was reasonable to deregulate them; they could monitor themselves. This reasoning failed to appreciate that one of the reasons that they had operated honestly was that they were being monitored by regulators.

Among the most egregious of the scams operated by S&Ls were the "land flips" in which they sold and resold the same property to each other, every time at a higher price, and then used the vastly inflated value of the land as collateral for loans that they often had no intention of repaying. Take the example of Erwin Hansen, who took over the once-conservative small-town Centennial Savings and Loan in Northern California in 1980. He hosted a $148,000 Christmas party for 500 people and otherwise engaged in wildly extravagant endeavors financed by company funds. To pay for these affairs, Hansen and a financier friend Sid Shah bought and sold one property worth $50,000 back and forth in the early 1980s until it reached a market "value" of $487,000. It was not unusual for a property, with the connivance of a corrupt appraiser, to be flipped in a single afternoon until its price was double or triple its original market value. The in-group jargon for such transactions was "cash for trash." Hansen died before he could be charged criminally with fraud.

In Texas and California, the states where the worst of the S&L scandals erupted, ADC loans (for acquisition, development, and construction) after deregulation often required no cash down payment, provided 100 percent financing including architects' and lawyers' fees, and offered prepaid interest for the first two years. The construction usually was on speculation rather than, as in former times, presold to awaiting occupants. These deals attracted only the most unreliable of borrowers who were unable to obtain loans from more demanding banks. If anything went wrong with the project, even slightly, the borrower, with no real financial stake at risk, would walk away from it. The result, as Kitty Calavita, Henry N. Ponell, and Robert H. Tillman report, was that "in the end, every thrift that concentrated on ADC loans and other direct investments, that experienced a change in ownership, and that grew rapidly in the 1980s, failed catastrophically." This occurred, they observe, both in Texas where the economy had gone from bad to worse and in California, where the economy was booming. In both states and elsewhere throughout the nation, taxpayers had to pick up the pieces.

DID YOU KNOW?

Rigging the System

The moneys poured into the coffers of the Keating Five by representatives of the savings and loan industry were compared by William Proxmire, an iconoclastic senator from Wisconsin, to a rigged baseball game:

> Imagine that you are watching a World Series baseball game. The pitcher walks over to the umpire before the game begins. The pitcher pulls a wad of $100 bills out of his pocket and counts out 100 of them, $10,000, and hands the whole fat wad to the plate umpire. The umpire jams the bills into his pocket, warmly thanks the pitcher and settles down to call the same pitcher's balls and strikes. What would be the reaction of the other team? Of the fans? The media? All would be furious. The game has been fixed. Far-fetched [compared to what goes on in Congress]? Not a bit. Yes, the game is fixed.

Source: U.S. House of Representatives, Committee on Banking, Finance, and Urban Affairs, October 1990, 79–80.

Calavita and her colleagues point out that the S&L debacle followed a different pattern than earlier instances of embezzlement and corporate crime. In embezzlement, offenders typically steal from the company that employed them, while corporate crimes, such as antitrust violations, are carried out by employees for the benefit of the organization that pays their salary. The S&L swindles commonly used the company as a vehicle—a weapon—for their own enrichment. The writers labeled this phenomenon "collective embezzlement."

The most notorious of the collective embezzlers was Charles Humphrey Keating Jr. who ran the Lincoln Savings and Loan in Irvine, California, a city known for regularly recording one of the lowest rates of street crimes in the nation and one of the highest rates of white-collar crime. Keating was arrested on September 20, 1990. When his bank's records were examined, investigators found thousands of forged documents. In one episode, he had flown employees from his Phoenix outlet to Irvine to alter thousands of pages of minutes of board meetings covering two years and to shred the originals. Signatures were forged and documents fabricated to provide the bank with an appearance of solvency. Keating maintained that he merely was tidying things up.

The spotlight came to fall on a quintet of U.S. senators who became known as the Keating Five because they had worked strenuously to thwart congressional efforts to raise the reserve requirements for savings and loan banks and to halt an investigation by the San Francisco U.S. Attorney's Office of Keating's operation. The senators all had been recipients of large campaign contributions from industry sources, including honoraria for speeches, money that they could retain as personal income. The complicity of the senators resulted in the marketing of playing cards featuring Keating holding a hand with the picture of each of the senators on a card. Alan Cranston (D-Calif.), Dennis DeConcini (D-Ariz.), and Donald W. Riegel Jr. (D-Mich.) did not run for reelection. John Glenn (D-Ohio) and John McCain (R-Ariz.) both emerged victorious in the next election, and McCain would run for president on the Republican ticket in 2008.

Keating was convicted both in a state court and in a federal court on criminal charges and received a 10-year and 12½-year sentence respectively. He was released after 4½ years when an appeals court ruled that there had been procedural errors in his trials. Fined huge amounts, Keating said that he could not pay them because he had no money; later in a retrial he would plead guilty to some of the charges and receive a sentence equivalent to the time he already had served in prison.

Relative calm came to the savings and loan industry with the enactment by Congress of the Federal Institution Reform, Recovery and Establishment Act of 1989 (FIRREA), which, among numerous other changes, moved regulatory authority from the Federal Housing Bank Board to an Office of Thrift Supervision to be located in the Department of Treasury and repealed many of the deregulatory statutes. It was now required that thrifts hold at least 70 percent of their assets in home mortgages or mortgage-backed securities to obtain federal loans and tax breaks.

FIRREA raised $50 billion through the sale of bonds that were to be paid back over the next 40 years. The law mandated that the states institute a set of licensing standards for appraisers and maintain a registry of certified appraisers. S&Ls were

DID YOU KNOW?

Enforcement Is Not Easy

One law enforcement agent indicated that when he dealt with the staggering extent of the S&L crimes he felt as if he was engaged in a cleanup of an Alaska oil spill armed only with a single paper towel. An FBI agent described the tortuous route that needed to be taken in order to obtain a conviction in a complicated savings and loan scam:

> When it comes to these insider, conspiratorial things, they are extremely complex, they are disguised ... The problem is figuring out what the crime is—what did they do, how did they do it. And then can I explain to a court of law, to people who are high school graduates or less. I spent, I think, about five and a half months when all day every day, I sat in a room with boxes and boxes of records. You look through these things to see where the money went ... It's difficult. To figure out what's happened to these things. It's really tough.

Source: Kitty Calavita, Henry N. Pontell, and Robert Tillman, *Big Money Crime* (Berkeley: University of California Press, 1997), 131.

required to maintain higher levels of reserves, and violations of various provisions of the new law could result in a civil penalty not to exceed $1 million or, if the offense was a continuing violation, $5 million. If the gain by the violator exceeded $5 million, the penalty could increase as well but could not be more than the amount of the gain. The bill also provided for increased penalties for financial institutional crimes (up from 5 years to 20 years for each offense) and lengthened the statute of limitations from 5 to 10 years. The result was that the number of prosecuted S&L managers rose rapidly. From October 1998 to April 1992, more than 1,100 defendants were formally charged in major cases, those involving losses of more than $100,000 or insolvency. Of the 1,100 charges, 839 people were convicted.

FURTHER READINGS

Black, William K. (2005). *The Best Way to Rob a Bank Is to Own One*. Austin, TX: University of Texas Press.

Calavita, Kitty, Henry N. Pontell, and Robert H. Tillman. (1997). *Big Money Crime: Fraud and Politics in the Savings and Loan Crisis*. Berkeley: University of California Press.

Mayer, Martin. (1990). *The Greatest Ever Bank Robbery: The Collapse of the Savings and Loan Industry*. New York: Scribner's.

Pizzo, Stephen, Mary Fricker, and Paul Muolo. (1991). *Inside Job: The Looting of American Savings and Loan* (2nd ed.). New York: HarperCollins.

Stewart, Alva W. (1991). *Savings and Loan Crisis: A Bibliography*. Monticello, IL: Vance Bibliographies.

Waldman, Michael. (1990). *Who Robbed America? A Citizen's Guide to the Savings & Loan Scandal*. New York: Random House.

White, Lawrence H. (1990). *The S&L Debacle: Public Policy Lessons for Bank and Thrift Regulation*. New York: Oxford University Press.

6

INSIDER TRADING AND RELATED CRIMES

INTRODUCTION

White-collar criminals enjoy the advantage of being able to make vast sums of money by illegal means without running the risk of being shot, robbed, or otherwise harmed. They can sit at their ornate desks in elegantly furnished offices and employ computers and telephones as their weapons. Insider trading, one of the lucrative forms of white-collar crime, involves nothing more complicated than one knowing or finding a person who possesses information not yet publicly announced about a pending deal that will enhance or reduce the value of a stock. It can be tricky to trade in the stock in ways that you presume will remain hidden. You might do the deal through an account in the Cayman Islands or Antigua or some other offshore bank or through a team of relatives and friends. The payoff amounts can be virtually guaranteed and very large.

This chapter discusses some of the intricacies of the law of insider trading, and then considers the notorious exploits of Ivan Boesky, Dennis Levine, and Michael Milken, three men who alerted the public to an understanding that the stock market is not always a level playing field and that it was being ripped off by unscrupulous insiders.

The Law of Insider Trading

- *Document:* Trading in securities by insiders who act on the basis of nonpublic information is forbidden by federal law and judicial rulings, but the exact nature of the criminal offense can prove difficult to pin down, and the Congress has never seen fit to provide a straightforward and clear definition of precisely what is not permitted. Document 6.1 offers an appraisal of the status of insider trading by two officials in the SEC, the agency responsible for enforcing the law.
- *Date:* September 19, 1998.
- *Where:* Document 6.1 originated as a speech before the 16th Symposium on Economic Crime, held at Jesus College in Cambridge University in England.
- *Significance:* The material offers the interpretation of insider trading as understood by officials charged with carrying out the legislative mandate, and it provides the legal background against which events discussed subsequently in this chapter played out.

DOCUMENT 6.1

An essential part of the securities market is the vigorous enforcement of our laws against insider trading . . . The enforcement program includes both civil and criminal prosecution of insider trading cases.

"Insider trading" is a term subject to many definitions and connotations and it encompasses both legal and prohibited activity. Insider trading takes place legally every day, when corporate insiders—officers, directors, or employees—buy or sell stock in their own companies within the confines of company policy and the regulations governing this trading.

The type of insider trading we discuss here is the illegal variety that most of us think of when we hear the term, the type of insider trading that achieved widespread notoriety in the 1980s with the SEC civil cases and the United States Department of Justice criminal cases against Michael Milken and Ivan Boesky and which inspired even Hollywood's imagination with the movie "Wall Street." It is the trading that takes place when those privileged with confidential information about important events use the special advantage of the knowledge to reap profits or avoid losses on the stock market, to the detriment . . . of the typical investors who buy or sell their stock without the advantage of "insider" information.

The American notion that insider trading is wrong was well-established long before the passage of the federal securities laws. In 1909, the United States Supreme Court held that a director of a corporation who knew that the value of the stock in his company was about to skyrocket committed fraud when he brought company stock from an outsider without disclosing what he knew. But the condemnation is not universal, even in the United States.

Those who oppose prohibiting insider trading advance many arguments, most of which fall on their own weight.

- Some say that insider trading is a legitimate form of compensation of corporate employees, permitting lower salaries that, in turn, benefit shareholders. It proves an incentive to innovation, some argue, by promising huge rewards for developing a plan or product that will lead to a precipitous rise in the stock. This argument, however, fails to address the real and significant hazard of creating an incentive for corporate insiders to enter into risky and ill-advised ventures for short-term personal gains, as well as to put off the public release of important corporate information so that they can capture the economic fruits at the expense of shareholders.
- Others have argued that American reliance on several antifraud provisions, and the absence of a statutory definition of insider trading, may lead to unfairly penalizing traders whose conduct comes close to the line. This seems an illusory concern. There are at least two compelling reasons for this. First, *scienter*, a fraudulent intent, is an element that must be proven. Second, given the inherent difficulties in investigating and proving insider trading cases, the result is that there is a significant amount of clearly illegal activity that goes undetected or unpunished. As SEC Chairman [Arthur] Levitt recently observed, "It's not as if insider traders wander innocently into the gray areas near the boundaries of legality. They willfully stride across the bright line of the law." . . .

One of the major reasons that capital is available in such quantity in the U.S. markets is basically that the investor trusts the U.S. markets to be fair. Fairness is a major issue . . . [I]t is a critical factor and one that is absent, really to a surprising degree in many of the sophisticated foreign markets . . .

While Congress gave us the mandate to protect investors and keep our markets free from fraud, it has been our jurists . . . who have played the largest role in defining the law of insider trading.

After the United States stock market crash of 1929, Congress enacted the Securities Act of 1933 and the Securities Act of 1934, aimed at controlling the abuses believed to have contributed to the crash. The 1934 act addressed insider trading directly through Section 16(b) and indirectly through Section 10(b).

Section 16(b) prohibits . . . any profits realized in any period less than six months by corporate insiders in their own corporation's stock, except in very limited circumstances. It applies only to directors or officers of the corporation and those holding greater than 10% of the stock and is designed to prevent insider trading by those most likely to be privy to important corporate information.

Section 10(b) . . . makes it unlawful for any person "to use or employ, in connection with the purchase or sale of any security registered on a national securities market or any security not so registered, any manipulative or deceptive device or contrivance in contravention of such rules and regulations as the [SEC] may prescribe" . . .

The breadth of the anti-fraud provisions leaves much room for interpretation and the flexibility to meet new schemes and contrivances head on. Moral imperatives have driven the development of insider trading laws in the United States.

In 1961, in the case of *In re Cady Roberts & Co.*, the Commission held that a broker who traded while in the possession of nonpublic information he received from a company director violated [the law] . . .

Direct evidence of insider trading is rare. There are no smoking guns or physical evidence that can be scientifically linked to a perpetrator. Unless the insider trader confesses the knowledge in some admissible form, evidence is almost entirely circumstantial. The investigation of the case and the proof presented to the fact-finder is a matter of putting together pieces of a puzzle. It requires examining inherently innocuous events—meetings in restaurants, . . . telephone calls, relationships between people, trading patterns—and drawing reasonable inferences based on the timing and surrounding circumstances to lead to the conclusion that the defendant bought or sold stock with the benefit of inside information wrongfully obtained.

Source: Thomas C. Newkirk and Melissa A. Robertson, *Insider Trading—A U.S. Perspective*. Paper presented at the 16th International Symposium on Economic Crime. Jesus College, Cambridge University, England, September 19, 1998 (http://www.sec.gov/news/speech/speecharchive/1998/spch221.htm).

ANALYSIS

Reading carefully between the lines in Document 6.1, one might sense an effort by the officials of the enforcement agency to defend the fairness and, certainly, to detail the obstacles they face in their work. They point out that the insider trading law is complex and that considerable difficulty is encountered when trying to enforce it because of the need to demonstrate guilty knowledge in order to sustain a criminal conviction. An accused person always can (and often does) maintain that he or she intended all along to sell or buy that stock at a particular time and that it was beside the point that it took a sharp rise or decline when the transaction occurred; that was just a coincidence. "I found another opportunity that seemed more promising," the accused might say; or "I had an unexpected medical bill"; or "I saw a yacht that I knew I had to have and sold the stock to be able to help purchase it."

As far back as 1987, the *Wall Street Journal* published an article with the headline "Demand Rises for Law Defining Insider Trading to Provide More Than a Gut Feeling as a Guide." The text of the article was more ambiguous. It quoted some Wall Street traders as being well aware of what the law prohibited. One noted that when he heard snippets of corporate gossip at a cocktail party, he had been a broker long enough to know that it was privileged information. "For me, it's easy to define," he said. Others believed that a clear definition was necessary to make persons who might be in jeopardy perfectly aware of what was legally permissible and what was not. John Shad, the SEC chairman at the time, disagreed. He maintained that the courts were doing a good job of refining the definition of insider trading and expressed misgivings about a more definitive definition: "Once you get one, it doesn't take sophisticated minds long to figure out where the edges are," Shad said. One of the SEC commissioners agreed: "I'm afraid we'll define ourselves into a box," she argued.

The authors of Document 6.1 take some pains to set out the objections to laws that make insider trading illegal and offer their rebuttal to these positions. We might note, in this regard, the observation of Milton Friedman, the conservative guru who was a winner of the Nobel Prize in economics: "You want more insider trading not less. You want to give the people most likely to have knowledge about deficiencies in the company an incentive to make the public aware of them." Friedman's point seems disingenuous. Surely the public can be informed about corporate conditions by means other than stock sales by insiders who are using nonpublic information to make money or to avoid losses. And Friedman well knows that insider sales or purchases of stock, depending on the situation, result in either gains or losses to outsiders who are not privy to the significant information.

To uncover insider trading, the SEC typically focuses on patterns of stock market trades that appear to be suspicious. Suspicion is most often aroused when there is a significantly higher volume of dealing in a particular stock a short time before news of a critical development brings about a considerable gain or loss in the price of the traded item.

The major criminological scrutiny of insider trading offenders studied persons who had been tried civilly or criminally during the decade from 1980 through 1989. It should be noted that the SEC is allowed to charge alleged offenders only civilly and must enlist the cooperation of the Department of Justice if there is to be a criminal prosecution. This turf differentiation can create problems. For one thing, SEC workers who have worked diligently to accumulate evidence may be reluctant to see the Department of Justice get the publicity and the credit for a successful prosecution. The result is that some cases that probably ought to be defined as criminal offenses are handled civilly. Further, the Department of Justice becomes the gatekeeper, and for whatever reason, such as limited resources or lack of expertise, it may decline to take on a case that the SEC regards as deserving a criminal charge.

A study of insider trading by Elizabeth Szockyj found that, contrary to popular perceptions, fewer than a third of those persons charged civilly with insider trading were corporate officers or directors. The usual civil defendant was a relative or an associate of an insider who was tipped about pending developments by an insider. One insider might tip numerous outsiders, who in turn tip others.

DID YOU KNOW?

Avoiding a Loss Is Preferred to Making a Gain

The finding that trading on nonpublic information to avoid a loss is more common than using insider information to roll up a profit fits with psychological research that has demonstrated that, all things being equal, people prioritize the avoidance of loss ahead of the achievement of gain. Two Nobel Prize–winning psychologists, Amos Tversky of Stanford University and Daniel Kahneman of Princeton, in a series of studies showed that a person who loses $100 will suffer more dissatisfaction than the pleasure gained by a person who obtains a $100 windfall. Similarly, individuals prefer a $5 discount to the avoidance of a $5 surcharge. The irrationality (but nonetheless emotional accuracy) of these kinds of preferences is illustrated by a consumer who will drive a great distance to purchase a $15 item with a $5 discount yet not undertake the same journey to buy a $125 item carrying a $5 discount.

Almost half of the insiders did not seek to help themselves; instead, they transmitted the information they had to others. The information about a pending development apparently was passed on in order to enhance a relationship rather than to entice someone into lawbreaking. Advance notice of a tender offer was most likely to generate tipping, probably because it involved the possibility of considerable profit. In situations of potential loss, loyalty to others, particularly if the insider had prompted family or friends to purchase shares in the first place, provided the tipping impetus.

Approximately a third of all defendants came from the business sector, while about 20 percent were associated with the securities industry. In the business sector, most insider traders were high-level company officials; only 18 percent were underling employees. In the securities industry, on the other hand, defendants were unlikely to be executives. Some of the lower-level securities personnel acquired the insider information as a result of illegal trades by their clients.

Trading to avoid losses was more frequent than trading to achieve profits. A possible explanation is that trading on anticipated losses is easier to detect by enforcement personnel than profitable ventures. Besides, those who trade to avoid losses have to trade on their own accounts, while they may locate others, family or friends, to take advantage on their behalf of nonpublic information about the likelihood of a rise in a stock price.

FURTHER READINGS

Macey, Jonathan. (2009). *Stock Market Efficiency: Insider Dealing and Market Abuse.* Burlington, VT: Gower.

Manne, Henry G. (1966). *Insider Trading and the Stock Market.* New York: Free Press.

Reingold, Dan, and Jennifer Reingold. (2006). *Confessions of a Wall Street Analyst: A True Story of Inside Information and Corruption in the Stock Market.* New York: HarperCollins.

Seyhoun, H. Nejat. (2000). *Investment Intelligence from Insider Trading.* Cambridge, MA: MIT Press.

Szockyj, Elizabeth. (1993). *Insider Trading: In Search of a Level Playing Field.* Buffalo, NY: Hein.

Vance, Mary. (1990). *Insider Trading: A Bibliography.* Monticello, NY: Vance Bibliographies.

Wang, William K. S., and Marc I. Steinberg. (2005). *Insider Trading.* New York: Practising Law Institute.

Ivan Boesky

- *Document:* John A. Mulheren Jr. was alleged to have been involved with Ivan Boesky in an illegal stock transaction. In response to the appeal of his criminal conviction of a Section 10(b) violation (see Document 6.1 regarding the nature of the offense), the judge, Joseph Michael McLaughlin, set forth the details of the activities that resulted in marked rampant manipulative behavior on Wall Street.
- *Date:* July 10, 1991.
- *Where:* U.S. Court of Appeals for the Second Circuit, New York City.
- *Significance:* The opinion provides details of the Wall Street crookedness that aroused public indignation and led to a tighter enforcement of the criminal laws prohibiting insider trading.

DOCUMENT 6.2

OPINION BY: [JOSEPH MICHAEL] McLAUGHLIN, Circuit Judge

In the late 1980's a wide prosecutorial net was cast upon Wall Street. Along with the usual flotsam and jetsam, the government catch included some of Wall Street's biggest, brightest, and now infamous—Ivan Boesky, Dennis Levine, Michael Milken, Robert Freeman, Martin Siegel, Boyd L. Jeffries, and Paul A. Bilzerian—each of whom either pleaded guilty to or was convicted of crimes involving illicit trading scandals . . .

[T]he following facts were established at trial.

In 1985, at the suggestion of his long-time friend, Carl Icahn, a prominent arbitrageur and corporate raider, Ivan Boesky directed his companies to buy G & W [Gulf and Western Industries] stock, a security that both Icahn and Boesky believed

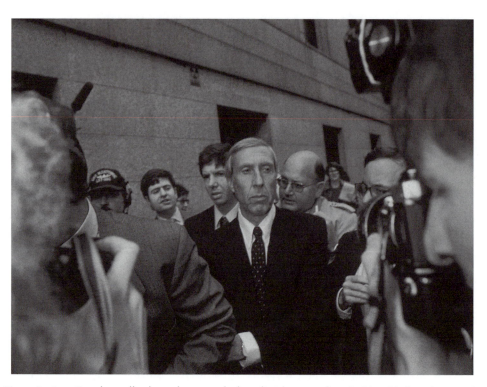

Financier Ivan Boesky walks through a crowd of media photographers in New York on January 1, 1987. Using inside information to gain from financial pursuits, he was eventually found guilty of securities fraud, tax evasion, and perjury. (AP/Wide World Photos)

to be "significantly undervalued." Between April and October 1985, Boesky's companies accumulated 3.4 million shares representing approximately 4.9 percent of the outstanding G & W shares . . .

On September 5, 1985, Boesky and Icahn met with Martin Davis, the chairman of G & W. Boesky expressed his interest in taking control of G & W through a leveraged buyout [a tactic for acquiring a company or securing controlling interest in it using a significant amount of borrowed money, usually 70% or more], or, failing that, increasing his position in G & W stock and securing a seat on the G & W board of directors . . . Davis said he was not interested in Boesky's proposal, and he remained adamant in subsequent telephone calls and at a later meeting on October 1, 1985.

At the October 1, 1985 meeting, . . . Boesky added a new string to his bow. If Davis continued to reject Boesky's s attempts at control, then G & W should buy out his position at $45 a share . . .

During—and for some time before—these negotiations, Mulheren and Boesky maintained a relationship of confidence and trust. The two had often shared market information and given each other trading tips. At some point during the April–October period when Boesky was acquiring G & W stock Mulheren asked Boesky what he thought of G & W and whether Icahn held a position in the stock. Boesky responded that he "thought well" of G & W stock and Icahn did indeed own G & W stock. Boesky never told Mulheren about his meeting or telephone conversations with Davis . . .

Shortly after 11:00 a.m. on October 17, 1985, Jamie (Mulheren's company) placed an order with Oliver Ihasz, a floor broker, to purchase 50,000 shares of G & W at the market price. . . . At 11:00 a.m., Ibasz purchased 16,100 shares at 44 ¾ per share. Unable to fill the entire 50,000 share order at 44 ¾, Ihasz purchased the remaining 33,900 shares between 11:04 a.m. and 11:08 a.m. at 44 7/8 per share . . . At 11:17 a.m., Boesky and Icahn sold their G & W stock—6,715,700 shares between them—back to the company at 45 per share. Trading in G & W closed on the NYSE [New York Stock Exchange] on October 17, 1985 at 43 5/8 per share. At the end of the day, Jamie's trading in G & W common stock at Mulheren's direction had caused it to lose $64,406.

Although we have misgivings about the government's view of the law, we will assume . . . that an investor may lawfully be convicted under Rule 10.5 [of the Securities Act of 1934] when the purpose of his transaction is solely to affect the price of a security. The issue then becomes one of Mulheren's subjective intent. The government was obligated to prove beyond a reasonable doubt that when Mulheren purchased 75,000 of G & W common stock on October 17, 1985, he did it with the intent to raise its price, rather than with the intent to invest. We conclude that the government failed to carry this burden.

Source: United States v. Mulheren, 938 Federal Reporter 2d 364 (1991).

ANALYSIS

The portrayal by Justice McLaughlin of the maneuvering between Boesky, the most infamous insider trader, and the president of G & W provides a sense of the hardball dealings that marked the behavior of Wall Street insiders hungry for the greatest profit that they could reap by the use of whatever tactics could work and could, hopefully, keep them free from entanglements with the law. John Mulheren was no babe in the woods in these dealing. He had, for instance, informed the G & W president that he could keep an eye on Boesky for him, and he and Davis apparently shared an unfavorable opinion of Boesky.

At the same time, the document indicates the problem involved in seeking convictions in complex white-collar crime cases—the difficult burden of establishing the intent of the perpetrator, what was in his or her mind when engaging in an act that, depending on that intent, could be perfectly legal or a criminal violation. Mulheren's criminal conviction was overturned by the court, and he harbored a burning resentment toward Boesky, who had

---

DID YOU KNOW?

Boesky: An All-Around Cheater

"Boesky sat on SEC panels when he was committing his most outrageous crimes. He did nothing to discourage his guests at the Harvard Club from believing he had spent years in Cambridge. Actually, he had gained membership, confined only to alumni and faculty, by becoming an honorary faculty member by means of a sizeable financial contribution to Harvard's School of Public Health. He charged his investors high management fees and then defrauded them by making some of his most profitable trades through an entity that siphoned their gains to his [own] account; later, in order to pay his lawyers, he may have defrauded his employees by draining $5 million to $10 million out of their salary-and-bonus account. He listed himself as an adjunct professor at Columbia University's School of Business when he was no more than a guest lecturer."

Source: Joyce Kornbluth Highly Confident: The Crimes and Punishment of Michael Milken (New York: Morrow, 1992), 68.

implicated him in this situation. Sometime after the appellate court ruling, Mulheren was stopped by the police with a shotgun in his car, allegedly en route to assassinate Boesky.

Ivan Boesky made his infamous mark as a premier arbitrageur, speculating in trades in stocks of companies that were believed to be likely to be eaten up in a merger or a hostile acquisition by another company. He fit the portrait of arbitrageurs painted by journalist James Stewart, that they "tended to be crass, excitable, street-smart, aggressive, and driven almost solely by the pursuit of quick profits." Stewart adds: "Their days were defined by the high-pressure periods between the opening and closing bells of the stock exchange during which they screamed orders into phones, punched stock symbols into their electronic terminals, scanned elaborate screens of constantly shifting data, and placed telephone calls to every potential source of information they could imagine."

Boesky brought insider trading from the shadows into the limelight and impelled the SEC to cast a much more diligent eye on insiders who were trading on information that had not yet been revealed to the public. Boesky amassed a huge fortune, estimated in 1986 at $200 million, by forming alliances with persons who had prior knowledge of mergers, acquisitions, and other developments on Wall Street that, once they became generally known, would cause the stock of the involved companies to skyrocket. His chief liaison was with Dennis Levine, the merger and acquisition specialist at the Drexel Burnham investment firm. In the spring of 1986, for information received and presumed to be forthcoming from Levine, Boesky paid him $2.4 million.

In a public speech in 1986 at the University of California–Berkeley, Boesky uttered a maxim that would become part of American culture when it became the mantra of Gordon Gekko in the 1987 motion picture *Wall Street*: "I think greed is healthy," Michael Douglas, playing a character obviously based on Boesky, declared. "You can be greedy and still feel good about yourself." He failed to mention that when the unlawful feeding of that greed came at other people's expense, they were not likely to feel so good about themselves—or about you. But then Gekko felt no need of approval from others: "If you need a friend," he told a coworker, "get a dog."

Interestingly, two economists, Sugato Chakravarty and John J. McConnell, determined that Boesky's purchase of Carnation stock in 1984, just before the company was acquired by Nestlé had no undue influence on the stock price. "Our tests are unable to distinguish the price effect of Boesky's (i.e., pre-informed) purchase of Carnation stock from the effect of non-insiders (i.e., uninformed purchasers)," they reported in the *Journal of Financial and Quantitative Analysis*. The authors note that their finding could be employed to argue for the legalization of insider trading. Opponents would

---

DID YOU KNOW?

The Arrogant Acts of Wealth

Boesky's wealth, self-importance, and all-out arrogance were clearly demonstrated in a report related by James Stewart in *Den of Thieves* regarding an evening meal involving Boesky, his wife, and some friends at the exclusive and extremely expensive Café des Artistes in Manhattan. As a waiter stood amazed, Boesky ordered for himself each of the eight entrees on the menu. When they all were wheeled to the table, he took a bite from each and selected one for his meal. He picked at that food, and paid the bill for all eight. His wife paid no heed, presumably because this was a commonplace performance by Boesky.

Source: Wall Street Journal, August 3, 2009.

maintain that the core issue is not necessarily the price effect of insider trading but rather the public's perception of its fairness. If the general public feels outgunned by insider trading, it may refrain from investing its money in the purchase of stocks to the detriment of the financial system.

Ivan Frederick Boesky was born in Detroit in 1937. According to Boesky his father, a Russian immigrant, owned a delicatessen. But that deli enterprise was his uncle's: Boesky's father ran a chain of bars called the Brass Rail that featured topless dancers and strippers. It was Boesky's wealthy wife's mother and father who backed him in 1975 by supplying $700,000 so that he was able to establish his own brokerage business, where he had great success, earning the reputation in the process as "Ivan the Terrible," referring to the cold-blooded and cruel onetime czar of Russia. He developed the tactic of consorting with persons who had early information of pending Wall Street deals at a time

when the merger mania was it is peak. In 1986, for instance, there were some 3,000 company mergers and buyouts, a new high.

The illegal exchange of information ended when Dennis Levine, the merger and acquisition specialist at Kidder, Peabody, was arrested on May 12, 1976. His attitude was sanguine: he told one of his sources: "We'll go to jail. I will be in one of those country club prisons. We'll be roommates, we'll play tennis, and get a tan." Levine supplied the authorities with information about his coconspirators. Soon after, Boesky and Martin Siegel, another Kidder executive, were placed under arrest. Boesky turned states' evidence, tattling to the authorities about persons who had fed him information. In exchange for his cooperation with the government, Boesky received a light prison sentence of three and a half years and a levy of $50 million as a fine, and had to disgorge $50 million of illegally earned profits. Boesky also was barred from ever again working in the securities field. The sentencing judge indicated that it no longer was acceptable to let convicted white-collar offenders escape with a slap on the wrist or a mere judicial scolding: "The signal must go out," the judge declared. "The time has come when it is totally unacceptable for courts to act as if prison is unthinkable for white collar defendants. To preserve not only the actual integrity of the financial markets, but the appearance of integrity in these markets, criminal behavior such as Mr. Boesky's cannot go unchecked."

Boesky, however, was allowed by government authorities to unload some $400 million in stocks from the estimated $2 billion that his company controlled, an arrangement that one critic called "the ultimate insider deal." In order to try to deter the kinds of frauds that Boesky had arranged, Congress later enacted legislation that allowed the confiscation of as much as six times the illegal profits gained from insider trading.

FURTHER READINGS

Boesky, Ivan, and Jeffrey G. Madick. (1985). *Merger Mania: Wall Street's Best Kept Money Market Secret*. New York: Holt, Rinehart and Winston.

Stevens, Mark, and Carol Brown Stevens. (1987). *The Insiders: The Truth behind the Scandals Rocking Wall Street*. London: Harrap.

Stewart, James B. (1991). *Den of Thieves*. New York: Simon & Schuster.

Michael Milken

- **Document:** The far-ranging stock manipulations by Michael Milken spawned a considerable barrage of litigation as various parties, including the government, sought to establish their right to be paid or reimbursed for the damages wrought by Milken. In the case from which the document is excerpted, the issue before the court was the liability of Milken's employer, Drexel Burnham Lambert. Drexel had filed for bankruptcy in 1990, and the SEC and the court had to adjudicate the more than 15,000 claims against it. To set the stage for his decision, the judge reviewed the significant aspects of Milken's actions.
- **Date:** May 26, 1993.
- **Where:** U.S. Court of Appeals for the Second Circuit, New York City.
- **Significance:** Milken was the superstar of the world of junk bonds and an adroit insider trader. The exposure of his actions set the stage for attempts at reform, improved monitoring, and the enhancement of penalties.

DOCUMENT 6.3

OPINION BY [RICHARD J.] CARDAMONE, Circuit Judge

This appeal concerns a $1.3 billion global settlement of civil actions that arose as a result of Michael Milken's illicit activities as head of Drexel Burnham Lambert's Group High Yield and Convertible Bond Department. Milken, who promoted the use of low-grade, high-yield junk bonds to finance takeovers and leveraged buyouts while serving as head of Drexel's junk bond group, had his office in Beverly Hills, California, far removed from and independent of Drexel's New York headquarters. He became the leading disciple of the theory that sheer greed is what drives our national securities market, and along the way created an enormous cash cow that yielded him monopoly profits in the hundreds of millions of dollars—$500 million reportedly, in a single year. . . .

[W]hile acting as a market professional Milken sought to exclude competition from the high-yield junk bond market and as a result of his control over entry to that market extracted monopoly profits from it illegally . . . Milken fed securities into investment partnerships he controlled (not telling the issuers or sponsors) thereby earning vastly greater returns than he would have earned were he acting simply as an investment banker. In this display of avarice, Milken plainly thought of money and of his own gain first, leaving integrity and his clients' interests a distant second. Such conduct contravened the fundamental notion that public securities markets are governed by principles of "fair and honest" dealings and should be "free and open" to competition. The proof of Milken's guilt was strong enough to force him to plead guilty in April 1990 to six serious felony charges including conspiracy to violate federal securities law, securities fraud, mail fraud, and filing false tax returns. In conjunction with his guilty plea, Milken agreed to pay a $200 million criminal fine and to establish a $400 million civil restitution fund [that he later declared as an income tax deduction] with the Securities and Exchange Commission.

Source: In re The Drexel Burnham Lambert Group v. Claimants, 995 Federal Reporter 2d. 1138 (1993).

ANALYSIS

Michael Milken began with a notably shrewd insight that he acquired while studying for an MBA at the prestigious Wharton School of Business at the University of Pennsylvania. He read a book by Walter Braddock Hickman, who held a PhD in economics from Johns Hopkins University and served as the president of the Federal Reserve Bank of Cleveland. Hickman's 1958 treatise, *Corporate Bond Quality Investor Experience*, demonstrated that low-grade bonds provided investors with a better financial return than the more-highly-regarded bonds of top-grade corporations. Since they were deemed much more risky investments, bonds issued by companies with iffy financial standards had to offer higher interest rates. Hickman showed that, nonetheless, their default rate was low and those who put their money in such bonds did well. Milken would make a vast fortune trading on this idea, becoming the king of the world of what came to be called "junk bonds."

Robert Michael Milken was born in Encino, a Los Angeles suburb, on July 4, 1946, and attended the local school before graduating from the University of California at Berkeley and getting his advanced business degree at Wharton. He did so well in establishing a lucrative market for high-yield junk bonds that in 1972 he was able to move his office from headquarters on Wall Street to Century City in Los Angeles and then to the posh environs of nearby Beverly Hills, in part to get back to where he had grown up and in considerable part to escape the closer oversight that could be used to monitor his activities in New York. Milken's California employees had to be at work promptly at 4:30 a.m. to synchronize with the opening of the stock market on the East Coast, and they often were still at work late into the evening.

Milken was charged with 94 counts of racketeering and securities fraud after Boesky turned informer against him. At a televised hearing before the House Energy and Commerce Subcommittee on Oversight and Investigation, Milken would decline to answer questions, invoking his Fifth Amendment privilege against self-incrimination. His shrewd lawyer located an obscure clause in a congressional law, subsequently repealed, that allowed witnesses to demand that television cameras be turned off at their request, so Milken was protected from having the public see him take the Fifth.

Milken bargained the felony counts down to six, three of them having to deal with his transactions with Boesky. He was sentenced to a 10-year prison term (but served less than two years) and was barred from any subsequent trading. The sentencing judge was Kimba Wood, who had been nominated for attorney general by President Clinton but had to withdraw when it was revealed that she had employed an illegal immigrant as a nanny. Wood's sentencing statement is a core consideration in the entire array of white-collar and corporate crimes considered in this volume. This is what she said to Michael Milken:

You were willing to commit only crimes that were unlikely to be detected . . . When a man of your power in the financial world, at the head of the most important department of one of the most important banking houses in the country, repeatedly conspires to violate, and violates, securities and tax laws in order to achieve more power and wealth for himself and his wealthy clients, and commits financial crimes that are particularly hard to detect, a significant prison term is required in order to deter others. . . . If the punishment for a particular crime is too light, however, then neither of deterrence's primary purposes will be served: the offender will not be reasonably deterred from changing his behavior, and society will learn that the particular criminal conduct may well be worth the risk of the light punishment . . . This still lacks sufficient deterrence value because far too many people would likely jump at the chance to walk away with hundreds of millions of dollars after serving forty-four months in prison . . . A corporate criminal will, given the economic analysis, weigh the potential benefits (e.g., economic gain) against the possibility of being caught

---

DID YOU KNOW?

Was Milken a Scapegoat?

On his release from prison, Michael Milken, still a very wealthy man from legitimate earnings in his personal stock trading, plunged deeply into philanthropic ventures, founding, among other enterprises, the Melanoma Research Alliance, dedicated to finding cures for deadly skin cancer conditions. A considerable contingent of writers seconded Milken's unsuccessful (so far) efforts to obtain a presidential pardon. Irwin Stelzer, an American economist who writes a column for the London *Sunday Times*, insisted that Milken had done wonders for the world of finance in America, that he "contributed mightily to converting American industry into a lean, mean, internationally competitive machine," and that there were those who now believed "that his punishment . . . was more the revenge of the establishment than the just deserts of willful law breaking." This remains a minority view; the prevailing opinion is that Milken milked the system by employing patently illegal tactics and that he thoroughly deserved the penalty imposed upon him.

multiplied by the price of punishment . . . The potential value for deterrence in the punishment of white-collar and corporate crimes is much higher than it is for blue-collar crimes.

FURTHER READINGS

Bailey, Fenton. (1992). *Fall from Grace: The Untold Story of Michael Milken*. Secaucus, NJ: Carol.

Bruck, Connie. (1988). *The Predators' Ball: The Junk Bond Traders and the Man Who Staked Them*. New York: Simon & Schuster.

Fischel, Daniel R. (1995). *Payback: The Conspiracy to Destroy Michael Milken and His Financial Revolution*. New York: HarperCollins.

Grant, R. W. (1993). *Bring Us the Head of Michael Milken: The Three Reasons behind the Downfall of Michael Milken*. Manhattan Beach, CA: Quandary House.

Kornbluth, Jesse. (1992). *Highly Confidential: The Crime and Punishment of Michael Milken*. New York: Morrow.

Stein, Benjamin. (1992). *A License to Steal: The Untold Story of Michael Milken and the Conspiracy to Bilk the Nation*. New York: Simon & Schuster.

Zey, Mary. (1993). *Banking on Fraud: Drexel, Junk Bonds, and Buyouts*. New York: Aldine de Gruyter.

Dennis Levine

- *Document:* Details of Dennis Levin's illegal insider trading activities were succinctly summarized by the judge in a case in which Levine challenged a levy by the IRS against him for unpaid income taxes.
- *Date:* August 2, 1989.
- *Where:* The Second Circuit of the federal appellate courts, New York City.
- *Significance:* Levine's exploitation of nonpublic information led to the subsequent enactment of legislation that sought to tighten up oversight procedures and increase penalties for the transfer and use of insider information to those who would exploit the advantage it offered them.

DOCUMENT 6.4

OPINION BY [Amalya Lyle] KEARSE
These appeals [are] by Dennis B. Levine and Robert M. Wilkis, defendants, in civil actions commenced by . . . [the] Securities and Exchange Commission.

BACKGROUND
The present appeals arise out of civil actions against Levine and Wilkis, New York investment bankers, accused of engaging in insider trading . . . The sequences of the procedural evens does not appear to be in dispute.

The Consent Judgment
On May 26, 1986, the SEC commenced its action against Levine and two of his companies . . . for alleged violation of the . . . securities laws. The complaint charged

that from May 1980 through May 12, 1986, Levine had purchased shares, or options for common stock of 54 companies that were targets of potential takeover offers or candidates for actual or contemplated mergers or other business combinations. It alleged that Levine had traded on the basis of material nonpublic information that he knew or should have known had been obtained through misappropriation or breach of fiduciary duty, and that he therefore defrauded other investors. The complaint alleged that Levine had gained more than $11 million in profits, and the SEC sought, *inter alia* [among other things], disgorgement by Levine and his companies of funds received as a result of his unlawful conduct.

On May 12, the day the complaint was filed, the Commission obtained a temporary restraining order prohibiting Levine from disposing of any of his assets. On May 29, the district court issued a preliminary injunction extending the temporary freeze order.

On June 4, 1986, Levine executed a Consent and Undertaking in which, without admitting or denying any of the allegations in the complaint, he consented to the entry of a "Final Judgment". . . . Levine also agreed to cooperate fully with the Commission in any other investigation conducted by or on behalf of that body.

Source: Securities and Exchange Commission v. Levine, 881 Federal Reporter 2d 1165 (2nd Circuit, 1989).

ANALYSIS

Dennis Levine had figured out a scheme of insider trading well before he began to feed confidential information to Ivan Boesky. Born in 1952 in the New York borough of Queens, Levine was a lackluster student, but earned a bachelor's degree and an MBA at Baruch College, a branch of the City University of New York. Like so many Wall Street traders, Levine bounced between various companies, each time moving up the hierarchy by actions that required demonstrated performance that was measured, like the batting average of a baseball player, by precise figures that indicated how much a person had earned—or lost—for his or her employer.

Levine was always dissatisfied with his progress toward power and an ever-higher rate of earnings. When Smith Barney dispatched him to its Paris office, he took a first step toward establishing an insider trading scheme by opening a secret Swiss bank account with Pictet & Co in Geneva that he would use to finance stock trades. Transferred back to New York, he inveigled a long-standing friend, Robert Wilkis, who worked at Lazard Freres, to set up an account in a branch of a Swiss bank in the Bahamas, under an alias, that would be used for trading. The Bahamas had one of the strictest bank secrecy laws in the world. When Levine's insider trading deeds were being investigated, the Bahaman attorney general decreed that the secrecy laws applied only to deposits and not to accounts that were used for stock trades— and Levine was doomed as incriminating documents now became available to prosecutors. Before their downfall Levine had supplied Wilkis with news of impending stock deals that he learned of at Smith Barney, and Wilkis would return the favor with reports from his firm. Always wanting to travel in a faster lane, Levine, with Wilkis serving as a frightened lookout, burglarized files at Lazard one evening and learned of a deal under which the French oil giant Elf Aquitaine might purchase

Kerr-McGee, a major American oil producer. His luck failed him on this occasion. The French government put pressure on Elf Aquitaine to back out of the deal, and Levine lost money. Later, when he had staked virtually all of his firm's capital on a supposedly pending merger involving Gulf Oil that fell through, Levine survived financially only when John Mulheren, who Boesky later would squeal about to the SEC, went to great lengths to bail him out.

Subsequently, Levine flourished financially. In one of his landmark endeavors, he purchased 150,000 shares of Nabisco three weeks before the company announced its takeover by R. J. Reynolds, the tobacco giant. Levine earned $2.7 million on the transaction.

Levin had only scorn for the SEC lawyers, who he saw as bumbling bureaucrats who lacked either ability or ambition or both and who failed to take what they had learned working for the government and turn it into a very much more lucrative job in private industry.

In *Den of Thieves*, James Stewart tells of Levine's encounter with an SEC official when the agency looked into the striking surge in his purchases of Textron, a takeover target, just before the transaction became public knowledge. Levine had made $200,000 on the deal, a relatively insignificant amount for him, but he had to face questions from the SEC about why he had purchased the stock. In Stewart's words, "lying repeatedly and flamboyant," Levine denied having any offshore trading accounts (he had one in the Cayman Islands at the Bank Leu under the name of Mr. Diamond). Levine told the SEC investigators that he had been sitting in the reception area of the investment firm of Drexel Burnham Lambert (he had no record of this visit on his calendar and no one to verify his claim). So located, he had overheard a conversation between two men dressed in business suits and carrying briefcases. The men mentioned the name of a director of Chicago Pacific, the acquiring firm in the Textron deal, that Levine claimed to have recognized, and then, in Levine's tall tale, the men supposedly said something about "fireworks in Rhode Island," which Levine interpreted as referring to Textron, which he maintained he knew was located in Rhode Island. The SEC was perfectly well aware that this preposterous story was a lie; indeed, one investigator said that in all his many working years he had never heard so far-fetched a tale. But the SEC agents had no witness to contradict Levine, and the investigation went nowhere.

When Levine's trading tactics were exposed, he pled guilty to four felony charges, but was sentenced lightly because of his cooperation in pointing the finger at coconspirators. He received four two-year prison terms to be served concurrently (he would stay in prison for 15 months) and a $362,000 fine that came on top of a civil penalty of $11.6 million levied by the SEC.

In the wake of the revelations about the plentitude of insider trading on Wall Street, Congress upped the penalties with the Insider Trading and Securities Fraud Enforcement Act of 1984 and the

DID YOU KNOW?

Dennis Levine: "I Became a Go-Go Guy"

In a May 1990 interview for *Fortune*, Dennis Levine sought to throw some light on his criminal behavior: "Wall Street went crazy in those days," he said. "These were the 1980s, remember, the decade of excess, greed, and materialism. I became a go-go guy, consumed by the high pressure, ultracompetitive world of investment banking." He added: "When the phone rang it was like a cash register going off."

Insider Trading and Securities Fraud Law Enforcement Act of 1999. After his release from prison, Levine started a consulting firm, providing advice to companies about the perils connected with doing what he had done. He also lectured extensively at colleges and universities, telling his audiences about the virtues of virtue.

FURTHER READINGS

Frantz, Douglas. (1987). *Levine & Co.: Wall Street's Insider Trading Scandal*. New York: Holt.

Levine, Dennis B., and William Hoffer. (1991). *Inside Out: An Insiders Account of Wall Street*. New York: Holt.

Reams, Bernard D., Jr. (Compiler) (1984). *Insider Trading and the Law: A Legislative History of the Insider Trading Securities Act of 1984, Pub. Law 98-376*. Buffalo, NY: Hein.

Martha Stewart

- *Document:* A grand jury hears evidence, usually only from the prosecutor, and then, if convinced that there are grounds for a prosecution,
  returns an indictment. In the case of Martha Stewart, who allegedly
  had engaged in insider trading, the prosecution decided that a more
  feasible route would be to charge her with obstruction of justice and
  perjury, that is, lying to government agents. Document 6.5 provides
  the specifics of the false statements. A similar charge was leveled
  against Peter Bacanovic, the Merrill Lynch broker who had handled
  Ms. Stewart's stock transactions.
- *Date:* June 4, 2003.
- *Where:* U.S. District Court in New York City.
- *Significance:* The grand jury indictment provides a setting for comprehension of Ms. Stewart's actions in regard to the alleged insider trading, her dissembling when questioned, and the rationale for the
  decision to charge her with perjury rather than insider trading.

DOCUMENT 6.5

The Grand Jury charges: . . .

STEWART'S False Statement on February 4, 2002.

On or about February 4, 2002, MARTHA STEWART accompanied by her lawyers, was interviewed in New York, New York by the SEC, the FBI, and the U.S.
Attorney's Office. In furtherance of the conspiracy, and with the intent and purpose
to conceal and cover up that, BACANOVIC had caused Stewart to be provided
information regarding the sale and attempted sale of the Waksal shares [Waksal
was the president of ImClone] and that STEWART had sold her ImClone stock

while in possession of that information. STEWART concealed and covered up the following material facts, among others:

    a. STEWART stated that she did not know whether the phone message BACA-NOVIC left for STEWART on December 27, 2001 was recorded in the phone message log maintained by her assistant. This statement was false and misleading in that, as STEWART well knew, but concealed and covered up, the message was recorded in the phone message log, the substance of which—"Peter Bacanovic thinks ImClone is going to start trading downward"—STEWART had reviewed when she temporarily altered the message four days before the interview.

    b. STEWART stated that on December 27, 2001, STEWART spoke to Bacanovic who told her that ImClone was trading a little below $60 a share and asked STEWART if she wanted to sell. STEWART stated that after being informed of ImClone's stock price, she directed BACANOVIC to sell her ImClone shares that day because she did not want to be bothered over her vacation. These statements were false and misleading in that, as STEWART well knew but concealed and covered up, STEWART spoke to Faneuil [Bacanovic's coworker], not BACANOVIC, on December 27, 2001, and STEWART sold her ImClone shares the day after Douglas Faneuil conveyed to her information regarding the sale and attempted sale of the Waksal shares.

    c. STEWART stated that before concluding their telephone conversation on December 27, 2001, BACANOVIC and STEWART discussed "how MSLO stock [Martha Stewart Living Omnimedia, Inc.] was doing" and Kmart. STEWART provided these false details of her purported conversation with BACANOVIC to conceal and cover up the fact that STEWART spoke on December 27, 2001 to Douglas Faneuil, who conveyed to her information regarding the sale and attempted sale of Waksal shares.

    d. STEWART stated that during the period from December 28, 2001 to the date of the interview, February 4, 2002, STEWART had only one conversation with BACANOVIC regarding ImClone, in which only publicly disclosed material in the "public arena" was discussed. STEWART further states that although BACANOVIC mentioned that Merrill Lynch had been questioned by the SEC regarding trading in ImClone generally, BACANOVIC did not inform STEWART that he had been questioned by the SEC or that he had been questioned regarding STEWART'S account. STEWART made these false statements to conceal and cover up that she and BACANOVIC had agreed to provide false information to the SEC, the FBI, and the U.S. Attorney's Office regarding STEWART'S sale of ImClone stock and conceal and cover up that BACANOVIC had caused STEWART to provide information regarding the sale and attempted sale of the Waksal shares and that STEWART had sold her ImClone stock while in possession of that information.

    Source: United States v. Stewart, 323 Federal Supplement 2d 606 (Southern District New York, July 6, 2004), 624–26.

ANALYSIS

One of the more interesting questions that arises from a reading of Document 6.5 is why Martha Stewart, in the presence of her lawyers, sought to extricate herself from the mess that she was in by lying to the government officials. The first advice that attorneys will give a client under investigation for a criminal offense is to refuse to respond to questions. The obligation is on the government to prove its case, and the accused is not required to participate in that endeavor. Commentators have suggested that Ms. Stewart, given her enormous success as a public figure, arrogantly assumed that she could maneuver her way out of the situation she was in. Others have faulted the lawyers, saying that Stewart should have been cautioned to remain silent or, if she refused, they should have withdrawn from the case.

The facts were these. Martha Stewart at age 61 was a wildly successful business entrepreneur, specializing in home décor and lifestyle elegance. She had her own company, which peddled upscale living styles. Her friend Samuel Waksal, who had received a PhD in immunology from Ohio State University, was the founder and the chief executive officer of ImClone Systems, Inc., a biotechnical company. On December 26, 2001, he learned that the Food and Drug Administration (FDA) was going to reject the marketing of the drug Eribtus (cetuximab), aimed at treating colon cancer. ImClone had

Celebrity homemaker, Martha Stewart, was charged with perjury and obstruction of justice for her part in the insider trader scandal involving her sale of ImClone stock, June 4, 2003. (Shutterstock)

wagered its future on the approval of the drug. Waksal sought to sell tens of thousands of his shares in the company and encouraged his father and daughter to do so as well. He later would plead guilty to insider trading, securities fraud, bank fraud, obstruction of justice, conspiracy, and wire fraud. He also was accused of avoiding $1.2 million in sales taxes in connection of his purchase of $15 million of artwork. Waksal received a prison sentence of seven years and three months and was ordered to pay $4 million in fines and back taxes. He was released after five years, and, ironically, the drug subsequently was approved to treat metastasized colon and head and neck cancer in conjunction with chemotherapy treatments. Currently, ImClone, whose stock has done very well, is attempting to get FDA approval of a drug for dealing with lung cancer. For his part, on release from prison, Waksal in 2010 was seeking to raise $50 million to fund Kadmon, the company of which he is the managing member. The company's prospectus indicated that it would pick up and try to develop for the market interesting drug compounds that other companies, for whatever reason, had lost interest in.

Tipped off regarding what Waksal was doing with his shares of ImClone stock, Stewart on December 27 sold the 3,928 shares that she held in ImClone at $58 a share for a total income of $228,000. She avoided a $45,673 loss, but the sales price represented a considerable increase on the purchase price, and at the same time was quite insignificant in terms of Stewart's great wealth, making her transaction puzzling, seeming to be nothing other than an act of irrational greed. Ironically, when

Stewart was convicted the stock in her own company dropped 23 percent, and overall Stewart was believed to have lost $200 million in her business's stock and $400 million all told as a consequence of the criminal allegation. That she should have known better is clear from the fact Stewart had earlier been a stockbroker, had served on the board of directors of the New York Stock Exchange, and was well acquainted with the regulations forbidding insider trading. She would claim, falsely, that she had an agreement with her Merrill Lynch stockbroker that they should sell her ImClone when it dipped below $60. A notation in the broker's log to that effect was declared by an expert in analysis of inks to have been entered after the entries surrounding it in the logbook.

A judge's summary expresses the core of the government's case:

> Faneuil testified that when he told Bacanovic that Sam Waksal and his daughters wanted to sell their ImClone stock, Bacanovic said: "Oh, my God, get Martha on the phone" . . . Later that morning, Bacanovic called Faneuil again. Bacanovic told Faneuil that Stewart would be calling and instructed Faneuil to "tell her what's going on." When Faneil asked whether that he should tell Martha "about Sam," Banovic replied, "Of course, you must. You've got to. That's the whole point."

When Stewart called later, Faneuil told her that Waksal was attempting to sell all his shares. "All his shares?" she wanted to know. Then she told him to sell all of her shares.

Faneuil offered to e-mail Stewart's assistant, Ann Armstrong, to confirm the sale, which angered Stewart, who informed him that he had no right to tell her assistant about her personal transactions.

Faneuil's examination by the government lasted some four hours. The defense counsel cross-examined him for more than nine hours over three days, seeking to impeach his credibility through evidence of his prior experiences with Stewart, his former drug use, and his agreement with the government to cooperate in the prosecution.

One commentator noted that "rather stunningly, Stewart was not charged with insider trading." But the U.S. Attorney handling the case maintained that an insider trading criminal charge would have been "unprecedented." He said that the Supreme Court rulings exempted Stewart's acts from the law of insider trading. First, she was not an insider who owed fiduciary duties to ImClone shareholders. Nor was Stewart a recipient of a tip from an insider who gave information to her in breach of that person's fiduciary duty. As Merrill Lynch employees, neither the broker nor his assistant owed fiduciary duties to ImClone shareholders. Nor could Stewart have been

---

DID YOU KNOW?

Was the Martha Stewart Prosecution Unjustified?

There were a host of onlookers who believed that Martha Stewart was the victim of an overzealous prosecution driven by the fact that being a celebrity her case would call considerable attention to the U.S. attorneys and to the SEC. There also was a belief that as a wondrously successful woman, Stewart had aroused envy, particularly in the male justice establishment, which regarded her stress on household elegance as over the top. Further, according to some, Stewart did not possess an ingratiating or appealing personality. *Newsweek* bitingly moralized that "if she had been nicer to people on the way up, they'd be nicer to her on the way down." Stewart was labeled, not altogether kindly, as the "domestic diva." In her interview with *New Yorker* writer Jeffrey Toobin, Stewart herself referred to what she saw as envy. "You know in China they say the thinner the chopsticks the higher the social status. Of course, I got the thinnest I could find." Then she paused before adding: "That's why people hate me."

charged with misappropriating information and then trading. All told, the lesson is clear: had Martha Stewart managed to keep her mouth shut, she would have ambled away with her ill-gotten gain, or more correctly, the avoidance of the loss.

As it was, after a five-week trial, Martha Stewart was sentenced to a five-month jail term and a subsequent five months under house arrest during which she had to wear an electronic monitoring device.

Stewart became the butt of commentary that played on her business and her current condition. Late-night comedian Conan O'Brien noted that her subpoena "should be served with a nice appetizer." When Stewart was sentenced, a mock magazine cover circulated indicating how she would redecorate her prison cell to make it more chichi than the government-supplied furnishings. More seriously and arguably, one commentator found the Stewart case to represent "a Rorschach test of women's and men's anxieties about female success."

DID YOU KNOW?

Was Martha Stewart a Recidivist?

The perjury and other convictions of Martha Stewart did not represent the only behavior that could be regarded as criminal. On May 21, 1997, Stewart, in her car, had accused Matthew John Munnich, a 22-year-old landscape gardener working for her neighbor, of having constructed a fence that intruded on her property. In his sworn deposition Munnich said that when he said he had nothing to do with the fence, Stewart started to get "extremely angry," called him "a fucking liar," and screamed that "you and your fucking illegal aliens are no good." Stewart then, according to Munnich, drove her car in a way that pushed him into a cement wall. As a result, he claimed, his right side had been injured when he was came up against an electronic security box and was black and blue.

The district attorney's office, in a formal statement, declared that Stewart's behavior, "as objectionable as it may appear," did not reach the level that he believed it should or could be prosecuted criminally. Munnich's civil suit against Stewart was reported to have been settled before it would have gone to trial.

FURTHER READINGS

Hemenway, Jane McLeod. (2003). "Save Martha Stewart? Observations about Equal Justice in U.S. Insider Trading Regulation." *Texas Journal of Women and the Law* 12:247–85.

Moohr, Geraldine Szott. (2006). "What the Martha Stewart Case Tells Us about White Collar Criminal Law." *Houston Law Review* 43:591–619.

Schroeder, Jerome L. (2005). "Envy and Outsider Trading." *Cardozo Law Review* 26: 2023–78.

Seller, Patricia. (2005, November 14). "Remodeling Martha." *Fortune*, 49–62.

Stabile, Carol A. (2004). "Getting What She Deserved: The News Media, Martha Stewart and Male Domination." *Feminist Media Studies* 4:315–22.

Strudler, Alan, and Eric W. Orts. (1999). "Moral Principle in the Law of Insider Trading." *Texas Law Review* 78:375–438.

Toobin, Jeffrey. (2003, February 3). "Lunch at Martha's: Problems with the Perfect Life." *The New Yorker* 78:38–43.

New Vigilance against Insider Trading

- *Document:* Toward the end of 2009, as the Obama administration began to get comfortable with its assumption of the reins of power, the SEC announced that hereafter it intended to bear down much harder on the practice of insider trading.
- *Date:* December 2, 2009.
- *Where:* *Wall Street Journal.*
- *Significance:* It is not uncommon for a new political party when it comes into office to announce that it will correct the alleged errors and shortcomings in the behavior of the previous administration, particularly when a different political regime assumes power. By the end of 2009, the SEC was receiving uniformly hostile comments for its failure to have responded to evidence, some of it having been fed directly to it, that there was a great deal of unsavory behavior going on the world of finance.

DOCUMENT 6.6

SEC STEPS UP INSIDER-TRADING PROBES
. . . Agency's Push Highlights New Aggressiveness

The Securities and Exchange Commission has sent at least three dozen subpoenas to hedge funds and brokerages within the past few months in an expanding sweep of potential insider-trading violations, according to people familiar with the matter.

At least some of the inquiries are focused on potential information leaks around health-care mergers of the past three years . . . Some of the subpoenas focus on . . . the role of Goldman Sachs Inc., bankers in roughly a dozen health-care deals since 2006 . . .

Since coming under new leadership this year, the SEC has become more aggressive in enforcement, including insider-trading cases. The SEC has faced attacks after fumbling an investigation into Bernard Madoff's multi-million dollar fraud [see chapter 11 for a Document and Analysis of the Madoff case].

Source: Kara Scannell and Jenny Strasburg, "SEC Steps Up Insider-Trading Probes," *Wall Street Journal*, December 2, 2009, C1, C5.

ANALYSIS

In the film *Wall Street*, actor Michael Douglas declares that "the most valuable commodity I know is information." This view is echoed in the first paragraph of an early 2010 news story in the business section of the *New York Times*: "The most precious commodity on Wall Street is information, and savvy players will do almost anything for it." The story's headline tells readers of the uncertainty of law regarding the use of such information: "A Thin Line Separates Insider Trading and Legal Research," it reads. The news report notes that today some investment funds query doctors to learn about the likely market for drugs produced by pharmaceutical companies while others pay meteorologists to forecast weather developments that will affect the price of oil and wheat.

Such tactics produce legitimate information. But there remains what is apparently a brisk business in the transmission to traders of nonpublic (or, more accurately, prepublic) insider information that predictably will influence the ups or downs of stock prices. Periodic federal crackdowns indicate that the temptation to trade on exclusive insider information is a difficult temptation for some people to resist. This undoubtedly is particularly true of business school graduates, who typically are attracted to the profession out of a desire to get rich, and who are confronted with opportunities to do so by breaking the law.

The promised stepped-up crusade against insider trading saw its first significant payoff in the May, 2011 conviction of Raj Rajaratnam, the founder of the Galleon group, a hedge fund company, who was found guilty of 5 counts of conspiracy and 9 counts of securities fraud after a two-month trial. Almost two dozen of his co-conspirators had earlier pleaded guilty, including Silicon Valley executives and a bevy of lawyers. As in the case of Martha Stewart, insider trading was not charged although it was at the heart of the prosecution. Conspiracy was much easier to prove to the jury. What made the case particularly noteworthy was that even though the more sophisticated participants used prepaid cell phones to avoid having their communications overhead, the prosecution was able to rely heavily on the results of wiretapping, a tactic previously almost exclusively employed against the activities of organized crime. The case demonstrated the emergent willingness of the Department of Justice to play hardball to develop criminal prosecutions of high-status culprits engaged in white-collar crimes.

Rajaratnam, 53-years-old, was born in Sri Lanka and become a billionaire, ranked 236th on the *Fortune* roster of America's wealthiest people. He was charged with having profited to the tune of $50 million by insider trading in the stock of companies such as Google, Goldman Sachs, Sprint Nextel, and Hilton Hotels. Typical of the tapes played to the jury was a conversation with Danielle Chiesi, a consultant at the New Castle Fund, with whom Rajaratnam had traded insider information:

"I mean this stock could go up $10, you know," he told her. "But we got to keep radio silence."

"Oh, please, this is my pleasure," Ms. Chiesi said.

"No, even for your little boyfriends," the defendant had said.

"No, believe me, I don't have friends," she replied.

The defense attorney maintained that what his client had done "happened every day on Wall Street," and declared: "There's nothing wrong with it." He planned to appeal the conviction.

DID YOU KNOW?

Prosecutors' Pronouncements

A former federal prosecutor offered his take on insider trading based on his courtroom experiences. "It's a very funny crime because you can't identify a victim. No one is looking in the wallet and saying I lost money. I lost $20 million."

Preet Bharara, a prosecutor in the Galleon case, observed that "people will probably ask just how pervasive insider trading is these days? Is this just the tip of the iceberg? We don't have an answer to that yet but we aim to find out." Cynics would regard this as no more than an expression of wishful thinking. They see illegal insider trading as so shadowy and so appealing a crime that its true extent will never be known.

FURTHER READINGS

Eads, Linda S. (1981). "From Capone to Boesky: Tax Evasion, Insider Trading, and the Problem of Proof." *California Law Review* 79:1421–84.

Rider, Barry Alexander K., and H. Leigh Ffrench. (1979). *The Regulation of Insider Trading.* Dobbs Ferry, NY: Oceana.

7

GOVERNMENT WHITE-COLLAR CRIMES

INTRODUCTION

Government crimes involve actions by the rulers and other top-level office holders that violate national or international criminal codes. The white-collar category is concerned with the abuse of the power of official position to achieve an end that, whether or not it is adjudicated by a criminal tribunal, self-evidently violates criminal laws. The problem here, of course, is that acts that reasonably could be seen as war crimes, for instance, are charged only against those who were on the losing side of the conflict. The victors are in a position to declare that what they have done was a perfectly legitimate enterprise and there rarely is anybody with the authority to counteract them and do something about it.

In this chapter we will look at three instances of government crime that exemplify the more flagrant aspects of such behavior. First, we consider the Abscam bribery case, which ensnared a bevy of federal and municipal legislators who were taken in by a scenario concocted by federal agents who were aware of the reputation of those they trapped for fiscal venery. Then we look at the notorious Watergate events that resulted in the first and only resignation of an American president who otherwise almost certainly would have been impeached and removed from office. And, finally, we consider extraordinary rendition, a procedure in which American agents kidnap persons on overseas territory and transport them to a country where it is known that they are almost assuredly likely to be tortured. We focus on an instance of extraordinary rendition in which the Italian government convicted a group of Americans in absentia for kidnapping when they snatched a Muslim cleric off the streets of Milan and flew him to Egypt where he was manhandled by the security forces there.

Watergate: Burglary and Cover-Up

- **Document:** Document 7.1 reproduces excerpts from the resignation statement of President Richard M. Nixon after his attempted cover-up of the Watergate burglary forced him either to resign or to face an impeachment process that would have stripped him of his office. Earlier, the president had memorably declared "I am not a crook," a startling exclamation for a man holding the most powerful position in the world, placed in a position where he had to defend his honesty against overwhelming evidence undermining it.
- **Date:** August 8, 1974.
- **Where:** The White House in Washington, DC.
- **Significance:** Document 7.1 represents a historic moment in American history when for the first and only time, a sitting president voluntarily gave up his office.

DOCUMENT 7.1

Good evening,

This is the 37th time I have spoken to you from this office, where so many decisions have been made that shaped he history of this Nation. Each time I have done so to discuss with you matters that I believe affect the national interest.

In all the decisions I have made in my public life, I have always tried to do what was best for the Nation. Throughout the long and difficult period of Watergate, I have felt it was my duty to persevere, to make every possible effort to complete the term of office to which you elected me.

In the past few days, however, it has become evident to me that I no longer have a strong enough political base in the Congress to justify continuing that effort. As long as there was such a base, I felt strongly that it was necessary to see the constitutional process through to its conclusion, that to do otherwise would be unfaithful to the spirit of the deliberately difficult process and a dangerously destabilizing precedent for the future.

But with the disappearance of that base, I now believe that the constitutional purpose has been served, and there is no longer a need for the process to be prolonged.

I would have preferred to carry through to the finish whatever the personal agony it would have involved, and my family unanimously urged me to do so. But the interest of the Nation must always come before any personal considerations.

From the discussions I have had with Congressional and other leaders, I have concluded that because of the Watergate matters I might not have the support of the Congress that I would consider necessary to back the very difficult decisions and carry out the duties of this office in the way the interests of the Nation would require.

I have never been a quitter. To leave office before my term is completed is abhorrent to every instinct in my body. But as President, I must put the interest of America first. America needs a full-time President and a full-time Congress, particularly at a time with problems we face at home and abroad.

To continue to fight through the months ahead for personal vindication would almost totally absorb the time and attention of the President and the Congress in a period when our entire focus should be on the great issues of peace abroad and prosperity without inflation at home.

Richard Nixon flashes his signature "V for Victory" symbol with his hands as he boards a helicopter after resigning the presidency on August 9, 1974. (National Archives)

Therefore, I shall resign the President's office at noon tomorrow. Vice President Ford will be sworn in as President at that time in this office . . .

By taking this action, I hope that I will have hastened the start of the process of healing which is so desperately needed in America.

I regret deeply any injuries that may have been done in the course of the events that led to this decision. I would say only that if some of my judgments were wrong, and some were wrong, they were made in what I believed at the time to be the best interest of the Nation.

To those who have stood with me during these past difficult months, my family, my friends, to many others who joined in supporting my cause because they believe it was right, I will be eternally grateful for your support . . .

To have served in this office is to have felt a very personal sense of kinship with each and every American. In leaving it, I do so with this prayer: May God's grace be with you, in all the days ahead.

Source: President Richard Nixon, Resignation Speech, August 8, 1974.

ANALYSIS

Perhaps the kindest thing that can be said about the involvement of President Richard Milhous Nixon, America's 37th president, in regard to the break-in at the

Watergate headquarters of the Democratic National Committee and the subsequent cover-up was that he was so obsessed with the belief that he more than anybody else could steer the nation through a period of severe crisis that any act that helped to keep him in office was in the service of the national well-being.

Nixon's resignation speech illustrates some of the doubletalk that characterized his time as president, a period of his life that has been thoroughly captured in the tapes that he ordered to be made of Oval Office conversations, conversations that were replete with exceedingly foul language on Nixon's part. The phrase in the resignation statement that reads "The constitutional purpose has been served" defies sensible interpretation, and nowhere is there to be found a clear admission of guilt and a strong sentiment of remorse. And it never is the "Watergate crime" or "Watergate burglary" or "Watergate cover-up," but rather the "Watergate matter." Or simply "Watergate."

The burglary in the Watergate housing and office complex took place before the 1972 presidential election and was orchestrated by Nixon operatives in order to plant recording devices and steal confidential information regarding the plans of the opposition Democratic Party for the election. An earlier break-in resulted in the placing of wiretaps on a number of telephones, but the results proved disappointing. Either the conversations could not be clearly heard or else the phones tapped were being used for personal and often very intimate discussions by staff members with partners of the opposite sex.

The burglary crew was headed by James W. McCord Jr. The crucial burglary began near midnight on Friday, June 16, 1972. But the night watchman, Frank Willis, noticed the taped latches that the burglars had placed on the Democratic National Committee office door and called the police, who took the intruders into custody at 2:30 the following morning. Each burglar had in his possession two $100 bills that he had been given to use to try to bribe his way out of any difficulty he might encounter.

The initial media reaction was tame until it became increasingly evident that the caper had been endorsed by the president's closest aides, who sought to distance themselves and him from the entire business, insisting to the media at first that McCord had once worked for them to install a security system, but otherwise that whatever he had been up to at Democratic National Committee headquarters had nothing to do with them. The Nixon aides told the burglars to say that they had sought to hinder the Democratic campaign because they thought some crazy man was going to become president and sell the country out to the Communists. That falsehood collapsed as the FBI gathered more evidence, so the Nixon team took another tack. They told Patrick Gray, a staunch ally who had succeeded J. Edgar Hoover as FBI chief, that the plot was part of a secret CIA maneuver and the need for national security dictated that the FBI immediately halt its investigation of the Watergate break-in. Nixon had set the ground rules earlier when he confided to Leonard Garment, a close aide: "You'll never make it in politics, Len. You just don't know how to lie."

With a certain slow and yet unstoppable movement, the true story behind the Watergate burglary began to become public. On October 15, Carl Bernstein and Robert Woodward, two *Washington Post* reporters, had begun to tie the threads together. They reported that "the FBI agents have established that the Watergate burglary incident stemmed from a massive campaign of political spying and sabotage on behalf of President Nixon's reelection and directed by officials of the White House and the Committee for the Re-Election of the President." One of the first developments to tie Nixon to the break-in was the discovery that a $25,000 cashier's check, apparently donated to the Committee to Re-Elect the President, had been deposited in the bank account of one of the burglars. But these early revelations hardly made a dent in Nixon's campaign for a second term. The following month he swamped George McGovern, obtaining 60% of the popular vote and the electoral votes of all states except Massachusetts. But the Democrats increased their control of both houses of Congress.

A Senate committee to investigate the Watergate affair was appointed, with Archibald Cox, a Harvard Law School professor, as special prosecutor. Testimony by John Dean, Nixon's counsel in the White House, mentioned that he had discussed the Watergate plan with the president at least 35 times. A witness then spilled the news to the investigative committee that Nixon had installed a tape recorder in the Oval Office. The president strenuously resisted turning the tapes over to Congress until ordered to do so by the Supreme Court. Eighteen and a half minutes were found to have been erased from the tapes. Nixon's longtime secretary, Rose Mary Woods, said that she had inadvertently made the erasure when she forgot to take her foot off a pedal while answering the telephone, but forensic evidence indicated that the tapes had been doctored on at least five separate occasions.

Nixon fired Cox in what became known as the Saturday Night Massacre, and both Nixon's Attorney General and the Attorney General's deputy resigned in protest. Facing impeachment, Nixon resigned his office on August 9, 1974. His successor, Vice President Gerald Ford, later would pardon Nixon.

DID YOU KNOW?

Deep Throat Coughs Up

Bob Woodward and Carl Bernstein, two extraordinarily enterprising reporters for the *Washington Post*, tumbled onto the Watergate story early when Bernstein, who covered the District of Columbia police, published the first stories about the burglary escapade. Thereafter, the two men established a stranglehold on inside information, relying heavily on an informant they identified as Deep Throat, oddly enough selecting the title of an early porn film to designate the individual feeding them news scoops.

Their work formed the plot of the highly acclaimed motion picture, *All the President's Men*, directed by Alan Pakula and starring Dustin Hoffman (as Bernstein) and Robert Redford (as Woodward). The film won four Academy Awards including one for Jason Robards for Best Supporting Actor.

Speculation was rife about Deep Threat, the source that was feeding the reporters highly confidential investigative information. The reporters identified Deep Throat merely as someone close to the White House, and noted that they signaled the need to talk to their source by placing the flower pot on Woodward's apartment balcony in a certain position.

More than 30 years down the road, W. Mark Feld, then sickly, announced that he was Deep Throat. Feld, born in Twin Falls, Idaho, had risen to the number two position in the FBI and had access to all the field reports concerning Watergate. Nixon's people had suspected him, but others had fastened on a wide variety of other persons who they believed were feeding information to Bernstein and Woodward. Woodward described Feld, who died in 2008, as a man with "a studied air of confidence, even what might be called a command presence." Interpretations of the reasons for Feld's providing confidential information to the *Post* vary. Some say that he reveled in being part of the action, others assert that he was angry that Nixon had not appointed him to replace J. Edgar Hoover, and still others insist that patriotic motives impelled him to make public presidential behavior that he considered unpalatable and a disgrace to the nation.

FURTHER READINGS

Ben-Veniste, Richard, and George T. Frampton Jr. (1977). *Stonewall: The Real Story of the Watergate Prosecution*. New York: Simon & Schuster.

Bernstein, Carl, and Bob Woodward. (1974). *All the President's Men*. New York: Simon & Schuster.

Genovese, Michael A. (1999). *The Watergate Crisis*. Westport, CT: Greenwood.

Kurland, Philip B. (1978). *Watergate and the Constitution*. Chicago: University of Chicago Press.

Merrill, William H. (2008). *Watergate Prosecutor*. East Lansing: Michigan State University Press.

Olson, Keith W. (2008). *Watergate: The Presidential Scandal That Shook America*. Lawrence: University Press of Kansas.

Perlstein, Rick. (2008). *Nixonland: The Rise of a President and the Fracturing of America*. New York: Scribner's.

Rosenberg, Kenyon C., and Judith K. Rosenberg. (1975). *Watergate: An Annotated Bibliography*. Litttleton, CO: Libraries Unlimited.

Abscam

- **Document:** Representative Michael Myers was the first major figure to be tried as a result of the Abscam sting operation. The Eastern District Court in New York City set forth the history of the operation and Myers's role in it. Except for slight variations, Document 7.2 encapsulates in general the events that led to the capture and conviction of the figures who participated in the Abscam bribery scandal.
- **Date:** 1981.
- **Where:** Federal courthouse, New York City.
- **Significance:** The document indicates the ingredients of the Federal Bureau of Investigation (FBI) operation and the responses of some of those who were ensnared. Equally important, it offers the reasoning that underlay the judicial system's denial of the legitimacy of the defenses that were offered by Myers and, subsequently, by others of those who had been arrested and charged.

DOCUMENT 7.2

Abscam was the code word assigned by the Federal Bureau of Investigation to an undercover sting operation conducted out of the FBI office at Haupauge, Long Island, New York, under the supervision of agent John Good. Abscam began after Melvin Weinberg in 1977 was convicted in the Western District of Pennsylvania on a plea of guilty to fraud. In return for a sentence of probation, Weinberg agreed to cooperate with the FBI in setting up an undercover operation similar to the London Investors, Ltd. "business" that Weinberg had conducted with remarkable success before his arrest and conviction in Pittsburgh.

For most of his life Weinberg had been a "con man" operating in the gray area between legitimate business and crude criminality. For a number of years in the 1960s and early 1970s he was an informant for the FBI and had provided his contact agent from time to time with intelligence about various known and suspected criminals and criminal activities in the New York metropolitan area and elsewhere, for which he received in return occasional small payments of money. When Weinberg was arrested his informant status was cancelled, later to be reinstituted after his guilty plea and his agreement to cooperate with the FBI. . . .

While operating outside the law in Huntington, Long Island as London Investors Weinberg's method had been a "front-end scam" for real estate investment wherein he would promise to obtain large loans for his victims and pick-up "appraisal" or "processing" fees of several thousand dollars, but without ever producing the final loans.

[T]he initial plan developed by Weinberg and the FBI that Weinberg was to present himself as a business agent for "Abdul Enterprises," an organization backed by two extremely wealthy Arab sheiks looking for American outlets for their cash . . .

At first Abscam's focus was upon stolen and forged securities and stolen art work. Other "investment" opportunities soon presented themselves . . . As word spread abut Weinberg's contact with the virtually inexhaustible Arab funds Angelo Errichetti, who was both mayor of Camden, New Jersey and a New Jersey state senator, came on the scene.

Errichetti and [Howard] Criden, [a Philadelphia lawyer], formed an alliance in which they undertook to produce . . . public officials who, in return for money, were willing to use their influence with the government on the sheik's behalf. Meetings were arranged . . . in New York, Philadelphia, and Washington where the FBI monitored the proceedings with concealed videotape cameras and microphones. When videotape was not feasible audio recordings were made.

U.S. v. MYERS, ERRICHETTI, JOHNSTON AND CRIDEN

The Myers trial involved four defendants. Michael O. Myers was a member of the United States House of Representatives from Philadelphia. He was brought to the undercover operatives through defendant Angelo J. Errichetti and defendant Howard L. Criden, who made contact with Myers through Criden's law partner, Louis C. Johnston.

Myers was the first congressman to take money in front of the Abscam TV cameras. He did so in a hotel room at Kennedy Airport on August 22, 1979 . . . All four defendants shared in the $50,000, with Errichetti receiving $15,000, Myers $15,000 and Johnston and Criden $20,000, part of which they shared with their law partner, Ellis Cook, who testified at the trial as an immunized witness.

Myers testified on his own behalf and attempted to convince the jury that when he appeared in the video tape and received the money in return for a promise to introduce a private bill to enable the sheikh to enter and remain in this country he was only "play acting" because he never intended ultimately to do the acts for which he was receiving the money. In other words, Myers defense was essentially that although he was swindling the sheikh, in no way was he compromising his congressional office . . . Ultimately, the jury resolved the credibility issues against Myers. . . .

CONCLUSION

[T]he congressional defendants were caught on videotape in flagrante delicto [Latin for in the very act of committing an offense], accepting money in relation to their conduct as public servants . . . None of the defendants was a "deprived" citizen. All of them occupied honored, well rewarded, and highly respected positions in our society. . . . Defendants' crass conduct here reveals only greed, dishonesty and corruption. . . .

The government's need to unmask such conduct more than justifies the investigative techniques employed in this case . . .

After careful consideration of the many problems raised about Abscam over the course of these cases, which have now covered approximately one year, this court is satisfied that all of the defendants were proved guilty beyond a reasonable doubt, that the trials accorded to them are fair, that the arguments advanced for setting aside the convictions and dismissing the indictments on "due process" grounds are without merit, and that there are no circumstances requiring a new trial for any of the defendants.

Source: United States v Myers, 527 Federal Supplement 2nd 1206 (Eastern District, New York, 1981).

ANALYSIS

The public's opinion of the moral character of persons prominent in public life has in recent years persistently been at the very low end of what might be called an integrity scale. The clamor running through a significant segment of the population takes the form of "Throw the Bums Out"; that is, replace incumbents with new faces, particularly faces that have not yet appeared on the lawmaking scene. The difficulty here, of course, is that soon the newcomers typically join with the old-timers in perpetuating behaviors that are related to the low esteem with which politicians in the United States are regarded.

Money lies at the heart of the problem. To get into and stay in important elective office requires very large sums of money. Those who are willing to donate such money are rarely altruistic; they give it to persons who they believe—too often correctly—will do something for them in return when they feel this support is necessary for their own good, although not necessarily, or likely, for the good of the public. The only real check on this state of affairs lies in the fact that many, perhaps most, politicians will defy their rich contributors if it seems essential that they must take some action that will convince the public to elect or reelect them, even if that action is unpopular with rich donors.

The Abscam scandal brought out into the open the mind-set of politicians savoring the scent of money. The term came from Abdul Enterprises, Ltd., a phony company created by the FBI as part of a sting operation. The sting, as noted, was directed by Melvin Weinberg, a former convicted conman, who was hired by the FBI. Weinberg set up a scheme involving a fictitious Arab who sought to purchase asylum in the United States, to involve the legislators in a number of business ventures, and to obtain help to get his money out of the country.

In one of the sidelights to the scam, a legislator asked a government agent posing as an Arab what country he was from. The agent had forgotten what he had been rehearsed to say and replied that he knew his homeland only by its Arabic name and not in its English rendition. The legislator, intent on getting his hands on some loot, failed to be alerted by this verbal gaffe to what actually was going on.

Abscam targeted legislators who had a reputation for being particularly vulnerable to bribery. In the end it captured one U.S. senator, five members of the U.S. House of Representatives, one New Jersey state senator, a member of the Philadelphia City Council, and a naturalization service inspector, among others. The senator was Harrison A. Williams Jr. (D-N. J.); the House members were John Jenrette (D-S.C.), Richard Kelly (D-Mo.), Raymond Lederer (D-Pa.), Michael Myers (D-Pa.), and Frank Thompson (D-N. J.). Only one lawmaker who was approached, Senator Larry Pressler, a Republican from South Dakota, turned down the bribery offer: "Wait a minute," Pressler was recorded as saying, "What you are suggesting may be illegal." Pressler, the first Vietnam veteran elected to Congress, had been a Rhodes scholar at Oxford and was a graduate of the Harvard Law School. He would serve in Congress for 22 years, from 1979 to 1997.

Most of those congressmen implicated in the scam resigned their seats or did not seek reelection, although Myers had to be expelled. Lederer was the only accused member of Congress who was reelected, but he resigned in the face of a House Ethics Committee recommendation that he be expelled. In a 1978 videotape Myers had informed the plotters: "I'm going to tell you something real simple and short—money talks in this business." He sought unsuccessfully to claim legislative immunity and maintained that he could not be convicted because "the Abscam investigation did not uncover criminal conduct, but instead created and instigated it." Neither position succeeded, and Myers was convicted and sentenced to three years in prison. Not long before, he had drawn a suspended sentence when he and a cousin pled guilty to dragging a hotel

DID YOU KNOW?

Was Abscam Entrapment?

The strongest defense that the Abscam defendants were able to mount was that they had been entrapped and therefore could not be convicted as charged. Entrapment is deemed to occur when an enforcement officer or other government agent suggests, encourages, or aids in the production of a crime that otherwise would not have been committed. The U.S. Supreme Court in 1932 in *Sorrells v. United States* handed down the landmark ruling on entrapment. A federal agent had approached the defendant in his rural North Carolina home and claimed that he was a furniture dealer and had served in the same Army unit as David Sorrells. The agent persistently sought to have Sorrells sell him liquor, which would have been a violation of the National Prohibition Act. After a number of visits Sorrells provided the agent with a gallon of whiskey, was arrested, and sentenced to 18 months in prison. The Supreme Court decision declared that the aim of the government should not be to create crime and called for a retrial.

To overcome an entrapment defense, the state must convince the judge or jury that the individual had a predisposition to commit the criminal act and that the inducement offered was not sufficient in itself to produce the result. This is known as the "subjective test" of entrapment.

The "objective test," advocated by dissenters in *Sorrells*, focuses on the decency and persuasive power of the tactics used to determine whether an entrapment defense will succeed. Its aim is not to excuse defendants but to monitor police behavior so that it comports with reasonable standards of decency and morality.

Do you believe that the federal courts favored Sorrells because what he had done was a minor wrong and involved an unpopular law while Abscam snared elites who violated the demands of their leadership position? Or was justice truly done in both instances?

security guard into an elevator and beating him up. Williams also drew a three-year sentence, thus becoming the first incumbent senator since 1905 to be convicted of a crime. He failed to prevail in his claim that the he was not really bribed since the share in a titanium mine that he had been given was worthless. Kelly at first was successful with an argument that he had been entrapped (see Sidebar 7.2) but subsequently was convicted. He received the lightest sentence of all the defendants: 6 to 18 months in prison. A videotape showed Kelly pocketing $25,000 and asking an FBI agent, dressed as an Arab, "Does it show?" Thompson received a three-year sentence, and Jenrette got two years in prison. Jenrette probably gained the most personal notoriety of the Abscam bribe takers when his wife posed nude for a *Playboy* centerfold.

A biography of Melvin Weinberg would detail a life of petty crime, beginning when he stole gold stars from his classroom teacher's desk to try to convince his parents that he was an outstanding student. Following the Abscam affair, Weinberg's wife claimed publicly that he had perjured himself in the Abscam case and had stolen some of the money supplied by the FBI; then, not long after, she committed suicide.

FURTHER READINGS

Caplan, Gerald M. (1983). *ABSCAM Ethics: Moral Issues and Deception in Law*. Cambridge, MA: Ballinger.

Greene, Robert W. (1981). *The Sting Man: Inside Abscam*. New York: Elsevier-Dutton.

Jones, Curtis C., and Alva W. Stewart. (1982). *ABSCAM: Its Operation and Political Consequences*. Monticello, IL: Vance Bibliographies.

Katzman, Gary S. (1985). *Understanding the Criminal Process: The Abscam Case*. New York: Pergamon.

Extraordinary Rendition

- *Document:* The U.S. government, operating through the Central Intelligence Agency (CIA), kidnapped a Muslim imam on the streets of Milan in Italy and flew him to Egypt. The U.S. government had considerable evidence and perhaps an agreement that the imam would be tortured in Egypt. The Italian government convicted the CIA agents in absentia for committing acts that were criminal offenses under Italian (and international) law. Document 7.3 is largely based on original Italian sources and interviews with the prosecuting attorney.
- *Date:* The rendition took place in Italy in 2003. The document was published in 2010.
- *Where:* Milan, Italy.
- *Significance:* The use of extraordinary rendition tactics, first inaugurated on a small scale by President Ronald Reagan, then employed widely by President George W. Bush, and subsequently endorsed by President Barack Obama, illustrates the employment of government resources to carry out acts on foreign soil that are crimes in those countries and, done without a warrant, would be domestic criminal violations as well.

DOCUMENT 7.3

On February 17, 2003, 42-year-old Moustafa Hassan Nasr, commonly known as Abu Omar, was kidnapped by American and Italian officials and flown from Italy through Germany to Egypt, where he was subjected to a brutal regime of torture . . .

[W]hat happened to Abu Omar was the commonplace fate of many people who United States agents or accomplices transported to overseas sites so that their interrogations would not be associated with American policy. Legal judgments of this practice, known as "extraordinary rendition," and sometimes labeled "torture by proxy," have reached varying conclusions. For our part, we regard extraordinary rendition as immoral and as a violation of both American and international law. . . .

Abu Omar, after stays in Albania and in Munich, had gained political asylum in Italy. He faced persecution if he returned to Egypt because of his onetime membership in a radical Islamic organization, Jamat al Islam. Omar had been a government informant for SHJIK, the Albanian intelligence agency, and there was speculation that the Italians and/or Americans might desire to induce him to play the same role in Italy in regard to possible Muslim terrorists . . .

Walking to noon prayer at a mosque on Via Guerzoni in Milan, Omar was confronted by men dressed a Italian police officers. One of those men later told prosecutors that Omar was lured to a van by asking him to show his identification papers. The man providing these details testified that he had been informed by the Central Intelligence Agency station chief in Milan, Robert Selden Lady, that the operation had "cover" [that is, the approval of the Italian government]. Numerous CIA agents were involved in the planning and execution of the rendition . . .

The kidnappers sprayed chemicals into Omar's face and thrust him into the minivan. He was then taken to Aviano, a joint American and Italian airport based northeast of Venice, then to the Ramstein air base in Germany. From there he was flown to Egypt. There he underwent a severe torture regimen that included electric shocks to his genitals, being hung upside down, being bombarded with loud noises, and being moved from a hot sauna into a refrigerated cell . . .

These details became known in a trial in Milan of the police officers who had taken part in the abduction. Also on trial, in absentia, were the CIA officials . . . In July 2005, Armando Spataro [the prosecutor] issued warrants for 13 Americans. Later, nine more Americans were added . . .

Source: Joseph F. C. DiMento, and Gilbert Geis, "Extraordinary Rendition: Legal and Moral Considerations," in *I Diritti Umani di Fronte al Giudice Internazionale,* ed. Tullio Scovazzi, Irani Papancolopulo, and Sabrina Urbaniti (Milan: Giuffré, 2009), 151–54.

ANALYSIS

The Abu Omar case is but one of a number of similar incidents that have come to light. Two of the more prominent episodes convey the U.S. government-approved nature of the events.

Khaled El-Masri, a Lebanon-born German citizen, was on vacation when he was removed from a bus on a border crossing into Macedonia on New Year's Eve in 2003. It would later turn out that he had been mistaken for a member of the Hamburg Al-Qaeda cell with almost the same name. He was held for five months in solitary

DID YOU KNOW?

CIA Shenanigans

The CIA operatives involved in the Omar kidnapping were astonishingly careless in covering their trail. Even if they assumed that there would be no repercussions, it would have been expected that they would be more discreet in their actions. They left a sloppy, telltale trail behind them. As a former CIA official noted: "They behaved like elephants stampeding through Milan. They left huge footprints." The Italian and the American media were particularly intrigued by the $144,984 bill for food and accommodations that the CIA agents had run up in a relatively short time span, and with the postabduction festive holidays at taxpayers' expense that a number of the agents took in Venice to celebrate their feat.

The Italian police obtained the telephone traffic records of the mobile phones of the CIA agents that were used on the day of the kidnapping. While traveling to Aviano, the agents used the mobile phones to call telephone numbers in Virginia (the home of the CIA headquarters). To identify those present at the crime several other sources of evidence were mined, including photocopies of identity papers (passports and driver's licenses) used in the hotels. There also were transcripts of phone calls the agents had made to their families in the United States.

Public identification was offered only of CIA agent Robert Lady. He had passed as a diplomat at the American consulate in Milan, and had retired 10 months after the Omar kidnapping. Lady had flown from Milan to Cairo five days following the Omar kidnapping. He owned a retreat in the Asti region in Italy where authorities found pictures of Omar and of the area where Omar lived and worked. Like the other accused Americans, Lady had fled the country. An appeal by his attorney to an Italian court claiming that Lady deserved diplomatic immunity was rejected on the ground that since he had retired he no longer was entitled to such protection. Another participant in the kidnapping, a 62-year-old man, had been assigned to the U.S. embassy in Tanzania, out of harm's way.

confinement in Kabul in Afghanistan. A Council of Europe report concluded that his allegation that he was beaten, stripped of his clothing, drugged, and sodomized was substantially correct. When finally released he was dumped off in a desolate area in Albania.

Syrian-born Arar, a telecommunications engineer, had lived in Canada for 17 years. In September 2002, during a stopover in John F. Kennedy airport in New York City en route to Montreal from Tunis, he was seized by FBI agents and held in detention for 20 days. He then was transported to Syria, where he was placed in a cell six feet long and seven feet high, damp and cold, with a feeble light and infested with rats. He then was subjected to torture. To obtain surcease he confessed to training with terrorists in Afghanistan although he never had been in that country. He was finally released in October 2003, never having been charged with anything. American courts rejected his appeal for compensation but a Commission on Inquiry in Canada supported his allegations and the government awarded him 10 million Canadian dollars as compensation.

FURTHER READINGS

Asim, Qureshi. (2007). *Rules of the Game: Detention, Deportation, Disappearance.* New York: Columbia University Press.

Grey, Stephen. (2006). *Ghost Plane: The True Story of the CIA Torture Program.* New York: St. Martin's.

Mayer, Jane. (2008). *Dark Side: The Inside Story of How the War on Terrorism Turned to a War on American Ideals.* New York: Doubleday.

Mazigh, Monia. (2008). *Hope and Despair: My Struggle to Free My Husband, Maher Arar.* Toronto, Ontario: McClellan & Stewart.

Paglen, Trevor, and A. C. Thompson. (2006). *Torture Taxi: On the Trail of CIA Rendition Flights.* New York: Melville House.

8

WHITE-COLLAR CRIME IN THE PROFESSIONS

INTRODUCTION

Power and prestige offer an abundant array of lifestyle advantages: luxurious house, fancy cars, a first-rate education, and high-style travel arrangements, among many other desirable pleasures. They also put a person in a position to commit crimes that are less risky, yield more money, and are more unlikely to result in arrest and harsh punishment than street crimes. Bank embezzlers steal many times more money than bank robbers, and they stand no chance of being shot by law enforcers who pursue the robbers' getaway car.

In a previous chapter we saw the multimillion-dollar yearly incomes that Wall Street magnates reaped when they violated the law by trading on nonpublic material insider information. In this chapter we examine lawbreaking found in the practice of medicine, in the practice of law, and in the political realm. Keep in mind that these are people who legally enjoy benefits far above those available to ordinary folk, and yet they feel compelled to grab more, to compete with their peers or neighbors who might have a bigger house, a better car, or a more luxurious yacht.

White-Collar Crime in Medicine

- *Document:* As a result of the horrors of the deadly experiments by Nazi doctors upon persons they dehumanized, such as the feeble-minded and Jews and gypsies, the General Assembly of the World Medical Association in 1948 adopted the Declaration of Geneva that sought to translate the Hippocratic Oath into a modern and comprehensive set of moral and ethical imperatives. The text of the Declaration has undergone several revisions. Document 8.1 represents the most recent iteration.
- *Date:* May 2006.
- *Where:* Divonne les-Bains, France.
- *Significance:* The Declaration sets out standards of conduct that represent principles that should be observed by all medical practitioners.

DOCUMENT 8.1

At the time of being admitted as a member of the medical profession:

- I solemnly pledge to consecrate my life to the service of humanity;
- I will give to my teachers the respect and gratitude that is their due;
- I will practice my profession with conscience and dignity;
- The health of my patients will be my first consideration;
- I will respect the secrets that are confided in me, even after the patient has died;
- I will maintain by all the means in my power, the honor and the noble traditions of the medical profession;
- My colleagues will be my sisters and brothers;

- I will not permit considerations of age, disease or disability, creed, ethnic origin, gender, nationality, political affiliation, race, sexual orientation, social standing or any other factor to intervene between my duty and my patient;
- I will maintain the utmost respect for human life;
- I will not use my medical knowledge to violate human rights and civil liberties, even under threat;
- I make these promises solemnly, freely and upon my honor.

Source: Declaration of Geneva, General Assembly of the World Medical Association at Geneva, 2006. Originally created in 1948. Revised in 1968, 1984, 1994, 2005, and 2006.

ANALYSIS

Flagrant violations by physicians of the Declaration of Geneva occurred in conjunction with the preemptive invasion of Iraq in 2002 by American military forces. The most comprehensive report of these violations has been by Dr. Stephen Miles, a professor of medicine and bioethics at the University of Minnesota, in his book *Oath Betrayed*. In an interview, Miles indicated that the routine torture by Americans of Iraqi prisoners had aroused his interest in regard to the role of doctors in the proceedings: "I found somewhat to my amazement that it was not just a matter of not reporting but it was actually a matter of being involved in setting the harshness of the interrogation plans and delaying repots of homicides, which would have been an important signal to the people of what was wrong inside the prison."

Miles examined 35,000 pages of government documents that he secured by filing a Freedom of Information request. He found that in numerous instances American doctors let their military situation override the dictates of their oath to serve as healers, not as accessories to torture. The situation unfolded when then-Secretary of Defense Donald Rumsfeld defied international conventions outlawing torture and specifically ordered that Army doctors should be involved in the torture of suspected terrorists taken captive in Iraq and elsewhere. A *Time* editorial caustically observed that "some of the medical involvement in torture defies belief."

At the notorious Abu Ghraib prison in Baghdad, according to the Army surgeon general, only 15 percent of the inmates were examined for injuries after they underwent interrogation. The incriminating photographs that surfaced—many of which were withheld from public scrutiny—indicated that severe physical harm inflicted on prisoners was commonplace.

One of the few logs that Miles was able to obtain dealt with the torture of Mohammed al-Ohatani. Al-Ohatani, a Saudi Arabian, was believed to have been slated to join one of the teams that carried out the 9/11 terrorist attacks, but he was turned aside at the Orlando airport in Florida, after arriving on a flight from Dubai, when the authorities decided that with only a one-way ticket and $2,000 in cash, he likely intended to remain in the United States illegally. He moved to Pakistan and was captured in the Tora Bora battle in Afghanistan.

Doctors were present when al-Ohatani was tortured. He was subject to periods of sleep deprivation that lasted for 49 days. His interrogators induced hypothermia (cooling the body below 95°F) and watched as he was threatened by dogs, among other torture routines. They took the prisoner to the hospital to treat the hypothermia and then returned him to the torture chambers.

At Guantánamo prison in Cuba, the notorious Gitmo facility, doctors allowed a prisoner's gunshot wound to fester for three days while he was being interrogated and withheld antibiotic treatments for prisoners in need of them. According to the Army surgeon general "an anesthesiologist repeatedly dropped a 2-lb bag of intravenous fluid on a patient, a nurse deliberately delayed giving pain medication, and medical staff fed pork to Muslim patients," whose religion forbade the eating of pork.

The filing of death certificates of the more than 150 prisoners who died in captivity was delayed, often for a year, and when issued, often were faked. The death certificate for a 63-year-old prisoner said that he died of "cardiovascular disease and the building of fluid around his heart." No mention was made of the fact that he had been stripped naked, doused with cold water, and kept outside in 40° weather for three days before he suffered cardiac arrest. A 2010 op-ed piece in the *New York Times* by a public health scholar and a psychiatrist who is a retired Army brigadier general sums up their criticism of the authorities for ignoring the medical involvement in the Army's torture regimen:

> No agency—not the Pentagon, the C.I.A., state licensing boards or professional medical societies—has instigated any action to investigate, much less to discipline, these individuals . . . they have ignored the gross and appalling violations by medical personnel. This is an unconscionable disservice to the thousands of ethical doctors and psychologists in the country's service.

The disgraceful record of the involvement of health care professionals in torture was summarized by the group Physicians for Human Rights:

> The earliest reports of torture and abusive interrogation by US personnel were accompanied by disturbing reports of health professional complicity, from withholding or modifying medical care to disclosure of confidential medical information about physical or mental vulnerabilities to interrogators to failure to report torture and ill-treatment. The Defense Department's

DID YOU KNOW?

The Hippocratic Oath

Newly minted doctors were at one time required to swear to an oath first promulgated in the late fifth century BCE, that is, more than 2,500 years ago. Steven Miles had reworked an earlier translation of the Greek into what he calls the vernacular, the common language of our time. I have placed italics into the oath in order to emphasize the phrase that is equivalent to the "Do no harm" injunction, a maxim that actually never was specifically part of the Oath. Today, few medical schools administer the Hippocratic Oath, but many require graduating doctors to swear allegiance to modern versions of ethical codes.

The Oath takes the following form:

> I will use treatment for the benefit of the ill in accordance with my ability and my judgment *but from what is to be their harm I will keep them.*
>
> In a purse and holy way I will guard my life and my art.
>
> To each clinical encounter I will go for the benefit of the ill and I will refrain from unjustly treating them, especially from sexual acts with my patients or their relatives. I will remain silent about the private things that I learn of them during treatment or in broader conversations. If I honor this and do not evade its spirit or violate it, may I enjoy the benefits of life and of the profession and be respected by all. If I transgress, the opposite be my lot.

Inspector General revealed in 2006 that military psychologists, including members of Behavioral Science Consultation Teams . . . played a central role in designing and implementing the regime [of] psychological torture that became "standard operating procedure" for interrogations at Guantanamo Bay and in Iraq and Afghanistan.

Besides these wartime brutalities and neglect, there are other forms of violence committed by physicians. A considerable portion of the medical malpractice settlements and verdicts against doctors could be tried as violations of the law against criminal assault, but patients overwhelmingly prefer to seek financial compensation rather than revenge that would involve a criminal conviction.

FURTHER READINGS

Jaffer, Jameel, and Amri Singh. (2007). *Administration of Torture: A Documentary Record from Washington to Abu Ghraib and Beyond.* New York: Columbia University Press.

Lifton, Robert Jay. (1998). *The Nazi Doctors: Medical Killing and the Psychology of Genocide.* New York: Basic Books.

Miles, Steven. (2004). *The Hippocratic Oath and the Ethics of Medicine.* New York: Oxford University Press.

Miles, Steven. (2008). *Oath Betrayed: America's Torture Doctors.* Berkeley: University of California Press.

Physician Fraud against Medical Insurance Programs

- **Document:** Some physicians have found a cash cow in the private insurance firms and government benefit programs that provide services to the elderly (Medicare) and to the indigent (Medicaid). These impersonal agencies can be overwhelmed with claims from doctors that inflate or otherwise misrepresent the treatment provided to a real or a make-believe patient. Document 8.2 provides details of one such case out of the many hundreds that are uncovered each year.
- **Date:** August 9, 2007.
- **Where:** Houston, Texas.
- **Significance:** The document illustrates a form of fraud in the field of medicine that has come into being since the advent of private health insurance companies and the establishment by the government of health care programs during the administration of President Lyndon Johnson. That the convicted defendant also sought to murder officials handling his case demonstrates how upper-class professionals, under threat, can resort to criminal tactics much more common in the underworld.

DOCUMENT 8.2

LOCAL PHYSICIAN SENTENCED TO PRISON FOR DEFRAUDING INSURANCE COMPANY OF $10 MILLION

A federal jury convicted Dr. Ira Klein, 61, of Houston, Texas, in November 2006 of 18 counts of medical fraud and 26 counts of health care fraud in connection with a scheme to defraud insurance companies of $10 million. Today, U.S. District Judge David Hunter sentenced Dr. Klein to 135 months in prison to be followed by a three-year term of suspended release. Klein was also ordered to pay $11,590,784 in restitution.

... The court found Dr. Klein had obstructed justice when he allegedly conspired with jailhouse inmates to murder the Assistant District Attorney prosecuting the case, one of the Federal Bureau of Investigation Special Agents investigating the case and his wife. ... Klein wired $250,000 from his bank account to the individual. What Klein did not know at the time was that the individual he discussed and sent payment to was a federal undercover agent. ... Prior to pronouncing sentence, Judge Hunter noted that ... Klein could face possible federal charges for the alleged plot to murder the prosecuting AUSA and the FBI agent.

... Dr. Klein specialized in treating patients diagnosed with Hepatitis C and billed insurance companies for services he did not provide to patients and misrepresented services that were actually provided. The fraudulent scheme involved ordering large quantities of medications used to treat Hepatitis C and providing medications to patients to self-administer at home and then billing the insurance companies as if the injections had been administered by him or his staff in his office. Trial evidence indicated that Dr. Klein ordered Hepatitis C treatment kits containing interferon and ribavirin at a cost of $695 each, but would unbundle the kit and submit claims to the insurance company for more than $3,840 for the components of the kits. The majority of the claims filed for services provided were for dates when patients were not in his office ...

Former patients testified that when their insurance company refused to pay Klein the exorbitant fees he cut off their treatment or told them to contact their respective insurance companies and demand that Dr. Klein be paid.

Patient files introduced during trial showed Klein did not have doctors notes for the majority of claims submitted for reimbursement. Moreover, where notes existed they uniformly documented the same blood pressure and pulse recorded for every patient—120/80 and 80 beats per minute—a virtual impossibility according to several physicians who testified at the trial.

Representatives from the Texas State Board of Medical Examiners and the Texas Board of Pharmacy testified Klein violated board rules and state law by acting as a pharmacy and ordering large quantities of prescription drugs that were available by prescription from a pharmacy. As a result of his fraudulent scheme, Klein billed insurance companies over $16 million and was paid $10 million.

Source: "Texas Physician Sentenced for $10 Million Scam," U.S. Attorney's Office, Southern District of Texas, Press Release, August 6, 2007, http://mathiasconsulting .com/node/2033 (accessed March 31, 2011).

ANALYSIS

The detection of fraud is viewed by many of the insurance agencies in cost-benefit terms. How much will it cost to detect violations compared to how much will be saved by trying to do so? The Klein case is so egregious that it could not be allowed to go unattended. But often the losses from fraud are much smaller, and the insurers can readily pass the costs on to their customers by means of higher premiums.

The work of physicians has a number of built-in opportunities for white-collar crime that are not available in most other kinds of work. Among their offenses are: (1) lying about their credentials; (2) performing unnecessary surgery and ordering unnecessary tests and procedures; (3) steering patients to specialists who then kick back a portion of their fee to the referring doctor; (4) faking reports of accident injuries in order to collect an examination fee and, at times, share in the insurance payment to the bogus patient; (5) sexually abuse patients, typically male doctors with female patients (as people sometimes say, what other stranger would most women undress for?); (6) conduct superficial visits in facilities for the elderly and charge as if these quick look-ins were full-fledged examinations; (7) treat a parent but bill for each member of the family as if they had been seen individually.

Doctors enjoy exceedingly high (but declining) status in American society. They rely on training and experience in matters that are well beyond the common understanding of most people, although the Internet has come to make amateur doctors out of many of us—not to mention the anxiety that a perusal of medical websites can induce in those given to a tendency toward hypochondria. Few doctors work on salary, so that their earnings are likely to vary with the type of treatment they offer. They learn quickly, for instance, that they cannot bill for leisurely discussions with patients, and many resort instead to arguably necessary but lucrative interventions.

Before the appearance of insurance programs, a doctor's income was primarily derived from the purses and wallets of patients they treated. There were social and moral barriers to taking advantage of an individual on a personal, face-to-face level. Besides, you could swindle a patient out of only so much money: they did not have the deep pockets of an insurance agency or a government benefit program. Nonetheless, physicians engaged in a number of practices that were against the law. The term "quackery" came into use as a label for doctors, or those who pretended to be doctors, or laypersons who offered useless nostrums said to be effective as cures for all kinds of diseases.

Today, estimates place the cost of medical fraud as high as $80 billion annually. In a comprehensive review of the subject, Stephen Rosoff and his colleagues noted wildly inflated prices on medical equipment that is billed to insurance companies, and scams on motorized scooters including an instance in which one elderly man obtained for free a scooter that he turned around and sold to a pawn shop. A Texas doctor prescribed wheelchairs that cost a good deal less but were billed to government insurance programs at a price of $7,000 each. The doctor made more than $1 million on the scheme and ended up with an 11-year prison sentence. A New York study showed that home treatment companies sold drugs from 157 to 1,006 percent more than the retail pharmacy price.

Hospital costs constitute the largest outlay of health care funds. Hospitals have been found to pay kickbacks to doctors who refer patients to them. Itemized bills given to discharged hospital patients are likely to be shocking: toothbrushes are priced as if they were inlaid with diamonds, Kleenex as if it were precious papyrus, and the patient's room as if it were the presidential suite at the Waldorf Astoria.

Unnecessary surgery is often performed by some physicians because it is a lucrative business. One of the worst cases involved a Los Angeles ophthalmologist who was convicted on charges of performing unneeded eye surgeries. The doctor subjected poor, mostly Hispanic patients to needless cataract surgery in order to collected $584 for each eye operated on. He "earned" about a million dollars over a period of five years. In one instance a 57-year-old woman was totally blinded after the doctor operated on her one good eye.

The typical investigative approach in regard to fraudulent medical practices is to pose as a patient with a faked ailment and determine whether the doctor handles your complaint in a way that conforms to accepted standards of practice. This tactic is not too difficult with psychiatrists who may charge for sessions that never took place or see the patient for half an hour but bill for an hour's therapy. It becomes more difficult with serious afflictions, first, because the undercover agent cannot pretend to be suffering from certain ailments without showing physical signs and, second, because few agents want to be probed and undergo examinations and tests that they do not actually require. Therefore investigations more often involve a review of claims. If a doctor bills for more hours than there are in a day (and some have done so) or for diaper rash treatment for a varsity football player (some have done this too), fraud inspectors will be alerted. But the more subtle medical offenses inevitably go undetected.

FURTHER READINGS

Baumann, Linda A. (2007). *Health Care Fraud and Abuse: Practical Perspectives.* Washington, DC: Bureau of National Affairs.

Busch, Rebecca S. (2008). *Healthcare Fraud: Auditing and Detection Guide.* Hoboken, NJ: Wiley.

Jesilow, Paul, Henry N. Ponttell, and Gilbert Geis. (1983). *Prescription for Profit: How Doctors Defraud Medicaid.* Berkeley: University of California Press.

Sparrow, Malcolm K. (1996). *License to Steal: Why Fraud Pervades America's Health Care System.* Boulder, CO: Westview.

Tomas, Hoyt W. (2003). *Health Care Fraud and Abuse: A Physician's Guide to Compliance.* Chicago: American Medical Association.

White-Collar Crime by Attorneys

- **Document:** The Model Rules of Professional Conduct set forth a very long list of the professional obligations of persons admitted to the bar as qualified to practice law. Rule 8.4, reproduced as Document 8.3, specifies the forms of misconduct that lawyers must avoid.
- **Date:** 1992.
- **Where:** Issued by the American Bar Association in Chicago.
- **Significance:** The areas of misconduct specified in Rule 8.4 form the basis for actions against errant attorneys by local and state bar associations, and often lie at the heart of state civil and criminal regulation of the practice of law.

DOCUMENT 8.3

Maintaining the Integrity of the Profession
Rule 8.4 Misconduct
It is professional misconduct for a lawyer to:

(a) violate or attempt to violate the Rules of Professional Conduct, knowingly assist or induce others to do so, or do so through the acts of another;

(b) commit a criminal act that reflects adversely on the lawyer's honesty, trustworthiness or fitness as a lawyer in other respects;

(c) engage in conduct involving dishonesty, fraud, deceit or misrepresentation;

(d) engage in conduct that is prejudicial to the administration of justice;

(e) state or imply an ability to influence improperly a government agency or official or to achieve results by means that violate the Rules of Professional Conduct or other law; or

(f) knowingly assist a judge or judicial officer in conduct that is a violation of applicable rules of conduct or other law.

Source: The Model Rules of Professional Conduct, Center for Professional Responsibility, American Bar Association, 2007.

ANALYSIS

In 2007 there were, according to the American Bar Association, almost one and a half million attorneys in the Unites States. The America Medical Association reports 853,187 doctors in the country in the same year. Thus, if only in terms of potential violators, the lawyers are likely to have more white-collar criminals in their ranks, a judgment that is probably accurate. Certainly public opinion would support that conclusion. Doctors continue to be highly regarded, while attorneys often are suspected of the worst.

The Rules of Professional Conduct for lawyers address various issues in more specific terms than those grouped under the rubric of misconduct. They cover such diverse matters as the responsibilities of a subordinate lawyer, advertising, duties to former clients, the safekeeping of property, trial publicity, and fairness to other parties and opposing counsel. Many set out specific restrictions, such as Rule 1.2(d) that prohibits an attorney from assisting or counseling a client to engage in conduct that the lawyer knows is criminal or fraudulent.

States that adopt the Rules may add further embellishments. In Illinois, for instance, among other additions, the State Code extends 8.4(d) by specifying that "in relation thereto, a lawyer shall not engage in adverse discriminatory treatment of litigants, jurors, witnesses, lawyers, and others, based on race, sex, religion or national origin." This section does not preclude legitimate adversarial actions when these or similar factors are issues in the proceedings. Illinois also includes as misconduct the avoidance in bad faith of the repayment of student loans. Kansas added an Item (g) to the list specifying that it is professional misconduct for a lawyer "to engage in any . . . conduct that adversely reflects on the lawyer's fitness to practice law."

In the past half century, two lawyer-presidents have had the right to practice law denied them. Richard Nixon was disbarred in 1976 on the ground of obstruction of justice. In early 2001, Bill Clinton's license to practice law in Arkansas was suspended for five years on the ground that he had violated Rules 8.4(c) and 8.4(d) by lying to a court in response to the allegation by Jennifer Flowers that he had sexually harassed her and that he had denied ever being alone with Monica Lewinsky and having sex with her. Clinton was also fined $25,000. Later that year, the U.S. Supreme Court withdrew Clinton's right to appear before it. He had been accorded the privilege in 1977 but never exercised it.

Courts also seek to convey their strong disapproval of attorney tactics that have in recent times made the profession the object of public scorn and ridicule. The New Hampshire Supreme Court noted, for instance, that "since no single transgression reflects more negatively on the legal profession than a lie, it is the responsibility of every attorney at all times to be truthful." Lying was one of the reasons that the Minnesota Supreme Court upheld the suspension of the license of Marion Haugen to practice law. The final straw was Haugen's failure on two occasions to pay court reporter fees, but earlier he had been found to have submitted an answer in a personal injury action denying factual allegations in the pleading on behalf of a client "when he knew the answer to be false." Haugen also was accused of publishing misleading advertising and mishandling and failing to keep adequate records of trust funds. The court decided that it was "highly probable that future violations will occur," but it allowed that although the suspension was for an indefinite period, Haugen could apply for reinstatement in twelve months' time.

A South Dakota case illustrates that the Rules may trump substantive criminal law, as the state courts concluded that what two attorneys had done may (or may not) have been a crime, but assuredly was unethical. The Arctic Cat sales company had withdrawn its franchise from Elliott Power Sports and awarded it to another business. Arctic, being sued by Elliott, hired a retired FBI agent to secrete a recording device and visit Elliott, posing as a customer. He was to try to obtain evidence from employees that the company was not satisfactorily pushing the Arctic product. The district court judge refused to admit at trial the recorded evidence and any other information that had been gathered as a product of the taped interviews. He accused the defendant's attorneys of engaging in "deceit and dishonesty" in violation of Section (c) of Rule 8.4 and suggested that the bar association might consider taking action against them.

Both defense and prosecuting attorneys become indoctrinated in an ethic that focuses on winning rather than on serving the cause of justice. At times, prosecutors will conclude that a defendant is obviously guilty even though they are unable to legitimately persuade a jury to endorse a criminal conviction. So they hide evidence, stretch the truth, and engage in other tricks of the trade, such as suggestive but misleading cross-examinations to see that their sense of the defendant's guilt is validated by a conviction. A well-known New York University law professor noted that by training and experience trial lawyers come to believe that if they can convince a jury or a judge that a fact is true, they themselves come to believe it is true—even if it is false.

Defense attorneys have their own ruses. Overwhelmingly, they are defending persons who are guilty as charged, but the ethics of the profession demand that they use whatever legitimate approaches they can conceive of to try to secure an acquittal. Ethics dilemmas arise when a defense attorney induces a client to plead guilty when he or she knows that there is a decent chance of convincing a jury that the person is innocent, but that the process will be expensive and time-consuming and the outcome somewhat uncertain. There is also a gray area in which clever defense attorneys secure the freedom of their client, as in the O. J. Simpson double-murder case, even though on the face of it the evidence of guilt is overwhelming. That dilemma can turn into tragedy if the person set free were to murder again.

The role played by defense lawyers in major white-collar crime cases raises a number of questions about fairness and the accuracy of the maxim that all of us are entitled to "equal justice under law." White-collar defense lawyers typically are trained at prestige law schools, such as Harvard, Yale, Michigan, and Duke, and then work for three to six years in U.S. Attorneys' offices, preferably in New York. After that they trade their experience for extremely high salaries in top-level Manhattan law firms. The fees they command defending corporate executives typically are paid by the companies themselves, so that shareholders bear the burden of the defense of persons who often have engaged in crooked practices.

White-collar defense attorneys, as Kenneth Mann discovered in interviews, almost invariably assume that their client is guilty and that their task is to get him or her the best deal possible. "Above all," Man writes, "the central theme of the white-collar defense work is to keep potential evidence out of government reach by controlling access to information." Mann adds: "For the defense attorney, winning almost always entails helping the client to conceal facts." He also indicates a common tactic and its implications:

> The attorney accepts that there are certain things he cannot and should not do—such as tell a client to alter his story—but if he explains to a client the legal significance of a particular story, manifestly a legitimate form of counsel, it is permissible, even if he could foresee that given the particular client the explanation may result in client improprieties.

Often white-collar defense attorneys negotiate with prosecutors who once worked with or for them, and their usual ploy is to make what is called a proffer, an offer to plead guilty, to implicate bigger fish or more extensive networks, in return for an indulgent sentence. As we have seen, Ivan Boesky's three-year prison term seems quite mild compared to the harm he had inflicted on the financial system.

The behavior of attorneys Melvyn Weiss and William Lerach provides a striking example of professional white-collar crime, of attorneys turned rotten. During 30 years working at the New York-based law firm of Milberg Weiss, a firm founded in 1965 that had grown to include some 200 attorneys, Lerach and Weiss became the most feared tort lawyers in the country. They would file class action suits against companies that would settle for very large sums rather than face the prospect of the negative publicity associated with a public trial and the possibility of even larger awards mandated by an uncertain jury decision. In 2008, Weiss and Lerach became the national symbol of the corruption and greed that underlay their work when they pled guilty to charges of operating a long-running succession of scams. They would scrutinize stock prices, looking for one that had plunged. Then they would locate an earlier optimistic statement from a company executive, find an inside trade or two, recruit shareholder plaintiffs, and claim investor fraud. They would hold out to the company the prospect of bankruptcy unless it settled for a hefty sum, most of which went to their law firm. The difficulty involved in locating plaintiffs was solved when a man volunteered—for a fee—to buy stock in target companies and act as plaintiff, an illegal arrangement. The man was a plaintiff in more than 70 cases. He had his kickback camouflaged by having it paid out by a law firm

DID YOU KNOW?

Portraying Lawyers in Motion Pictures

Law professor Patrick Schultz of Notre Dame University in an article with the catchy title of "On Being a Happy, Healthy, and Ethical Member of an Unhappy, Unhealthy, and Unethical Profession" in the May 1994 issue of the *Vanderbilt Law Review* notes that law school courses on legal ethics are among the least popular offerings in the curriculum, sometimes disliked even more than the arcane intricacies taught in classes on taxation. Schultz also observes that recent motion pictures have been providing portraits of unethical lawyers. The film title *The Rainmaker* refers to the term used to describe a grungy process of finding new clients and is based on a best-selling novel by John Grisham. Matt Damon plays the attorney who hunts in the local hospitals for potential clients who can press insurance claims, and Danny DeVito is a paralegal who has failed the bar exam six times. On orders from the boss of the law firm, he operates the same kinds of shady recruitment tactics, also called ambulance chasing. Bill Murray destroying evidence in *Wild Things*, and Al Pacino destroying evidence in *Devil's Advocate* offer other examples of unflattering movie portrayals of a profession that is said to have the highest rate of unhappy practitioners among equivalent kinds of occupations.

cooperating with Milberg Weiss. All told, Milberg Weiss paid some $11.4 million in illegal kickbacks to persons to act as plaintiffs in 180 cases over 25 years.

Weiss received a 30-month prison sentence and had to pay $10 million in restitution. Lerach received a two-year sentence, a fine of $250,00, and the requirement that he perform 1,000 hours of community service. Milberg Weiss was not charged but agreed to pay $75 million in restitution. Thereafter it changed its name to only Miliberg, and saw more than half of its staff attorneys resign.

Astute lawyers also lobby strenuously to try to influence the law in ways that protect the companies for which they work from effective government oversight. The Sarbanes-Oxley Act sought to curb corporate excess and attorney's evasive tactics in the wake of a series of major scandals (see chapter 10). The act at first ordered the SEC to adopt a rule requiring lawyers who become aware that the company that employed them was breaking the law to notify the SEC of that situation. Corporate lawyers protested vociferously and got the government to back down. The original rule offered a simple definition of the information that a lawyer would be obligated to report. "Evidence of a material violation," it read, means "information that would lead an attorney reasonably to believe that a material violation has occurred, is occurring, or is about to occur." That was too straightforward for the legal lobby. Under pressure, it was altered to read: "Evidence of a material violation means credible evidence, based upon which it would be unreasonable, under the circumstances, for a prudent and competent attorney not to conclude that it is reasonably likely that a material violation has occurred, is occurring, or is about to occur." The change now means that an attorney who reasonably believes his client is a crook can keep quiet so long as he can show that it would not be unreasonable for another attorney to have doubts about this. The double negative in the revision makes its interpretation complicated and seriously undermines the cleansing effect of the original idea.

FURTHER READINGS

American Bar Association. (2007). *Model Rules of Professional Conduct, Including Preamble, Scope and Comment.* Chicago, IL: American Bar Association.

Cohen, George M., and Susan P. Koniak. (Eds.) (2004). *Foundations of the Law and Ethics of Lawyering.* New York: Foundation Press.

Dillon, Patrick, and Carl M. Cannon. (2009). *Circle of Greed: The Spectacular Rise and Fall of the Lawyers Who Brought Corporate America to Its Knees*. New York: Broadway Books.

Hazard, Geoffrey C., Jr., Susan P. Koniak, Roger C. Cramton, and George M. Cohen. (2003). *The Law and Ethics of Lawyering* (4th ed.). New York: Foundation Press.

Mann, Kenneth. (1985). *Defending White-Collar Crime: A Portrait of Attorneys at Work*. New Haven, CT: Yale University Press.

Corrupt Politicians and Other Criminal Officials

- *Document:* Sir Joseph Rotblat (1908–2005), a Polish-born physicist who worked on the Manhattan project in New Mexico that led to the creation of the atomic bomb, lived his professional life in England. His vigorous efforts to call attention to the danger of nuclear weaponry led to his being awarded the Nobel Peace Prize. Rotblat founded the Pugwash Conference on Science and World Affairs, an annual gathering of leading physical scientists. At one meeting he introduced the conference's theme that year by noting a number of biting comments that characterized public opinion about the integrity of political figures.
- *Date:* 1992.
- *Where:* Fifty-second annual meeting of the Pugwash conference in Halifax, Nova Scotia, Canada.
- *Significance:* These brief remarks reflect the generally critical attitudes that people hold in regard to the integrity of their elected and appointed representatives.

DOCUMENT 8.4

Pundits on Politicians

It is a very sad reflection on the reputation of politicians in the Western World that the title of this session "Ethics and Politics" is perceived as an oxymoron, a figure of speech, which links two contradictory concepts. . . . Politicians are generally considered to be the least trustworthy professionals. This is a long—and widely—held view expressed in many aphorisms.

Jonathan Swift, the author of Gulliver's Travels, said: "Politicks, as the Word is commonly understood, are nothing but Corruption."

George Orwell said: "Political language . . . is designed to make lies sound truthful and murder respectable, and to give an appearance of solidity to pure wind."

The American essayist, H. L. Mencken said: "If experience teaches us anything at all, it teaches us that a good politician, under democracy, is quite as unthinkable as an honest burglar."

Source: Joseph Rotblat, "Ethics and Politics," 1992. http://britishpugwash.org/documents/EthicsandPolitics.pdf.

ANALYSIS

Money and politics go together like the proverbial horse and carriage. As the song goes, "You can't have one without the other." Two fundamental considerations are involved. For virtually all politicians except those who age out, are fed up, or find more lucrative pastures in which to graze, the single most prominent concern is to get elected and then to get reelected. And to get elected and reelected requires money: money to hire staff, pay for telephones and office equipment, travel continuously in the preelection period, and book television time, buy newspaper advertising, and mount billboards and posters.

The money that flows into the coffers of a politician very often carries a quid pro quo element: we've done this for you; now what are you going to do for us? Relatively few donors donate money for altruistic reasons; more usually, they anticipate that the person they support will push or favor measures that are financially beneficial to them—tax cuts, subsidies, deregulation, or similar advantages—and will oppose measures that the donors object to, either on ideological grounds or because they cut into their profits. In these regards, campaign contributions do not differ dramatically from the criminal offense of bribery, except that those who decide what constitutes bribery are the same persons who rely upon campaign contributions.

The payment of money or the provision of other perks, such as free travel, stock tips, and speaking honoraria, reasonably can be viewed as legal bribery. Criminal bribery occurs when under-the-table payments are made to covertly buy specific endeavors by persons holding a political office. Extortion is the other side of the coin. It signifies the use of pressure, often in the form of threats, to be carried out if the person being threatened does not do specified things.

In the political realm the most common form of bribery involves a corporation rewarding a political figure for his or her cooperation. While both parties are equally culpable, research indicates that almost invariably it is the person who accepts the bribe who is regarded as having committed the more serious wrongdoing. Presumably, the public presumes that the offer of the bribe is a somewhat reasonable attempt to advance whatever cause is involved, while the acceptance of the bribe is a betrayal of the trust bestowed upon a person elected or appointed to a political position. This discrepancy exists despite the opinion of writers such as John Flynn who insisted: "The average politician is the merest amateur in the gentle art of graft, as opposed to his brother in business."

It would take endless pages to provide a roster of political corruption in any given decade. Two recent cases are illustrative of the behavior. Representative James A.

Trafficant Jr. of Ohio accepted money, equipment for his farm, and other material expressions of gratitude for doing favors for corporate executives. He became only the second member of Congress since the Civil War to be expelled by a vote of his colleagues. Virtually all others resign before they have to be voted out. Randy Cunningham of San Diego, California, had gone that route, resigning from the House of Representatives in 2005 after pleading guilty to tax evasions, conspiracy to commit bribery, and mail and wire fraud for having accepted several million dollars in bribes. The charge of conspiracy illustrates that it often is much easier to convict a malefactor for planning to do something illegal—others can be found to testify to their involvement—than it is to prove that the deed was done.

Eighty-four of the 1,000 people studied by a research team at the Yale Law School in a comprehensive inquiry into varieties of what were defined as white-collar crimes had been charged with bribery. The cases all involved offenses against federal law. In most instances, the person arrested had offered a bribe, and in 4 of 10 cases it was not taken. Most instances involved attempts to have rules waived or changed; and in 10 the bribes were offered to a certified public accountant or an Internal Revenue Service agent.

The Old Testament mentions bribery several times. Exodus 23:8 commands "Do not take bribes for bribes blind the clear-sighted and upset the peace of the just." This warning is repeated in Leviticus 16:19, where it is directed specifically to officials and judges.

In England, a parliamentary inquiry in the early eighteenth century into the machinations involved in what was known as the South Sea Bubble case found that about 50 members of the two legislative houses—Lords and Commons—had been bribed to support the company, which had made what was one of the earliest offerings of stock shaeres to the public. A major discovery was that there was no law that would allow criminal proceedings to be launched against the malefactors. A parliamentarian who had lost a considerable sum when the bubble burst plunged into the legal gap, unsuccessfully as it turned out, by arguing that the company directors should be charged with parricide, since they had strangled the country, the father of all English citizens. If found guilty, he declared, they should receive the penalty decreed in ancient Rome for that offense by being sewn into sacks with a monkey and a snake and cast into the river.

Bribery and treason are the only offenses specified by name in the U.S. Constitution. In federal law, bribery is codified as "corruptly attempting to influence a public official in the performance of official acts through the giving of valuable considerations. It is barter for an official act or omission to be taken other than on its merits." Extortion in American law is a considerably more complex doctrine than bribery, and has no precise statutory definition. One writer has made a stab at pinning the term down. James Lindgren writes: "Broadly speaking, coercive extortion [the form almost invariably charged] can refer to any illegal use of threat or fear to obtain property or advantages from another, short of violence, that would be robbery."

Typically, the more important and/or powerful an official, the more money it will require to have him or her do what you want. In some places in some times, contesting parties would both bribe the judge, who then had to determine which was the better deal. The hierarchy of bribery payouts is noted by Liz Smith, a celebrity gossip columnist, who earlier had worked as a gofer for a television producer:

> I hated our show and begged to be given the job nobody wanted, going out on the street "shaking hands" with the cops. ("Shaking hands" is a euphemism for paying off he police for looking the other way . . . to not move our trucks, not to harass our crews and cameramen). I'd step up to each policeman, shake hands and give him $20. When the big brass with gold braid on their hats and shoulders showed up, I shook hands holding $50 bills. I would be out on the streets with thousands in cash.

The ambiguity in determining what is a corrupt and illegal act of bribery and a reciprocal return of a favor can be seen in the fact that slipping money to a headwaiter to get a desired table is considered legitimate, but slipping money to a legislator to get a favorable vote is not. In his comprehensive study of bribery, John Noonan, now a federal judge, challenges his readers by asking whether "prayer and sacrifice to God are different from bribes."

DID YOU KNOW?

Shakespeare on Bribery

One of the better known references to bribery is found in William Shakespeare's *The Tragedy of Julius Caesar* when Brutus confronts Cassius with an accusation:

> "Let me tell you, Cassius," Brutus declares, "you yourself Are much condemn'd to have an itching palm. To select and mart [sell] your offices for gold To unde-servers."

Gaius Cassius Longinus, a Roman senator, was the instigator of the plot to kill Caesar on the fatal Ideas of March— March 15, 44 BCE. Brutus (his full name was Marcus Junius Brutus) was also a senator, and he allegedly turned against Caesar because he believed that Caesar was power-hungry and a threat to the state when Caesar declared himself emperor for life. The term "itching palm" is said to derive from the belief of the ancients Saxons that the way to cure a skin disease was to rub silver over it.

FURTHER READINGS

Bull, Martin J., and James Newell. (2003). *Corruption in Contemporary Politics*. New York: Palgrave Macmillan.

Carswell, John C. (1960). *The South Sea Bubble*. Stanford, CA: Stanford University Press.

Harris, Robert. (2003). *Political Corruption in and Beyond the States*. New York: Routledge.

Heidenheimer, Arnold J., and Michael Johnston. (2002). *Political Corruption: Concepts and Context*. New Brunswick, NJ: Transaction.

Huffington, Arianna S. (2003). *Pigs at the Trough: How Corporate Greed and Political Corruption Are Undermining America*. New York: Crown.

Kaiser, Robert G. (2009). *So Damn Much Money: The Triumph of Lobbying and the Corruption of American Government*. New York: Crown.

Noonan, John T., Jr. (1984). *Bribes*. Berkeley: University of California Press.

Williams, Robert. (2006). *Party Finance and Political Corruption*. New York: St. Martin's.

Corruption on the International Scene

- *Document:* The Corruption Perceptions Index (CPI) is an annual rating of what now are 180 countries in regard to the perceived level of corruption prevailing in each. The CPI describes itself as a "survey of surveys," indicating that it is based on a composite of information gathered from experts and businesspeople within the country and abroad. The results, the CPI analysts state, "show how one country compares to others included in the index" and is based on as many as thirteen different surveys of opinions regarding corruption levels. The document lists the top 30 and the bottom 35 among the 180 sites surveyed.
- *Date:* 2009.
- *Where:* Transparency International, which constructs the index, is based in Berlin, Germany.
- *Significance:* The CPI provides countries with a standard by which they can determine their progress or regress in controlling corruption and can see how they rate in comparison with nearby and the world's nations. Its public proclamation can prod countries with poor records to strive harder and can support public calls for aggressive reforms.

DOCUMENT 8.5

Rank	Country/Territory	Score
1	New Zealand	9.4
2	Denmark	9.3
3	Singapore	9.2
3	Sweden	9.2
5	Switzerland	9.0
6	Finland	8.9
6	Netherlands	8.9
8	Austria	8.7
8	Canada	8.7
8	Iceland	8.7
11	Norway	8.6
12	Hong Kong	8.2
12	Luxembourg	8.2
14	Germany	8.0
14	Ireland	8.0
16	Austria	7.9
17	Japan	7.7
17	United Kingdom	7.7
19	United States	7.5
20	Barbados	7.4
21	Belgium	7.1
22	Qatar	7.0
22	St. Lucia	7.0
24	France	6.9
25	Chile	6.7
25	Uruguay	6.7
27	Cyprus	6.6
27	Estonia	6.6
27	Slovenia	6.6
30	United Arab Emirates	6.5
146	Cameroon	2.2
146	Ecuador	2.2
146	Kenya	2.2
146	Russia	2.2
146	Sierra Leone	2.2
146	Timor-Leste	2.2
146	Ukraine	2.2
146	Zimbabwe	2.2
154	Côte d'Ivoire	2.1
154	Papua New Guinea	2.1

(Continued)

(Continued)

Rank	Country/Territory	Score
154	Paraguay	2.1
154	Yemen	2.1
158	Cambodia	2.0
158	Central Africa Republic	2.0
158	Laos	2.0
158	Tajikistan	2.0
162	Angola	1.9
162	Congo Brazzaville	1.9
162	Democratic Republic of Congo	1.9
162	Guinea-Bisseau	1.9
162	Kyrgyzstan	1.9
162	Venezuela	1.9
168	Burundi	1.8
168	Equatorial Guinea	1.8
168	Guinea	1.8
168	Haiti	1.8
168	Iran	1.8
168	Turkmenistan	1.8
174	Uzbekistan	1.7
175	Chad	1.6
176	Iraq	1.5
176	Sudan	1.5
178	Myanmar	1.4
178	Afghanistan	1.3
180	Somalia	1

Source: The Corruption Perceptions Index, Transparency International (Berlin, Germany, 2009).

ANALYSIS

Transparency International was founded in 1993 by Peter Eigen, a German lawyer, and now has some 100 branches throughout the world that monitor local instances of corruption, which is defined as "the abuse of entrusted power for private gain."

The 2009 tabulation indicates some rather rough geographic correlations. Most notable is the bunching of African nations on or near the bottom of the list as these countries continue to seek to carve out peaceable existences after having won the struggle to free themselves from colonial rule. The two countries in which

Somali pirates stand on the deck of the Ukrainian merchant vessel *NV Faina* in October 2008. Somalia was found to be the most corrupt country of the 180 countries surveyed by Transparency International and measured against the Corruption Perception Index in 2009. (AP/Wide World Photos)

Americans have been at wa—Afghanistan and Iraq—stand out as among the most corrupt places in the world. Afghanistan is 179th on the list and Iraq is tied at 178th.

Some conditions seem to contribute to the fact that New Zealand lands at the very top of the pyramid as the least corrupt nation in the world, and Somalia finds itself occupying the lowest rung at the bottom of the pack.

It is easy to describe conditions in New Zealand that appear to be tied to the low level of corruption, but it is more difficult to indicate with confidence how these conditions came about and in what combination they exist to produce such law-abiding results.

New Zealand is a relatively isolated nation with a population estimated to be 4.25 million. The country has long been known for benefits conferred by a compassionate welfare system that provides free care for victims of crime, accidents, disaster, and disease. Its reputation undoubtedly brings to its shores people attracted by that social climate who are unlikely to become involved in corrupt activities.

The country is relatively homogeneous and has stringent requirements for those seeking permanent entry. New Zealand has no contiguous border with another country; its nearest neighbor, Australia, is 1,200 miles away, a geographical reality that makes hiding or fleeing after committing a street crime difficult and may inhibit white-collar offenses. This is not to say that such offenses never occur. In the early 2000s, for instance, Taito Philip Field, a onetime member of parliament, was found guilty after a 14-week trial of easing the immigration requirements for Thais and as payment having them work for free on his property. He received a six-year sentence, four for corruption and two for obstruction of justice.

DID YOU KNOW?

Corruption in India

India stands near the middle of the roster on the Corruption Index, but it has a reputation in the Western world of being more corrupt than it actually is, perhaps because the language is English and there is a large resident population of British and Americans to report on their experiences with itching palms.

We get a very good flavor of corruption in India from some of the classic fiction writers who have depicted life on the subcontinent. Rudyard Kipling, for instance, in *Kim*, tells the story of a young man born in India to an aristocratic English couple, who is raised by an Indian ayah after his parents die, is educated in an English military academy, and returns to India as an Army officer. Corruption figures in a vignette in which Kim purchases a train ticket for a lama he has befriended:

> Kim asked and paid for a ticket to Umballa. A sleepy clerk grunted and flung out a ticket to the next station, just six miles distant.
>
> "Nay," said Kim, scanning it with a grin. "This may serve for farmers, but I live in the city of Lahore. It was cleverly done, Babu. Now give me the ticket to Umballa.
>
> The clerk snorted and dealt the proper ticket.

A lengthy episode in *A Fine Balance*, a novel by the Parsi author Rohinton Mistry, portrays a commonplace incident of police corruption. It involves a collision between a bicycle and a luxury car:

> The chauffeur . . . emerged boldly from the car . . . "You have eyes or marbles?" he screams. "Can't you see where you're going? Causing trouble to other people's property!"
>
> A policeman arrives. A man . . . in the back of the car fished out his wallet. He paid the policeman some money, then beckoned the chauffeur to the window. The chauffeur put something in Om's [the bicyclist] hand.
>
> Om looked down at what was in his shaking hand. Fifty rupees.

The same author notes how a pharmacist resolved matters after he had made a fatal error in filling a prescription. When the police came to investigate, they and the manager discussed the situation. "Manager offered money, police took money, and everybody was happy." The last line seems a bit odd. We can presume that not everybody was happy: very likely the family and friends of the deceased were not joyous.

The Police Act of 1886 provided for New Zealand's first national police force, but it is notable that in 1968 the Police Act mandated that the word "force" be eliminated from the agency's name, that it thereafter be known as the New Zealand Police. There are 400 community police stations located throughout the rather small country. As a local commentator points out, a person trying to bribe a police officer (see Sidebar 8.4) would be arrested on the spot. "Everybody knows this," he writes, "which is why nobody tries to." The same writer observes that the judiciary is "fiercely independent."

An economic report notes that the New Zealand government is renowned for its efforts to create transparent and competitive procurement policies. The lesson is that the country's leaders make strenuous efforts to treat people with exceptional decency, and in return they get decent behavior from the people.

Interpreting the world-leading level of corruption in Somalia, which borders on the Indian Ocean and the Gulf of Aden, usually begins with an inventory of the absence of forces that might control corruption: a strong government, a free press, a peaceful population, and similar barriers to rampant wrongdoing. Somalia has none of these, but does have a roster of other elements of disarray. It is a conflict-ridden, war-torn country, ruled by clans that plunder the people and each other. Clans, warlords, merchants, and religious groups each mount their own militia forces. Iran and expatriate Somalis pour money into the country to support insurgency and unrest. Somalia has gained international notoriety for acts of maritime piracy. These began when foreign vessels intruded on waters essential for the livelihood of Somalia's fishermen and continued when the ransoms demanded for the release of ships and their crews became an attractive source of national income. Only the sparse African Union troops offer some semblance of oversight in Somalia. A newspaper story opened with a sentence that encapsulated the sorry condition of Somalia and that feeds into its dismal rating on the CPI corruption scale. It read: "Somalia has been named as the world's most corrupt country as war-torn nations proved once again that conflict provides for all manner of dishonest dealings."

FURTHER READINGS

Little, Walter, and Eduardo Posada Carbó. (1992). *Political Corruption in Europe and Latin America*. New York: St. Martin's.

Morris, Stephen D. (2009). *Political Corruption in Mexico: The Impact of Democratization*. Boulder, CO: Rienner.

Manion, Melanie K. (2004). *Corruption by Design: Building Clean Government in Mainland China and Hong Kong*. Cambridge, MA: Harvard University Press.

Williams, Robert. (1987). *Political Corruption in Africa*. Brookfield, VT: Gower.

9

ENVIRONMENTAL AND CONSUMER CRIMES

INTRODUCTION

The use of the criminal law to protect people from the ravages of contaminated air, unhealthy drinking water, toxic fumes, greenhouse gases, building materials containing asbestos, dangerous chemical waste inadequately stored, atomic fallout, and any number of other perils is in most regards a relatively new phenomenon. In earlier times, life-threatening conditions that we see today did not exist: there were no automobiles to spew carbon dioxide into the atmosphere and no pollutants from factories to feed into rivers and streams, killing fish and eating into the well-being of people who unknowingly drank the tainted water. Technology brought dramatic improvements—not insignificantly, the extension of the human life span produced by advances in medicine. But the new technology also introduced hazards unimaginable in earlier centuries.

Issues of white-collar and corporate crime play an important part in attempts to deal with environment threats in cases where the danger resulting from uncontrolled business or other entrepreneurial activities poses a serious and at times dramatic threat to the population. It is a truism that it often takes a catastrophe to move legislators to penalize the kinds of conditions—such as the marketing of poisonous food products—that led in 1916 to enactment of the Pure Food and Drug Act.

Today, evidence has been accumulating regarding the laxity, incompetence, and corruption associated with many government regulatory agencies. Typical is the observation of a *New Yorker* writer that the now-defunct Minerals Management Service, the agency that was in charge of offshore drilling, during the past decade had let oil companies short-change the government on leases and get away with inadequate safety plans. The writer notes that when President Franklin Roosevelt installed Joseph P. Kennedy, the father of the future president, as head of the SEC, he did so with the observation that you had to "set a thief to catch a thief." The situation today at times seems to be worse like setting a thief to help other thieves get their way.

Noteworthy is the fact that the Food and Drug Administration (FDA), said to be one of the few consistently efficient regulatory groups, has leaders and staff that pride themselves on their record and, as political scientist Daniel Carpenter notes in his comprehensive study *Reputation and Power*, the respect the FDA engenders has led the industries it monitors to attend respectfully and carefully to its requirements.

Disagreement continues to mark responses to many environmental hazards, and disputes arise over whether the benefits of certain arrangements outweigh the risks they pose. A key concern is whether extremely tough enforcement polices cause companies to try very hard to hide their violations, thereby often increasing the hazards, or whether more lenient enforcement encourages companies to believe that they can readily get away with lawbreaking behaviors. The usual compromise answer is that one policy is appropriate for some companies and the other for other companies; the difficulty is to determine which companies are best monitored by which approach—and to do so before a catastrophe occurs, not afterward.

This chapter considers some of the major issues in the area of environment crime, beginning with the Love Canal disaster and the *Exxon Valdez* oil spill in Alaskan waters, the latter the precursor of the much more devastating 2010 BP Deepwater Horizon oil rig explosion in the Gulf of Mexico. However catastrophic—besides the torrent of oil released into the Gulf waters, 11 persons were killed when the rig blew up—and whatever might have been the level of negligence no criminal charges were brought. Thereafter we consider the Clean Water Act, the Resource Conservation and Recovery Act, and the Clean Air Act. The chapter concludes with a discussion of the McNeil Consumer Healthcare recall of drugs for children, such as Tylenol, in which the FDA reported that it gave serious consideration to lodging criminal charges.

The Unlovely Story of Love Canal

- **Document:** Report by the New York State Commissioner of Health to the governor in regard to Love Canal.
- **Date:** September 1978.
- **Where:** Albany, New York.
- **Significance:** The report of the investigation of the Love Canal tragedy by the New York State Department of Health provides details on the conditions that had undermined the health and reproductive outcomes of so many families living atop the waste deposited in the ground by the Hooker Chemical and Plastic Company. The Love Canal horrors were instrumental in the subsequent enactment by Congress of the measure that created a billion-dollar Superfund to clean up similar situations.

DOCUMENT 9.1

LOVE CANAL—PUBLIC HEALTH TIME BOMB

To Governor Hugh L. Carey and Members of the New York State Legislature

In accordance with Chapter 487 of the New York State Law of 1978, I hereby submit to you a Special Report on the Love Canal crisis.

The profound and devastating effects of the Love Canal tragedy, in terms of human health and suffering and environmental damage, cannot and probably will never be fully measured.

The lessons we are learning from this modern-day disaster should serve as a warning for governments at all levels and for private industry to take steps to avoid repetition of these tragic events. They must also serve as a reminder to be ever watchful for the tell-tale signs of potential disasters and to look beyond our daily endeavors and to plan for the well-being of future generations.

We must improve our technological capability, supplant ignorance with knowledge and be ever vigilant for those seemingly innocuous situations which may portend the beginning of an environment nightmare.

The issues confronting our citizens and their elected and appointed leaders in the Love Canal situation are unprecedented in the State's health annals. We can be proud of the swift and compassionate response to the crisis by our leaders and the agencies they direct in easing the plight of those of those affected and removing the hazards to their health and safety . . .

We cannot undo the damage that has been wrought at Love Canal but we can take appropriate preventive measures, so that we are better able to anticipate and hopefully prevent future events of this kind. . . .

Robert P. Whalen, M.D.
Commissioner of Public Health . . .

Love Canal: A Brief History . . .

There was a partially dug section of canal in the southeast corner of Niagara Falls. For several decades of the Twentieth Century, this portion of the canal reportedly served as a swimming hole for the children living in the La Salle section of the city.

But in the 1920's the excavation was turned to a new and ominous use. It became a chemical and municipal dumping site for several chemical companies and the city of Niagara Falls. Chemicals of unknown kind and quantity were buried at the site for a 25-year period, up until 1953. After 1953, the site was covered with earth.

In the late 1950s homebuilding began directly adjacent to the Love Canal landfill. Over a period of time about 100 homes were built and an elementary school was opened.

And Then the Rains Came . . .

Today . . . this 16-acre rectangular piece of land, located only a few miles from the world famous waterfall which each year attracts thousands to the honeymoon mecca of Niagara Falls, has . . . become the focus of international attention . . .

[T]he center of attention is an ominous array of chemicals buried within the boundaries of the unfinished canal for more than 25 years—toxic ingredients which are infiltrating scores of nearby homes, posing a serious threat to human health and upsetting the domestic tranquility of hundreds of families living in this middle-class community.

The Love Canal problem began to surface in recent years as chemical odors in the basements bordering the sites became more noticeable. This followed prolonged heavy rains and one of the worst blizzards ever to hit this section of the country.

Thus began a series of events and momentous decisions involving city, country, State and Federal governments to cope with what can only be described as a major human and environmental tragedy without precedent and unparalleled in New York State's history . . .

Environmental Sampling

As data flowed in, it became evident that unacceptable levels of toxic vapors associated with more than 80 compounds were emanating from the basements of many homes in the first ring directly adjacent to the Love Canal. Ten of the most prevalent and most toxic compounds—including benzene, a known human carcinogen—were selected for evaluation purposes . . .

Findings of Fact . . .

1. A slight increase in risk for spontaneous abortion was found among all residents of the Canal, with the overall estimated risk 15 times greater than that expected.
2. A significant excess of spontaneous abortions was localized among residents of 99th Street South.
3. The miscarriage experience in the 90th Street North and South sections approximated that which could be expected.
4. A significant excess of spontaneous abortions occurred during the summer months of June through August.
5. Congenital malformations were found among 5 children of adults presently residing on the Love Canal . . .

Conclusion

A review of all of the available evidence respecting the Love Canal Waste Landfill site has convinced me of the existence of a great and imminent peril to the health of the general public residing near the said site as a result of exposure to toxic substances emanating from such site and, pursuit to the authority conferred upon me by Public Health Law 1388, enacted by Chapter 487 of the laws of 1978, the existence of an emergency should be declared by me.

Source: Robert P. Whalen, "Love Canal—Public Health Time Bomb: A Special Report to the Governor and Legislature," Albany, New York, September, 1978.

ANALYSIS

Writing in the *EPA Journal*, the news outlet for the federal Environmental Protection Agency, Eckardt C. Bock observed: "Quite simply, Love Canal is one of the most appalling tragedies in American history." "But that's not the most disturbing fact," he added. "What is worse is that it cannot be regarded as an isolated event. It can happen again—anywhere—unless we move expeditiously to prevent it."

The extensive report of the Health Commissioner at best merely glances over the forces that produced the tragedy at Love Canal. Those who dumped the very dangerous chemicals into the pit apparently were well aware of the possible terrible consequences of what they had done.

The back story of the Love Canal tragedy starts with William T. Love, who in 1890 sought to build a utopian community on the site, a development that he hoped would in time house a million people and draw power from the nearby thundering Niagara Falls. When the plan fell apart because of financial problems, the City of Niagara Falls purchased the site and in time began to use the deep pit that had been dug as part of the canal design as a dumping ground, The Hooker Chemical and Plastic Company then bought the property and placed its chemical waste into the pit. By 1950, Hooker had buried nearly 20,000 tons of waste in the site. When it was filled, it was sealed with what were assumed to be impermeable clay linings and a topping of dirt. Hooker then sold the site to the city for $1. Evidence that it may have been aware of possible dangers can be inferred from the fact that the sale contract included a disclaimer exempting Hooker from liability for any side effects from chemical exposure.

Homes were built atop the pit, and in 1955 the city Board of Education constructed the 99th Street public school on the site. As Document 9.1 indicates, heavy rains and a record-breaking blizzard caused the chemicals to rise to the surface. Eventually, more than 1,500 families living in the contaminated area were relocated with the aid of state funds.

Despite the sale contract clause, Occidental Chemical Company, which had taken over Hooker, reached an agreement with New York State authorities over the cost for the cleanup of the Love Canal area. Occidental agreed to pay $98 million as reimbursement for state expenses.

Particularly significant was the impetus provided by the Love Canal tragedy for the passage of the Comprehensive Environmental Response, Compensation and Liability Act that mandated the creation of a Superfund with a $1 billion budget to locate and repair the damage created by hazardous waste conditions similar to those at Love Canal. Among the criminal offenses specified in the act were failure to notify the Environmental Protection Agency (EPA) of hazardous waste release and falsifying records related to such events. Whistle-blowers who provide information on secret hazardous waste disposal can qualify for a monetary reward under the bill's provisions.

The Superfund was to be financed by funds from offending companies, but in 2003, with the original funds now expended, Congress exempted the companies from footing the Superfund cleanup bill for waste havoc they may have created.

DID YOU KNOW?

Love Canal 30 Years Later

Lois Kenney, a Love Canal survivor, lost both her son and her husband to health problems that she is convinced were the result of chemicals that leaked into their backyard in their Love Canal neighborhood. Thirty years later, she has a vivid and disturbing memory of that period.

Lois Gills, also a Love Canal survivor and now executive director of the Center for Health, Environment and Justice, points out: "When you move away from a site, it's not over," she says, "because you're carrying the chemicals in your body and they're affecting generation after generation and that's pretty scary when you think about it." Gibbs would like the government to contact all of the youngsters who lived at the toxic dump to alert them to the continuing health dangers they may face. "We know the young men and women from Love Canal have two times higher a risk of having a birth-defective child and they're not telling them."

Source: Richard Clapp (2009). "The Love Canal Story is not Finished," *Environment Health Perpectives* 117: A5–54.

FURTHER READINGS

Barnett, Harold C. (1994). *Toxic Debts and the Superfund Dilemma*. Chapel Hill: University of North Carolina Press.

Blum, Elizabeth D. (2008). *Love Canal Revisited: Race, Class and Gender in Environmental Activism*. Lawrence: University of Kansas Press.

Clark, Karen K. (2011). Environmental Crime. In David Shichor, Larry Gaines, and Andrea Schoerfer (Eds.), *Reflections on White-Collar and Corporate Crime: Discerning Readings* (342–358). Long Grove, IL: Waveland Press.

Culllen, Craig E., and Peter N. Skinner. (1996). *The Road to Love Canal: Managing Industrial Waste before EPA*. Austin: University of Texas Press.

Gibbs, Lois Mary, and Murray Levine. (1982). *Love Canal: My Story*. Albany: State University of New York Press.

Levine, Adeline Gordon. (1982). *Love Canal: Science, Politics, and People*. Lexington, MA: Lexington Press.

Mazur, Allan. (1998). *A Hazardous Inquiry: The Rashomon Effect at Love Canal*. Cambridge, MA: Harvard University Press.

The *Exxon Valdez* Oil Spill

- *Document:* The *Exxon Valdez* Oil Spill Trust Council is made up of six members, three appointed by the Alaska state government and three by the federal government. The Council's task has been to coordinate and oversee the handling of efforts to deal with the consequences of the oil spill. Document 9.2 is a release for public consumption by the Council to inform people about elements of the disaster and some of the work that had been and is being done to remedy the situation.
- *Date:* 2001.
- *Where:* *Exxon Valdez* Oil Spill Trust Council Headquarters, Anchorage, Alaska.
- *Significance:* The document offers an official response to many of the basic questions about the *Exxon Valdez* oil spill.

DOCUMENT 9.2

Questions and Answers...

How did the accident happen?

The National Transportation Safety Board investigated the accident and determined that the probable causes of the grounding were:

1. The failure of the third mate to properly maneuver the vessel, probably due to fatigue and excessive workload.
2. The failure of the master to provide a proper navigational watch, probably due to impairment from alcohol.

The *Exxon Valdez* is seen in Prince William Sound after running aground on Bligh Reef on March 24, 1989. The ship spilled 11 million gallons of crude oil into the ocean. (U.S. Coast Guard)

3. The failure of the Exxon Shipping Company to supervise the master and provide a rested and sufficient crew for the *Exxon Valdez*.
4. The failure of the U.S. Coast Guard to provide an effective traffic system.
5. The lack of effective pilot and escort services.

Okay. But What Actually Happened?

The *Exxon Valdez* departed from the Trans Alaska Pipeline terminal [in the town of Valdez in Alaska and bound for Long Beach, California] at 9:12 pm, March 23, 1989. William Murphy, an expert ship's pilot hired to maneuver the 986-foot vessel through the Valdez Narrows, was in control of the wheelhouse. At his side was the captain of the vessel, Joe Hazelwood. Helmsman Harry Clear was steering. After passing through Valdez Narrows, pilot Murphy left the vessel and Captain Hazelwood took over the wheelhouse. The *Exxon Valdez* encountered icebergs in the shipping lanes and Captain Hazelwood ordered Chase to take the *Exxon Valdez* out of the shipping lanes to go around the icebergs. He then handed over control of the wheelhouse to Third Mate Gregory Cousins with precise instructions to turn back into the shipping lane when the tanker reaches a certain point. At that time, Clear was replaced by Helmsman Robert Kagan. For reasons that remain unclear, Cousins and Kagan failed to make the turn back into the shipping lanes and the ship ran aground on Bligh Reef at 12:04 a.m. March 24, 1989 . . . Captain Hazelwood was in his quarters at the time.

Was the captain drunk?

The captain was seen in a local bar, admitted to have had some alcoholic drinks, and a blood test showed alcohol in his blood even several hours after the accident.

The captain has always insisted that he was not impaired by alcohol. The state charged him with operating a vessel while under the influence of alcohol. A jury in Alaska, however, found him NOT GUILTY. The jury did find him guilty of negligent discharge of oil, a misdemeanor. Hazelwood was fined $50,000 and sentenced to 1,000 hours of community service in Alaska. . . . He completed the community service ahead of schedule in 2001. He picked up trash along the Seward Highway and worked at Bean's Café, a "soup kitchen" for the homeless in Anchorage, Alaska . . .

How much oil was spilled?

Approximately 11 million gallons or 257,000 barrels. *Picture your swimming pool at your school or in your community. The amount of spilled oil is roughly equivalent to 125 olympic-sized swimming pools.*

How much oil was the Exxon Valdez carrying?

53,094,510 gallons . . .

How does oil harm birds and animals?

1. The oil gets on the fur and feathers and destroys the insulation value. Birds and mammals then die of hypothermia (they get too cold).
2. They eat the oil, either while trying to clean the oil off their fur or while scavenging on dead animals. The oil is poison that causes death.
3. The oil impacts them in ways that do not lead to quick death, such as damaging their liver or causing blindness. An impaired animal cannot compete for food and avoid predators. Oil also affects animals in non-lethal ways such as impairing reproducing.

Source: Questions and Answers, Alaska Oil Spill Trustee Council, 2001, http://www.evostc.state.ak.us/facts/qanda.cfm (accessed March 31, 2011).

ANALYSIS

The *Exxon Valdez*, as the document indicates, ran aground in Prince William Sound in southeastern Alaska after leaving the port town of Valdez, the northernmost site in Alaska with an ice-free port, and the southern terminus of the Alaska oil pipeline. The ship's hull was split, and oil poured out into some of the most ruggedly beautiful coves and fjords in the world. Not only were the beaches contaminated, thousands of birds were killed, including many bald eagles that became disoriented when they ingested oil as they fed. The bodies of more than 1,000 oilsoaked sea otters were recovered; many others just fell to the bottom of the sea. Fishermen also were unable to work because the polluted water killed fish they depended on for a living. A later study documented a decline in traditional social relationships among family members, friends, neighbors, and coworkers. The greater the loss from the disaster, the larger was the increase in problems such as drinking, drug use, and domestic violence, as well as medical conditions. Their work suggested, the study authors wrote, that the oil spill's impact on the psychological environment was as significant as its impact on the physical environment.

The *Exxon Valdez* disaster was by no means the first nor by far the most extensive oil spill from a tanker, but the fact that it occurred in an American territory marked by pristine natural conditions and at a time when citizens were becoming acutely aware of environmental dangers and degradation made the spill a cause of international concern. Among numerous other oil spills, there was the one from the *Torrey Canyon* in 1966 near the Scilly Isles off England with 119,000 tons spewing into the ocean, and the loss of about twice as much oil from the *Amoco Cadiz* in 1978 off the coast of France. In February 1977 the *Honolulu Patriot*, en route to Hawaii, caught fire and exploded, killing a crew member and dropping 18,000 tons of oil into the ocean.

Besides the punishments meted out to the ship's captain, the Exxon Corporation was hit with a civil judgment totaling more than $1.1 billion as well as a criminal fine of $12.5 million.

The disaster also was directly responsible for passage by Congress of the Oil Pollution Act of 1990. The act toughened the roster of white-collar crimes, increasing the maximum penalty for a failure to notify the appropriate federal agency of a discharge from $10,000 to $250,000 for an individual and $500,000 for an organization. The maximum prison term was raised from one year to five years.

More than two decades later, in the spring of 2010, a newspaper reporter found lingering remnants of the *Exxon Valdez* spill in Cordova, Alaska. Suicides and bankruptcies had surged after the disaster, the herring fishery was gone, as were Dungeness crabs, while prawns remained scarce. A local fisherman, Mike Webber, who also does wood carvings had constructed what he called a "shame pole" to protest against Exxon. The pole depicted dead eagles, herrings with lesions, and the head of an Exxon executive, upside down. Webber told the reporter that people were asking him to do a "healing pole" but that he "couldn't come up with any character for it."

The *Exxon Valdez* spill returned to the limelight with the 2010 explosion of an oil rig in the Gulf of

DID YOU KNOW?

Postmortem on the *Exxon Valdez*

The *Exxon Valdez* went into dry dock for repairs in San Diego where it had been built in 1986. The ship was banned by the U.S. Congress from ever again operating in Alaskan waters, a ban that in 1998 its owners sought unsuccessfully to overturn. It made 190 trips worldwide after its return to operation, carrying oil from the Middle East to Europe, and did so without further untoward incidents. Exxon removed the company name from all its ships after the Alaskan oil spill, and the *Exxon Valdez* became known as the *Sea River Mediterranean* or *S/S Mediterranean*, Sea River being an Exxon subsidiary. In 2005, the ship was sold to the Hong Kong Bloom Company, registered under the flag of Panama, renamed the *Dong Fong Ocean*, and refitted to carry ore rather than oil.

Captain Joseph Hazelwood's trash cleanup on the highway lasted but one day Locals and tourists had tied up traffic—as Hazelwood put it—"ogling me in an orange jumpsuit" picking up trash. He worked some as a teacher at a maritime academy and later served as an investigator and technical exert for a maritime law firm in New York. On the 20th anniversary of the oil spill, the *Anchorage Age* reported that Hazelwood had talked with writers putting together the book *Spill*. He was now in his 60s and offered his "very heartfelt apology" for the disaster.

Hazelwood also turned aside statements that he had been the scapegoat in the episode. "Occasionally, people have called me a scapegoat, but I've never felt comfortable with that term applied to me in regard to the oil spill," he said. "I was captain of the ship that ran aground and caused a horrendous amount of damage. I've got to be responsible for that. There's no way around it."

Somewhat more than 30 years after the spillage from the *Exxon Valdez* cleanup efforts continue, but the area has gradually resumed its original ecological nature. Birds such as the arctic tern and the Kittlitz's Murrelet are now back, the last a rather mysterious, chubby brown and white seabird that nests high up in craggy mountain areas and is rarely seen.

Mexico off the coast of Louisiana. BP [British Petroleum] had ownership and oversight over Transocean Ltd., the rig owner that carried out the drilling operation at a depth of more than a mile. The amount of oil released far exceeded that from the Alaska spill and devastated the fishing and tourist trade as it invaded the beaches and marshes, killing off wildlife. It seemed obvious that somebody was responsible, but the question that so often figures in white-collar crime cases was front and center: Who should be held criminally liable? And precisely for what? Enormous harm had been done, there was clear evidence of negligence—the drillers had employed a less effective control strategy, for instance, because it was cheaper to do so than to use the most expensive procedure. Authorities were reported to be weighing the likelihood of criminal charges against BP for skirting regulations and misleading the government by maintaining that it could effectively cope with any disaster. Investigators also were interested to determine if there had been an unauthorized destruction of incriminating documents.

FURTHER READINGS

Bushell, Sharon, and Stan Jones. (2009). *The Spill: Personal Stories from the* Exxon Valdez *Disaster*. Kenmore, WA: Epicenter Press.

Carr, Terry. (1991). *Spill!: The Story of the* Exxon Valdez. New York: Watts.

Davidson, Art. (1990). *In the Wake of the* Exxon Valdez: *The Devastating Impact of the Alaska Oil Spill*. San Francisco: Sierra Club Books.

Hunt, Joe. (2009). *Mission without a Map: The Politics and Policies of Restoration Following the* Exxon Valdez *Oil Spill*. Anchorage, AK: *Exxon Valdez* Oil Spill Trustee Council.

Keeble, John. (1991). *Out of the Channel: The* Exxon Valdez *Oil Spill in Prince William Sound*. New York: HarperCollins.

Loughlin, Thomas R. (1994). *Marine Animals and the* Exxon Valdez. San Diego, CA: Academic Press.

Ott, Riki. (2008). *Not One Drop: Betrayal and Outrage in the Wake of the* Exxon Valdez *Oil Spill*. River Junction, VT: Chelsea Green.

Owen, Bruce M., David A. Argue, Harold W. Furchtgott-Roth, and Gloria A. Hurdle. (1995). *The Economics of a Disaster: The* Exxon Valdez *Oil Spill*. Westport, CT: Quorum Press.

Clean Water, Resource Conservation, and Clean Air

- *Document:* The federal Environmental Protection Agency (EPA) sought to alert the public to possible criminal behaviors that fell within its jurisdiction by soliciting information from those who might be aware of such offenses and providing examples of three of the major statutes that it was charged with enforcing.
- *Date:* May 10, 2010.
- *Where:* Washington, DC.
- *Significance:* The document provides an authoritative and informative overview of the assignments that Congress has given the EPA to protect people against environmental hazards.

DOCUMENT 9.3

WHAT IS AN ENVIRONMENTAL CRIME?

The Criminal Enforcement Program focuses investigative resources on cases that involve negligent, knowing or willful violations of federal environmental law. Generally speaking, knowing violations are those that are deliberate and not the product of accident or mistake. Knowledge of the specific statutes or regulations that prohibit the wrongful conduct is not required. When the violator is aware that the wrongful conduct is prohibited the law, the violation is said to be willful . . .

Frequently, the investigations of environmental crimes will uncover other crimes, such as lying to the government, fraud or conspiracy. These crimes could also be prosecuted. Some examples of types of criminal investigations are noted below.

Reporting a Possible Crime

We encourage you to report a suspected crime, even if you are not sure which law has been violated or which federal or state agency is responsible for investigating such crimes. EPA will direct the matter to the appropriate investigative authority.

Examples of Investigations

Clean Water Act: A plant manager at a metal finishing company directs employees to bypass the facility's wastewater treatment unit in order to avoid having to purchase the chemicals that are needed to run the wastewater treatment unit. In so doing, the company sends untreated wastewater directly to the sewer system in violation of the permit issued by the municipal water authority. The plant manager is guilty of a criminal violation of the Clean Water Act.

Resource Conservation and Recovery Act (RCRA): In order to avoid the cost of paying for proper treatment of its hazardous waste, the owner of a manufacturer of cleaning solvents places several dozen 5-gallon buckets of highly flammable and caustic waste into its dumpster for disposal at a local, municipal landfill that is not authorized to receive hazardous waste. The owner of the company is guilty of a criminal violation of RCRA.

Clean Air Act: The owner of an apartment complex solicits bids to remove 4,000 square feet of old ceiling tiles from the building. The bidders inspect the building, determining that the tiles contain dangerous asbestos fibers, and bid with the understanding that, in doing the removal, they would be required to follow the work practice standards that apply to asbestos removal. The fourth bidder proposes to save the owner money by removing the tiles without following the work practice standards. The owner hires the fourth bidder on this basis and so, the work is done without following the work practice standards. The owner is guilty of a criminal violation of the Clean Air Act.

In addition to the investigate samples above, investigations may also involve, but are not limited to:

- Illicit disposal of hazardous waste.
- Export of hazardous waste without the permission of the receiving country
- Illegal discharge of pollutants to a water of the United States; the removal and disposal of regulated asbestos containing materials in a manner inconsistent with the laws and regulations
- Illegal importation of certain restricted or regulated chemicals into the United States
- Tampering with a drinking water supply
- Illegal importation of certain restricted or regulated chemicals into the United States
- Tampering with a drinking water supply
- Mail fraud

- Wire fraud
- Conspiracy
- Money laundering relating to environmental crime activities

Source: Criminal Enforcement, Environment Protection Agency, Updated May 11, 2010.

ANALYSIS

The request by the EPA that citizens report possible violations "even if you are not sure which laws has been violated or which federal or state agency is responsible" offers several important lessons about the distinction between street crimes, such as robbery, and white-collar crime. No one who is robbed or burglarized is likely to be uncertain whether a crime has been committed and what that crime is known as. Nor are people likely to be uncertain to whom they should report the crime: it almost always is either the local police or the sheriff. In white-collar crimes these matters are rather more complicated. The EPA report also lets us know that the agency is more dependent than the local police on acquiring information about committed crimes.

The examples offered by the EPA have a common thread; in each case the violator chooses to evade the requirements of the law in order to save money. In this regard the regulations tend to operate in favor of the larger businesses that are better able to bear the expenses associated with following the law in regard to protecting the environment.

> ### DID YOU KNOW?
>
> **White-Collar Crime Leads to Street Crime?**
>
> Jessica Wolpaw Reyes, an economist at Amherst College, believes that lead poisoning, even at low levels, can cause brain damage that renders children more impulsive and aggressive. The major source of lead in the air was not paint but rather leaded gasoline, until it was phased out under the Clean Air Act, which reduced the lead in the blood of Americans to a much lower level. Reyes found that the rise and fall in lead-exposure rates matched the arc of violent crime, but with a 20-year lag—the time needed for children who were exposed in 1973 to high lead levels to attain their most violent crime-prone years.
>
> *Source*: Jessica Wolpaw Reyes, "Environmental Policy as Social Policy? The Impact of Childhood Lead Exposure on Crime," *B.E. Journal of Economic Analysis & Policy* 7, no. 1 (2007): Article 51, doi:10.2202/1935-1682.

FURTHER READINGS

Adler, Robert W., Jessica C. Landman, and Diane M. Cameron. (1983). *The Clean Water Act 20 Years Later*. Washington, DC: Island Press.

Bryner, Gary C. (1993). *Blue Skies, Green Politics: The Clean Air Act of 1990*. Washington, DC: CQ Press.

Clifford, Mary. (Ed.) (1998). *Environmental Crime: Enforcement, Policy and Social Responsibility*. Gaithersburg, MD: Aspen.

Copeland, Claudia. (2003). *Clean Water Act; Current Issues and Guide to Books*. New York: Nova Science.

Lipton, James P. (2006). *Clean Air Act: Interpretation and Analysis*. New York: Nova Science.

Yeager, Peter C. (1991). *The Limits of Law: The Public Regulation of Private Pollution*. New York: Cambridge University Press.

Ralph Nader

- *Document:* Ralph Nader, a crusader who inspired a generation of associates and followers, typically young persons, to attend to the rape of the environment, sponsored a series of books that investigated the manner in which regulatory agencies were doing their job in protecting the residents of American from pollution and similar environment hazards. The document reproduces Nader's introduction to his group's study of the enforcement of the Clean Air Act.
- *Date:* 1970.
- *Where:* Grossman Publishers, New York.
- *Significance:* The hard-hitting campaign by the Nader forces ignited and led a crusade for enhanced protection of people from environmental hazards, in time giving birth to a vigorous "green" movement that agitated for reform through the world.

DOCUMENT 9.4

Air pollution (and its fallout on soil and water) is a form of domestic chemical and biological warfare. The efflux from motor vehicles, plants, and incinerators of sulfur oxides, hydrocarbons, carbon monoxide, oxides to nitrogen, particulates, and many more contaminants amounts of compulsory consumption of violence by most Americans. There is no full escape from such violent ingestions, for breathing is required. This damage, perpetrated increasingly in direct violation of local, state, and federal law, shatters people's health and safety but still escapes inclusion in the crime statistics. "Smogging" a city or town has taken on the proportions of a massive crime wave, yet federal and state statistical compilations of crime pay attention to muggers and ignore "smoggers." As a nation that purports to apply laws for preserving health, safety, and property, there is a curious permissiveness toward passing and enforcing laws against the primary polluters who harm our society's more valued rights.

Source: Ralph Nader, "Foreword," In John C. Esposito, *The Vanishing Air* (New York: Grossman, 1970), viii.

ANALYSIS

Ralph Nader is one of the best known people in the United States based on his continuous and highly visible populist campaigns, focused particularly on alerting college students to the necessity to improve the quality of life in the United States. Nader's power appears to have diminished with the passing years, not because his message is less powerful or less important, but because people tire of being reminded of the crusades they ought to be mounting, the money they ought to be contributing to worthy causes, and the outrage they ought to be (but no longer are if they ever were) expressing about unsettling evidence of white-collar and corporate crime. An ardent reformer and prophet in time can be seen as a nag, an uncomfortable reminder of our own inadequacy, of our pursuit of self-interested rather than social goals.

Nader was born in Connecticut in 1934 to a family from Lebanon. He was a brilliant student, graduating from Princeton and Harvard Law School. At Harvard, he became interested in automobile safety and later published *Unsafe at Any Speed*, a stinging critique of the performance of car manufacturers. The book would be voted the 38th most outstanding piece of journalism in the twentieth century.

General Motors, a major target, hired private investigators to tap Nader's telephone, dig into details of his personal life, and try to lure him into sex with a prostitute. He sued the company and won a settlement of $284,000 for what an appellate court would label "overzealous surveillance."

Nader used the money to establish a group of young activists who set to work scrutinizing the activities of a variety of federal regulatory agencies. They became known as "Nader's Raiders" and generally concluded that the agencies were not doing an adequate job.

DID YOU KNOW?

Nader for President?

Ralph Nader has now run for president of the United States in the past four campaigns. He justifies the obviously doomed effort as an opportunity to secure a podium from which to preach to the largest possible audience. Critics say that he draws votes from candidates who are nearest to his own position and thereby benefits their more conservative opponents. Nader's response is that both the Democrats and Republicans stand for pretty much the same things and that he presents the only decent political platform.

Nader ran twice on the Green Party ticket. In 1996, he received 685,297 votes (0.7% of the total); in 2000 he got 2,885,105 votes (2.74%). The next two times he ran as an independent, and in 2004 received 433,656 votes (0.38%) and in 2008 had 738,474 votes (0.56%) were cast for him.

FURTHER READINGS

Hawkins, Howard. (2006). *Independent Politics: The Green Party Strategy Debate*. Chicago, IL: Haymarket.

Marcello, Patricia Cronin. (2004). *Ralph Nader: A Biography*. Westport, CT: Greenwood.

Martin Justin. (2002). *Nader: Spoiler, Crusader, Icon*. Cambridge, MA: Perseus.

Nader, Ralph. (2007). *Crashing the Party: Taking on Corporate Government in an Age of Surrender*. New York: St. Martin's,

Nader, Ralph, and Mark J. Green. (1973). *Corporate Power in America*. New York: Grossman.

Whiteside, Thomas. (1972). *The Investigation of Ralph Nader, General Motors vs. One Determined Man*. New York: Arbor House.

Tainted Tylenol

- *Document:* The recall by McNeil Consumer Healthcare of several of its pharmaceutical products prompted a hearing by the U.S. House of Representatives to look into this matter as well as other problems alleged to involve McNeil. Document 9.5 offers the opening and closing remarks of Edolphus Towns, a Democrat from New York and chair of the House Committee on Oversight and Government Reform, as well as excerpts from the prepared statement by Coleen A. Goggins, an executive of Johnson & Johnson, the company that owns McNeil.
- *Date:* May 27, 2010.
- *Where:* U.S. House of Representatives, Washington, DC.
- *Significance:* The case had been referred to the Department of Justice to consider whether there was sufficient reason to lay a criminal charge in regard to the alleged violations. Either way, whether charged criminally or otherwise handled, the case illustrates the complex ingredients of white-collar crime despite what can often be very serious consequences of its behavior under review.

DOCUMENT 9.5

STATEMENT OF
CHAIRMAN EDOLPHUS TOWNS . . .

"Johnson & Johnson's Recall of Children's Tylenol and
Other Children's Medicines"

Good morning and thank you for being here.

Any time we give our children or grandchildren medicine, we expect it to be safe and we expect it to help our children get better.

Worldwide Chairman of Johnson & Johnson's Consumer Group, Colleen Goggins, testifies before the House Oversight and Government Reform Committee about the phantom recall of children's medicine on Capitol Hill on September 30, 2010. (AP/Wide World Photos)

When questions are asked about whether children's medicine is safe, parents need immediate answers. Almost every household in this country has these children's products in their medicine cabinets. And everyone has the same questions: Are these products safe, and what are we doing to ensure safety in the future.

While we don't want to cause unnecessary alarm, we cannot ignore the troubling facts before us,

Less than a month ago a Johnson & Johnson company known as McNeil Consumer Healthcare recalled over 40 variations of children's medicine, including such widely used products as Children's Tylenol, Children's Motrin, Children's Benadryl and Tylenol Infant's Drops,

The recall was carried out because of production problems at McNeil that affected the quality, purity and potency of the medicine. McNeil received dozens of consumer complaints about foreign particles in children's medicine, which were later confirmed by McNeil.

In addition, tests at the plant show that three batches of Infant's Tylenol were found to be "super potent," meaning that they contained an overdose of the active ingredient.

McNeil's production of children's medicine was shut down by the company and a month later it is still shut down. The FDA is currently investigating any possible links between the recalled medicine and adverse health effects on children who took that medicine.

The FDA is also currently receiving reports of children who died to determine if there is any connection between those deaths and this recall. At this point, the FDA is not aware of any connection between the recalled medicine and the death of a child.

One document the Committee received from the FDA refers to the case of a 1½ year old girl who died. The document reads, "coroner's office called to report the death of a 1½ year old female that is suspected to be related to a Tylenol product."

Just last night, the Committee obtained from the FDA even more disturbing information. According to an FDA document, McNeil knew there was a potential problem with one of the Motrin products that was on the market in 2008, but rather than issue a public recall, McNeil allegedly sent contractors out to stores to buy the product back and told the stores "not to mention" a recall.

After the FDA confronted McNeil about this, McNeil announced a recall of the affected products.

The "phantom recall" warrants further investigation by this Committee. Who at McNeil and Johnson & Johnson knew about this scheme? How high in the corporate suite was this scheme hatched? Is this standard operating procedure for McNeil? . . .

Both Johnson & Johnson and the FDA will be asked difficult questions today and I hope they are prepared to give the answers we need. . . .

There is nothing this Committee will investigate that is more serious than the health of our children. I can assure you that as Chairman of this Committee . . . we will use all of our authority to find out what went wrong and do everything we can to ensure that it doesn't happen again.

Thank you.

Johnson & Johnson

Testimony of

Ms. Colleen A. Groggins

Worldwide Chairman, Consumer Group, Johnson & Johnson

. . . I am pleased to testify on behalf of Johnson & Johnson to point out our understanding of the events.

All of us at the Johnson & Johnson family of companies realize that we have a responsibility to provide customers with the highest quality products possible, and we have worked hard to fulfill that responsibility for more than a century . . . In this instance, we have not lived up to that responsibility, and the recall is therefore a disappointment to our Chairman Bill Weldon, to me personally, and to the thousands of employees in the Johnson & Johnson family of companies.

The quality and the process issues that we found at McNeil, those which led to the recall and others, are unacceptable On behalf of McNeil and Johnson & Johnson, I apologize to the mothers, fathers, and caregivers for the concern and inconvenience caused by the recall . . .

I would like to stress . . . four key points. First, as the FDA noted last month, the health risks to customers from the recalled products were remote. Second, McNeil has no indication of a serious medical event caused by any of the issues referenced in the recall announcement. Third, no raw materials that tested positive for objectionable bacteria were ever used in the manufacture of McNeil's pediatric products. And finally, McNeil rejected the products that it found had excess active ingredients . . .

The recall last month was implemented because of the presence of minor metal particles detected in a small portion of product. To be clear, the quality issues, including the minor particles, are unacceptable to us . . .

Even though we were relieved that the medical risks are remote, we recognize that quality process deficiencies are important and must be corrected. Tylenol and the other brand names produced by McNeil are among the most trusted names in over-the-counter medicine. Millions of families rely on our products to treat those dearest to them.

Mr. Chairman, I want to stress that even before the recent recall, Johnson & Johnson and McNeil have been working together to improve the quality of McNeil's products. The Johnson & Johnson parent company is committed to providing McNeil with the resources and personnel needed to improve quality, work with the FDA, and ensure that these products meet our high standards. McNeil's quality expenditures and investments relating to the Fort Washington plant [a McNeil production site in Pennsylvania] have increased. Johnson & Johnson and McNeil will expend whatever resources are necessary to ensure that this facility provides, once again, high quality medicine . . .

McNeil will update the FDA about its progress implementing the plan at least once a month. McNeil also intends to use the support of a third party in making product release decisions during the first six months of operation. Third-party involvement may include review of investigations, complaints, completed batch records, and changes that have the potential to affect products or processes . . .

Mr. Chairman, I would like to close in the same manner that our company's chairman . . . concluded his letter to the people who use our products: "We will work hard to earn back your confidence."

CLOSING STATEMENT [BY COMMITTEE CHAIR]

Frankly, what we have heard today is not reassuring.

The initial story was bad enough. On April 30, Johnson & Johnson announced the largest recall of children's medicine in history. But it turns out there wasn't just one recall. What we have heard about today is rolling recalls, a phantom recall, a plant shut down and management firings.

I was hoping that J&J would be completely forthcoming today, but I think there are still unanswered questions.

J&J told the Committee staff that the most recent recall involved only 6 million bottles. That's a huge number. But today we learned from the FDA that it was more than 20 times that, nearly 136 million bottles.

Regarding the phantom recall. J&J testified that there was no attempt to hide anything. But we uncovered a J&J document showing that they told their contractor not to say this was a recall.

J&J says that none of its contaminated products has had any adverse health effects. But the FDA testified today that the issue of whether any of these products caused deaths is still being investigated . . .

One thing we know now is that the FDA needs mandatory recall authority. They shouldn't have to persuade a company to recall suspect products. I intend to introduce legislation to give FDA that authority . . .

Source: U.S. House of Representatives, Committee on Oversight and Government Reform, Hearings, May 27, 2010.

ANALYSIS

In the tainted Tylenol case, McNeil Consumer Healthcare, one of the 250 far-flung units of the New Brunswick, New Jersey, pharmaceutical giant Johnson & Johnson, at the end of April 2010 recalled more than 136 million bottles of liquid Tylenol for children as well as several similar children's drugs. The products were admitted to contain metal particles, among other faults. There also had been lengthy delays over the past two years in the company reporting problems to the FDA. It might be noted in the document above that toward the end of her testimony, the company spokeswoman indicates, putting an upbeat face on the matter, that Johnson & Johnson had been at work trying to straighten out McNeil.

It is worth noting that the spokeswoman for Johnson & Johnson, who had recently ranked 37th on *Fortune* magazine's list of the nation's 50 most powerful women, did not refer in her prepared congressional committee testimony to one of the more culpable acts alleged against her employee: a surreptitious attempt in 2008 to remove Motrin, a painkiller, from drugstore shelves without notifying the FDA regarding the action or the reason for what the committee chair called the "phantom recall." Contractors hired to do this task were instructed in writing to "simply 'act' like a regular customer" and in capital letters were told "THERE MUST BE NO MENTION OF THIS BEING A RECALL." Under questioning, the J&J spokeswoman said that the company had told the FDA that the contractor had been employed to do statistical sampling.

As the committee chair indicated in his closing remarks, the issue of the harmful consequences of the recalled drugs was still up in the air. Despite Ms. Groggins's assurance, the FDA had noted

---

DID YOU KNOW?

Fraud in Drug Testing

The tension between safety and utility is particularly pronounced in the realm of pharmaceutical products. Virtually all of the costs for the publication of medical journals are paid by income from drug company advertisements in their pages (about 30% of the average medical journal is made up of ads). The companies would be displeased and very likely retributive if a journal published negative information about one of its products. The companies also pay out millions of dollars for reprints of favorable reports of drugs they offer for sale.

Great sums of money are invested by drug manufacturers in research that is necessary to obtain FDA approval for their products. Positive testing results can prove to be very lucrative or they can cause heavy financial losses if they fail to meet federal regulatory standards. Doctors have published in respectable medical journals articles testifying to the admirable qualities of a drug in which they disregarded any contrary evidence and discussed only early test outcomes that were contradicted by longer-term conclusions. In the lawsuit of *Alaska Electric Pension Fund v. Pharmacia Corp.*, for instance, investors claimed that Pharmacia trumpeted data from the first six months of a study to claim that the drug Celebrex had fewer gastrointestinal side effects than other medications to treat arthritis. It was alleged that Pharmacia knew that a 13-month study contradicted that conclusion. There also have been recent reports of articles written by the marketing branch of a company that manufactures a drug and submitted to a journal under a doctor's name, for which he or she was paid a fee.

Typically, drug testing is carried out by an "independent" medical research scientist but is paid for by the manufacturer, creating an obvious conflict of interest. The drug companies also court doctors by paying them cushy lecturing fees, providing free samples, and subsidizing their trips to conventions in such posh sites as Caribbean resorts.

hundreds of adverse effects and 37 deaths since January 1, 2008, that may or may not have been a consequence of the ingestion of the recalled McNeil medications.

The FDA's criminal investigations office also was determining whether the case should be referred to the Department of Justice for possible criminal action.

FURTHER READINGS

Abramson, John. (2004). *Overdosed America: The Broken Promises of American Medicine.* New York: HarperCollins.

Braithwaite, John. (1984). *Corporate Crime in the Pharmaceutical Industry.* Boston: Routledge & Kegan Paul.

Kassirer, Jerome. (2004). *On the Take: How Medicine's Complicity with Big Business Can Endanger Your Health.* New York: Oxford University Press.

Szockyj, Elizabeth, and James G. Fox. (1996). *Corporate Victimization of Women.* Boston: Northeastern University Press.

10

THE ENRON DECADE OF CORPORATE DEBACLES

INTRODUCTION

Beginning in 2001 with the collapse into bankruptcy of Enron, the Houston-based company dealing in natural gas and a range of other products, there followed a cascade of corporations that were found to be riddled with corrupt and criminal practices. The roll call included Arthur Andersen, one of the country's leading auditing organizations, whose personnel were found to have conspired with Enron officials to camouflage the Houston company's woeful financial condition.

The fallout from the failures of these two and other companies was far-reaching. The greatest burden fell on investors and on employees who found themselves out of a job and in many instances bereft of money that they had put into the company's stock to support their retirement. The government was diligent, with mixed success, in taking measures to convict executives who it deemed to have engaged in criminal actions—unlike the hands-off posture in regard to alleged criminal behaviors that would mark responses to the subsequent economic meltdown that we discuss in chapters 11 and 12.

The torrent of corporate scandals induced Congress to enact the Sarbanes-Oxley Act (typically abbreviated as SOX), which sought to rein in some of the worst excesses exposed by the Enron and the post-Enron corporate crimes and torts. In this chapter we look at the Enron failure and the offenses of Arthur Andersen, as well as the wrongdoing of four other major companies—Adelphia, HealthSouth, Tyco, and WorldCom. We also examine the heralded whistle-blowing performance of Sherron Watkins at Enron and discuss the Sarbanes-Oxley law that sought to head off future business crimes.

Enron

- **Document:** Kenneth Lay, the founder and former chairman and CEO of Enron Corporation, and Jeffrey Skilling, who had served as CEO from February to August of 2001 before abruptly resigning, faced criminal charges for unloading their own stock while acting to persuade investors to put their money into a company that they knew but did not publicly announce was in very serious financial difficulty. Document 10.1 spells out the allegations by the SEC in a court decision that denied Skilling's motion to have the insider trading charges against him dismissed.
- **Date:** July 7, 2004.
- **Where:** U.S. District Court in Houston, Texas.
- **Significance:** The document details the alleged criminal behavior that would result in the conviction and imprisonment of Jeffrey Skilling.

DOCUMENT 10.1

I. Factual Allegations

The [indictment] alleges that Enron hired Skilling in August of 1990, that Skilling held various executive and management positions at Enron until January of 1997 when he became President and Chief Executive Officer . . . , and that from February to August of 2001 Skilling served as Enron's President and Chief Executive Officer. The offenses charged . . . arise from an alleged scheme to deceive the investing public, including Enron's shareholders, the Securities and Exchange Commission, and others "about the true performance of Enron's businesses by: (a) manipulating Enron's publicly reported financial results; and (b) making public statements and representations about Enron's financial performance and results that were false and misleading in that they did not fairly and accurately reflect Enron's actual financial condition and performance, and they omitted to disclose facts necessary to make those statements and representations fair and accurate."

The [indictment] charges the defendants with having "enriched themselves as a result of the scheme through salary, bonuses, grants of stock and stock options, other profits, and prestige within their profession and communities." The [indictment] alleges that "between 1998 and 2001, SKILLING received approximately $200 million from the sale of Enron stock options and restricted stock, netting over $89 million in profit, and was paid more than $14 million in salary and bonuses."

Source: United States v. Richard Causey, Jeffrey K. Skilling, and Kenneth L. Lay, CRIMINAL H-04-025-SS, U.S. District Court, (Texas, 2004).

ANALYSIS

At the time it began to fall apart publicly, Enron was the seventh-largest company in the United States, employing more than 20,000 people. From 1996 through 2001 *Fortune* magazine had named it the country's Most Innovative Company, and in one year indicated that it was one of the 100 best companies in America to work in. Despite that glowing tribute, Enron was a cutthroat operation: employees were rated every six months, and those who found themselves in the bottom 20 percent were fired. The company had run up huge debts, but avoided including them in its financial reports by transferring them to paper partnerships that had been formed to hide the company's true financial condition.

The resignation of Jeffrey Skilling as CEO, as Sherron Watkins's letter to Kenneth Lay, the former Enron president (reproduced as Document 10.2) indicated, was the first peal of the death knell for Enron. Skilling sought to deal with the suspicions that he had quit because he knew trouble was ahead with a statement that was patently false. He claimed that "the numbers, the earnings show that the company is in just excellent shape right now" and that his resignation was "entirely a personal matter." Skilling, a graduate of Southern Methodist University and the Harvard Business School, was drawing a yearly salary of $132 million when he abruptly walked away from his job.

Skilling later would claim that he had no knowledge of the illegal financial maneuvers that pervaded Enron's accounting methods, including, for instance, what was called "mark to market" accounting, a

DID YOU KNOW?

Mrs. Lay Gets Involved

The spillover onto family members that can take place in white-collar crime cases. Kenneth Lay's second wife, Linda, to whom he had been married for 22 years, became an object of ridicule when she told an NBC television interviewer about the family wealth: "It's all gone. We lost everything. Everything we had was mostly in Enron stock." A media reporter called in at Just Stuff, an antiques shop opened by Mrs. Lay and her daughter, where they were disposing of some of the valuable possessions that they had accumulated to furnish the 15 homes that they owned—two of which were in Aspen, Colorado—one of which had brought a price of $11 million. The Lays also had millions in stock in companies besides Enron. The reporter also observed that Mrs. Lay had hired an expensive public relations firm to try to peddle an image of her family as desolate, an image repudiated by a former Enron employee who had lost all her retirement savings and said angrily that she deliberately crossed the street when she was walking on the side where the Just Stuff store was located.

practice by means of which an anticipated profit was booked as an actual asset even though in time it might turn out to be a loss. In a statement that later became the object of scorn in the face of information about crooked dealings at Enron, Skilling had said: "We were doing something special. It wasn't a job—it was a mission. We were changing the world. It was God's work." One can hope that in heaven they don't cook the books.

Enron also had robbed California blind when the state underwent an energy emergency and had to deal with Enron. Skilling was quoted as making a dismissive remark about the crisis in California. "At least when the *Titanic* went down," he was heard to say, "the lights were on."

Skilling was tried by a jury on 35 criminal counts of fraud, insider trading, and other offenses. Found guilty on 19 of the counts, he was fined $40 million and sentenced to 24 years and 4 months in prison. In his appeal, he claims that a woman was allowed to sit on the jury in his trial even though she had said that she had lost $50,000 to $60,000 when Enron went under. Skilling's lawyers also objected to the failure of the judge to transfer the trial to another venue because the "degree of passion and prejudice in the community" worked against Skilling obtaining a fair trial. His appeal pointed out that the local newspaper, the *Houston Chronicle*, had printed a headline reading: "Your tar and feathers ready? Mine are," and that Skilling at various times had publicly been compared to "Al Qaida, Hitler, Stalin, child molesters, rapists, embezzlers, and terrorists." Skilling's attorneys also argued that the use of a standard of "honest service" by which Skilling's conduct was judged was unconstitutionally vague.

Skilling prevailed in a unanimous Supreme Court decision that agreed that the requirement for "honest service" was unconstitutionally vague. The Court put some flesh on the term by decreeing that it might well involve such behavior as accepting a bribe or a kickback, neither of which had been done by Skilling. The ruling did not release him from prison, but could reduce the time he has to serve.

Kenneth Lay, Enron's onetime chief executive officer, who was tried with Skilling in the case that the government required four and a half years to prepare, was a graduate of the University of Missouri in economics who had gone on to receive a PhD from Houston University. He had divested himself of stock and stock options worth more than $200 million shortly before the company collapsed. In 1999, his salary and other perks added up to $42.4 million. One of Lay's better known statements setting out his goal in life was: "I don't want to be rich. I want to be World Class rich." Lay was found guilty of 10 charges

DID YOU KNOW?

Enron: Movie and Theater

The Enron story was a sufficiently compelling moral tale and dramatic situation to impel the production of two documentary films and a theater production that ran to rave reviews in London and an admirable if more restrained critical response when it opened on Broadway.

One documentary, *Enron: The Smartest Guys in the Room*, based on a book with that title, was released in April 2005 and relied heavily on tapes and audio recordings to re-create the shady dealings that marked the collapse of Enron. So did the documentary *The Crooked E: The Unheralded Truth about Enron*.

Five years after appearance of *The Smartest Guys*, the theater production *Enron: The True Story of False Profits* had its opening performance at the Broadhurst Theater on Broadway. Written by Lucy Prebble, the show had first been acted in England's Chichester Festival, then moved to the avant garde Royal Court Theater. One critic called the play "stunning" and "an astonishing thrill ride through the high-flying nineties and a chilling precursor of everything that would follow." Jeffrey Skilling was played as "a cool scoundrel of the most thoroughgoing duplicity," although a "good father and a boy genius." The headline of the review in the *New York Times* aptly labeled the Enron executives "Titans of Tangled Finance."

and faced a sentence that likely would have kept him in prison for the remainder of his life. However, he suffered a heart attack while vacationing in Colorado several months before he was to be sentenced, and under the law the case against him had to be abated—that is, treated as if it had never taken place.

Enron declared bankruptcy late in 2001. It was at the time the largest such filing in American history in terms of the amount of money involved. Enron Field no longer remained the name of the baseball park of the Houston Astros: it was changed to Minute Maid Field. When Enron emerged from bankruptcy three years later it was rechristened the Enron Creditors Recovery Corp., and announced that its "sole mission is to reorganize and liquidate the remaining operations and assets of Enron."

FURTHER READINGS

Bryce, Robert. (2002). *Pipe Dream: Greed, Ego, and the Death of Enron*. New York: Public Affairs.

Cruven, Brian. (2002). *Anatomy of Greed: The Unheralded Truth from an Enron Insider*. New York: Carroll & Graf.

Eichenwald, Kurt. (2005). *Conspiracy of Fools: A True Story*. New York: Broadway Books.

Fox, Loren. (2003). *Enron: The Rise and Fall*. Hoboken, NJ: Wiley.

McLean, Bethany, and Peter Elkind. (2003). *The Smartest Guys in the Room: The Amazing Rise and Scandalous Fall of Enron*. New York: Portfolio.

Salter, Malcolm S. (2008). *Innovation Corrupted: The Origin and Legacy of Enron's Collapse*. Cambridge, MA: Harvard University Press.

Sterling, Theodore F. (2002). *The Enron Scandal*. New York: Nova Science.

Sherron Watkins

- *Document:* The e-mail warning that Sherron Watkins sent to Kenneth Lay, the leading figure in Enron, pinpointed the failure of company executives to respond to information presented to them by reliable sources regarding the illegal activities going on in their realm. Watkins, a trained and experienced accountant who had once worked for Arthur Andersen, was able to interpret auditing information that was camouflaged and hidden in the required Enron financial reports.
- *Date:* January 20, 2002.
- *Where:* Inside Enron's corporate offices in Houston, Texas.
- *Significance:* Ms. Watkins's forewarning of trouble ahead at Enron came to represent for the public the "good" side of the case—the willingness of an employee to put herself in jeopardy by informing her bosses about things that they obviously preferred to ignore—and Ms. Watkins became a national celebrity for what she had dared to do.

DOCUMENT 10.2

Dear Mr. Lay:

Has Enron become a risky place to work? For those of us who didn't get rich over the last few years, can we afford to stay?

Skilling's abrupt departure will raise suspicions of accounting improprieties. The spotlight will be on us, the market can't accept that Skilling is leaving his dream job.

I think that the valuation issues can be fixed and reported with other good will write-downs to occur in 2002. How do we fix the Raptor and Condor deals? They unwind in 2002 and 2003, we will have to pony up Enron stock and that won't go unnoticed.

(From left to right) Former Enron Vice President of Corporate Development Sherron Watkins, Enron Chief Executive Officer Jeffrey Skilling, and Enron President and Chief Operating Officer Jeffrey McMahon are sworn before the Senate Commerce Committee hearing in Washington D.C. on February 26, 2002. (AP/Wide World Photos)

To the man in the street, it will look like we recognized funds flow of $800 million from merchant asset sales in 1999 by selling to a vehicle (Condor) that we capitalized with a promise of Enron stock in later years. Is that really funds flow or is it cash from equity issuance? We have recognized over $555 million of fair value gains on stocks via our swaps with Raptor. Much of that stock has declined significantly—Avici by 98 percent from $178 million to $5 million; the New Power company by 80 percent from $40 a share, to $6 a share. The value in the swaps won't be there for Raptor, so once again Enron will issue stock to offset these losses . . . It sure looks to the layman on the street that we are hiding losses in a related company and will compensate that company with Enron stock in the future.

I am incredibly nervous that we will implode in a wave of accounting scandals. My eight years of Enron work history will be worth noting on my resume, the business world will consider the past successes as nothing but an elaborate accounting hoax. Skilling is resigning now for "personal reasons" but I would think he wasn't having fun, looked down the road and knew this stuff was unfixable and would rather abandon ship now than resign in shame in two years.

Is there a way our accounting gurus can unwind these deals now? I have thought and thought about a way to do this, but I keep bumping into one big problem—we booked the Condor and Raptor deals in 1999 and 2000, we enjoyed wonderfully high stock price, many executives sold stock, we then try and reverse or fix the deals in 2001, and it's a bit like robbing the bank in one year and trying to pay it back two years later. Nice try, but investors were hurt, they bought at $70 and $80 a share looking for $120 a share and now they're at $38 a share. We are under too much scrutiny and there are probably one or two disgruntled "redeployed" employees who know enough about the "funny" accounting to get us in trouble.

What do we do? I know this question cannot be addressed in the all-employee meetings, but can you give some assurance that you and [Richard A.] Causey [a former Andersen auditor and then an Enron executive vice president and chief accounting officer] will sit down and take a good hard objective look at what is going to happen to Condor and Raptor in 2002 and 2003 . . .

I realize that we have a lot of smart people looking at this and a lot of accountants including AA & Co. [Arthur Andersen] have blessed the accounting treatment. None of that will protect Enron if these transactions are ever discussed in the bright light of day. (Please review the problems of Waste Management—where AA paid $130 million plus in litigation re: questionable accounting principles.)

The overriding basic principle of accounting is that if you explain the "accounting treatment" to a man in the street, would you influence his investing decisions? Would he sell or buy the stock based on thorough understanding of the facts? If so, you best present it correctly and/or change the accounting.

My concern is that the footnotes don't adequately explain the transactions. If adequately explained, the investor would know that the "Entities" described in our related party footnote are thinly capitalized, the equity holders have no skin in the game, and all the value in the entities comes from the underlying value of the derivatives (unfortunately in this case, a big loss) AND Enron stock . . . Looking at the stock we swapped, I also don't believe any other company would have entered into the equity derivative transactions with us at the same prices or without substantial premiums from Enron. In other words, the $500 million in reserve in 2000 would have been much lower. How much lower?

I firmly believe that executive management of the company must have a clear and precise knowledge of the transactions and they must have the transactions reviewed by objective experts in the fields of securities law and accounting. I believe Ken Lay deserves the right to judge for himself what he believes the probabilities of discovery to be and the estimated damages to the company from those discoveries and decide one of two courses:

1.   The probability of discovery is low enough and the estimated danger too great; therefore we find a way to quietly reverse, unwind, write down these positions/transactions.

DID YOU KNOW?

The Triumphant Trio

In its first issue of each year, *Time* magazine features the person who it deems to have been the most significant figure during the previous 12-month period. In 2002, it chose three women—Sherron Watkins, Cynthia Cooper, who had been a whistle-blower in the drama of WorldCom (see below), and Coleen Rowley, an FBI staff attorney who had sought to alert her employer to terrorist threats facing the nation. "They took huge professional and personal risk to blow the whistle," *Time* declared at the head of its report, adding: "and in so doing helped remind us what American courage and American values are all about."

Time went on to note "the black comedy of corporate fraud" that had marked the past year. "You could laugh about the CEOs in handcuffs and the financial analysts who turned out to be fishier than storefront palm readings," *Time* intoned, "but after a while the laughs came hard." Then *Time* launched into a moral conclusion:

> These women . . . were people who did right just by doing their jobs rightly—which means ferociously, with eyes open and with the bravery all the rest of us always hope we have and may never know if we do. Their lives may not have been at stake. . . . but [they] put pretty much everything else on the line. Their jobs, their health, their privacy, their sanity—they risked all of these to bring us badly needed word of trouble inside crucial institutions.

The magazine brought the three women together in a Minneapolis hotel, and they decided after firsthand acquaintance that at heart none of them was a publicity-seeking rebel and that they became public figures only because their memos leaked. All three had grown up in small Midwest towns. All turned out to be firstborns and, of course, all three were female. Two of the three had husbands who were stay-at-home fathers.

2.   The probability of discovery is too great, the estimated damages to the company too great; therefore, we must quantify, develop containment plans and disclose.

I firmly believe that the probability of discovery significantly increased with Skilling's shocking departure. Too many people are looking for a smoking gun. . . .

I have heard one manager-level employee from the principal investments group say, "I know it would be devastating to all of us, but I wish we would get caught. We're such a crooked company."

Source: Sherron Watkins, e-mail to Kenneth Lay, January 20, 2002, released to the public by the House of Representatives Energy and Commerce Committee, Hearing 489 (February 14, 2002).

ANALYSIS

Sherron Watkins, who forewarned the leaders at Enron that something was seriously rotten in their midst, would be featured on the cover of *Time* magazine with two other women whistle-blowers as the most eminent persons of the year. Despite her attempt to get the powers-that-were at Enron to do something about the financial mess that had been created by underhanded maneuvers, it is worth noting that Watkins did not go public with her reservations but rather sought to have internal remedies put into operation. She suggested to Lay that there was a possibility that the wrongdoing would go undiscovered and remedial measures could be secretly and discreetly taken.

Forbes magazine deplored the continuous labeling of Watkins as a whistle-blower and the adulation she received. A true whistle-blower, the magazine maintained, is someone who sees a bank robber at work and alerts the police. What Watkins did, they insisted, was to "write a memoir to the bank robber suggesting ways to avoid getting caught." In this sense, Watkins was a team player but one who wanted the team to straighten up and fly right before its excesses were discovered by outsiders. She quit her Enron job in late 2002 and began a consulting business focused on corporate compliance.

FURTHER READINGS

Swartz, Mimi, and Sherron Watkins. (2003). *Power Failure: The Inside Story of the Collapse of Enron*. New York: Doubleday.

Watkins, Sherron S. (2005). *Power Source: Enron's Whistle Blower Reveals Her Story of Finding Reason amid the Ruins*. Nashville, TN: Nelson.

Watkins, Sherron S. (2003). Ethical Conflicts at Enron: Moral Responsibility in Corporate Capitalism. *California Management Review* 45:6–19.

Watkins, Sherron S. (2003). Pristine Ethics. *Vital Speeches of the Day* 69:435–39.

Arthur Andersen

- **Document:** In complicated white-collar and corporate crime cases, prosecutors typically outline for a grand jury, a body of citizens appointed by a judge, the ingredients of the case that they desire to pursue. Members of grand jury deliberate and almost invariably return an indictment, or what is called a true bill, that indicates it believes there are satisfactory grounds to proceed against the accused. Document 10.3 represents the indictment returned by the grand jury against the Arthur Andersen accounting firm.
- **Date:** April 24, 2001.
- **Where:** U.S. District Court, Houston, Texas.
- **Significance:** The grand jury indictment sets out the precise legal case that the prosecutors charged against Arthur Andersen in regard to its work with Enron.

DOCUMENT 10.3

THE GRAND JURY CHARGES:

I. ANDERSEN AND ENRON

1. ARTHUR ANDERSEN ... is a partnership that performs, among other things, accounting and consulting services for clients that operate businesses through the United States and the world. ANDERSEN has its headquarters in Chicago, Illinois, and maintains offices throughout the world, including Houston, Texas.

2. Enron Corp. was an Oregon operation with its principal place of business in Houston, Texas. For most of 2001, Enron was considered the seventh largest corporation in the United States based on reported revenues. In the previous ten years,

Enron had evolved from a regional natural gas provider to, among other things, a trader of natural gas, electricity and other commodities, with retail operations in energy and other products. . . .

3.   For the past 16 years, up until it filed for bankruptcy in December 2001, Enron retained ANDERSEN as its auditor. Enron was one of ANDERSEN'S largest clients worldwide, and became ANDERSEN'S largest client in ANDERSEN'S Gulf Coast region. ANDERSEN earned tens of millions of dollars from Enron in auditing and other fees.

4.   ANDERSEN performed both internal and external auditing work for Enron mainly in Houston, Texas. ANDERSEN established within Enron's office in Houston a work space for the ANDERSEN team that had primary responsibility for performing audit work for Enron. In addition to Houston, ANDERSEN personnel performed work for Enron in, among other locations, Chicago, Illinois, Portland, Oregon, and London, England.

II.   THE ANTICIPATION OF LITIGATION AGAINST ENRON AND ANDERSEN.

5.   In the summer and fall of 2001, a series of significant developments led to ANDERSEN'S foreseeing imminent civil litigation against, and government investigations of, Enron and ANDERSEN.

6.   On or about October 6, 2001, Enron issued a press release announcing a $618 million net loss for the third quarter of 2001. The same day, but not as part of the press release, Enron announced that it would reduce shareholder equity by approximately $1.2 billion. The market reacted immediately and the stock price of Enron shares plummeted.

7.   The Securities and Exchange Commission . . . opened an inquiry into Enron the very next day, requesting in writing information from Enron.

8.   In addition to the negative financial information disclosed by Enron to the public and analysts on October 16, 2001, ANDERSEN was aware by this time of additional significant facts unknown to the public.

•   The approximately $1.2 billion reduction in stockholder equity . . . was necessitated by ANDERSEN and Enron having previously improperly categorized hundreds of millions of dollars as an increase, rather than a decrease, to Enron shareholders equity.

•   The Enron October 16,2001, press release characterized numerous charges against income for the third quarter as non-recurring even though ANDERSEN believed the company did not have a basis for concluding that the charges would be in fact non-recurring. Indeed, ANDERSEN advised Enron against using that term, and documented its objections internally in the event of litigation, but did not report its objections or otherwise take steps to cure the public statement.

•   The ANDERSEN team handling he Enron audit directly contravened the accounting methodology approved by ANDERSEN'S own specialists working in its Professional Standards Group. In opposition to the view of its own experts, the ANDERSEN auditors had advised Enron in the spring of 2001 that it could use a favorable accounting method for its "special purpose entities."

- In 2000, an internal review conducted by senior management within ANDERSEN evaluated the ANDERSEN team assigned to audit Enron and rated the team as only a "2" on a sale of one to five, with five being the highest rating.

III. THE WHOLSALE DESTRUCTION OF DOCUMENTS BY ANDERSEN

9.   By Friday, October 19, 2001, Enron alerted the ANDERSEN audit team that the SEC had begun an inquiry regarding the Enron "special purpose entities" and the involvement of Enron's Chief Financial Officer. The next morning an emergency conference call among high-level ANDERSEN management was convened to address the SEC inquiry. During the calls, it was decided that documentation that could assist Enron in responding to the SEC was to be assembled by the Andersen auditors.

10.   After spending Monday, October 22, 2001 at Enron, ANDERSEN partners assigned to the Enron engagement team launched on October 23, 2001, a wholesale destruction of documents at ANDERSEN offices in Houston, Texas. ANDERSEN personnel were called to urgent and emergency meetings. Instead of being advised to preserve documentation so as to assist Enron and the SEC, ANDERSEN employees on the Enron engagement team were instructed by ANDERSEN partners and others to destroy immediately documentation relating to Enron, and told to work overtime if necessary to accomplish the destruction. During the next few weeks, an unparalleled initiative was undertaken to shred physical documentation and delete computer files. Tons of paper relative to the Enron audit were promptly shredded as part of the orchestrated document destruction. The shredder at the ANDERSEN office at the Enron building was used virtually constantly and, to handle the overload, dozens of large trucks filled with Enron documents were sent to ANDERSEN 's main Houston office to be shredded. A systematic effort was also undertaken and carried out to purge the computer hard-drives and E-mail system of Enron-related files.

11.   In addition to shredding and deleting documents in Houston, Texas, instructions were given to ANDERSEN working on Enron audit matters in Portland, Oregon, Chicago, Illinois, and London, England to make sure that Enron documents were destroyed there as well. Indeed, in London, a coordinated effort by ANDERSEN partners and others, similar to the initiative undertaken in Houston, was put in place to destroy Enron-related documents within days of notice of the SEC inquiry. Enron-related documents also were destroyed by ANDERSEN partners in Chicago.

12.   On or about November 8, 2001, the SEC served ANDERSEN with the anticipated subpoena related to its work for Enron. In response, members of the Andersen team on the Enron audit were alerted finally that there could be "no more active shredding" because the firm had been "officially served" for documents.

THE CHARGE: OBSTRUCTION OF JUSTICE

13.   On or about and between October 10, 2001, and November 9, 2001, within the Southern District of Texas and elsewhere, including Chicago, Illinois, Portland,

Oregon, and London, England, ANDERSEN, through its partners and others, did knowingly, intentionally, and corruptly persuade and attempt to persuade other persons, to wit ANDERSEN employees, with intent to cause and induce such persons (a) to withhold records, documents and other objects from official proceedings, namely regulatory and criminal proceedings and investigations, and (b) alter, destroy, and conceal objects with intent to impair the objects integrity and availability for use in such official proceedings.

Source: United States v. Arthur Andersen, LLP, Grand jury indictment, U.S. District Court (Texas, 2001).

ANALYSIS

Arthur Andersen, a limited partnership, was founded in 1913 and was one of the so-called "Big Five," the leaders in the country's auditing business. Andersen had 340 offices in 34 countries and 85,000 employees. The firm had been the auditor for Enron since 1985, and the relationship between the two companies had grown increasingly cozy. There was a pattern that saw employees, such as Sherron Watkins, move casually from jobs in one of the companies to the other. Meanwhile, Andersen endorsed the patently fraudulent bookkeeping schemes that Enron executives were concocting.

Andersen received $52 million a year in auditing and consulting fees from Enron, which was its major client. In time, government authorities essentially got fed up with Andersen's repetitive wrongdoing. A year before its Enron troubles erupted, Arthur Andersen had paid $110 million to settle a class action suit brought by stockholders of Sunbeam, an appliance firm. Sunbeam's accounting gimmick was to sell a product worth about $1 million or $2 million to a company for, say, $12 million and then tally that sum as income. But the purchasing company was given the right to (and would) cancel the deal after Sunbeam had completed its earning statement for the relevant time period.

In regard to the telecommunications company Global Crossing, another Andersen client, a similar kind of maneuver prevailed. Global would sign a contract to provide service over the next 20 years and count the anticipated income for the full period as earnings; but when it purchased a product it would list only the yearly cost on its financial statements. Global Crossing paid Andersen $2.1 million for its auditing indulgence. Andersen also earned another $12 million from the Bermuda-based company Global Crossing for nonaudit consulting. The company filed for bankruptcy early in 2002, although its founder walked away with $734 million before the company went bust and was sold to an Asian firm.

Andersen's auditors also had failed to detect a Ponzi scheme run by the Baptist Foundation of America and had settled complaints in that case for $217 million. Abraham Kennard, the originator of the scheme, was charged with cheating 1,600 African American churches and many individuals out of nearly $9 million. After Kennard's arrest, the government seized 20 upper-end automobiles that he owned.

Kennard's defense was that the authorities were mistaking a dream for a scheme. A jury convicted him of money laundering, conspiracy, tax evasion, and mail fraud, and he received a 17-year prison sentence.

Then there was a $7 million payment in a suit involving an inflated earnings statement by Waste Management, a conglomerate controlling regional garbage collections. As part of that settlement, Andersen had specified that it would not again engage in such behavior. At the Enron trial, the prosecutor stressed that Andersen was well aware of how investigations proceeded—it had been the object of a number of them, and this earlier experience led them to destroy Enron evidence that might incriminate them.

The end for Arthur Andersen came after a six-week criminal trial and 10 days of jury deliberations when Andersen was found guilty of complicity in the Enron lawbreaking. The prosecution focused its case on the shredding of relevant papers in various Andersen offices after managers had learned that the government was suspicious of their audits of Enron's books. The shredding had begun when 37-year-old Nancy Temple, one of the 20 in-house Andersen lawyers (see Sidebar 10.4), initiated an e-mail that reminded company officials that they ought to pay heed to the company's "document retention" policy, which allowed the shredding of materials after the lapse of a certain time.

Temple did not say that the employees ought to make haste to destroy incriminating documents, but the implication of the message seemed very clear, an implicit but self-protecting move to achieve the desired end. For Ms. Temple, her legal obligation was to Arthur Andersen, not to government investigators; it was the moral and ethical implications of the activity that proved worrisome. But the attorney was never charged with a violation. When she gave a deposition before the trial she often relied upon the Fifth Amendment protection against self-incrimination to decline to answer questions.

More than a ton of documents were destroyed as well some 30,000 e-mails and computer files. One of the jurors noted: "We wanted to find Andersen not guilty and find that they stood up to Enron. But it's clear that [the lawyer who ordered the shredding] knew investigators were coming and told Andersen to abort the evidence." The judge imposed a fine of $500,000 and a sentence of five years' probation. Andersen clients fled to other auditors, and the company went under. Criminologist Stephen Rosoff and his colleagues have aptly summed up what happened to Andersen: "The company now acknowledges that it made what it terms 'errors in judgment.' One could respond that wearing a striped tie with a plaid shirt is an 'error in judgment.' What Arthur Andersen did was a *crime*." Twenty-eight thousand Andersen employees found themselves without a job.

DID YOU KNOW?

A Young Auditor's Report

Vincent Daniel, who later made a killing by betting short on the downfall of Wall Street investment banks, had worked for Arthur Andersen in his first job. He was assigned as a junior member of an audit team looking over the books of Salomon Brothers, a huge Wall Street enterprise. Michael Lewis in *The Big Short* reports that Daniel was immediately struck by the opacity of the Salomon Brothers' books and the auditors' inability to comprehend what Salomon was doing and why it was doing it. He concluded that there was no way for an accountant assigned to such a task to determine accurately whether the company was making money or losing money, that their books were "giant black boxes, whose hidden gears were in constant motion." His manager, who did not have any better comprehension of the true picture, finally told him to stop asking questions and just do the best he could, that that was what he had been hired for.

The auditing company also became the butt of a presidential joke. Speaking to a charity group in 2002, George W. Bush declared: "I just received a message from Saddam Hussein. The good news is that he is willing to have nuclear, biological, and chemical weapons inspected. The bad news is that he wants Arthur Andersen to do it."

But the story did not end there. In mid-2005 a unanimous U.S. Supreme Court agreed with the claim of Andersen lawyers that the shredding of papers—the core of the government's case—could have been no more than a routine act that was part of the company's "document retention policy" and not necessarily a cover-up. The Court declared that "the jury instructions at issue simply failed to convey the requisite consciousness of wrongdoing required to convict." Given the information in the indictment that is set forth as Document 10.3, it seems extraordinarily far-fetched to suggest that the shredding was anything but a deliberate and strenuous attempt to keep the SEC from looking at incriminating materials. But the Supreme Court also relied on a more compelling technical point: that the trial court's instructions to the jury had failed to convey the requisite consciousness of wrongdoing that was needed to be proven in order to convict. The decision again underlined the considerable difficulty in regard to white-collar offenses that is connected to the need to establish mens rea— criminal intent. If someone enters your house without permission and walks out with a bagful of your possessions, it is obvious that the intent was to commit a crime. But as we have seen earlier, to get a conviction on insider trading, for instance, the prosecution must prove that the nonpublic information was the cause for the transaction. And with Andersen it had to prove that the disposal of documents was not just one of those things that happened regularly but rather was an illegal attempt to thwart the investigators.

There was a further irony. The reversal by the Supreme Court was almost totally meaningless. The company was dead and there was no possibility of resurrection. The decision was much like the centuries later action by the Massachusetts legislature to overturn the verdict that condemned persons hanged as witches in Salem in 1692. The affected were no longer around to appreciate the legislative pardon.

DID YOU KNOW?

Nancy Temple Thereafter

Following the demise of Arthur Andersen, Nancy Anne Temple, in the words of an interviewer, "hit bottom." But she rebounded and a decade afterward had established herself as a partner in a six-person law firm on Dearborn Street in Chicago.

Temple was a graduate of the University of Illinois with a major in accounting and holds a JD degree from Harvard Law School. She worked for 11 years for the law firm Sidley Austin handling accountant liability cases. With that experience and her twin specialties, she was a natural for a powerful position at Arthur Andersen, but there she encountered an environment that demanded unquestioning support for the company's behavior even in the face of personal doubt that it was desirable, even legal behavior.

After the Andersen trial, Ms. Temple found herself outside the circle of elite so-called white-shoe prosperous attorneys and tried a solo practice, handling whatever came through the door—criminal cases and contingency claims where the attorney gets a cut of the award, but only if there is an award. She trained for the Chicago marathon and the Ironman Triathlon, where she met Mitchell Katten, who was also preparing for the grueling competition, and who would become her partner in the law firm they launched: Katten and Temple. She also took a five-day trek in the Andes. "I just tried to get through each day," she would tell an interviewer. "If I stepped back and thought about what I was going through, I probably would have been frightened to death."

Katten & Temple's website advertises the firm in boilerplate prose: "We serve as attorney and counselor. We take care and time at the outset of the representation to understand the relevant facts . . . We work closely with our clients to ensure each strategy takes into account applicable business goals and needs." More informative is a comment by a fellow lawyer regarding Ms. Temple: "She's smart and tough. Her experience in learning how the winds of fate can turn on anybody certainly helped her perspective."

FURTHER READINGS

Arthur Andersen LLP v. United States, 544 United States Reporter 686 (May 31, 2005), reversing 374 Federal Reporter 3d 281 (Fifth Circuit, June 24, 2004).

Squires, Susan E., Cynthia Smith, Lorna MacDougall, and William B. Yeack. (2003). *Inside Arthur Andersen: Shifting Values, Unexpected Consequences.* Upper Saddle River, NJ: Prentice Hall.

Toffler, Barbara Ley, and Jennifer Reingold. (2003). *Final Accounting: Ambition, Greed, and the Fall of Arthur Andersen.* New York: Broadway Books.

Adelphia Communications Corporation

- **Document:** John Rigas, the founder of the Adelphia Communications Corporation, was convicted of robbing the company's treasury. After this and similar cases are concluded, the question of compensating victims arises. Document 10.4 demonstrates how the office handling the prosecution informs possible victims of their rights and summarizes the events that led up to this communication to them.
- **Date:** April 8, 2008.
- **Where:** U.S. Attorney's Office, New York City.
- **Significance:** Document 10.4 is a wrap-up explanation of the government's case against the Adelphia Communications Corporation and its two leading executives. The document also is significant in showing the emerging concern by law enforcers with making victims aware of the course of events. In earlier days, a common complaint was that a victim, once she or he had aided the enforcers, was never told of what had later occurred, and that this negligence deterred some citizens from cooperating with the authorities.

DOCUMENT 10.4

RE: *United States v. John Rigas, et al.,* S102 Cr. 1236 (LBS)

Dear Investor:

We are writing to you because you may have suffered a financial loss as a direct result of the Adelphia Communications Company securities fraud. The purpose of this letter is to notify you of an opportunity to petition to recover a portion of your financial losses and to inform you of the status of the criminal prosecutions of those who are primarily responsible for the fraud.

On July 2, 2003, ... [an] indictment was filed against John Rigas, Timothy Rigas and others, charging them with conspiracy to commit securities fraud, conspiracy to make false statements in filings with the Securities and Exchange Commission, and other offenses in connection with the management and control of Adelphia Communications Corporation ... On July 8, 2004, following a jury trial, John Rigas and Timothy Rigas were convicted of conspiracy to commit securities fraud and other offenses. On June 20, 2005, the District Court sentenced John Rigas to fifteen years' imprisonment, six months' suspended release, and a $1,800 special assessment. The same day, Judge Sand sentenced Timothy Rigas to twenty years' imprisonment, two years' suspended release, and a $1,800 special assessment.

The investigation and prosecution of the Adelphia fraud has resulted in criminal forfeiture of asses that the Government intends to use to provide partial compensation to holders of Adelphia publicly traded securities who suffered a pecuniary loss as a direct result of the fraud, in accord with the provisions of Part 9 of Article 28 of the Code of Federal Regulations. These regulations ... provide for the disbursement of forfeited money to qualified victims. The regulations spell out who is a qualified victim, and under what circumstances such a victim can recover ... A copy of these regulations is available on the website www.adelphiiafund.com If you do not have internet access you may obtain a copy of the regulations by calling (866) 446-4884 or writing the Adelphia Victim Fund, P.O. Box 697, Syracuse, New York 13217-6977. The decision as to which victims receive funds and in what amounts is within the discretion of the DOJ [Department of Justice], and is determined by the Chief of the Asset Forfeiture and Money Laundering Section. While it is the Office's view that victims of fraud should recover their lost funds under the petition for remission and mitigation process, there are no guarantees that each victim will receive reimbursement or that each victim will receive a full recovery.[1] ...

If you have any questions, please do not hesitate to call the phone number listed on the petition form.

Very truly yours,

MICHAEL L. GARCIA
United States Attorney
Southern District of New York

Source: Michael L. Garcia, letter to investor regarding *United States v. John Rigas, et al.*, S102 Cr. 1236, U.S. Department of Justice, U.S. Attorney, Southern District of New York, New York City, April 8, 2008.

---

[1]"The United States Securities and Exchange Commission has obtained additional funds in civil enforcement actions it brought in connection with the Adelphia securities fraud. ... These funds are subject to the jurisdiction of he Federal District Court presiding over the SEC enforcement action. The SEC intends to seek permission from he Federal District Court to distribute those funds to victims of the fraud. To be considered for a distribution from the SEC fund, you do not need to do anything at this time other than petition DOJ for a distribution as set forth in this letter and accompanying documents."

ANALYSIS

The brazen scams perpetuated by two members of the Rigas family who operated the Adelphia Communications Company stands as a model of flagrant managerial arrogance. The company had been founded in 1952 by John J. Rigas and his brother, Gus, sons of Greek immigrants who had lived over a small hot dog stand that they operated. The Rigas brothers started with the $300 purchase of a cable television franchise, and in the 1980s John bought his brother out. In time, Adelphia grew to be the fifth-largest cable television marketer in the nation. It was headquartered in Coudersport in north central Pennsylvania, a two-stoplight town, and employed 2,000 people in a city with a population of fewer than 500 people. Coudersport was five hours away from Buffalo, New York, where the nearest airport was located. Rigas so dominated the town that it would sometimes take him an hour to traverse a couple of blocks on the main street as people stopped him to talk and pay their respects.

Its website notes that Adelphia "owns, manages, and operates cable television systems in mid-sized and suburban areas where non-cable reception is weak." At its peak Adelphia had 5.7 million subscribers and stations in 32 states. In its earlier days, before it took on shareholders, the company finances and those of its founder were one and the same. The management continued with that policy, dipping recklessly into the company assets whenever they felt like doing so. As one commentator put it, the cheating was "plain vanilla old-fashioned self-dealing."

In 2002, Adelphia declared bankruptcy and John Rigas and his two sons, Timothy and Michael, as well as Michael Mulcahey, the former treasurer, were charged with a host of criminal offenses, including falsifying profit-and-loss numbers supplied to investors and regularly withdrawing money from the company for personal use. John, for instance, pulled from the company funds $1 million each month without indicating that this was a loan and that the funds were to be repaid—neither of which statements would have been accurate.

At the trial, evidence showed that the company airplane had been used to ship a Christmas tree to the home of one of the Rigas family members at a cost of $6,000. John and Timothy Rigas were said to own 22 automobiles. The company also was billed for the $40,000 annual salary of a personal family masseuse. The real estate taxes on the 12 houses owned by Rigas family members were paid with a single check drawn on the company.

After a four-month trial, the jury convicted John and Timothy Rigas, but could not reach a verdict on their brother Michael, who in his defense showed that he routinely reimbursed the company for his personal expenses, including a check that he wrote to Adelphia for $3.45 for postage. Timothy Rigas

> ## DID YOU KNOW?
>
> ### The Dismemberment of Adelphia
>
> Shortly after Adelphia declared bankruptcy, the remnants of the company moved to Greenwood Village in Colorado where some 275 employees attended to liquidation details. A major rearrangement came with the sale of the cable operation to Time Warner and Comcast for some $17 billion. Time Warner, the second-largest cable company in the world, acquired 3.3 million subscribers as a result of the purchase. Comcast got 1.7 former Adelphia clients. Soon after, the long-distance telephone business of Adelphia was sold to Pioneer Telephone for $1.2 million. Adelphia Field, the name bestowed on a Nashville sports stadium, ceased to bear the company signature until it found a new sponsor in 2006. It became LP Field when the Louisiana-Pacific company, a Nashville company dealing in building materials, paid for the right to have its trade name assigned to the stadium.

had found to have purchased 100 pairs of slippers and charged them to the company. There also was the expenditure of $3 million of company money for the Rigas daughter to use to produce a film.

Mulcahey, the only defendant to take the stand, was acquitted of all 23 counts. John Rigas, then 79 years old and under treatment at the Mayo Clinic in Minneapolis for bladder cancer, was convicted and sentenced to 15 years in prison, with the judge indicating that if his health seemed to necessitate it, he would agree to release Rigas after he had served two years in custody. Timothy received a 20-year sentence. Michael later pled guilty to making a false entry on company records and received a sentence of 10 months of house confinement.

FURTHER READINGS

Frank, Robert. (2002, May 28). "In Coudersport, PA, Adelphia Chief is Hometown Hero." *Wall Street Journal*, A1, A4.

Jennings, Marianne M. (2008). "Adelphia: Good Works Via a Hand in the Till." In Marianne M. Jennings, *Business Ethics: Case Studies and Selected Readings* (6th ed., pp. 93–97). Mason, OH: South-Western/Cengage.

Kidwell, Robert E., and Christopher L. Martin. (2005). *Managing Organizational Deviance*. Thousand Oaks, CA: Sage.

Leonard, Devin. (2003, August 12). "The Adelphia Story." *Fortune* 146:137–46.

Mahoney, Philip. (2005). In re Adelphia Communications Corporation. *New York Law School Law Review* 49:1007–18.

Sarbanes-Oxley

- *Document:* The cascade of bankruptcies and the revelations about irregularities perpetrated by business executives cried out for some kind of federal action to prevent a repetition of such behaviors, to, if not successful in achieving that goal, punish more severely those who engaged in similar kinds of acts, and to deter those who might contemplate doing so. The Sarbanes-Oxley Act was designed to deal with corrupt corporate conduct that had been uncovered in 2002. The excerpt below includes Section 302 of the act, which discusses corporate responsibility.
- *Date:* The Sarbanes-Oxley Act was passed by Congress in 2002.
- *Where:* U.S. Congress.
- *Significance:* The act was seen as a strong response to the accounting and other devious manipulations practices by some of the major corporate entities in the United States. It has been duplicated with adjustments to local conditions in several European and Asian countries.

DOCUMENT 10.5

Sarbanes-Oxley Act
SEC. 302. CORPORATE RESPONSIBILITY FOR FINANCIAL REPORTS.

(a) REGULATIONS REQUIRED.—The Commission shall, by rule, require, for each company filing periodic reports under section 13(a) or 15(d) of the Securities Exchange Act of 1934 (15 U.S.C. 78m, 78o(d)), that the principal executive officer or officers and the principal financial officer or officers, or persons performing similar functions, certify in each annual or quarterly report filed or submitted under either such section of such Act that—

(1) the signing officer has reviewed the report;

(2) based on the officer's knowledge, the report does not contain any untrue statement of a material fact or omit to state a material fact necessary in order to make the statements made, in light of the circumstances under which such statements were made, not misleading;

(3) based on such officer's knowledge, the financial statements, and other financial information included in the report, fairly present in all material respects the financial condition and results of operations of the issuer as of, and for, the periods presented in the report;

(4) the signing officers—

(A) are responsible for establishing and maintaining internal controls;

(B) have designed such internal controls to ensure that material information relating to the issuer and its consolidated subsidiaries is made known to such officers by others within those entities, particularly during the period in which the periodic reports are being prepared;

(C) have evaluated the effectiveness of the issuer's internal controls as of a date within 90 days prior to the report; and

(D) have presented in the report their conclusions about the effectiveness of their internal controls based on their evaluation as of that date;

(5) the signing officers have disclosed to the issuer's auditors and the audit committee of the board of directors (or persons fulfilling the equivalent function)—

(A) all significant deficiencies in the design or operation of internal controls which could adversely affect the issuer's ability to record, process, summarize, and report financial data and have identified for the issuer's auditors any material weaknesses in internal controls; and

(B) any fraud, whether or not material, that involves management or other employees who have a significant role in the issuer's internal controls; and

(6) the signing officers have indicated in the report whether or not there were significant changes in internal controls or in other factors that could significantly affect internal controls subsequent to the date of their evaluation, including any corrective actions with regard to significant deficiencies and material weaknesses.

(b) FOREIGN REINCORPORATIONS HAVE NO EFFECT.—Nothing in this section 302 shall be interpreted or applied in any way to allow any issuer to lessen the legal force of the statement required under this section 302, by an issuer having reincorporated or having engaged in any other transaction that resulted in the transfer of the corporate domicile or offices of the issuer from inside the United States to outside of the United States.

(c) DEADLINE.—The rules required by subsection (a) shall be effective not later than 30 days after the date of enactment of this Act.

Source: U.S. Congress, *Congressional Record*, 107th Cong., 2nd Sess. (2002).

ANALYSIS

The most obvious and depressing aspect of the Sarbanes-Oxley Act was that it did not prove to be successful in preventing the egregious acts by corporate America that resulted in the most serious economic crisis the United States has experienced since the Great Depression of the 1930s (see chapter 12). Even so, corporate lobbyists complained that the act imposed too strenuous and too costly an array of burdens on them that cost jobs and depleted the vitality of the capitalistic economic engine.

Prior to Sarbanes-Oxley, episodes of corporate malfeasance had been shrugged off as rare occurrences, the misbehavior of a few bad apples in an otherwise untainted barrel, but the scandals before and subsequent to passage of the act indicated that these were not uncommon events but had remained in the dark during periods of financial prosperity. Corporate earning statements might be wildly inflated, but the manipulations could be ignored so long as investors were seeing their holdings increase considerably in value. Ironically, problems arose for executives in companies competing with the outlaws. They were being downgraded for their failure to show a growth rate equivalent to that of the cheaters.

The Sarbanes-Oxley Act, more formally known as Public Company Reform and Investor Protection Act, established norms for publicly held companies and certified public accountants, though businesses not registered in the United States remain beyond its reach. The law forbids auditing firms to engage in consulting activities for a client unless the activities are approved by the client's board of directors. Most important, the law requires that a company's executive officer and chief financial officer attest to the honesty of a company's quarterly financial statement. If the statement is false, the attesting officers must reimburse the company for any equity-based compensation and any profit from the sale of stock during the year following the noncompliant report. Critics maintain that this requirement is unfair: how can a chief executive guarantee that his fiscal officers are not cheating in the profit-and-loss statements they submit to him? College professors wonder if it is a true parallel to suggest that they would resent a law that penalized them if they accepted and gave a good grade for a term paper that the student had cribbed off the Internet.

Sarbanes-Oxley also prohibits executives and other specified company officers from accepting employment with the company's auditor for at least two years after they have given up their corporate position. Lead auditors must be rotated every five years, and an audit cannot be done by a firm for whom the CEO or CFO worked within the past five years. Also, audit documents must be retained for at least five years.

Sarbanes-Oxley created two new criminal felonies. The first punishes any person or organization that knowingly alters, destroys, mutilates, conceals, or covers up any document or tangible object with the intent to obstruct or impede procedures of federal agencies or bankruptcy investigations. The second relates to the willful destruction or secreting of corporate audit records. The new statute also indicated that if a company formulated and vigorously taught and enforced compliance guidelines, this could play a role in reducing the punishment inflicted upon it for criminal behavior. Most companies immediately set about creating guidelines insisting on legal and ethical actions, but it remains arguable whether these are likely to be particularly effective. The best thinking in the field is that the moral tone set by the highest officers in a company is the key to how underlings will act.

The language in SOX seeking to protect whistleblowers, who often seem to suffer severe retaliation, tries to deal with the ironic maxim that "no good deed goes unpunished." Section 1107 of SOX under the title "Retaliation against Informants" reads:

> Whoever knowingly, with the intent to retaliate, takes any action harmful to any person, including interference with the lawful employment or livelihood of any person, for providing to a law enforcement officer any truthful information relating to the commission or possible commission of any Federal offense, shall be fined under this rule or imprisoned not more than ten years.

DID YOU KNOW?

Senator Sarbanes and Representative Oxley

Paul Spyros Sarbanes served as a Democratic senator from Maryland from 1977 until 2007, the longest tenure for a person holding that position in the state's history. He was descended from a family of Greek immigrants, attended Princeton University, was a Rhodes Scholar in England, and a graduate of Harvard Law School.

In an interview in 2008 with Tom Shean of the *Virginia Pilot*, Sarbanes was asked about his experiences in getting SOX enacted into law:

> When I took over the chairmanship of the Senate Banking Committee in June 2001, I didn't expect to be dealing with this issue. Enron at the time was reporting 20 percent increases in earnings quarter to quarter. By December of 2001, they had declared bankruptcy, so these figures were phony. Lots of people lost their jobs. People's retirements were severely affected, so there are very real consequences for not doing things the right way.
>
> In the end, the bill was passed without dissent, but getting there was not that easy. As it turned out, just a few days before we were able to report the bill out of the Senate committee, the WorldCom scandal broke. That gave tremendous momentum for moving the legislation through the Senate and then through the conference committee with the House.

Michael Garner Oxley, who sponsored the reform measure in the House of Representatives, was a Republican from Ohio. He had graduated from Miami University in Oxford, Ohio, and in Congress rose to be chair of the House Financial Services Committee. On SOX he had this to say when he was interviewed by Liz Alderman while he was attending a meeting in France in March 2007:

> Everybody felt like Rome was burning. It was unlike anything I had ever seen in Congress in the 25 years in terms of the heat from the body politic. And all the members were for it.

FURTHER READINGS

Fletcher, William H., and Theodore N. Plette. (2003). *The Sarbanes-Oxley Act: Implementation, Significance and Impact.* New York: Nova Science.

Prentice, Robert A., and Dean Bredeson. (2008). *Student Guide to the Sarbanes-Oxley Act.* Mason, OH: Homson/West.

Rezaee, Zabihollah. (2007). *Corporate Governance Post-Sarbanes-Oxley Regulations, Requirements, and Integrated Processes.* Hoboken, NJ: Wiley.

Thibodeau, Jay, and Deborah Freir. (2007). *Auditing After Sarbanes-Oxley: Illustrative Cases.* Boston: McGraw-Hill/Irwin.

Welytok, Jill Gilbert. (2008). *Sarbanes-Oxley for Dummies.* Hoboken, NJ: Wiley.

HealthSouth

- *Document:* The case against Richard Scrushy, the former CEO of HealthSouth, is spelled out in the complaint filed by the SEC.
- *Date:* March 19, 2003.
- *Where:* U.S. District Court, Northern District of Alabama, Birmingham.
- *Significance:* A major question facing the government was whether the Sarbanes-Oxley Act, when used as the basis for a court case, could effectively produce the curative result it sought to achieve by punishing a wrongdoer and, much more difficult to determine, whether it could inhibit others from engaging in the same kind of unacceptable act.

DOCUMENT 10.6

The Securities and Exchange Commission . . . files this Complaint for Injunctive and Other Relief as follows.

INTRODUCTION

1. Since 1999, HealthSouth Corp ("HRC"), one of the nation's largest healthcare providers, has overstated its earnings by at least $1.4 billion. This massive overstatement occurred because HRC's founder, Chief Executive Officer and Chairman of the Board, Richard M. Scrushy insisted that HRC must meet or exceed earnings expectations established by Wall Street analysts. When HRC's earnings fell short of such estimates, Scrushy directed HRC accounting personnel to "fix it" by artificially inflating the company's earnings to match Wall Street expectations. To balance HRC's books, the false increases in earnings were matched by false increases in HRC assets. By the third quarter of 2002, HRC's assets were overstated by at least

$800 million, or approximately 10 percent of total asserts. HRC's most recent reports filed with the Commission continue to reflect the fraudulent numbers...

2.   Despite the fact that HRC's financial statements were materially misstated, on August 14, 2002, Scrushy certified under oath that HRC's 2001 Form 10-K contained "no untrue statement of a material fact." In truth, the financial statements filed with this report overstated HRC's earnings, identified on HRC's income statement as "Income Before Income Taxes And Minority Interests," by at least 4,700%....

THE DEFENDANTS

9.   HealthSouth Corporation was incorporated in Delaware in 1984 and is head-quartered in Birmingham, Alabama. HRC is the nation's biggest provider of outpatient surgery, diagnostic and rehabilitative healthcare services. It owns or operates over 1,800 different facilities throughout the United States and abroad, including inpatient and outpatient rehabilitative facilities, outpatient surgery centers, diagnostic centers, medical centers and other healthcare facilities.

11.   Richard M. Scrushy, 49, founded HRC and has served as Chairman since 1994. He served as HRC's Chief Executive Officer from 1994 until August 27, 2002. On January 6, 2003, he resumed the position of HRC's CEO...

13.   The approximate amounts of overstated [income] since 1999... are as follows:

...16.   Pursuant to the scheme, on a quarterly basis HRC's officers would present Scrushy with an analysis of HRC's actual, but as yet unreported, earnings for the quarter as compared to Wall Street's expected earnings for the company.

17.   HRC senior accounting personnel then convened a meeting to "fix" the earnings shortfall. By 1997, the attendees referred to these meetings as "family meetings" and referred to themselves as "family members"...

25.   HRC's accounting personnel designed the false journal entries to the income statement and balance sheet accounts in a manner calculated to avoid detection by the outside auditors. For example, instead of increasing the revenue account directly, HRC inflated earnings by increasing the "contractual adjustment" amount. Because the amounts booked to this account are estimated, there is a limited paper trail and the individual entries to this account are more difficult to verify than other entries.

26.   Additionally, each inflation of earnings and corresponding increase in fixed assets were recorded through several intermediary journal entries in order to make the false inflation more difficult to trace...

Income (Loss) before Income Taxes and Minority Interests (in $ Million)	1999 Form 10-K	2000 Form 10-K	2001 Form 10-K	For Six Months Ended June 30, 2002
Actual	$(191)	$194	$9	$157
Reported	230	559	434	340
Misstated Amount	421	365	425	183
Misstated Percentage	220%	188%	4,722%	119%

29. HRC also created false documents to support its fictitious accounting entries. For example, during the audit of HRC's 2000 financial statements, the auditors questioned an addition to fiscal assets at one particular HRC facility. HRCs accounting personnel, knowing that this addition was fictitious altered an existing invoice . . . to fraudulently indicate that the facility in question had actually purchased the asset. . . .

30. In the fall of 1997, when HRC's accounting personnel advised Scrushy to abandon the earnings manipulation scheme, Scrushy refused, saying in substance: "Not until I sell my stock."

Source: United States v. HealthSouth Corporation, Complaint for Injunctive and Other Relief, Civil Action No. CV-03-J-0615-S, U.S. District Court (Alabama, 2003).

ANALYSIS

Richard Martin Scrushy became the first major corporate kingpin prosecuted for violation of the Sarbanes-Oxley Act. He was charged with 36 counts, including having certified fraudulent accounting reports that were said to involve misstatements involving $2.3 billion.

Scrushy was born in Selma, Alabama, a site that would become famous for its central role in the civil rights campaign by Africa Americans, and he was educated at the University of Alabama in Birmingham. By the time he was heading HealthSouth, he had been married three times and sired eight children. He started the company with an investment of $50,000 and drove it forward relentlessly. *Fortune* magazine would note that he confronted employees with a picture of a wagon with two men pulling it while eight others sat inside. He told employees: "Everyone has to pull the wagon." HealthSouth would adopt that idea as its motto: "Pull the wagon together."

Scrushy was the founder, chairman, and chief executive officer of HealthSouth, the nation's largest rehabilitative hospital facility. HealthSouth employed more than 50,000 people worldwide and had earned more than $267 million between 1996 and 2002. Scrushy's name was prominent all over Birmingham: There was the Richard Scrushy Building on the University of Alabama campus; the Richard Scrushy Parkway; and a museum behind the HealthSouth headquarters that was devoted to Scrushy's career. There also was a statue of Scrushy in Birmingham that would be pulled down after someone spray-painted the word "Thief" on it. Commentators joked that if he were to be imprisoned, in no time Scrushy would have the penal facility being named for him. His worldly success was exemplified by a 49-room house in Vestavia, Alabama, that became a tourist attraction after Scrushy was incarcerated.

When he was tried on the charges leveled by the SEC, Scrushy's lawyers claimed that the requirements of the Sarbanes-Oxley Act were "so vague as to defy comprehension." Their client was acquitted on all counts after a six-month trial, again demonstrating the difficulty that can arise when the government tries persons it believes are guilty of white-collar crimes. The situation was exemplified during the voir dire examinations to select the jury. A person who later was chosen to be on the jury was asked: "Are you going to hold it against Mr. Scrushy that he hired that many lawyers?" "Certainly not," the prospective juror answered. "That's the way our system works. You hire the best." The implied end of the answer was "that you are able to afford."

Matters took various other turns after Scrushy's acquittal. He was sued by stockholders for equity losses at the same time that he was suing HealthSouth for $70 million, claiming that he had been unfairly terminated. The stockholders won a $2.87 billion award, and the SEC hit Scrushy with a $40 million penalty on a charge of "unjust enrichment."

On top of this, four months later Scrushy was charged with bribery, money laundering, extortion, obstruction of justice, and racketeering for allegedly giving Alabama governor Don Siegelman half a million dollars in exchange for a seat on the state board that regulated hospitals. The jury twice told the judge that it was hopelessly deadlocked, with the foreman indicating that some jurors were being "lackadaisical" about their duty. The judge sent them back to try some more, and the panel managed to reach a guilty verdict. Siegelman was sentenced to seven years in prison; Scrushy got six years and 10 months and a $150,000 fine. He also was required to pay for the expense of his imprisonment.

Scrushy's reaction to these events was in character: "There is no evidence to tie me into any of these changes. It is very sad that this could happen in America." Note might be made that the did not claim innocence; only that the evidence to establish guilt was not sufficient. Scrushy's mélange of lawyers might well have warned him of the danger of perjury charges if he lied flat out,

An Internet biography by Answer.com on Scrushy sums up his career nicely, noting that "he represents the true American success story, albeit one with a less-than-happy ending." The same source pinpoints his aspirations: "When Scrushy was working as a bricklayer and living in a trailer, his guests did not get a beer and pretzels but rather a serving of wine and cheese."

DID YOU KNOW?

Why Was Scrushy Acquitted?

Postmortems on the Scrushy case sought to understand why he had been acquitted when Bernard J. Ebbers, the former CEO of WorldCom, and Dennis Kozlowski of Tyco both had been convicted on evidence no more compelling than that against Scrushy. It was noted that both Ebbers and Kozlowski had taken the witness stand in their own defense and thereby had offered prosecutors the opportunity to pinpoint their lies, evasions, and discomforts when confronted with possibly incriminating evidence. Scrushy had declined to testify, a matter that in the United Kingdom now may be commented upon by the judge as a possible adverse circumstance, but cannot be mentioned by American judges. And both Ebbers and Kozlowski had been tried in New York City whereas Scrushy's case was heard in Birmingham, where he was admired for his philanthropy. In addition, right before and during the trial Scrushy had become affiliated with an African American church; 7 of the 12 jurors were African Americans.

FURTHER READINGS

Cherry, Brenda, and Patricia Nearing. (2003, July 7). "The Insatiable King Richard: He Started as a Nobody. He Became a Hotshot CEO. He Tried to Be a Country Star? Then It All Came Crashing Down: The Bizarre Rise and Fall of Health South's Richard Scrushy." *Fortune* 48: 76–80, 82, 84.

Taylor, Jaclyn. (2005). "Fluke or Failure?: Assessing the Sarbanes-Oxley Act After *United States v. Scrushy.*" *University of Missouri Kansas City Law Review* 74:411–34.

Tyco International

- **Document:** Document 10.7 is part of New York Court's ruling regarding legal aspects of a suit filed by Tyco International against Frank E. Walsh Jr., a former member of its board of directors, to recover money that the company claimed had not legally been awarded to Walsh. The document concerns Walsh's challenge of the right of this particular court to deal with the issue.
- **Date:** February 28, 2003.
- **Where:** U.S. District Court, Southern District of New York, Manhattan.
- **Significance:** The case focuses a spotlight on a member of Tyco's board of directors, a group that often fails miserably in its duties to safeguard the interests of investors. Directors typically are appointed by a company's top officials and acquiesce to whatever is asked of them. The Walsh-Tyco case also shows the much greater complexity of legal wrangling that tends to be associated with white-collar and corporate crimes compared to street offenses.

DOCUMENT 10.7

OPINION AND ORDER
DENNIS COTE, District Judge

Defendant Frank E. Walsh, Jr. has moved to dismiss this action on the ground of a lack of personal jurisdiction and improper venue, or, in the alternative, for a transfer of this case to the District of New Jersey. The plaintiff Tyco International Limited asserts personal jurisdiction in this diversity action pursuant to New York's long-standing statute . . .

Background

The complaint arises out of Tyco's payment to Walsh on or about July 31, 2001, in connection with Tyco's acquisition of CIT Group, Inc. on or about June 1, 2011. Walsh was allegedly paid this amount for introducing Tyco's Chairman and CEO, Dennis Kozlowski to CIT's chairman and CEO and otherwise promoting the acquisition. Walsh was a member of the Board of Directors of Tyco at the time, having been a board member since 1997, and having been a board member of its predecessor since 1992. The complaint alleges that Walsh knew that the payment of the $20 million, half of which went to a New Jersey charity designated by Walsh, had to be disclosed to and approved by the Board, but that he and Kozlowski agreed that the Board would not be informed. Outside directors learned of the payment in January 2002. At the Board meeting on January 16, 2002, in Florida, the Board asked Walsh to return $10 million and he refused. The complaint contains causes of action for restitution, breach of fiduciary duty, conversion, unjust enrichment, constructive trusts, and inducing breach of fiduciary duty. . . .

On August 27 Walsh filed a motion to dismiss.

In support of his motion to dismiss Walsh asser4ts that he is a resident of New Jersey and had no residence in New York. His business office is in New Jersey and his involvement with the CTT acquisition took place outside of New York. The last Tyco meeting that he attended in New York was on October 13, 1999. The CTT transaction was approved by Tyco at a Board meeting in Bermuda, the place of incorporation since 1997.

To support the assertion of personal jurisdiction and venue in this jurisdiction in this district, Tyco points to Walsh's regular attendance at Tyco board meetings in New York through 1997, and attendance at a board committee meeting in New York in 1999. It asserts that Walsh negotiated payment of the $20 million in telephone calls with Kozlowski and Tyco's Chief Financial Officer while the latter two men were in New York. The invoice that Walsh prepared for payment of the fee was addressed to Tyco's Treasurer in New York, although sent by Walsh to Florida for transmittal to New York. While in New York, the Treasurer approved the payment. Tyco also relies on the fact that the CTT acquisition was negotiated and closed in New York. . . .

[Readers might find it interesting to pause at this point in their review of the case and decide what decision they themselves would reach based on the facts outlined above by the presiding judge. The next paragraph offers his conclusions.]

Defendant has not shown that he would be seriously inconvenienced or that it would be unfair to litigate this case in New York. Indeed, the defendant has not presented any argument to support his motion for transfer. Based on this and the facts in the record, the defendant's motion for transfer is denied.

Source: Tyco International Limited v. Frank E. Walsh, Jr., 02 CIV. 463 (DL), U.S. Dist. LEXIS 207 (2003).

ANALYSIS

The first major inkling of trouble at Tyco International surfaced early in 2001 when it paid $9.2 billion in cash and stock to purchase CIT Group, a commercial finance company. Tyco, although incorporated in Bermuda, had its headquarters since 1998 in Exeter, New Hampshire—New Hampshire being one of the nine American states without an income tax. Tyco was a conglomerate with 250,000 employees that marketed products such as medical supplies, home security systems, fiber-optic cable, and steel fence posts.

The smoking gun that began Tyco's undoing was the fact that Frank E. Walsh Jr., a director of Tyco, had helped arrange the deal. Walsh, a graduate of Lehigh University in Bethlehem, Pennsylvania, with a degree in accounting, had founded and chaired the Wesray Capital Corporation, located in Morristown, New Jersey, and specializing in acquisitions. It would soon come to light that Walsh had received $10 million as a fee. Another $10 million had been given to the Community Foundation of New Jersey, a charity in which Walsh was a director. He would testify that he was told by Tyco's CEO not to inform any other members of the board of directors of the arrangement. In late 2002, Walsh would plead guilty to having attempted to hide the $20 million and was fined $2.5 million. It was speculated that Walsh, who headed the compensation committee at Tyco, was given the $20 million to buy his silence in regard to his awareness of the depredations that Tyco's CEO, CFO, and other company officers were inflicting on the company.

Ironically, in January 2002, L. Dennis Kozlowski, the CEO of Tyco, had been named one of the 25 top corporate managers in the United States for the previous year. Perhaps that judgment was predicated on approval of Kozlowski's business philosophy: "Money is the only way to keep score," he had proclaimed.

In that same month as the accolade, Kozlowski and Mark H. Swartz, Tyco's chief financial officer, were reported to have sold more than $100 million worth of their own stock during the prior fiscal year despite their public pronouncements that they rarely sold their stock. Six months later Kozlowski resigned in the face of reports that he was under investigation by the Manhattan district attorney's office for sales tax evasion. Kozlowski had purchased paintings by Monet and Renoir for $13.1 million and pretended to have bought them from Tyco's New Hampshire office to avoid the higher tax in New York.

In September 2002, Kozlowski and Swartz were criminally indicted for allegedly stealing more than $170 million from Tyco and obtaining $470 million by fraud involving the sale of company stock. At their first trial the prosecution showed videos of a birthday party in Sardinia for Kozlowski's wife with the guests all adorned with Roman togas. Singer Jimmy Buffett provided some of the entertainment. In all, Tyco paid out about $1 million to underwrite the party. Also presented to the jury was a picture of what became a notorious shower curtain in the Kozlowski home, a $6,000 purchase paid for by Tyco. In April, 2004, however, the judge declared a mistrial. The vote was 11 to 1 for conviction. The holdout was a lawyer and former teacher who reported that she had received a message pressuring her to convict the defendants.

Interviews with jurors found that they had ignored the eye-catching evidence about Kozlowski's bash and shower curtains as beside the point in regard to his guilt for criminal behavior. The jurors, one said, considered that information "a waste of time." In the subsequent trial, the prosecution dropped the Sardinia and shower curtain evidence, concentrating instead on the money the two men had stolen from the company, calling their behavior "kleptomaniac management." This time the prosecution sped up its presentation. The second trial occupied 13 weeks compared to 18 for the initial hearing.

Unlike in the first trial, Kozlowski took the witness stand on his behalf, a maneuver that failed to save him and may have contributed to his conviction. Jurors can be somewhat forgiving of what they see as financial irregularities, but in an odd way they can be much less tolerant when they listen to a defendant seemingly lying about persuasive prosecution evidence. "I have never intended to commit a crime at all when I was chief executive officer of Tyco," Kozlowski said on the witness stand, a statement hardly fully exonerating him, given the qualifier of "intended." "Did you ever steal money from Tyco?" his lawyer asked Kozlowski. "No, I did not," the witness replied. "I never conspired with anyone at Tyco to commit a crime." Again, this is hardly a rousing statement of outraged innocence.

In mid-June the jury, after 11 days of deliberation, found both men guilty of stealing more than $150 million from Tyco. They were sentenced to a maximum of 25 years in prison with the possibility of release in 8 years and 4 months. Together they were required to pay $140 million in restitution; Kozlowski was fined $70 million, Swartz $35 million.

DID YOU KNOW?

Tyco Today

Arthur Andersen went up in flames; Tyco not only survived the crimes of its executives, it has thrived in post-Kozlowski times. Why is this so?

One reason is that auditing firms such as Arthur Andersen in their competition for clients rely upon prevailing judgments of their honesty and fair dealing. It matters to a corporation to not have to say that they were being audited by a company that was charged with flagrant violations of accounting regulations. On the other hand, it is quite unlikely that a customer will buy a product from a company other than Tyco, presuming the product is so available, because Tyco's former CEO and CFO are serving time in prison for fraudulent insider manipulations. The consequences may be unfair and uneven, but in this regard, unfortunately, they reflect many other inequities that pervade contemporary life.

Tyco in the wake of Kozlowski's departure split into three companies, each with its own management and own stock exchange listing: Covidien, Ltd. (formerly Tyco Healthcare); Tyco Electronics; and Tyco International. The latter two relocated in Schaffhausen in northern Switzerland, and in mid-2010 Tyco International announced its purchase of Brink's Home Security, thereby adding 1.5 million customers to its base of 4.5 million clients.

FURTHER READINGS

Eisenberg, Daniel, Daren Fonda, and Adam Zagorin. (2002, June 17). "Dennis the Menace." *Time* 159:46–49.

Greenberg, Herb. (2002, April 1). "Does Tyco Play Accounting Games?" *Fortune* 145–83.

McEntegart, Peter. (2002, April 12). "One Angry Man," *Time* 163:47–48.

Sweeney, Paul. (2002). "The Travails of Tyco," part 4, *Financial Executive* 18:20–23.

WorldCom

- *Document:* Document 10.8, excerpted from a law review article by an experienced communications attorney, focuses on the role of the Federal Communications Commission in monitoring (or, more accurately, failing to adequately monitor) WorldCom and notes how that federal agency suffered virtually no blame for its inaction. The document highlights the theme that the public perception and media construction of events such as corporate crime depend on conditions that do not necessarily reflect the true picture in terms of who did or did not do what.
- *Date:* June 2006.
- *Where:* *Federal Communications Law Journal.*
- *Significance:* The document inspects from a different angle and perspective another in the series of corporate crimes that we have looked at in this chapter.

DOCUMENT 10.8

HIGHLIGHT: WorldCom's disclosure of billions of dollars of financial fraud on June 25, 2002 challenged the Federal Communications Commission ("FCC") in several major ways. The FCC proclaimed its commitment to enforce its rules to protect consumers against service disturbances as well as the priority of rooting out corporate fraud. The FCC rules required WorldCom to file accurate financial information and to show that it had financial and character qualifications necessary to hold FCC licenses. Despite numerous related proceedings and other actions in 2001 and early 2002, the FCC had not detected nor deterred WorldCom's fraud. After the disclosure that WorldCom violated the FCC's rules by filing false financial information, the FCC did not take enforcement action against WorldCom and did not tighten its regulations related to such financial fraud ... Four partial explanations for the FCC's responses involve the actions of the Securities and Exchange Commission and Justice Department, downturns in the telecommunications industry, long-term deregulation, and political accountability ...

I. INTRODUCTION

The FCC is the principal federal agency responsible for fostering reliable, universally available telecommunication services, as well as competition and growth in the communications and related Internet services industry. A wide range of FCC policies, proceedings, and capabilities were implicated in the accounting fraud and resulting bankruptcy of WorldCom ... During the quarter century prior to the disclosure of fraud, advocacy by WorldCom and MCI Communications reshaped telecommunications regulations ...

The securities laws and regulations and the competence of the Securities and Exchange Commission were the focus of the public debate following WorldCom's disclosure. There was relatively slight attention to the FCC's enabling statute, regulations, and performance. The spotlight was instead directed at public companies' audited financial statements filed with the SEC. Perhaps this occurred because WorldCom's disclosure was preceded by disclosures at Enron and many other companies, as well as the criminal prosecution of Arthur Andersen LLP.

The failures within the communications industries were largely treated as further examples of problems with the securities laws, accounting standards, and the SEC. The FCC's public response to WorldCom's disclosure focused primarily on continuity of telecommunications services to the public, with secondary concerns about punishing and preventing fraud ...

The picture that emerges shows an agency that had responsibilities and made findings related to WorldCom's financial accounts but which was unaware and unsuspecting of the criminal conduct until WorldCom's public disclosure. Following the disclosure ... the FCC did not reform its analyses or regulations with the goal of protecting against future occurrences of similar harmful conduct. On the contrary, as part of its efforts to decrease unnecessary regulatory burdens and promote market force, the FCC applied streamlined requirements related to financial qualifications and accounting ... ,

[O]n a political level, high profile investigations and rule changes at the FCC would have put the agency more in the spotlight of what it, rather than the SEC, could have done to prevent accounting fraud by major telecommunications carriers; the FCC needed its political credibility as an effective regulator and industry analyst to push forward deregulation.

Source: Warren G. Lavey, "Response by the Federal Communications Commission to WorldCom's Accounting Fraud," *Federal Communications Law Journal* 58 (2007): 614–18.

ANALYSIS

The low-key response by the Federal Communications Commission to the unscrupulous behavior at WorldCom left the playing field to the Department of

Justice and the SEC, both of which were coming under increasing fire for alleged negligence in monitoring and inertia in prosecuting. WorldCom proved an easier target than usual because rebellious insiders took a role in exposing the wrongdoing and the criminal acts.

WorldCom for a time was the second-largest company in the long-distance telephone business, behind AT&T. The company had been founded by Bernie Ebbers in 1982 in Hattiesburg, Mississippi, under the name Long Distinct Discount Services. It subsequently renamed itself WorldCom. But when there was a downturn in telecommunications profits, Ebbers was plagued with margin calls on personal business investments in timber holdings and other acquisitions; that is, he had purchased these holdings by putting down only a percentage (the margin) of their price, and when that price dropped he was dunned for more capital. In 2001, Ebbers got the WorldCom board of directors to "loan" him $400 million; then in the following year he was ousted from the company.

Internal auditors had learned and reported in 2002 that by various ruses the company had cooked its books to inflate income and ignore expenses to the tune of $3.2 billion. The failure of regulatory agencies to tumble to the WorldCom accounting tricks led David Ackman, writing in *Forbes*, to observe that "during its swift rise and even faster fall, WorldCom has been one of the world's most scrutinized companies. Still Tuesday it managed to shock the world with an accounting fraud."

When WorldCom filed for bankruptcy, people possessing stock in the company were wiped out, and bondholders received 37 cents for each dollar of their holdings.

Ebbers was sentenced in 2005 to 25 years in prison. His chief financial officer, Scott Sullivan, who turned state's evidence, got one-fifth that sentence. Sullivan insisted that he had fudged the books because Ebbers persistently insisted that he "hit the numbers," that is, show earnings equivalent to what Wall Street analysts had predicted for the company. He claimed that he had constantly warned Ebbers to desist from this finagling effort, and that he had been "ashamed and embarrassed" by what he did. A more cynical commentator said that the lesson Sullivan's situation conveyed was: "If you do something very bad in your company and know you're gonna get whacked, find someone above you to rat out." A WorldCom accounting officer, Betty Vinson, one of

---

DID YOU KNOW?

Worldwide Reaction to the WorldCom Fraud

Worldwide repercussions from the collapse of WorldCom and the surrounding corporate scandals created a malevolent glee in editorial writers for newspapers around the world. They took delight in calling attention to what they deemed to be an ugly flaw in a country that they believed had arrogantly exalted its virtue far and wide. The critical responses came from Communist papers, where they could be expected, to middle-of-the road outlets. A sample was reproduced by the World Press Review in September 2002:

Dublin, Ireland: *Irish Times:* The crisis has put the spotlight on suspect accounting standards throughout the capitalist world. It presents Mr. Bush with a stern test of domestic credibility.

Manila, The Philippines: *Manila Times:* The problem the Bush government truly faces is how to stave off the steady declining public trust and confidence in corporate America.

Sofia, Romania: *Dnevik:* Until recently America was pretending that it was offering the world an indisputable model of success. More than a thousand U.S. companies have admitted that they published false figures in the '90s. This means that the much-hyped and lucrative growth of Clinton's "New Economy" may prove to be a hot air balloon, and one overblown with foreign money.

Havana, Cuba: *Gramma International:* These scandals are not a sudden, passing illness of the major U.S. corporations, but revelations of their true character.

Bogota, Colombia: *El Tiempo:* Americans must be wondering if their prodigious prosperity of the past decade is more the work of manipulative executives, banks, and accountants than a system that rewards hard work.

Peking, China: *China Daily:* The revelations of corporate misdeeds of Enron and WorldCom confirm that there is an urgent need to rein in greedy and powerful chief executives, and curb rampant abuses of stock options.

the very few women to become involved in corporate crimes (in part because women less frequently than men hold executives offices), received a five-year prison term, five months of house arrest, and three years' probation. As Vinson put it, she had "pulled numbers out of the air" to include in her profit-and-loss calculations.

Ebbers was forced to sell the $15 million house he was building in Boca Raton, Florida, and to contribute the ultimate sales price, $9.7 million, to a fund to repay WorldCom stockholders. The 30,000-square-foot house located in the exclusive Le Lac enclave had 14 bedrooms, seven fireplaces, and a six-car garage. On his release from the Jessup, Georgia, medium-security prison, Sullivan returned to Boca Raton and a considerably more modest dwelling.

WorldCom became MCI in April 2003 and moved from Mississippi to Dulles, Virginia. In 2005 Verizon purchased the company for $7.6 billion.

FURTHER READINGS

Cooper, Cynthia. (2008). *Extraordinary Circumstances: The Journal of a Corporate Whistle-blower*. Hoboken, NJ: Wiley.

Jeter, Lynn W. (2003). *Disconnected: Deceit and Betrayal at WorldCom*. Hoboken, NJ: Wiley.

Marik, Om. (2003). *Broadbandits: Inside the $75 Billion Telecom Heist*. Hoboken, NJ: Wiley.

Rezaee, Zabihollah, and Richard Riley. (2010) *Financial Statement Fraud: Prevention and Detection* (2nd ed.). Hoboken, NJ: Wiley.

Walker, Pavlo, Jr., and Neil Weinberg. (2007). *Stolen without a Gun: Confessions from Inside History's Biggest Accounting Fraud: The Challenge of MCI/World Com*. Tampa, FL: Etika Books.

11

OUTDOING PONZI: BERNIE MADOFF, R. ALLEN STANFORD, AND BOSS JEZDA

INTRODUCTION

Ponzi schemes flourish best when an economy is prospering mightily. An inflow of money can reasonably be accumulated in sufficient quantity to allow payouts to be offered to old investors at rates better than those generally otherwise available, and this arrangement will attract additional investors by word-of-mouth endorsement from those who see their statements reflect a continuing healthy rate of increase. There typically is a wondrous amount of cash that can be siphoned off by the person operating the scam to support a dazzling lifestyle. It is an axiom of the business world that wariness and skepticism are placed on hold when money is coming to clients in regular intervals and in satisfying amounts.

The difficulty arises when there is a sharp economic downtown such as occurred toward the end of the first decade of the twenty-first century. People are wont to withdraw their investments in order to offset losses elsewhere, and at the first strong sign that something might be fishy about the operation that has prospered so long and so well, there will be a run on the bank, a snowball effect of concerned people wanting to get their hands on the money they have invested. And that's when the bubble breaks.

Bernard Madoff's Ponzi Scheme

- *Document:* In federal law, the process of allocution is one by which a guilty plea is accepted in a criminal action: the defendant offers his or her explanation of the illegal behavior as part of the process by means of which the judge gathers information that will be employed to determine the sentence. The document offers Bernard Madoff's summary of what he had done that brought him to this fate and, as is almost invariably the case in white-collar crime, he offers his apology to his victims. This assumption of personal responsibility is a mandatory requirement if there is to be any hope of leniency, and its terms are carefully crafted by the attorney representing the defendant.
- *Date:* March 12, 2009.
- *Where:* The federal district court in the Southern District of New York, New York City.
- *Significance:* Madoff's statement provides his only public attempt to somewhat explain his criminal activity.

DOCUMENT 11.1

Your Honor, for many years up until my arrest on December 11, 2008, I operated a Ponzi scheme through the investment advisory side of my business, Bernard Madoff Securities, L.LC, which was located here in Manhattan, New York, at 885 Third Avenue. I am actually grateful for this first opportunity to publicly speak about my crimes, for which I am deeply sorry and ashamed. As I engaged in my fraud, I knew what I was doing was wrong, indeed criminal. When I began the Ponzi scheme I believed it would end shortly and I would be able to extricate myself and my clients from the scheme. However, this proved difficult, and ultimately impossible, and as

Bernard Madoff (right) arrives at federal court for his hearing in New York on January 14, 2009. (AP/Wide World Photos)

the years went by I realized that my arrest and this day would inevitably come. I am painfully aware that I have deeply hurt many, many people, including members of my family, my closest friends, business associates and the thousands of clients who gave me their money. I cannot adequately express how sorry I am for what I have done. I am here today to accept responsibility for my crimes by pleading guilty, and with this plea allocution to explain the means by which I carried out and concealed my fraud.

The essence of my scheme was that I represented to clients and prospective clients who wished to open investment advisory and individual trading accounts with me that I would invest their money in shares of common stock, options and other securities of large well-known corporations, and upon request, would return to them their profits and principal. These representations were false because for many years up until I was arrested, . . . I never invested their funds in the securities, as I had promised. Instead these funds were deposited in a bank account in the Chase Manhattan Bank. When the clients wished to receive the profits they believed they had earned or to redeem their principal I used the money in the Chase Manhattan Bank account that belonged to them or to other clients to pay the requested funds . . . The victims of my scheme involved individuals, charitable organizations, trusts, pension funds and hedge funds. Among other means, I obtained their funds through interstate wire transfers . . .

To the best of my recollection, my fraud began in the early 1990s . . . I received investment commitments from certain institutional clients and understood that these clients, like all professional investors, expected to see their investments outperform the market. While I never provided a specific rate of return to my any client, I felt compelled to satisfy my clients' expectations, at any cost. I therefore claimed that I employed an investment strategy I had developed called a "split-spike conversion strategy"...

To further cover-up the fact that I had not executed trades on behalf of my investment advisory clients, I knowingly caused false trading confirmations to be created and sent to clients...

In more recent years I used...another method to conceal my fraud. I wired money between the United States and the United Kingdom to make it appear as though these were actual securities transactions...

Your Honor, I hope I have covered with some particularity in my own words the crimes I have committed and the means by which I have committed them. Thank you.

Source: Bernard L. Madoff, plea allocution, *U.S. v. Madoff*, 09-cr-00213, U.S. District Court, Southern District of New York, New York City, March 12, 2009.

ANALYSIS

As far as it goes, Madoff's allocution provides an unemotional skeletal outline of his rogue activities. Most notable is the absence of any information about the extravagant, elegant, and self-indulgent lifestyle that he enjoyed by bilking his customers. Those who attended the court hearing found what they believed to be the absence of any real emotional sympathy and empathy with their plight, indicative of the character trait that allowed Madoff to cold-bloodedly swindle them. They remembered how he had at times not accepted large sums that some people wanted him to invest for them, thereby creating a sense in those whose money he accepted that they were particularly special and fortunate.

The Madoff allocution needs to be fleshed out with further details to convey a more thorough portrait of what he was about. For 40 years, Bernie Madoff, an affable crook who mingled with the country club elite, operated the Ponzi scheme that is estimated to have defrauded investors of $65 billion. Madoff enticed the careless and the gullible with a campaign that, among other things, maintained that his company used sophisticated computer systems to monitor prices and identify trading opportunities around the world. Much Madoff business was generated by endorsements from satisfied customers. By the time the law caught up with Madoff, he owned apartments on New York's exclusive Upper East Side and near Wall Street, an elegant house in Montauk on Long Island, three properties in Palm Beach, Florida, a house in Kay Largo, also in Florida, and another in Antibes, France. To gain political advantages, between 1997 and 2008 Madoff spent $590,000 on lobbying efforts, plus from 1991 forward another quarter of a million on political campaign contributions.

When taken into custody in late 2008, Madoff posted $10 million in bail money that allowed him to remain under house arrest in his penthouse apartment. He had been turned in by his sons Mark and Anthony, who worked in his investment company and reported to their attorney their father's confession to them of his frauds. The attorney informed the authorities.

Critics were appalled that the SEC had never caught on to Madoff's crooked scheme even though the agency had been alerted many times over the years about the wrongdoing (see Document 11.2 below and the following information).

In November 2009, David G. Friehling pleaded guilty to conspiring with Madoff in cooking his company's books, a task for which he was paid a monthly fee of $12,000 to $14,000. It took two years before Friehling's CPA license was revoked by the state board of auditors. His sentencing was continuously postponed—now set for September 2011—because he had been cooperating with the federal authorities in their investigation of other possible participants in Madoff's scheme.

When Madoff pled guilty and offered his allocution, his lawyer noted that at age 71 his client had a life expectancy of 13 years and asked the judge to impose a 12-year sentence. Ignoring this recommendation, on June 29, 2009, Judge Denny Chin imposed the maximum possible sentence of 150 years on Madoff, declaring that the defendant was "extraordinarily evil." The judge granted that 150 years was symbolic, an overkill of a life sentence, but he said that he considered it a gesture that might convey a lesson to other actual or potential white-collar criminals.

Madoff's prison term was far from a record for a financial fraud perpetrator. In 2000, Sholam Weiss received an 845-year sentence for a scheme that bilked $450 million from the National Heritage Life Insurance Company in Wilmington, Delaware. A coconspirator, Keith Pound, got a 700-year term. Weiss, who has appealed the length of the sentence, would under its terms be eligible for release in 2754. He had fled the United States near the end of a nine-month trial, shaved his beard, and lost 50 pounds before being apprehended in Austria and extradited back to the United States. In 2008, Norman Schmidt of Denver, Colorado, was dealt another death-in-prison sentence, this one 330 years for his role in a fraudulent investment scheme. A law enforcement officer who worked the case drew this lesson from the Schmidt scam: "If you can't afford to lose it, don't invest it. That's the safest way to avoid being a victim of an investment scheme." Compared to the Weiss and Schmidt sentences, the 50-year term imposed on Thomas J. Peters in 2010 seems mild. Peters was convicted of operating a Ponzi scheme that inveigled investors by claiming to buy surplus appliances and merchandise and reselling them to retailers.

Madoff was incarcerated in the medium-security section of the Federal Correctional Complex in Butner, North Carolina, a prison known for its up-to-date medical facilities for disabled and elderly inmates. There Madoff could have the company of a coterie of other white-collar crooks, including one-time Rite Aid vice chairman Franklin C. Brown and Al Parish of Charleston, South Carolina, a former university business school professor, who was serving a two-year sentence for having fleeced some 630

DID YOU KNOW?

Victims Speak Out

During the court hearing prior to the point where the judge imposed sentence on Madoff, there were wrenching presentations by victims of his nefarious acts. One victim said that the funds he had deposited with Madoff were to be used for the care of his mentally disabled brother. "I hope Madoff's sentence is long enough so that his jail will become his coffin," the victim declared. One woman told the judge: "I now live on food stamps. I scavenger in Dumpsters at the end of the month." Others labeled Madoff a "monster" and "low life."

The roster of Madoff's victims included many celebrities. One of the nastier elements of his actions was that he betrayed friendships and preyed upon Jewish co-religionists and organizations. Yeshiva University lost $110 million of its endowment fund to Madoff; the Mortimer Zuckerman charity, run by the owner of the *New York Daily News*, took a $30 million hit; while the Jewish Family Foundation of Los Angeles lost $18 million. Entertainment figures such as Larry King, Steven Spielberg, and Zsa Zsa Gabor were among those swindled. The biggest loss—$75 billion—was suffered by the Fairfield Greenwich Group, which had put funds from its investors directly into Madoff's coffers. The Massachusetts attorney general charged the company civilly for "flagrant and recurring misrepresentation to its investors [that] rises to the level of fraud." The managing director of Fairfield, who paid himself $45 million a year, maintained that he had no knowledge of the true nature of Madoff's scheme.

people out of a total of $66 million. Two corporate executives from Adelphia also were in residence at Butner.

FURTHER READINGS

Arvedlund, Erin. (2009). *Too Good to Be True: The Rise and Fall of Bernie Madoff*. New York: Portfolio.

Kirtzman, Andre. (2009). *Betrayal: The Life and Lies of Bernie Madoff*. New York: Harper.

LeBor, Adam. (2009). *The Believers: How America Fell for Bernie Madoff's $65Billiion Investment Scheme*. London: Weidenfeld & Nicolson.

Oppenheimer, Jerry. (2009). *Madoff with the Money*. Hoboken, NJ: Wiley.

Ross, Brian. (2009). *The Madoff Chronicles: Inside the Secret World of Bernie and Ruth*. New York: Hyperion.

Sander, Peter J. (2009). *Madoff: Corruption, Deceit, and the Making of the World's Most Notorious Ponzi Scheme*. Guilford, CT: Lyons Press.

Strober, Deborah H., and Gerald S. Strober. (2009). *Catastrophe: The Story of Bernard L. Madoff, the Man Who Swindled the World*. Beverly Hills, CA: Phoenix Books.

Harry Markopolos, Madoff's Nemesis

- *Document:* Harry Markopolos, a financial analyst or, as they now tend to be labeled, a forensic accountant, for more than a decade had warned authorities and the media that Madoff was running a crooked operation. They ignored him. Document 11.2 reproduces a portion of Markopolos's testimony before a congressional committee after Madoff had confessed.
- *Date:* February 4, 2009.
- *Where:* Rayburn Office Building, U.S. Congress, Washington, DC.
- *Significance:* Markopolos's appearance before the House committee publicized the obviously insubstantial operation that Madoff had been operating and provided an unflattering view of the inadequacy of government regulatory oversight of the Ponzi scheme.

DOCUMENT 11.2

Why did BM [I do not know whether Markopolos used this abbreviation merely to avoid having to repeat continually his subject's name or whether he somewhat slyly wanted to suggest to readers the common usage of the initials to refer to a bowel movement] suddenly turn himself in Thursday, December 11, 2008? Clearly, it was because he could not meet cash redemption by the feeder funds and fund of funds [the latter term refers to an investment strategy of holding a portfolio of other investment funds rather than investing directly in stocks, bonds, or other securities]. Due to the seductive steadiness of his returns and the purported liquidity of his strategy the rest of the funds, in a down market, would consider him the best in their lineup of managers and would most likely go to him first with their redemption requests. Many hedge funds invest in illiquid securities for which they might have

DID YOU KNOW?

Markopolos on Markopolos

The following are excerpts from a question-and-answer interview with Harry Markopolos:

Q: Now you're triumphant, a hero in investment circles who exposes the S.E.C. as the most futile of agencies.

A: It was a trip through the twilight zone.

Q: Why do you think the S.E.C. failed to wake up to Madoff's $65 billion Ponzi scheme until he turned himself in.

A: They weren't asleep at the switch, they were comatose. They didn't respond to heat and light, much less evidence of wrongdoing. They were not engaged in the fight.

Q: This was when William Donaldson was head of the S.E.C.?

A: Donaldson was tough on Wall Street, so he got the ax. Then you had Christopher Cox, because he wasn't going to do his job. That's why he got the job.

Q: In the year since you testified before Congress about the S.E.C.'s failures, many of the agency employees have been replaced.

A: They've redisorganized. They redisorganized the enforcement unit.

Q: Are you saying the S.E.C. . . . is not about to catch fraud on Wall Street?

A: She [Mary Schapiro, the new S.E.C. head] has the wrong staff. They're a bunch of idiots there.

Q: What do you mean?

A: The five commissioners of the S.E.C. are securities lawyers. Securities lawyers never understand finance. They don't have the math background. If you can't do math and if you can't take apart the investment product of the 21st century backward and forward and put them together in your sleep, you'll never find frauds on Wall Street.

Q: Has anyone contacted you about making a film based on your book?

A: Yes. All the major studios. Sony, Paramount, Tom Hanks, you name it.

Q: Where did you learn about finance?

A: You don't learn much in grad school. Half the formulas they teach you are false. It's a lot of self-study. I read a lot of finance books and I usually read them with a calculator because I go through the math to make sure I master the formulas.

Q. Were you always a math whiz?

A: I needed a tutor in 7th and 8th grade. Whatever it was, I was having big problems with algebra.

Source: Deborah Solomon, "Math Is Hard," *New York Times Magazine*, February 25, 2010.

trouble finding buyers in a down market. Therefore, rather than sell in a down market where there may be no buyers and drive prices even lower than they were already, the fund of funds managers feel that they will have less of an impact by asking BM to redeem what they considered to be their "safe" investments. BM's strategy of investing in highly liquid, blue chip stocks seemed tailor made for easy redemptions. Therefore, the fund of funds managers went to BM first . . . and that is what caused his downfall. Too many hedge fund investors were asking to redeem their money and BM ended up with too many of these redemption requests which brought the entire house of cards down around him. . . .

Government has coddled, accepted, and ignored white collar crime for too long. It's time that the nation woke up and realized it's not the armed robbers or drug dealers who cause the most economic harm, it's the white collar criminal living in the most expensive homes which have the most impressive resumes who harm us the most. They steal our pensions, bankrupt our companies, and destroy thousands of jobs, ruining countless lives . . .

To the victims, words cannot express our sorrow at your loss. Let this be a lesson to us all. White collar crime is . . . a cancer on the nation's soul and our tolerance of it speaks volumes about where we need to go as a nation if we are to survive the current economic troubles we find ourselves facing; because these troubles were of our own making and due solely to unchecked, unregulated greed.

Source: Harry Markopolos, Testimony before the U.S. House of Representatives, Subcommittee on Capital Markets, Insurance, and Government Sponsored Enterprise. Hearing on Assessing the Madoff Ponzi Scheme and Regulatory Failure, 111th Cong., 1st Sess., February 4, 2009.

ANALYSIS

Harry Markopolos, 52 years old at the time that Madoff pled guilty, was born in Erie, Pennsylvania, and earned a graduate degree in finance from Boston

College. He worked from 1991 to 2004 in Boston for the Rampart Management Investment Company where he was charged with the task of determining how Madoff had so consistently, in up markets and down markets, returned comfortable profits to his investors. Rampart wanted to learn Madoff's secret, which they assumed involved legal practices, so that they could do the same thing.

Working with information that was publicly available, Markopolos and several colleagues concluded in May of 2000 that Madoff was either operating a Ponzi scheme or taking advantage of front-running tactics. Front running, the Free Dictionary of Falex indicates, involves entering into an equity trade with advance knowledge of a block transaction that will influence the price of the underlying security. The practice is forbidden by the SEC. Front running was not what Madoff was doing; he was merely using newly placed funds to pay off earlier investors when they requested a redemption.

In November 2005, Markopolos submitted a 21-page paper to the SEC with the title: "World's Largest Hedge Fund Is a Fraud." It produced hardly a flutter of reaction: in personal interviews Markopolos was met with indifference and condescension by government officials. They believed that as a competitor he was jealous of Madoff's success, or that he was a quack or a publicity hound. Markopolos described his interview with the SEC branch chief in New York in these terms: "She never expressed even the slightest interest in asking me questions."

DID YOU KNOW?

The Revolving Door at the SEC

The woeful inadequacy of the SEC led to later attempts to try to figure out why the agency had been so lax and what might be done about this. The Senate Finance Committee in mid-2010 focused on the "revolving door" policy whereby numerous SEC regulators move from the agency into jobs with the companies they had been charged with monitoring. A press release by Senator Charles Grassley highlighted the problem: "We need to ensure that SEC officials are more focused on regulation and enforcement than on getting their next job in the industry they are supposed to oversee," Grassley said. It was noted that when employees move into private industry, they take with them essential information about SEC policies and priorities that help their new employers formulate tactics that might otherwise have been blocked by SEC monitoring.

FURTHER READINGS

Kamel, Roberta S. (1982). *Regulation by Prosecution: The Securities and Exchange Commission vs. Corporate America.* New York: Simon & Schuster.

Katz, H. David. (2009). *Investigation of Failure of the SEC to Uncover Bernard Madoff's Ponzi Scheme.* Washington, DC: U.S. Government Printing Office.

Markopolos, Harry. (2010). *No One Would Listen: A True Financial Thriller.* Hoboken, NJ: Wiley.

Shapiro, Susan. (1984). *Wayward Capitalists: Target of the Securities and Exchange Commission.* New Haven, CT: Yale University Press.

Stanford Investment Bank

- **Document:** This initial court complaint filed by the SEC sought to halt what it regarded as the outrageously illegal Ponzi scheme being carried on by the Stanford Investment Bank.
- **Date:** February 9, 2009.
- **Where:** The U.S. District Court for the Northern District of Texas, located in Dallas.
- **Significance:** The document offers the official conclusions of the enforcement agencies about the scheme being perpetrated by the three top executives of the Stanford investment group.

DOCUMENT 11.3

Plaintiff Securities and Exchange Commission alleges:

SUMMARY

1. The Commission seeks emergency relief to halt a massive, ongoing fraud orchestrated by R. Allen Stanford and James M. Davis and executed through companies they control, including Stanford Investment Bank, Ltd. ("SIB") and its affiliated Houston investment advisor, the Stanford Group Company ("SGC") and Stanford Capital Management ("SCM"). Laura Pendergest-Holt, the chief investment officer of a Stanford affiliate, was indispensable to this scheme by helping to preserve the appearance of safety fabricated by Stanford and by training others to mislead investors. For example, she trained SIB's senior investment officer to provide false information to investors.

2. Through this fraudulent scheme, SIB, acting through a network of SGC financial advisors, has sold approximately $8 billion of self-styled "certificates of deposit" by promising high return rates that exceeded those available through the true certificates of deposit offered by traditional banks.

3. SIB claims that its unique investment strategy has allowed it to achieve double-digit returns on its investments over the past 15 years allowing it [to] offer high yields to CD purchasers . . . SIB claims that its "diversified port-folio of investments" lost only 1.3% in 2002, a time during which the S&P [Standard and Poor's, a securities price and rating index] lost 39% and the Dow-Jones STOXX Europe 500 Fund lost 41%.

4. Perhaps even more strange, SIB reports identical returns in 1965 and 1966 of exactly 15.71%. As Pendergest-Holt . . . admits, it is simply "improbable" that SIB could have managed a "global diversified" portfolio of investments in a way that returned identical results in consecutive years . . . Yet SIB continues to promote its CDs using these improbable returns.

5. The improbable results are made even more suspicious by the fact that, contrary to assurances provided to investors, at most only two people—Stanford and Davis—knew the details concerning the bulk of SIB's investment portfolio. And SIB goes to great lengths to prevent any true independent examination of these portfolios. For example, its long-standing auditor is reportedly based on a "relationship of trust" between the head of the auditing firm and Stanford.

6. Importantly, contrary to recent public statements by SIB, Stanford and Davis (and through them SGC) have wholly failed to cooperate with the Commission's efforts to account for the $8 billion of investor funds purportedly held by SIB. In short, approximately 90% of SIB's claimed investment portfolio resides in a "black box" shielded from any independent oversight.

7. In fact, far from "cooperating" with the Commission's enforcement investigation (which Stanford has reportedly tried to characterize as only involving routine examinations), SGC appears to have used press reports speculating about the Commission's investigation as [a] way to further mislead investors, falsely telling at least one customer during the week of February 9, 2009, that his multi-million dollar CD could not be redeemed because "the SEC has frozen the account for two months" . . .

8. This secrecy and recent misrepresentations are made even more suspicious by extensive and fundamental misrepresentations SIB and its advisors have made to CD purchasers. In order to lull them into thinking their investments are safe. SIB and its advisors have misrepresented to CD purchasers that their deposits are safe because the bank (i) re-invests client funds primarily in "liquid" financial investments . . . (ii) monitors the portfolio through a team of 20-plus analysts, and (iii) is subject to yearly audits by Antiguan regulators. Recently, as the market absorbed the news of Bernard Madoff's massive Ponzi scheme, SIB attempted to calm its own investors by claiming that the bank had no "direct or indirect" exposure to Madoff's scheme.

9. These assurances are false. Contrary to these representations, SIB's investment portfolio was not invested in liquid financial instruments or allocated

in the manner described in its promotional material and public reports. Instead, a substantial portion of the bank's portfolio was placed in illiquid investments, such as real estate and private equity. Further, the vast majority of SIB's multi-billion dollar investment portfolio was monitored not by a team of experts, but rather by two people—Allen Stanford and James Davis. And contrary to SIB's representations, the Antiguan regulator responsible for oversight of the bank's portfolio, the Financial Services Regulatory Commission, does not audit SIB's portfolio or verify the assets SIB claims in its financial statements. Perhaps most alarming is that SIB has exposure to losses from the Madoff scheme despite the bank's public assurances to the contrary.

10. ...Alarmingly, recent weeks have seen an increasing amount of liquidation activity by SIB and attempts to wire money out of its investment portfolio. The Commission has received information indicating that in just the last two weeks, SIB has sought to remove over $178 million from its accounts...

11. Stanford's fraudulent conduct is not limited to the sale of CDs. Since 2005, SCG advisors have sold more than $1 billion of a proprietary mutual fund wrap program, called Stanford Allocation Strategy ("SAS"), by using materially false and misleading historical performance data. The false data helped SCG grow the SAS program from less than $10 million in around 2004 to over $1.2 billion, generating fees for SCB (and ultimately Stanford) in excess of $25 million...

12. The Commission, in the interest of protecting the public from any further unscrupulous and illegal activity, brings this action against the defendants, seeking temporary, preliminary and permanent injunctive relief, disgorgement of all illicit profits defendants have received plus accrued prejudgment interest and civil monetary penalty. The Commission also seeks an asset freeze, an accounting and other incidental relief, as well as the appointment of a receiver to take possession and control of defendants' assets for the protection of defendants' victims.

Source: Securities and Exchange Commission v. Stanford International Bank, Ltd., et al., Complaint, U.S. District Court for the Northern District of Texas, Dallas Division, February 9, 2009, 1–5.

ANALYSIS

The Madoff scandal had been instrumental in leading law enforcement authorities to the alleged Ponzi scheme operated by the Stanford Investment Bank, Ltd. (SIB). The SEC had been put on the alert when SIB lied to it in declaring that it had no exposure to Madoff's scheme.

Earlier, the American enforcement agencies, much like they did in regard to Harry Markopolos's warnings, had ignored a scathing denunciation of SIB by Alex Dalmady. Dalmady had been asked by a friend to vet his investment with Stanford, and he was appalled by what he found. Dalmady, who worked out of Florida, had published his findings in *VenEconomy*, a Venezuelan business magazine. Nor had the authorities responded when two employees of SIG in a discrimination suit told of "various unethical and illegal business practices" engaged in by the company.

In 2009, the Department of Justice filed a 21-count criminal judgment against financier Robert Allen Stanford, the 59-year-old Texas billionaire, and five other persons. Stanford was accused of masterminding a Ponzi scheme that bilked some 30,000 investors, a large portion of them from Latin American countries, out of an estimated $7 billion. The government convinced James M. Davis, SIB's chief financial officer, to plead guilty in return for a lesser sentence than he likely would have received if convicted, and to testify against Stanford. Among Stanford's investors were major league baseball players Johnny Damon and Xavier Nady.

SIB had its headquarters in St. John's, the capital of the Caribbean island-nation of Antigua and Barbuda, with investment offices in Venezuela, Houston, Panama, and Miami. *Fortune* magazine had labeled Stanford as the 250th wealthiest person in the United States. He had grown up Mexia, Texas, a town of about 6,000 people some 50 miles west of Waco, and claims to have played quarterback with the Baylor University Bears in Waco, a claim that could not be substantiated by the university's alumni office. Stanford also claims to have genealogical records that show his kinship to the robber baron Leland Stanford (see chapter 2), a kinship that Stanford University officials deny. Stanford lives in St. Croix, and when he came to Antigua he stayed on his luxurious boat, the *Sea Eagle*. He and others were giving to the Caribbean island the description that the writer Somerset Maugham applied to the French Riviera: "a sunny place for shady people."

The head of the Antiguan Financial Services Authority, Leroy King, indicted with Stanford, allegedly was paid more than $100,000 to supply confidential information to the company. King had helped craft a response to the SEC that said that SIB was "in compliance with all areas of depositor safety and solvency."

SIB's so-called certificates of deposit typically paid 10 percent interest. The company officers were accused of having engaged in "round-trip" real estate transactions, buying undeveloped real estate for $6.5 million and then "selling" the property to its own subsidiaries for $2 billion, and carrying that sum on its books as an asset.

Just as had Bernie Madoff, Stanford relied exclusively on an out-of-the-way auditor to check (or, more accurately, not to check) his company's books. The company had a relationship that went back over a decade with a 72-year-old accountant, recently deceased, even though major international firms such as PriceWaterhouseCoopers and KPMG maintained offices on Antigua.

In the words of an SEC spokeswoman, Stanford was said to have operated "a fraud of shocking magnitude that has spread its tentacles through the world."

DID YOU KNOW?

Sir Allen and Cricket

Allen Stanford is known variously on Antigua as a patron saint or as a freebooting six-foot-four pirate. He has been the island's largest employer and was rewarded by the government with a knighthood at a ceremony attended by England's Price Edward.

Stanford was responsible for putting up the largest prize money ever when he offered $20 million to the victorious team in a November 2008 cricket match between the English national team and the Stanford Superstars, whose roster was composed of the best players in the West Indies. The Superstars trashed the English, and each of the 11 players on the West Indies team received a million dollars with the remainder going to coaches, the cricket board, and others associated with the team. The loser got nothing.

Stanford was incarcerated in the same federal prison in North Carolina as Madoff and reports had him in and out of the hospital for treatment for anxiety and nervous disorders, matters that were used to justify requests to postpone his trial.

The Stanford story had taken bizarre turns months before he went to trial. By June 2010 Stanford had fired a total of about 120 lawyers, paralegals, and clerks from some 10 law firms. An exasperated judge was offered this explanation: "I am a man who has been treated like a piece of meat with attorneys who are more concerned with representing themselves to the public than representing me," Stanford claimed, adding, "Almost all my attorneys have effectively left me on my own to try to fight the biggest fight of my life." One of the former defense attorneys thought that the trouble lay in the fact that Stanford was accustomed to giving orders, not accepting advice. For its part, Lloyd's of London and another insurance firm that had paid out more than $6 million so far in Stanford's legal fees were beginning to balk.

FURTHER READINGS

Benner, Katie. (2009, March 16). "Temptation Island: In Antigua Allen Stanford Was Just Another Shady Ex-Pat," *Fortune* 159:24.

Burrough, Bryan, and Christopher Bateman. (2009, July). "Pirates of the Caribbean," *Vanity Fair* 587:76–82.

Wilkinson, Alec. (2009, March 8). "Not Quite Cricket," *New Yorker* 85:24–31.

Boss Jezda (Jezdimir Vasiljevic)

- *Document:* "Boss Jezda," as he called himself, operated a Ponzi scheme in Belgrade, then the capital of a united Yugoslavia, and now the capital of Serbia. The document and the following analysis pinpoint the complex international maneuvers involved in white-collar crimes that cross international borders.
- *Date:* May 3,1993.
- *Where:* *Time* magazine.
- *Significance:* The case indicates the global reach of frauds that in the past were almost invariably operated within national boundaries. Some of Madoff's victims were Europeans and Asians, while Stanford, also an American, operated offshore and tended to bilk people in Latin America. Like Allen Stanford, Jezdimir Vasiljevic is awaiting trial.

DOCUMENT 11.4

Back when he was running one of the hottest banks in Belgrade, before its spectacular collapse, Jezdimir Vasiljevic was known for his financial bravado, his wild ties and his even wilder statements. But last week the stocky and shadowy man known as "Jezda the Boss" was holed up in Israel . . . and hatching plans to preside over a government-in-exile. Such grandiose plans come naturally to Vasiljevic, 45, the maverick entrepreneur . . .

Shock waves from the failure of Vasiljevic's Jugoskandik Bank continue to rumble in Belgrade. Thousands of furious depositors took to the streets to demand their money and stirred panicky runs on other banks . . . When Vasiljevic fled to Israel at the height of the Jugoskandik scandal, the departure only fueled his ever growing legend. No sooner had he left town than local papers breathlessly reported rumors that a Tel Aviv-bound Sabena Airlines flight had made an unscheduled stop in Belgrade and taken off with bags bulging with cash, presumably taken directly from the vaults of Jugoskandik. Sabena said the plane landed in response to a hijacking threat and denied picking up any money . . .

Ravaged by 20,000% hyperinflation, whipped up by United Nations sanctions, the desperate Serbs on the home front have turned to shady banks like Jugoskandik to help put food on the table. In return for deposits of hard currencies such as U.S. dollars and German marks, Jugoskandik paid up to 15% in monthly interest. Customers could thus earn $150 a month on a $1,000 deposit, or about four times the wages of an average worker.

Vasiljevic had little trouble meeting the interest payments at first. Western experts say his bank ran a classic Ponzi scheme, using new deposits to pay the interest on old ones. At the same time, diplomats say, Vasiljevic used his customers' hard currency to buy sanctioned goods like oil on the black market and sell it for a handsome profit.

Source: John Greenwald, Ann Blackman, James L. Graff, and Robert Slater, "Mystery of the Moneybags," *Time* May 3, 1993.

ANALYSIS

The word "grandiose" in the report on the scheming of Boss Jezda is meaningful as an appellation that applies equally well to the other two men who engaged in major Ponzi schemes, as well as to Ponzi himself, the elegant man-about-town with the very fancy canes, the finest automobile available, and a mansion in the Boston suburbs. Madoff and Stanford lived wildly extravagant lives, with private jets, numerous homes, and other glamorous trappings. One might have presumed, knowing they were engaged in crime, that they would have sought to keep a reasonably low profile. But perhaps they figured that they were destined to be caught and they ought to seize whatever advantages and pleasures their ill-gotten wealth could command. Both Stanford and Boss Jezda were six foot four inches tall: does such human height create a sense of command and invulnerability? Jezda's idea of his self-importance was manifest in the 1992 election when he ran for the presidency of Serbia. He finished a poor fifth out of seven candidates, getting 61,729 votes, or 1.31 percent of the total.

Boss Jezda was accused of stealing more than $130 million. He had earned the government's backing in Serbia because of his ability to import military equipment from Israel, such as infrared mine-clearing equipment and bugging devices, in violation of UN trading sanctions against Serbia for its ruthless aggression in its war with Bosnia-Herzegovina. The media had turned Jezda into a mythical figure. Vidosav Stevanović notes that long lines would form in front of Jezda's bank. "To reach the counter," he notes, "you had to wait all night, fight those in front and behind you or buy a numbered ticket. But somehow everyone managed to invest his or her money. Over the next few months the investors basked in the sweet illusion of becoming rich by staying at home and watching television."

In early 2010 Jezda was extradited from the Netherlands to Serbia, where he was incarcerated in the Belgrade Central Prison. In 2007, he jumped bail and fled from Serbia to Israel shortly after his criminal trial had gotten under way. He was arrested in Holland in April 2009 and put under home detention for submitting false documents in an effort to secure asylum. He sought to avoid return to Belgrade by requesting that he be sent to Ecuador. His wife had Ecuadorian citizenship and by marriage so did he. Nonetheless, he was returned to Belgrade where he awaits trial.

FURTHER READING

Lane, Charles. (1986). "Deadline Belgrade: Mob Rule." In Nader Mousavzadeh (Ed.), *The Black Book of Bosnia: The Consequences of Appeasement* (pp. 80–83). New York: Basic Books.

DID YOU KNOW?

The Legendary Chess Championship Matches

If he is known to Americans at all, Boss Jezda is probably recalled as the man who financed to the tune of $5 million the world championship chess matches between the American Bobby Fischer and the Russian Boris Spassky, held in 1992 in the Hotel Maestral in the resort town of Sveti Stefan on the Yugoslavian coast. As with Allen Stanford, it was the staging of a high-profile sports event—the attendant publicity that this garnered—that apparently sold the sponsorship idea to Jezda.

Charles Lane, writing in the *New Republic* in 1992, described Jezda as having the look of a small-town banker. Lane noted his "fireplug frame" and his cheap suit with the pants flopping over his shoes. He sported a very large gold watch that dangled from his wrist, and his hair, which was his own, impressed Lane as seeming to be a cheap wig.

12

THE GREAT ECONOMIC MELTDOWN: 2007–2009

INTRODUCTION

The economic collapse that brought the United States to its knees beginning in the summer of 2007 has been tied to home loans in what became known as the subprime lending market. Subprime lending involved mortgage brokers courting potential homebuyers who ordinarily would not qualify for traditional 30-year, 20 percent-down loans. The sellers offered these people seductively easy terms, low interest rates that later escalated steeply, interest-only loans, and low or nonexistent down payments. Later inquiries found that in 43 percent of the subprime loans, the lender never even bothered to obtain written verification of the borrower's income.

Banks and other lending institutions participated in the seducing of individuals and families to purchase homes that they could not afford by promoting the idea that the stunning escalation in real estate values would continue indefinitely and the new home owners would be able to make their payments by withdrawing cash based on the value of a home that in short order would be worth a great deal more than what they paid for it. This led to the great refi (refinancing) boom during which families used the wildly increasing values of their homes like ATMs.

The bubble burst when home began to go "underwater," the term indicating that they now were worth less than what was owed on them. It soon became evident that the investment industry, driven by a lust for lucre, irresponsibly and stupidly—and at times criminally—had taken risks that placed them in serious financial jeopardy and forced them to seek help from the government (that is, the taxpayers) to keep themselves solvent. This chapter looks at several of the major financial fiascos that marked the great economic meltdown, a meltdown that has been characterized as a recession but, as the eminent jurist-economist Richard Posner declares, is actually a depression. That word, he notes, was taboo because it conjures up frightful images of destitute out-of-work people selling apples on city streets in order to earn a pittance.

Bank of America

- **Document:** Bank of America, apparently under pressure from government officials and with their financial assistance, had purchased Merrill Lynch, a leading investment firm on the verge of bankruptcy. Prior to its purchase, Merrill Lynch had awarded huge bonuses to many of its executives, a situation known to Bank of America's top officials but not disclosed to stockholders in material that they received as background for their vote on whether or not to approve the merger. The SEC then negotiated a $33 million settlement with the Bank of America as a penalty for this failure. The settlement required the approval of a federal judge. Judge Jed S. Rakoff refused to endorse the proposed agreement for the reasons set out in Document 12.1.
- **Date:** February 9, 2009.
- **Where:** U.S. District Court for the Southern District of New York, New York City.
- **Significance:** The judge's opinion vividly pinpoints the self-serving tactics of a corporate entity working to protect its executives at the expense of the public and its stockholders.

DOCUMENT 12.1.

JED S.RAKOFF, U.S.D.J. [United States District Judge]

In the complaint in this case ... the Securities and Exchange Commission ("S.E.C.") alleges, in stark terms, that defendant Bank of America Corporation materially lied to its shareholders in a proxy statement of November 3, 2008 that solicited the shareholders' approval of the $50 billion acquisition of Merrill Lynch & Co. ... The essence of the lie, according to the Complaint, was that Bank of

America represented that Merrill had agreed not to pay year-end performance bonuses or other discretionary incentive compensation to its executives prior to the closing of the merger without Bank of America's consent when in fact, contrary to the representation . . . , Bank of America had agreed that Merrill could pay up to $5.8 billion—nearly 12% of the total consideration to be exchanged in the merger—in discretionary year-end and other bonuses to Merrill executives for 2008. Along with the filing of these very serious allegations, however, the parties, on the very same day, jointly sought this court's approval of a proposed final Consent Judgment by which Bank of America, without admitting or denying the accusations, would be enjoined from making future false statements in proxy solicitations and would pay to the S.E.C. a fine of $33 million.

In other words, the parties were proposing that the management of Bank of America—having allegedly hidden from the bank's shareholder's that as much as $5.8 billion of their money would be given as bonuses to the executives of Merrill who had run that company nearly into bankruptcy—would now settle the legal consequences of their lying by paying the S.E.C. $33 million more of the their shareholders' money.

This proposal to have the victims of the violation pay an additional penalty for their own victimization was enough to give the Court pause. The Court therefore heard oral argument on August 10, 2009 and received extensive written submissions . . . Having now carefully reviewed all these materials, the Court concludes that the proposed Consent Judgment must be denied . . .

. . . [T]he Court . . . is forced to conclude that the proposed Consent Judgment is neither fair, nor reasonable, nor adequate.

It is not fair, first and foremost, because it does not comport with the most elementary notions of justice and morality, in that it proposes that the shareholders who are the victims of the Bank's alleged misconduct now pay the penalty for that misconduct . . . But the S.E.C. argues that this is justified because "[a] corporate penalty . . . sends a strong signal to shareholders that unsatisfactory corporate conduct has occurred and allows shareholders to better assess the quality and performance of management." This hypothesis, however, makes no sense when applied to the facts here: for the notion that Bank of America shareholders, having been lied to blatantly in connection with the multi-billion dollar purchase of a huge, nearly bankrupt company need to lose another $33 million of their money in order to "better assess the quality and performance of management" is absurd.

The S.E.C., while also conceding that its normal policy in such situations is to go after the company executives who were responsible for the lie, rather than innocent shareholders, says it cannot do so here because "[t]he uncontroverted evidence in the investigative record is that lawyers for the Bank of America and Merrill Lynch drafted the documents at issue and made their relevant decisions concerning disclosures of the bonuses." But if that is the case, why are the penalties not then sought from the lawyers? . . .

Bank of America, for its part . . . vigorously asserts that the proxy statement, when read carefully, is neither false nor misleading or that, even if it is false or misleading, the misstatements were immaterial because "[it] was widely acknowledged in the period leading up to the shareholder vote that Merrill Lynch intended to pay

Settling the Bank of America Case

The September 2010 agreement by Judge Jed Rakoff to the terms of a settlement between the SEC and Bank of America offers significant insights on issues core to consideration of white-collar and corporate crime. It also includes enforcement prose that stands as some of the hardest-hitting and most honest appraisal of underhanded tactics employed in the corporate world. Before being appointed as a judge, Rakoff had served as a federal prosecutor, and in a newspaper interview he told how that experience had influenced him. "Once I really got into securities fraud prosecutions," he said, "I came to realize how crucial they were to the maintenance of a free market and how, in many ways, they are far more important to the welfare of our society than many of the more sensational crimes that one hears about."

Rakoff strongly believes that individuals ought not to be able to hide behind a corporate institution when wrongdoing is involved. In the same interview he said: "If crimes are committee they are committed by individuals, they are not committed by some free-floating entity. These companies and other entities don't operate on automatic pilot. There are individuals that make decisions—and some make the right decisions and some make the wrong decisions. If the decisions they make break the law, they are the ones who are responsible."

In the SEC case, Bank of America lawyers insistently pointed out that legal precedent indicated that a judge should endorse regulatory arrangements unless there were very compelling reasons to do otherwise. Rakoff thought there was much "otherwise" in the "somewhat tortured background of the cases." He introduced his consideration of some of those issues by a quotation from "the great philosopher," the former New York Yankee catcher Yogi Berra, who had told reporters: "I wish I had an answer to that because I am getting tired of answering that question."

Rakoff said he had agreed with the renegotiated terms only "reluctantly" and that if he had been presented with the case originally, he might well have ruled differently. He noted the "cozy refusal" of the corporate attorneys to admit obvious episodes of wrongdoing. Most significantly, Rakoff took heart from the civil action filed by the New York attorney general against Bank of America, its former chief executive officer Kenneth D. Lewis, and its former chief financial officer John L. Price, who were said to have "masterminded a massive fraud and manipulation" and to have done so because they were "motivated by self-interest, greed, hubris, and a palpable sense that the normal rules of fair play did not apply to them."

year-end incentive compensation." The S.E.C. responds, however, that these statements are hollow. The Bank's argument that the proxy statement was not misleading rests in material part on reference to a schedule that was not even attached to the proxy statement, and "[s]hareholders are entitled to rely on the representations in the proxy itself, and are not required to puzzle out material information from a variety of external sources . . ."

Moreover, it is noteworthy that, in all its voluminous papers protesting its innocence, Bank of America never actually provides the Court with the particularized facts that the Court requested, such as precisely how the proxy statement came to be prepared, exactly who made the relevant decisions as to what to include and not include so far as the Merrill bonuses were concerned, etc.

But all of this is beside the point because, if the Bank is innocent of lying to its shareholders, why is it prepared to pay $33 million of its shareholders' money as a penalty for lying to them? All the Bank offers in response to this obvious question is that "Because of the SEC's decision to bring charges, Bank of America would have to spend corporate funds whether or not it settles," . . . —the implication being that the payment was simply an exercise in business judgment, as to which alternative would cost more: litigating or settling. But, quite aside from the fact that it is difficult to believe that litigating this simple case would cost anything like $33 million, it does not appear . . . that this decision was made by disinterested parties. It is one thing for management to exercise its business judgment to determine how much of its shareholders money should be used to settle a case brought by former shareholders or third parties. It is quite something else for the very management that is accused of having lied to its shareholders to determine how much of those victims' money should be used to make the case against the management go away.

Overall, indeed, the parties' submissions, when carefully read, leave the distinct impression that the proposed Consent Judgment was a contrivance to provide the S.E.C. with the façade of enforcement and the management of the Bank with a quick resolution of an embarrassing inquiry—all at the expense of the sole alleged victims, the shareholders ...

[T]he Consent Judgment would effectively close the case without the S.E.C. adequately accounting for why, in contravention of its own policy it did not pursue charges against either Bank management or the lawyers who allegedly were responsible for the false and misleading proxy statements. The S.E.C. says this is because charges against individuals for making false proxy statements require, at a minimum, proof that they participated in the making of the false statements knowing the statements were false or recklessly disregarding the high probability the statements were false. But how can such knowledge be lacking when ... executives at the Bank expressly approved Merrill's making year-end bonuses before they issued he proxy statements denying such approval? ...

On December 5, 2008, shareholders of Merrill Lynch, which had been founded in 1914, approved their buyout by Bank of America. It later became known that Merrill Lynch had paid 170 executives a total of $3.6 billion in bonuses despite the fact that the company had lost $28 billion during the year. Critics of this cozy arrangement were met with the response that such staggering sums were necessary to return the best and the brightest. The critics wondered how bright a person needed to be in order to inflict losses of billions of dollars on a company. As one wisecrack put it: "As a general rule, only the very smartest people can make catastrophic mistakes." Others noted that the U.S. Supreme Court manages to attract quite competent members with a salary very far below the millions taken home by corporate executives. Ultimately, the hullabaloo over the hidden bonuses played a prominent part in the mid-2010 resignation of Kenneth Lewis as Bank of America's chief executive officer.

Oscar Wilde once famously said that a cynic is someone "who knows the price of everything and the value of nothing." Oscar Wilde, *Lady Windemere's Fan* (1892). The proposed Consent Judgment in this case suggests a rather cynical relationship between the parties: the S.E.C. gets to claim that it is exposing wrongdoing on the part of the Bank of America in a high-profile merger; the Bank's management gets to claim that they have been coerced into an onerous settlement by overzealous regulators. And all this is done at the expense, not only of the shareholders, but also of the truth.

Source: Securities and Exchange Commission v. Bank of America Corporation, Memorandum Order, Case 09 Civ. 6929 (JSR), U.S. District Court, Southern District of New York, New York City, February 8, 2010.

ANALYSIS

Judge Rakoff ultimately agreed to allow the case between the SEC and the Bank of America to be settled with a penalty of $150 million, an insignificant sum when measured against the $40 billion of bailout money that the government had given the bank, an amount that, as we have seen, embraced the wildly extravagant bonus money that went to Merrill Lynch executives. The new terms also required that the independent auditor hired by the bank had to be "fully acceptable" to the SEC. Obviously, the final settlement was even more harmful to shareholders than the original $33 million figure. It has been argued too that Bank of America executives, when they learned of the bonus arrangement, decided not to go ahead with the merger but that the government offered them an additional $20 billion to persuade them otherwise.

FURTHER READINGS

Farrell, Greg. (2010). *Crash of the Titans: How the Decline and Fall of Merrill Lynch Crippled Bank of America and Nearly Destroyed America's Financial System*. New York: Random House.

Lowenstein, Roger. (2010). *The End of Wall Street*. New York: Penguin Press.

Bear Stearns

- *Document:* For some people, one of the most disturbing aspects of the response to the great economic meltdown was the failure to invoke the criminal law against corporate executives who had recklessly and irresponsibly betrayed the trust of whose funds they controlled. An exception arose in the case of Bear Stearns when two hedge fund managers were charged with an array of criminal acts. Both were acquitted after an eight-hour jury deliberation. Document 12.2 deals with a pretrial determination that possibly incriminating evidence seized by investigators not be admissible at trial because of flaws in the warrant under which the search was conducted.
- *Date:* October 26, 2009.
- *Where:* U.S. District Court for the Eastern District of New York.
- *Significance:* Document 12.2 illustrates the excellent quality of the defense that persons accused of white-collar crime can command.

DOCUMENT 12.2

[FREDERIC] BLOCK, Senior District Judge

Defendant Matthew Tannin . . . moves to suppress evidence seized from his personal email account on the ground that the warrant authorizing the seizure did not comply with the Warrants Clause of the Fourth Amendment [of the U.S. Constitution]. For the following reasons the motion is granted.

I

On July 7, 2009, FBI Special Agent Mark Munster applied to Magistrate Judge Cheryl Pollak for a warrant to search Tannin's personal email account. An affidavit executed by Munster accompanied the application.

A. The Affidavit

. . . First, the affidavit expressly incorporated by reference the 27-page indictment to demonstrate probable cause that Tannin had committed the charged crimes. To connect these crimes to Tannin's personal email account, the Affidavit alluded to . . . an email sent by Tannin from his personal computer account to Cioffi on April 22, 2007:

> [T]he subprime market looks pretty damn ugly . . . If we believe the [CDO report] [editor's note: CDO stands for collateralized debt obligation, a security backed by a pool of debt securities, such as mortgages: the report involved an evaluation of the condition of Bear Stearns's CDOs], ANYWHERE close to accurate I think we should close the funds now. The reason for this is that if [the CDO Report] is correct than the entire subprime market is toast. If AAA bonds [the highest rating] are systematically downgraded then there is simply no way for us to make money—ever.

The government had introduced the April 22nd Email as evidence of Tannin's knowledge and intent.

As recounted in the Affidavit, the April 22nd Email was provided to the BSAM [Bear Stearns Assets Management fund, operated by Tannin and Cioffi] counsel in the course of an investigation of the funds' collapse. BSAM turned the email over to the Securities Exchange Commission and the United States Attorney's Office in November 2007. Munster opined that Tammin's use of his personal email account, instead of his Bear Stearns account, made it "likely that Matthew Tannin personally used THE SUBJECT EMAIL ACCOUNT to facilitate the charged conspiracy" because the conspirators "were able to communicate privately using THE SUBJECT EMIAL ACCOUNT, in that their communications would not be subject to capture and review by Bear Stearns."

B. The Warrant

The Warrant authorized Munster ("or any Authorized Officer of the United States") to seize from Tannin's email accounts the items set forth in Attachment A to the Warrant. The attachment listed seven categories of "records and other stored information" relating to Tannin's account; the category pertinent here was described as all e-mail up through August 12, 2007, including any attachments, and all instant messages, sent and received by the accounts . . . , "whether saved or deleted, whether contained directly in the e-mail account or in a customized 'folder.'" There was no provision limiting the emails to be seized to those containing evidence of the crimes charged in the indictment or, indeed, of any crime at all . . .

C. Execution of the Warrant

Members of the prosecution team searched the account . . . During an "initial look" at the account the government isolated a November 23, 2006 email from Tannin to himself. The lengthy email is essentially a diary entry, in which Tannin recorded his thoughts about such sundry matters as recent vacations and medical issues; however, seven paragraphs were devoted to Tannin's anxiety and the state of the market.

Since I conclude that the search that yielded the November 23rd Email violated the Fourth Amendment [regarding search and seizure] it would be inappropriate to repeat the contents of the email.

D. The Motion to Suppress

On October 8, 2009, the government informed me and defense counsel that it intended to offer the November 23rd Email into evidence as bearing on Tannin's "knowledge and intent on all pending charges against him." Tannin moved to suppress the email; . . . he argued that the Warrant was "invalid on its face because it failed to describe with particularity the materials that would be the proper subject of a search" and that "such warrant is unreasonably broad and therefore is unconstitutional."

II
The Warrant Clause

The Fourth Amendment's Warrant Clause provides that "no Warrants shall issue, but upon probable cause, supported by Oath or affirmation, and particularly describing the place to be searched, and the persons or things to be seized." The clause was intended as a bulwark against "the 'general warrant' abhorred by the colonists" and protects against "a general exploratory rummaging in a person's belongings." Its overarching purpose is to ensure that "those searches deemed necessary shall be as limited as possible." . . .

The dawn of the Information Age heightened those concerns. The risk of exposing intimate (and innocent) correspondence to prying eyes is magnified because "computers . . . often contain significant intermingling of relevant documents with documents that the government has no probable cause to seize."

C. Application

The Warrant did not, on its face, limit the items to be seized from Tannin's personal email account to emails concerning evidence of the crime charged in the indictment or, indeed, any crime at all . . .

Both Munster and the prosecution team were undoubtedly aware that they were to seize Tannin's personal email account only for evidence relating to [charged] crimes.

CONCLUSION

Tannin's motion to suppress is granted. The government is barred from introducing the November 23rd Email into evidence in the case-in-chief.

Source: United States of America v. Cioffi, 668 Federal Supplement 2d 385 (2009).

ANALYSIS

For Ralph R. Cioffi and Matthew M. Tannin, the senior managers of the Bear Stearns hedge funds, their alleged persistent lies to stockholders about the condition of their holdings led to a criminal indictment. Both men were charged with security fraud, conspiracy, and wire fraud, and Cioffi also was charged with insider trading for taking $2 million of his own money out of a hedge fund without informing investors that he had done so and advising them to stay with their investment. For 18 months the pair was said to have indicated in their monthly statements to investors that only 6 percent of their holdings were in subprime mortgages when the true figure was 60 percent.

DID YOU KNOW?

Much Wrongdoing, Few Criminal Charges

The trial of Ralph Cioffi and Matthew Tannin has been the only criminal proceeding by the federal government against major players in the face of the economic meltdown. During a congressional hearing on the collapse of the investment bank Lehman Brothers, Texas Democrat Al Green sounded a note that reflects a common public belief that a platoon of Wall Street thieves were never going to have to face criminal charges for what they had done. Green put it this way: "My concern is that no one has been arrested. It's about as close as you can get to fraud."

Green's choice of words is telling. "As close as you can get" may not be enough to persuade a jury to a finding of guilt when the standard is "beyond a reasonable doubt."

The Cioffi-Tannin trial is instructive. The jury of eight women and four men took nine hours to reach a verdict. They did not buy into the declaration regarding the defendants: "If you are trusted with other people's money," the prosecutor said, "you can't defraud them." She said the two men acted like "masters of the universe" and "thought the laws and rules applied to everyone else but them."

Questioned by the media after they delivered their verdict, two jurors offered sound bites that suggested they saw the case as the government picking on two relatively minor Wall Street players while the big fish went unattended. "They were scapegoats for Wall Street," indicated one of the jurors; while another asked rhetorically, "How much can two men do?"—this a puzzling remark given the awful harm that at various times one person alone has inflicted on others throughout human history.

Nonetheless, the two Bear Stearns men still faced civil charges where the standard of proof was lower—the need to show liability by a preponderance of evidence. Perhaps in anticipation of a civil judgment, Cioffi had put his house in Southampton on Long Island up for sale at a price of $11,875,000, about $2 million more than he had paid for it two years earlier.

Nonetheless, both men were acquitted in a three-week jury trial in late 2009. The jury based its verdict on a judgment that the defendants had made poor investment decisions but that doing so did not constitute a criminal offense. A member who talked with the media indicated that the jury had found the evidence against the defendants flimsy and contradictory—in part, of course, because some of the stronger evidence, as noted in Document 12.2, could not be placed before the jury.

For cynics, it was the skill of the top-notch, well-paid lawyers, the poise and appearance of the defendants, and the complexity of arcane economic matters that was largely responsible for the not-guilty verdict. Others agreed with the idea that investments inevitably constitute a risky enterprise and that losers should grin and bear it—well, they need not grin if they did not feel like it but they had to bear it.

The earliest major investment bank meltdown had involved the collapse in March 2008 of the New York-based Bear Stearns, a company founded in 1923 that had become the fifth-largest institution of its kind in the United States. Bear Stearns had never, until then, registered a quarterly loss, and ironically it only recently had been honored by *Fortune* as the "most admired" securities firm, based on employee talent, the quality of risk management, and its business innovations. But by 2008, Bear Stearns's risk management team, while taking home spectacular paychecks, had run up a $1.5 billion company debt. As one onlooker observed: "The holy grail of investment banking had become increasing short-term profits and short-term bonuses as the expense of long-term health of the firm and its shareholders." There was so much money to be made as the housing bubble continued to expand before it burst. Greed readily trumped prudence.

Prodded and aided by federal subsidies, Bear Stearns merged with JPMorgan Chase, which paid

$10 for a share that once had sold at a high of $177.69. It did not escape the public and most certainly people and entities that owned Bear Stearns stock that the company's assets had been bled by a magnificently compensated management team that had engaged in reckless and irresponsible conduct. One commentator, playing on the Wall Street theme of bulls and bears, noted that the five top executives of Bear Stearns paid themselves more than the entire roster of the Chicago Bulls during the same year that the Bulls won the National Basketball Association championship.

From a white-collar crime perspective, perhaps the most telling observation was made by the son of a former managing partner of Bear Stearns in a comment on the culture of the firm: "Few came honest," he said. "None leave honest." The board meetings at Bear Stearns were so scripted that the minutes often were written out in advance and directors were asked to read from prepared comments. One observer noted: "It became a dictatorship as opposed to a corporation."

FURTHER READINGS

Bumber, Bill, and Andrew Spencer. (2009). *Bear Trap: The Fall of Bear Stearns and the Panic of 2008*. New York: Black Tower Press.

Cohan, William D. (2009). *House of Cards: A Tale of Hubris and Wretched Excess on Wall Street*. New York: Doubleday.

Goodman, Laurie S., Shuman Li, Thomas A. Zimmerman, and Douglas Lucas. (2008). *Subprime Mortgage Credit Derivatives*. Hoboken, NJ: Wiley.

Greenberg, Alan C. (2010). *The Rise and Fall of Bear Stearns*. New York: Simon & Schuster.

Kelly, Kate (2009). *Street Fighters: The Last 72 Hours of Bear Stearns, the Toughest Firm on Wall Street*. New York: Portfolio.

Mallaby, Sebastian. (2010). *More Money than God*. New York: Penguin.

Tavakoli, Janet M. (2003). *Collateralized Debt Obligations and Structured Finance: Developments in Cash and Securitization*. Hoboken, NJ: Wiley.

Countrywide Financial

- **Document:** The U.S. House of Representatives' investigation of Countrywide Financial pinpointed the crimes and sins that had marked the company's engagement in lending practices that led to the great economic meltdown. Document 12.3 also takes note of the dubious dealings between Countrywide and members of the Senate and other government officials.
- **Date:** March 19, 2009.
- **Where:** Washington, DC.
- **Significance:** The document provides information and an official judgment on the activities undertaken by a major lending company that demonstrated a pattern of wrongdoing that characterized the catastrophic crisis in the financial world at the end of the first decade of the twenty-first century.

DOCUMENT 12.3

Executive Summary

- With Countrywide-originated loans serving as the fuel and Government-Sponsored Enterprises (GSEs) Fannie Mae and Freddie Mac [two agencies that insured housing loans: both were shown to have operated irresponsibly] acting as a furnace, the alliance of the companies created an enormous fire that eventually consumed the American economy. Many of the people in a position to reform the GSEs and extinguish the flames before the danger spread were receiving perquisites from a VIP loan program operated by Countrywide under the supervision of Chairman and CEO Angelo Mozilo.

These included Fannie Mae Chief Executive Franklin D. Raines and two Senators with legislative jurisdiction over the issues at the heart of the emerging financial crisis—Christopher Dodd and Kent Conrad.

- ...Countrywide dispersed favors to VIPs who it believed might be worthwhile to the company. The group of borrowers included legislators, congressional staffers, lobbyists and other opinion leaders. Countrywide also distributed benefits to business partners, local politicians, homebuilders, entertainers and law enforcement officials. Countrywide's voice was heard in the debate on Capitol Hill about reforming the GSEs. When reform was considered by the 108th Congress, Members publicly expressed faith in Fannie and Freddie. Congressman Barney Frank (D-Ma), for example, described them as "not facing any kind of financial crisis." He was wrong.

- Countrywide's VIP loan program was a tool with which the company built relationships with Members of Congress and Congressional staff. It was also a tool it used to protect its relationship with Fannie Mae. Some Countrywide officials as well as the company's lobbyists openly and explicitly weighed the value of relationships with personally influential borrowers against the cost to Countrywide in terms of forfeited fees and payments. Preferential treatment for these potentially influential borrowers, the most important of whom were referred to internally as "Friends of Angelo," was part of an expansive effort by Countrywide to "ingratiate [Countrywide] with people in Washington who might help the company down the road."

- Countrywide loan officers waived fees and knocked off points for VIP borrowers at no cost, amounting to thousands of dollars in savings for them. For VIPs, Countrywide fast tracked the loan process and ignored their own documentation policy. Countrywide customers ordinarily paid hundreds of dollars in upfront fees. Not the VIPs. Regular customers paid one percent of the total amount of the loan to reduce the interest rate by one point. But not the VIPs...

- Borrowers whose loans were processed by Countrywide's VIP loan unit were aware they received preferential treatment. Countrywide VIP account executive Robert Feinberg testified VIP loan officers explicitly communicated to "Friends of Angelo" they were receiving special pricing and preferential treatment. Documents obtained by the Committee confirm this. VIP borrowers were informed Angelo Mozilo priced their loans personally...

- Accepting the discounts made exclusively available to "Friends of Angelo" violated applicable ethical rules for certain VIP borrowers. Senate rules prohibit acceptance of loans at discounted rates not available to the general public. The Fannie Mae Code of Conduct applicable to directors and executives bars any gift made in order to influence behavior, especially when accepting such a gift appears to create a conflict of interest.

- Involvement in the VIP loan program casts a cloud of suspicion over the actions—or in many instances non-actions—of those charged with policymaking, legislative, or oversight responsibility for the mortgage industry and the GSEs. The scope and intent of the "Friends of Angelo" and other VIP programs at Countrywide Financial Corporation represent a systematic attempt by the mortgage giant to gain favor from those entrusted to protect the public through oversight and regulation of the home mortgage industry.

Findings

- … Countrywide's Washington lobbyist Jimmie Williams identified influential borrowers for VIP treatment. Williams justified his referrals to the director of the VIP program by explaining the borrower's position and how he or she could be valuable. Among others, Williams referred the Chief Counsel to the House Financial Services Housing and Community and Opportunity Subcommittee Clinton Jones, HUD Secretary Alphonso Jackson's daughter Annette Watkins, U.S. Rep. Melvin Watts Chief of Staff Joyce Brayboy, and former Democratic National Committee official and Director of White House Political Affairs under President Clinton Minyon Moore.

Conclusion

- Countrywide CEO Angelo Mozilo originated a deliberate and calculated effort to establish relationships with key participants in the GSE-reform debate by affording decision-makers and other influential opinion leaders preferential mortgage loan terms. The effort was successful.
- His friends … in many instances returned the favor. In Congress, for example, legislation adverse to Countrywide's interests was blocked. At Fannie Mae, Chief Executive Franklin D. Raines—a "Friend of Angelo"—adopted strategies that assisted the continued growth of Countrywide …
- The gift and disclosure rules applicable to Congress do not merely prohibit quid pro quo exchanges of gifts in exchange for specific action. The rules prohibit accepting any gifts to avoid the appearance of quid pro quo expectation. The rules are restrictive because the stakes are high. In this case, the health of the American economy was at stake.
- We now know the economy was not adequately protected by some of the very people who could have made a difference—several influential "Friends of Angelo."

Source: Friends of Angelo: Countrywide's Systematic and Successful Effort to Buy Influence and Block Reform, United States House of Representatives, Staff Report, Committee on Oversight and Government Reform, 111th Congress, March 19, 2009.

ANALYSIS

Investment companies kept failing as the effects of the great economic meltdown kept snowballing. Countrywide Financial Corporation (CFC), which at its height financed one out of every five American home loans, had to be rescued with a $4 billion takeover (or, as some put it, a "takeunder") purchase by the Bank of America in the summer of 2008. Founded in 1969, Countrywide's stock had risen 23,000 percent between 1982 and 2003, largely as a result of its involvement with subprime mortgages. As Adam Michaelson, a Countrywide senior vice president, would subsequently note, Countrywide's "system of loans, and Refis [refinances] awarded to anyone with a pulse was, in retrospect, long-term madness driven by short-term profit." Michaelson described Countrywide as "a profit-hungry corporate beast." Countrywide's stated mission was to "Help All Americans Achieve the Dream of Home Ownership." Unstated were two other elements of that mission: "At a Magnificent Profit for Us" and "Without Being Concerned that They Could Readily Lose Their Home Ownership."

The financial hanky-panky by Countrywide executives resulted in charges by the SEC and the Department of Justice in 2009. The most prominent of those cited was Angelo Mozilo, who had cofounded CFC and was its chief executive officer and chairman of the board of directors. Mozilo had worked in his father's butcher shop in the Bronx when he was 10 years old and would tell audiences that his family had been unable to afford a home and that his goal at Countrywide was to see to it that other Americans could realize a goal that his own family had been unable to achieve.

The Department of Justice charged Mozilo with insider trading and securities fraud for an alleged failure to disclose CFC's lax lending standards in its annual report. Mozilo himself between 2005 and 2007, when he was or should have been well aware that his company was in dire trouble, had sold some of his own shares for a profit of $125 million. In a press release, the SEC portrayed Mozilo as a man who bet the chips of investors on ever crazier schemes while quietly accumulating personal wealth.

The case against Mozilo was largely based on the discrepancy between his public statements about the health of CFC and the private messages he had dispatched to insiders regarding the true condition of the subprime loans that were massacring the company's profit-and-loss statements. One internal e-mail read: "In all my years in the business I have never seen a more toxic product." In another he wrote: "Frankly I consider that product line to be the poison of our time."

Then there was the "Friends of Angelo" scandal whose parameters are set out in Document 12.3. Prominent politicians, including Christopher Dodd, chair of the Senate Banking Committee, and Kent Conrad, chair of the Senate Finance Committee, were given sweetheart loans by CFC that waived fees and carried especially low interest rates. Dodd had gotten a mortgage on houses in Washington, DC, and Connecticut that was $75,000 less than it would have been under normal conditions.

A Senate Ethics Committee investigation found no wrongdoing on Dodd's part except that he should have "avoided the appearance that you were receiving preferential treatment based on your status as a senator." That very mild rebuke seems shameful; perhaps it was predicated on Dodd's announcement that he would not run for reelection, a decision undoubtedly triggered in some measure by a wave of constituent disapproval regarding his dealings with Countrywide.

The *New York Post* reported that Mozilo and his codefendants had hired a brigade of 19 lawyers to mount their defense and that at least indirectly American taxpayers would foot the estimated $50 million attorney fees. The Bank of America, which had received $40 billion in bailout money, had agreed when taking over CFC that for six years it would be responsible for any legal expenses incurred by the company and its officers. In mid-2010, the Bank of America settled the civil suit against Countrywide with a payment of $108 million.

DID YOU KNOW?

A Countrywide Victim

The story of Edward Jordan, a retired postal worker living in New York City, puts a human face on predatory Countrywide tactics. Jordan was close to paying off his home when a broker told him that he was paying altogether too much interest on his loan. She offered him a 1 percent rate. Jordan refinanced his home, ending up with a fee of $20,000 for doing so. He soon found that the interest rate would quickly escalate to a high of 9.9 percent. Charles Morris, who discusses the case in his *The Two Million Dollar Meltdown*, says bluntly about the Jordan scam: "On any construction of the deal, he was robbed by Countrywide."

FURTHER READINGS

Bruck, Connie. (2009, June 29). "Angelo's Ashes: The Man Who Became the Face of the Financial Crisis," *The New Yorker*, 46–55.

Michaelson, Adam. (2009). *The Foreclosure of America: The Inside Story of the Rise and Fall of Countryside, Home Loans, the Mortgage Crisis, and the Default of the American Dream*. New York: Berkley Books.

Morris, Charles R. (2008). *The Two Trillion Dollar Meltdown: Easy Money, High Rollers, and the Great Credit Crunch* (Rev. ed.). New York: Public Affairs.

Muolo, Paul, and Mathew Padilla. (2008). *Chain of Blame: How Wall Street Caused the Mortgage and Credit Crisis*. Hoboken, NJ: Wiley.

American International Group

- *Document:* Document 12.4 is a letter from the Secretary of the Treasury, reprinted in a report issued by a committee of the U.S. House of Representatives. The bonuses paid by Wall Street firms to their employees fueled a sense of public outrage when details of the amounts given to top executives became a matter of public knowledge during the economic crisis. These extraordinary sums were seen as being subtracted from assets that properly belong to shareholders and to customers in the form of reduced prices. Document 12.4 is one of the rare detailed accounts of how much one company—in this case, AIG—distributed in the form of bonuses. The document maintains that AIG used the bonuses in order to keep the best and the brightest of their managers and staff in the firm; given the meltdown one may well ask how bright a person needs to be in order to participate in the loss of billions of dollars.
- *Date:* October 14, 2009.
- *Where:* Washington, DC.
- *Significance:* The document provides detailed insight into an important element associated with public reactions to the great economic meltdown.

DOCUMENT 12.4

According to information provided by Ernst & Young, LLP [a limited partner accounting firm], AIGFP [FP stands for Financial Products, the division of AIG that was responsible for its serious problems] retention awards total approximately $475 million and would be distributed over a period of two years. AIGFP retention awards were reportedly not designed to reward employees solely based on performance, and the rewards were not designed to increase with the employee's level of responsibility. Rather, the awards were designed to retain all AIGFP employees who would wind down the complex trades and/or continue AIGFP's general operations. Approximately half of the total retention awards were distributed among 400 employees in two installments: nearly $69 million in retention awards in December 2008 and approximately $168 million in March 2009. According to AIG officials, individual awards paid in March 2009 ranged from $700 for one File Administrator to more than $4 million for one Executive Vice President, with total awards divided across total award recipients averaging just over $400,000. Within that range AIG's data indicates that award amounts varied greatly. For example, $7,700 was awarded to one Kitchen Assistant, $59,500 to one Assistant Vice President, and $980,000 to one Managing Director. Approximately 62 percent of the AIGFP employees received retention awards of greater than $100,000, according to data provided by AIG. The retention awards paid in March 2009 range from as little as 1 percent of a recipient's base salary to as great as 36 times base salary. Awards paid in March 2009 averaged 2.5 times total base salary . . .

CONCLUSIONS

When . . . officials began examining AIG's executive compensation structure after making substantial loans to AIG in the fall of 2008 [the loan amount was $40 billion], they found a complex, decentralized system consisting of more than 630 separate compensation and bonus plans covering more than 50,000 employees and involving expected payments of more than $1.75 billion. . . .

Looking forward, legitimate concerns exist over large bonus and retention payments to corporate employees of organizations that are now supported by large-scale financial assistance from the Federal Government, particularly at firms such as AIG, which, but for the Government's extraordinary intervention, would be in bankruptcy . . .

Source: Extent of Federal Agencies' Oversight of AIG Compensation: Varied and Important Challenges Remain, Special Inspector General for the Troubled Asset Relief Program, SIGTARP—10-002, printed in *AIG Bonuses* Hearing, U.S. House of Representatives, Committee on Oversight and Government Reform, October 14, 2009.

ANALYSIS

AIG was the largest insurance company in the United States and the 18th-largest public company in the world. It had a colorful background, having been founded in Shanghai in China in 1919 by Cornelius Vander Starr, a young expatriate American who, among other things, correctly presumed that a fortune could be made by insuring Chinese on the basis of then-current estimates of longevity because improved hygiene and other amenities would enable them to live a good deal longer in the future. The company opened a branch in New York in 1929 that insured only risks to Americans working or traveling overseas, but in 1939, with the Japanese targeting China, it relocated its offices in New York City.

Maurice Raymond Greenberg, nicknamed Hank Greenberg after a popular former Detroit Tigers home run slugger, subsequently ran AIG for 37 years, the longest term of any contemporary leader of a major American corporation. In time, Greenberg's personal holdings of AIG stock were worth more than $3 billion, placing him 47th on the *Fortune* magazine's roster of the richest Americans. One of Greenberg's working maxims was: "All I want in life is an unfair advantage." He was forced to resign as AIG's chief executive officer in 2005 when the company admitted intentionally giving false information to regulators and misrepresenting earnings. The board of directors turned against Greenberg when it learned that he planned to take the Fifth Amendment against self-incrimination when called to testify before a congressional committee.

In August 2009, Greenberg and Howard Smith, AIG's former chief financial officer, paid $15 million to the SEC to settle the charge that they had misstated the financial condition of the company. Had the truth been revealed, AIG would have failed to meet key earnings and growth targets.

For people interested in the dynamics of white-collar crime, it was noteworthy that Greenberg did not admit guilt (but why else would he pay the financial penalty?) and insisted that had he been charged criminally for securities fraud he would have fought the case rather than settle. This view might be regarded as a piece of evidence favoring the view that the most effective tactic against white-collar offenders is a criminal charge. Corporate bigwigs find notably onerous and oppressive the stigma associated with a criminal label, while a financial penalty can be written off as not more than the relatively small price of doing business—especially monkey business. Earlier, four former executives of General Reinsurance Corporation (often called General Re), a reinsurance company, and one AIG executive were convicted, following six days of jury deliberation, of inflating AIG's reserves by $500 million, thereby boosting AIG's stock price. Christian Miller, head of AIG's reinsurance division, received a four-year prison term.

AIG had been deeply involved in the credit derivative market. Warren Buffett, the second-richest man

DID YOU KNOW?

The AIG St. Regis Gathering

Two AIG actions epitomize the belief that large organizations such as AIG exist in a world spectacularly different from that inhabited by more ordinary people and entities.

The first was an eight-day company "outing" for favored employees that took place at the St. Regis Monarch Beach Resort in Dana Point, California, just five days after the company accepted billions of dollars in taxpayer money. The total cost of the boondoggle came to almost half a million dollars (excluding airfares to the site) and included $135,000 for hotel rooms (an ordinary St. Regis room is priced at $425 a night plus tax; an ocean-view room at $565), $147,301 for banquets, and $23,380 for spa treatments. The company's response to revelations of the celebration is worth noting. It read:

> This type of gathering is standard practice in the industry and was planned a year in advance of the Federal Reserve loan to AIG. We recognize, however, that even activities that have long been considered practice may be perceived negatively. As a result, we are reevaluating various aspects of our operation in light of the new times in which we operate.

The defense that something is acceptable because everybody else in the industry is doing it and has been for some time might be viewed much the same as a burglar saying that his thievery is fine because all the burglars he associates with are persistently engaged in the same activity. The statement that AIG will be thinking twice about continuing the enormously expensive indulgence is grudging, as evidenced by the phrase "may be perceived" rather than a flat-out admission that the spending orgy was inexcusable.

The second episode involved the expenditure by AIG of $165 million in bonuses. The top payout to one person was $6.4 million, while 73 employees received at least 1 million dollars each. The action led to comments in Congress that AIG was like an Alice in Wonderland business, that its behavior was surreal and demonstrated unbridled greed, that the bonuses boggled the mind, and that they rewarded incompetence.

in America (Bill Gates of Microsoft is the richest), has called derivatives "weeds priced as flowers" and branded them "financial weapons of mass destruction." Financier Felix Rohatyn similarly described derivatives as "financial hydrogen bombs, built on personal computers by twenty-six-year olds with MBAs." Derivatives, complex packaging deals, became the hottest thing around in the investment world. Because of their risky nature, they paid hefty commissions to sellers. AIG, besides its exposure to derivative losses, was discovered to have placed reinsurance funds with companies that it misrepresented as independent but that actually were owned by AIG. In the fall of 2008, the government bailed AIG out of its dire liquidity crisis to the tune of $173 billion. The government thereby came to own nearly 80 percent of the company.

FURTHER READINGS

Goodman, Laura S., Li Shumin, Thomas A. Zimmerman, and Douglas J. Lucas. (2008). *Subprime Mortgage Derivatives*. Hoboken, NJ: Wiley.

Shelp, Ronald K., and Al Ehrbar. (2009). *Fallen Giant: The Amazing Story of Hank Greenberg and the History of AIG*. Hoboken, NJ: Wiley.

Lehman Brothers

- *Document:* The bankruptcy of Lehman Brothers following its failure to attract a government bailout or to entice other firms—such as Barclays Bank of England—to purchase them spurred Congress to launch an inquiry into what had gone wrong. Document 12.5 presents the opening remarks of Henry Waxman, the chair of House of Representatives Committee on Oversight and Government Reform, which sought to determine the dynamics of the Lehman Brothers collapse.
- *Date:* October 6, 2008.
- *Where:* U.S. House of Representatives.
- *Significance:* The distinctive fate of Lehman Brothers raised intriguing questions regarding why it had not been rescued and what the consequences of this neglect might prove to be. The government's persistent position that it was necessary to use vast sums of taxpayer money to fend off even worse economic consequences if they did not aid failing companies was a core issue in the congressional hearings on the singular fate of Lehman Brothers.

DOCUMENT 12.5

Opening Statement of Rep. Henry A. Waxman

On Friday, Congress passed a $700 billion rescue package for Wall Street. This was something no member wanted to do. If Wall Street had been less reckless or if federal regulators had been more attentive, the financial crisis could have been prevented.

But we voted for the $700 billion rescue because the consequences of doing nothing were even worse. The excesses on Wall Street had created a credit freeze that threatened our entire economy.

Media and pedestrians gather in front of the Lehman Brothers headquarters in New York, on September 15, 2008, the day the 158-year-old financial firm filed for bankruptcy. (AP/Wide World Photos)

The $700 billion rescue plan is a life-support measure. It may keep our economy from collapsing, but it won't make it healthy again.

To restore our economy to health, two steps are necessary. First, we must identify what went wrong. Then we must enact real reform of our financial markets . . .

Today's hearing examines the collapse of Lehman Brothers, which on September 15 [2008] filed for bankruptcy, the largest bankruptcy filing in American history.

Before the Lehman bankruptcy, Treasury Secretary Paulson and Federal Reserve Chairman Bernanke told us our financial system could handle the collapse of Lehman.

It now appears they were wrong. The repercussions of this collapse have reverberated across our economy. Many experts think that Lehman's fall triggered the credit freeze that is choking our economy and made the $700 billion rescue necessary. Lehman's collapse caused a big money market fund to "break the buck," which caused investors to flee to Treasury bills and dried up a key source of short-term commercial paper. It also spread throughout the credit markets, driving up the costs of borrowing.

Over the weekend, we received the written testimony of Richard Fuld, the CEO of Lehman Brothers. Mr. Fuld takes no responsibility for the collapse of Lehman. Instead, he cites a "litany of destabilizing factors" and says: "In the end, despite all our efforts, we were overwhelmed."

In preparation for today's hearing, the Committee received thousands of pages of internal documents from Lehman Brothers. Like Mr. Fuld's testimony, the documents portray a company in which there was no accountability for failure.

In one e-mail exchange from early June, some executives from Lehman's money management subsidiary, Neuberger Berman, made this recommendation.

Top management should forgo bonuses this year. This would serve a dual purpose. Firstly, it would represent a significant expense reduction. Secondly., . . . it would send a strong message to both employees and investors that management is not shirking accountability for recent performance.

The e-mail was sent to Lehman's executive committee. One of its members is George H. Walker, President Bush's cousin, who was responsible for overseeing Neuberger Berman. Here's what he wrote to the executive committee: "Sorry team. I'm not sure what's in the water at 605 Third Avenue today . . . I'm embarrassed and apologize."

Mr. Fuld also mocked the Neuberger suggestion that top management should accept responsibility by giving up their bonuses. . . .

Another remarkable document is a request submitted to the compensation committee of the board on September 11, four days before Lehman filed for bankruptcy. It recommends that the board give three departing executives $20 million in "special payments."

In other words, even as Mr. Fuld was pleading with Secretary Paulson for a federal rescue, Lehman continued to squander millions on executive compensation.

Other documents obtained by the Committee undermine Mr. Fuld's contention that Lehman was overwhelmed by forces outside its control. One internal analysis reveals that Lehman "saw warning signs" but "did not move early/fast enough" and lacked "discipline about capital allocation."

In 2004, the Securities and Exchange Commission relaxed a rule limiting the amount of leverage that Lehman and other investment banks could use. . . . That proved to be a temptation the firm could not resist.

At first, Lehman's bet paid off. As Mr. Fuld's testimony recounts, Lehman achieved "four consecutive years of record-breaking results" between 2004 and 2007.

These were lucrative years for Lehman's executives and Mr. Fuld. Lehman paid out over $16 billion in bonuses. Mr. Fuld himself received over $30 million in cash bonuses. His total compensation during these four years exceeded $250 million.

But while Mr. Fuld and other Lehman executives were getting rich they were steering Lehman Brothers and our economy toward a precipice.

Leverage is a dangerous double-edged sword. When it works—as it did from 2004 to 2007—it magnifies investment gains. But when assert values decline—as the subprime market did—leverage rapidly consumes a company's capital and jeopardizes its survival.

Mr. Fuld's actions during this crisis were questionable. In a January 2008 presentation, he and the Lehman board were warned that the company's "liquidity can disappear quite fast." Yet despite this warning, Mr. Fuld depleted Lehman's capital reserves by over $10 billion through year-end bonuses, stock buybacks, and dividend payments.

In one document, a senior executive tells Mr. Fuld that if the company can secure $5 billion in financing from Korea "I like the idea of aggressively going into the market and spending 2 to 5 in buying back lots of stock . . . This action would have burned through even more capital. Mr. Fuld's response: "I agree with all of it."

What's fundamentally unfair about the collapse of Lehman is its impact on the economy and the taxpayers. Mr. Fuld will do fine. He can walk away from Lehman a wealthy man who earned over $500 million. But taxpayers are left with a $700 billion bill to rescue Wall Street and an economy in crisis.

Risk-taking has an important role in our economy. But federal regulators are supposed to ensure that these risks don't become so large they can imperil our entire economy. They failed miserably. The regulators had a blind faith in the market and a belief that what was good for Mr. Fuld and other executives on Wall Street was good for America. We are now all paying a terrible price.

We can't undo the damage of the past eight years. That's why I reluctantly voted for the $700 billion rescue plan. But we can start the process of holding those responsible to public account and identifying the reforms we need for the future.

These are the goals of today's hearing and the other hearings we will be holding this month.

Source: Henry Waxman, Opening Statement, *Causes and Effects of the Lehman Brothers Bankruptcy*, U.S. House of Representatives, Committee on Oversight and Government Reform, Hearing, October 6, 2008.

ANALYSIS

The rescue operation that bailed out irresponsible investment houses came to a momentary halt when Lehman Brothers went broke. Richard Posner, a federal judge with a strong background in economics, has observed that the government "decided to allow Lehman Brothers to slip into bankruptcy, a decision yet to be explained, that looms as the single biggest blunder to date in response to the gathering storm." In the language of crime, the situation might be regarded as murder or, at least, negligent manslaughter. Another, perhaps more realistic appraisal would label the demise of Lehman Brothers as suicide.

Lehman Brothers had been founded in the 1850s by three brothers from Bavaria as a dry goods store and cotton trader in Montgomery, Alabama. The company moved to New York in 1868 and grew to be the country's fourth-largest investment bank. In 2007, in dire financial straits, it failed to find a buyer and was allowed by the government to go under. Lehman Brothers had been fudging its balance sheet, inflating its financial position by accounting chicanery, and was short $650 billion. The casino capitalism of Lehman Brothers was aided and abetted by the rating agencies, which gave top scores to the company's toxic holdings. A pair of observers had their idea about what was up at the rating agencies: "Maybe it was something spectacularly dishonest, like taking that colossal amount of fees in return for doing what Lehman and the rest wanted, given those [bonds] an utterly undeserved rating."

Lehman also played fast and loose with its accounting practices. For instance, it created a firm called Hudson Castle that appeared to be an independent business but was an alter-ego of Lehman, with a board of directors controlled by Lehman and a staff stacked with former Lehman employees. Hudson operated beyond the reach of bank regulators and enabled Lehman to exchange investments for cash and to make their earnings appear healthier.

An important element of the unwillingness of the government to come to the rescue of Lehman as it had with other entities lay in the company's culture. Lehman Brothers, led by Richard S. (Dick) Fuld Jr., was an insular organization, lacking close contact with the other Wall Street players and internally riven. Fuld operated his fiefdom as if he were engaged in a war with competitors rather than as an enterprise in which they could jointly become fabulously wealthy. He was dubbed the "gorilla" because he tended to grunt rather than to speak in full sentences, and he told his underlings: "Every day is a battle. You've got to kill the enemy." To make his point, he handed out plastic swords to staffers. For his own part, Fuld had taken home some $480 million during the six years before 2007 and owned six houses, including a 20-room mansion in Greenwich, Connecticut.

The vastness of the Lehman Brothers empire can be realized by the fact that after it had to evacuate three floors of the World Trade Center when the building was destroyed on September 11, 2001 (one Lehman employee was killed), it rented offices throughout Manhattan, including 650 rooms in the Sheraton Hotel, so that it could continue operating.

When Lehman Brothers had been torpedoed so that it could no longer rip off those with whom it did business, vultures swooped down from the nearby office skyscrapers to have themselves an exceedingly healthy meal on the corpse. In a story headlined: "Who Knew Bankruptcy Paid So Well? *New York Times* reporters in May 2010 noted that firms dealing with the resolution of the Lehman Brothers bankruptcy had billed for $263,000 in photocopying bills in four months. One firm partner had run up a $2,010 limousine tab in a single month. Someone else had charged $48 merely to leave a message. In September 2008, the New York law firm Weil, Gotschal & Manges paid a car-service company more than $500 a day while, as the reporters put it, "limo drivers cooled their heels waiting for meetings to break (and this in a city overflowing with taxis)." It was estimated that the fees commanded by those involved in dealing with the Lehman debacle could readily exceed $1 billion.

DID YOU KNOW?

William Black on Liars' Loan Operations

A former federal prosecutor with a PhD in criminology presented what the media labeled a "scorching" indictment of the manner in which Lehman Brothers had acted and the way the authorities had reacted. William K. Black had handled the case of William Keating in the infamous savings and loan scandals (see Chapter 5) and now was an associate professor of economics and law at University of Missouri–Kansas City School of Law.

Testifying in April 2010 before the House Financial Services Committee, Black noted that he had not heard any blunt words during the previous hours of testimony before the committee and that he intended to remedy that situation. "Lehman's failure," Black said, "is a story in large part of fraud" involving "subprime and liars' loan operations." He told the committee that "Lehman was the leading purveyor of liars' loans in the world." Black maintained that the SEC could not have dealt with such fraud by continuing business as usual, but that they had done business as usual, and were now dealing in excuses. On that point, he said: "The SEC, we're told they've only 24 people in their comprehensive program. Who decided how many people there would be in the comprehensive program? The SEC did. To say that we only had 24 people is not to create an excuse—it is to give an admission of criminal negligence. Except it's not criminal, because you're a federal employee."

FURTHER READINGS

Auletta, Ken. (1985). *Greed and Glory on Wall Street: The Fall of the House of Lehman Brothers*. New York: Random House.

Fishman, Steve. (2008, December 1). "Burning Down His House: Is Lehman's CEO Dick Fuld the Villain in the Collapse of Wall Street, or Is He Being Sacrificed for the Sins of His Peers?" *New York* 29:39–48.

McDonald, Lawrence G., and Patrick Robinson. (2009). *A Colossal Failure of Common Sense: The Inside Story of the Collapse of Lehman Brothers*. New York: Crown.

Tibman, Joseph. (2009). *The Murder of Lehman Brothers: An Insider's Look at the Global Meltdown*. New York: Brick Tower Press.

Ward, Vicky. (2010). *The Devil's Casino: Friendship, Betrayal, and the High Stakes Games Played inside Lehman*. Hoboken, NJ: Wiley.

Goldman Sachs

- **Document:** Blogging Stocks is an organization that tracks stocks and events on Wall Street. They posted an insider's interpretative view of the dynamics of the Goldman Sachs case that is missing from news reports that rely primarily on official, legal filings and the comments of the prosecutor and the attorneys and public relations figures representing those being charged.
- **Date:** April 16, 2010.
- **Where:** BloggingStocks.com.
- **Significance:** Document 12.6 provides the context and an appraisal of the meaning of the SEC filing against Goldman Sachs.

DOCUMENT 12.6

Chasing Value: Goldman Sachs Fraud Charges Creates Opportunity

It always amazes me how "group think" sways the market to do stupid things, or at least jump to foolish conclusions.

Today it was announced that Goldman Sachs (GS) had been charged by the Securities and Exchange Commission with defrauding investors alleging that they knowingly misstated and omitted key facts about securities tied to sub prime mortgages during the rupturing of the housing bubble when they structured and marketed a synthetic collateralized debt obligation (CDO) tied to the performance of sub-prime residential mortgage-backed securities (RMBS).

The SEC says Goldman "failed to disclose to investors vital information about the CDO, most notably that "a major hedge fund played in the portfolio selection process and the fact that the hedge fund had taken a short position [that is, had bet that it would lose value] against the CDO."

The stock is down dramatically from yesterday's close $184.27, trading between $155 and $160 a share . . .

Looked at another way, the stock has lost over $12 billion in value or capitalization based on investor reaction to the Federal charges. But this makes no sense to me, and might create a buying opportunity in what some would say was already an undervalued stock.

Let's consider some facts. If Goldman is found guilty it will pay a severe penalty. Before it is found guilty, several years may pass. It is in Goldman's best interest financially and in terms of its sullied reputation to do it. If the government is intent on making an example of Goldman, they will prosecute this case to a final judgment. I do not believe that this matter can be resolved in the near future unless there is a compromise between the parties that in today's fog may not be easy.

What are the potential financial costs to Goldman Sachs? Let's start by remembering that the largest fine ever paid by any institution was the recent $160 million paid by Washington Mutual, now a part of J. P. Morgan Chase (JPM) for its admitted guilt in laundering foreign drug money.

So what if Goldman Sachs is found guilty as charged and has to pay five times that figure, or $800 million. What if it had to pay 10 times the largest award of all time, or $1.6 billion. It will mean nothing. To get some perspective, looking back to January—"*Despite a record 2009, the bank announced that it had set aside only $16.2 billion to reward its employees.*"

I guess if it is forced to pay the largest fine by a magnitude of 1,000 it might mean cutting the bonus pool by 10%. This is laughable, so you see why I say this may be a buying opportunity. Why should the market slap Goldman with a $12 billon (or more) haircut because they left some change on the counter for the guy that sweeps the floor?

Source: Sheldon Liber, "Chasing Value: Goldman Sachs Fraud Charge Creates Opportunity," BloggingStocks.com, April 16, 2010. http://www.bloggingstocks .com/2010/04/16/chasing-value-goldman-sachs-opportunity/.

ANALYSIS

Goldman Sachs even before its heavily publicized problems had been described by *Rolling Stone* as "a great vampire squid wrapped around the face of humanity." When it was alleged to have committed fraud in its securities trading, an English newspaper, the *Daily Telegraph*, wrote that the company was "admired, envied, feared, despised and hated in equal measure" and that it was "too powerful for anybody's good." The revelation of their double-dealing was said to reinforce the burgeoning suspicion among the public that the Wall Street game is rigged, the odds heavily stacked in favor of the banks and investment companies and against investors.

There were a number of particularly unusual twists involved in the charges by the SEC in April of 2010 against the Goldman Sachs investment firm, a big money maker that was at the center of power on Wall Street, in a case in which Fabrice

Tourre, a Goldman vice president, was also charged. "Fabulous Fab" (as he called himself in an e-mail to a friend) was described by *New York Times* op-ed columnist David Brooks as a person who "seems to be the product of the current amoral Wall Street culture in which impersonal trading is more important than personal service to clients, and in which any product you can sell to some poor sucker is deemed to be admirable and O.K." Commentators presumed that the SEC's strategy was to convince Tourre, no more than a middle-level manager, to implicate higher-ups in the company who, all reports indicate, took an active role in overseeing the maneuvers that he carried out in regard to CDOs.

Unlike the companies we have discussed earlier in this chapter, Goldman did not lose money and have to go hat in hand to try to persuade government authorities to provide large sums to keep them from going belly up. Goldman made money, but it was how it accomplished that feat that got it into trouble. As one outsider saw the Goldman Sachs behavior that drew the charges from the SEC: "This is way beyond recklessness. This is beyond incompetence. This is cynical, selfish exploitation." Nighttime comedian Jay Leno also took a shot at Goldman: "Well, the government said today Somali pirates being held in U.S. custody will be brought home to the United States for prosecution and they will be tried by a jury of their peers," Leno told viewers, adding: "So I'm guessing, that's what, Goldman Sachs?"

In addition, Goldman's alleged wrongdoing did not produce an official reaction until the dust had cleared in regard to the other companies in the same kind of business. Goldman was charged after these companies had repaid some of the funds given them, and, infuriatingly for many people, were again paying out strikingly large bonuses to their top executives.

The fact that Goldman chose to contest the SEC allegations rather than settle by paying the financial penalty being sought was contrary to common practice. Virtually every solvent organization charged by the SEC prefers to pay what is asked, request that it be made clear that they neither deny nor admit the accuracy of the allegations, and get that matter out of the way. They want to avoid being in the limelight

DID YOU KNOW?

Scapegoat or Scamp?

The naming of only Fabrice Tourre in the SEC charges against corporate Goldman Sachs illustrates the intricate game and the often unscripted drama that attend high-profile cases such as this alleged white-collar crime.

Tourre, 31 years old, claimed to descend from a prominent French family. He was described as "a slight man with a flair for salesmanship," and said to be something of a party animal. He held a degree in mathematics from the highly regarded École Centrale in Paris and had earned a master's degree in operation research at Stanford University. He was a middle manager in the Goldman Sachs New York office and personally responsible for many of the subprime maneuvers involving his company and John Paulson, but nobody seriously doubted that persons higher up in the organization were perfectly aware of what he was doing. That he himself knew he was on thin ice is reflected in an e-mail that he dispatched to a friend in which he said: "The whole building is about to collapse anytime now ... [I am] the only potential survivor standing in the middle of all these complex, highly leveraged, exotic trades [I] created without necessarily understanding all the implications of these monstrosities!!!"

Testifying before a Senate committee investigating what went on in Goldman Sachs, Tourre was asked by Republican Susan Collins of Maine whether he had written an e-mail indicating that he preferred to sell stocks that he knew were bad risks to less sophisticated investors because they were more gullible. "This sounds like a deliberate attempt to sell your product to less-sophisticated clients who would not understand the product as well so that you could make more money," Collins maintained, and then asked Tourre: "Would you like to comment on that?"

But Tourre would not respond directly to the question, a tactic also adopted by other Goldman Sachs witnesses when confronted with demonstrated charges. Senator Collins complained to the committee chair that what she was getting from Tourre was irrelevant talk that ate up the time each senator had to quiz him. He had been well coached.

Tourre had moved to the Goldman Sachs office in London in 2008 with an exalted title—but a position still in middle management. His yearly salary was 1.5 million pounds (about $2.24 million) and his monthly rent for an apartment some $4,500.

In early 2010, Goldman Sachs announced that an internal investigation had found that Tourre had done nothing wrong and that he had taken a "bit of a leave" of absence. The company stressed that the leave decision was entirely personal, not the result of its pressure. An analyst noted that this scenario was dictated by the fact that had Goldman Sachs coerced the leave, it would have been admitting that Tourre was guilty of at least some infraction. And to turn its back on him ran the risk for Goldman Sachs that he would implicate higher-ups in the company in the wrongdoing.

At the same time, Goldman Sachs positioned itself to sacrifice Tourre as a scapegoat, if necessary. A press release noted that the core of the SEC allegations was that "one of our employees" had misled two professional investors. The release subtly blames Tourre for the entire affair without saying he had done anything wrong.

as a possible wrongdoer for the lengthy period of time that a trial typically consumes—even if they believe that they are likely to beat the rap. But, contrary to common procedure, Goldman was not offered settlement negotiations prior to the public announcement of its alleged malfeasance. It then vigorously denied the allegations. "The SEC's charges are completely unfounded in law and fact," it claimed, promising to contest them and defend the firm and its reputation.

Goldman's maneuvers were arcane and complex, but they can be summarized in a somewhat simplified manner by noting that they played both ends against the middle—the middle being the unsuspecting customers who were cajoled into purchasing toxic housing equities, time bombs ready to explore. Their seller, Goldman Sachs, made profits on the sales, and then bet against what they had marketed by wagering that the housing market would collapse. They profited on this investment as well. But they were charged with having failed to disclose that the CDOs they were peddling to investors such as foreign banks, pension funds, and insurance companies were being shorted by John A. Paulson, a billionaire, who was betting that the bonds would sharply decrease in value. Paulson had urged Goldman to market the CODs that he believed were doomed to hemorrhage. He was also instrumental in choosing the bonds that Goldman sold and, according to the SEC complaint, he selected those most likely to fail. Paulson paid Goldman $15 million for creating and marketing the CDO that went under the name of Abacus 2001-ACI. As writer Gregory Zuckerman would point out, Paulson's personal take amounted to more than $10 million a day, "more than the earnings of J. K. Rowling, Oprah Winfrey and Tiger Woods put together."

Investors were said by the SEC to have lost about $1 billion in the deal. Goldman knew what Paulson, a client of theirs, was doing, and did the same itself, but nonetheless worked hard to unload the CDOs. Paulson personally made a profit of $3.7 billion on the deal in 2007 and an additional $2 billion the following year.

Paulson, a New York native and a graduate of the Harvard Business School, first went to work on Wall Street for Bear Stearns as a junior executive in its investment banking unit. Later he would buy a $41 million home on Long Island to go with his Manhattan residence. Like so many other billionaires throughout American history—the Rockefellers, the Morgans—he has made very generous financial contributions to various organizations, including, ironically, a $15 million donation to the Center for Responsible Lending, which is devoted to providing assistance to homeowners facing foreclosure.

Paulson was not named in the SEC complaint because he had not made misrepresentations to clients of his investment group. A law professor invoked a more direct explanation of Paulson's situation: "He was not devious," she said. "He was smart."

Goldman insisted that it did not know—and could not have predicted—that the bonds it was selling were in jeopardy of suffering a serious downturn in value. The company maintained that its short selling was no more than a reasonable effort to protect itself in the event that the housing market collapsed. Goldman obviously had bet against its clients, but it claimed that this was no more than a sensible business practice in an uncertain market. Paul Krugman, the Nobel Prize–winning economist who writes op-ed columns for the *New York Times*, drew an astringent conclusion from the Goldman Sachs affair: "For the fact is that much of the financial industry has become a racket," wrote Krugman, "a game in which a handful of people are lavishly paid to mislead and exploit consumers and investors. And if we don't lower the boom on these practices, the racket will just go on."

Another critic of the Goldman tactics compared what the company had done to a car dealer who allows an outsider to dismantle some of the safety features in a vehicle and who then takes out a life insurance policy on the car's new owner. The analogy, of course, is not altogether on target: with Goldman Sachs the loss was money; in the hypothetical it was a human life that was put at risk. But from an ethical viewpoint it makes a strong point regarding how some persons regarded Goldman's performance.

FURTHER READINGS

Ellis, Charles D. (2009). *The Partnership: The Making of Goldman Sachs*. New York: Penguin Press.

Fisher, June Breton. (2010). *When Money was in Fashion: Henry Goldman, Goldman Sachs, and the Founding of Wall Street*. Houndsville, Hampshire: Palgrave Macmillan.

McGee, Suzanne. (2010). *Chasing Goldman Sachs: How the Masters of the Universe Melted Wall Street Down —and Why They'll Take Us to the Brink Again*. New York: Random House.

Zuckerman, Gregory. (2009). *The Greatest Trade Ever: The Behind-the-Scenes Story of How John Paulson Defied Wall Street and Made Financial History*. New York: Broadway Books.

DID YOU KNOW?

A Word to Those Who Would Be Wise

Brett Arends, writing in the *Wall Street Journal* in the wake of the revelations about Goldman Sachs's questionable activities, had four lessons that he believed could be drawn from the situation:

1. Never put too much faith in a bank.
   There are few banks that are likely to double-deal the way Goldman Sachs did, Arends says, but nonetheless they are peddling "products that are created to be sold to the public for the benefit of the bank." The lesson: "Don't take too much on trust."
2. Think twice before buying any complicated financial product.
   As a rule of thumb, Arends says, the more complex a product is the worse the deal. He adds that if the problem is not the hidden traps, it is probably the hidden fees.
3. Be wary of investing in something you do not understand.
   Humility and common sense are recommended. You probably will be better off investing in some boring blue-chip dividend stock of a company that sells hamburgers or shampoo.
4. When in doubt . . .
   It is a good idea, the writer recommends, to ask the person selling the stock: "How much of your own money are you putting into this?" The answer could be very revealing.

Source: Brett Arends, "Four Lessons from the Goldman Case," *Wall Street Journal*, May 2, 2010.

13

DOING SOMETHING ABOUT IT

INTRODUCTION

It often takes a disaster to fuel a remedial legislative response. Two recent disasters indicate the spur provided by tragedy for the development of remedies that hopefully will prevent a repetition of what had gone wrong.

In early April 2010, the collapse of a wall in the Upper Big Branch coal mine in West Virginia operated by the Massey Energy Company killed 29 miners and led to stricter safety requirements and more severe penalties for violations of these requirements. Authorities believed that the mine explosion was caused by a buildup of methane, a colorless, odorless gas found naturally in coal seams, and that the mine owners had not taken adequate advantage of detection devices nor responded to numerous citations they had been given by mining inspectors.

Then there was the massive oil spill when the Deepwater Horizon oil rig, operated by British Petroleum, exploded on April 20, 2010, and sank six days later. The oil bed was 5 mile underwater and leaked what would amount to 20,000 barrels of oil each day. The rig was located 50 miles offshore in the Gulf of Mexico, and the oil moved into the Mississippi River delta in Louisiana and then into the shorelines of the states of Mississippi and Alabama, devastating the wildlife and other living things in the coastal regions. The president declared a moratorium on offshore drilling until the cause of the tragedy was determined, and new laws and regulations were put in effect that hopefully would prevent a repetition of the spill. We have seen how the WorldCom economic difficulties provided the impetus for rapid passage of the Sarbanes-Oxley reform measure. The current meltdown triggered enactment of the most sweeping economic reform measure in the United States since the presidency of Franklin Roosevelt in the early 1930s.

This chapter opens with a satirical essay by humorist Art Buchwald, who reflects the understanding that white-collar criminals and crooked corporations are treated very gingerly by the authorities. It then reproduces the testimony by a criminologist before a U.S. Senate subcommittee seeking input on tactics that might most effectively deter future wrongdoing of the kind that led to the horrific economic meltdown that rocked the world markets and pulverized the pocketbooks of the public in 2008 and thereafter. Finally, the chapter provides details and analysis of the reform package that tortuously worked its way into law in the fall of 2010.

A Satirical Jab at White-Collar Crime Enforcement

- *Document:* The nationally syndicated satirical columnist Art Buchwald provides a humorous, but also telling commentary on the common belief that prevailed several decades ago and persists today about the failure of the criminal justice system to take tough measures against white-collar criminals who cause serious financial and physical damage to their victims.
- *Date:* November 20, 1986.
- *Where:* Los Angeles Times.
- *Significance:* The Buchwald column reflects a segment of public opinion that would surface in the wake of the economic meltdown with its call for more effective oversight and tougher penalties for elites who famously enrich themselves by breaking and/or blocking laws that would rein in their injurious acts.

DOCUMENT 13.1

JUSTICE SPECIALS ON WHITE COLLAR CRIME

If you have committed a white collar crime or are thinking of committing one, now is the time to do it. The reason is the Justice Department has run out of gas and is willing to settle with anyone who seems to have gotten into trouble.

Trinka, a lawyer for the American White Collar Crime Defense League, told me that this is the best time for me to make my deal with the government attorneys.

"But I haven't done anything," I protested.

Trinka said, "They'll give you a good deal anyway. I have a client who flies around in a helicopter doing TV commercials telling everyone what a great country this is."

["My client] bilked his stockholders out of a bundle and was fined, given a censure and suspended from playing squash for 10 days."

Aerial view of a building and garden at Alderson federal prison camp. Alderson, located in West Virginia, is said to have some of the nicest amenities, including a softball field. (AP/Wide World Photos)

"What's such a good deal about that?"

"The government agreed not to stop him from doing his helicopter commercials."

"But he manipulated stock. I didn't do anything. Why should I try to make a deal with the government?"

"This is the opportunity of a lifetime. [The Justice Department] will roll over for a white-collar criminal."

"Why is the Justice Department so easy on white-collar criminals?"

"Because they're pro-family. Almost everyone who commits a white-collar crime has a family. Do me a favor, let me go down and talk with them. I know they are in a good mood. What have you got to lose?

"I keep telling you I didn't do anything."

"You know Ivan Boesky? Violated all sorts of laws on the books. They stuck him with a $100 million fine."

"That's a lot of money."

"To you that's a lot of money. To him it's less than what he puts in parking meters every day. Besides, now that he's turning state's evidence there's a rumor the government is doing to redecorate his house in Palm Springs."

"That's fine for Boesky—but I still can't figure what's it to me if I confess to committing a felony."

"It won't be a felony. We'll go see the Justice people and if you act contrite they'll knock it down to a misdemeanor and give you a seven-day cruise on the QE2."

"You're just saying that because you're a lawyer."

"I'm looking after your interests. I've never known white-collar settlements to be so easy to get. We won't see anything like this again."

DID YOU KNOW?

Buchwald v. Paramount Pictures

Art Buchwald's comedic fulminations against the indulgence of white-collar crime turned personal when he subsequently sued Paramount Pictures for what he claimed was the theft of his idea for a feature movie. Buchwald had submitted a two-and-a-half page plot summary tailored for the comedian Eddie Murphy. Paramount had taken an option on the film but let it expire without further action. Then the studio in 1988 produced *Coming to America* starring Murphy and Arsenio Hall. The story line diverged considerably from Buchwald's submission, but he argued that Paramount had been inspired by his original idea and had, as studios do, refined and fleshed it out.

The movie told the story of an African prince—Murphy—from the fictitious country of Zamada who spurns an arranged marriage in his homeland and comes to the New York borough of Queens to seek a bride of his own choice. He finds his quarry working in McDowell's, a prototype of McDonald's, and, after a series of humorous episodes, persuades her to marry him.

Two legal issues were involved in Buchwald's lawsuit that occupied the courts for three years. The first concerned whether the picture was a breach of the contract that he originally had entered into with Paramount. The court ruled in Buchwald's favor. The second concerned payment. Paramount argued that box office receipts for the film were $288 million, and that this amount did no more than allow the studio to break even. The judge found that Paramount used "unconscionable" accounting methods to deprive authors of what should have been their share of the take, that what they did made it mathematically impossible to ever "earn" any money on a movie. The court told Buchwald that he had a legitimate claim against Paramount and that he could pursue it in a tort action, but he decided to settle for a sum that never has been made public.

I was losing my patience. "But I haven't committed a crime."

Trinka said, "Then go out and commit one so you can take advantage of their sale. Let me plead you now."

"No way. Even if you could make a good deal with the feds, I don't want my name in the papers."

"Did I tell you that if you commit a white-collar crime on Wall Street before Christmas they give you a ticker tape parade down Broadway."

"But if I plead guilty to a white-collar crime that I didn't commit, won't the other white-collar criminals get mad at me?"

"Why should they when every American is entitled to equal plea bargaining under the law?"

Source: Art Buchwald, "Justice Offering Chance to Beat White Collar Rap," *Los Angeles Times Syndicate*, November 20, 1986.

ANALYSIS

Art Buchwald's wry observation was but one of the chorus of expressions of concern, at times rising to the level of outrage, at what was seen as the indulgent attitude that law enforcement agencies and the courts have toward white-collar crooks in contrast to the fates of people who commit crimes such as burglary and robbery.

Commentaries from the time period in which Buchwald's column appeared reinforce his observations. In *Public Citizen*, Joan Claybrook wrote that "corporate crime continues apace in America because the government metes out mild penalties in most cases, ignoring the fact that corporate misbehavior is far more abusive of citizens than street crime."

U.S. News & World Report ran a full-page story on July 1, 1985, with the headline "Are White-Collar Crooks Getting Off Too Easy?" and the subhead "Fines, probation—or a 'cushy' prison at the very worst. That's the fate of most corporate wrongdoers."

The *U.S. News* article noted that in recent cases, while corporations had been fined for violations of federal laws, corporate officials escaped any criminal penalties. "Those rare ones who received short prison sentences," it observed, are placed in facilities that "boast more amenities than the average lockup." The prisons that typically house elite white-collar offenders have been dubbed "Club Fed," places to improve your tennis backhand and develop a healthy tan beside the swimming pool. To illustrate its points, the article included a *New Yorker* cartoon that showed a judge sentencing a white-collar criminal. It bore the cut line: "Warrington Trently, the court has found you guilty of price-fixing, bribing a government official and conspiring to act in restraint of trade. I sentence you to six months in jail suspended. You will now step forward for the ceremonial tapping of the wrist."

FURTHER READINGS

Buchwald, Art. (1993). *Leaving Home: A Memoir*. New York: Putnam.

Buchwald, Art. (2006). *Too Soon to Say Goodbye*. New York: Random House.

O'Donnell, Pierce, and Dennis McDougal. (1992). *Fatal Subtraction: The Inside Story of Buchwald v. Paramount*. New York: Doubleday.

Testimony to a Senate Committee on the Meltdown

- *Document:* Congressional committees in the United States often solicit persons with various views on proposed legislation to present those views in public hearings so that the legislators can learn how opponents and proponents evaluate different suggested legal approaches to a matter of public importance. Document 13.2 reproduces the testimony of Professor Henry N. Pontell of the Department of Criminology, Law and Society, University of California–Irvine, an academic specializing in the study of white-collar crime, about what he believes should be done to help curb such crime. The Senate committee was chaired by Arlen Specter, a former Pennsylvania prosecutor, who would soon thereafter be defeated for reelection in a primary election.
- *Date:* May 4, 2010.
- *Where:* U.S. Senate.
- *Significance:* The document presents the views of a scholar who was the coauthor of an authoritative book on the savings and loan debacle regarding tactics that might be employed to reduce the disastrous practices that led to a global economic crisis.

DOCUMENT 13.2

White-collar and corporate crimes impose an enormous financial burden on citizens, and it must be appreciated that they constitute a more serious threat to the well-being and integrity of our society than traditional kinds of street crime. As a Presidential Commission put the matter, "White-collar crime affects the whole moral climate of our society. Derelictions by corporations and their managers, who usually occupy leadership positions in their communities, establish an example which tends to erode the moral base of the law ... "

There are several major themes that I want to address in this brief presentation.

First, I want to support the infliction of criminal penalties on white-collar and corporate criminals who violate criminal laws. To do so requires that the Congress enact further legislation that imposes criminal sanctions on financial actions that have been demonstrated to seriously harm the public and are known to produce such consequences by their perpetrators. The current spate of financial sanctions is no more than an additional and mildly bothersome cost of doing business.

Second, I want to emphasize that persuasive anecdotal evidence indicates that particularly for potential white-collar offenders the prospect of criminal penalties can be effective deterrents. There is no definitive empirical evidence to prove this—to mount a satisfactory experiment on the subject would violate ethical standards. But we know that upper-class businesspersons fear shame and fear incarceration and will attend to credible threats of such consequences if they knowingly break the law; they are par excellence rational calculators.

Third, I would endorse the notion that regulatory agencies, most notably the Securities and Exchange Commission, be empowered to mount criminal prosecutions with internal personnel. Too often inter-agency agendas that must be negotiated between an agency and the Department of Justice inhibit effective deterrent responses to white-collar and corporate crime.

Fourth, I believe the public is growing increasingly restive about the failure of the criminal law to be tied to the crimes of those who engaged in them. The war on drugs snared a vast horde of financially marginal people. There has been no similar war on financial thugs. Cynics suggest in fact that imprisoning some of the Wall Street malefactors might help to upgrade the way prisons are run. To make a decisive move toward deterring fraud in the higher echelons of business, a significant influx of enforcement resources is necessary to allow investigators and prosecutors to bring major cases. Representative Marcy Kaptur has proposed legislation to do just this with H.R. 3995, the "Financial Crisis Criminal Investigation and Prosecution Act."

Much remains to be criminally investigated and dealt with in regard to the widespread financial frauds in the mortgage industry and on Wall Street, the failure of regulatory oversight, the continued general reluctance and slow response by government to identify white-collar and corporate crimes, particularly those acts constituting insider, or "control frauds."

A central concern about white-collar and corporate crime is that the risk-reward ratio is out of balance—that is, potential rewards greatly outweigh the risks. Given the low probability of apprehension and the likelihood of no, or light punishment, white-collar crime is seen as a "rational" action in many cases. The comparative leniency shown white-collar offenders has been attributed to several factors related to their status and resources including their high educational level and occupational prestige which produces a "status shield" that protects them from the harsh penalties applied with greater frequency to common criminals. White-collar defendants' high incomes and the willingness often of corporations to pay their exorbitant legal expenses with shareholder funds enable them to secure expensive legal counsel, whose level of skill and access to defensive resources is generally unavailable to lower-class defendants. Finally, white-collar crimes frequently involve complicated financial transactions in which the victims are either aggregated classes of unrelated persons, such as stockholders, or large government agencies, such as the IRS. These victims do not engender the kind of commiseration that individual victims of street crimes can elicit from judges and juries.

Empirical evidence supports the leniency hypothesis. A study of persons suspected by federal regulators in Texas and California to be involved in serious financial crimes during the savings and loan crisis of the 1980s revealed that between only 14 percent and 25 percent were ever indicted. The study also examined the sentences imposed in S&L cases involving mean losses of a half-million dollars and found that the average sentence was 3 years—significantly less than the average prison terms handed to convicted burglars and first-time drug offenders tried in federal court.

The U.S. Sentencing Guidelines can enhance penalties for financial crimes based on losses attributable to fraud, the number of victims, whether the fraud involved special skills or sophisticated means, and whether the defendant worked in the investment business or as an officer or director of a public company. Critics argue that such penalties can have a chilling effect on productivity. In fact, some financial writers have labeled past reactions of politicians to corporate scandals as "hysterical," arguing that "penalties for failure are not merely lower earnings, but lawsuits, prosecution, huge fines, and long prison terms." They may be correct about failure causing lawsuits and fines; but they're mistaken about prosecution. Long prison terms are not caused by mere failure; they are caused by serious criminal behavior.

Certainly, the risk-reward ratio is central to capitalism. Economist John Maynard Keynes was a proponent of risk-taking, which he called "animal spirits." Historian Walter A. McDougall maintains that the U.S. economy was built by "scramblers, gamblers, scofflaws, and speculators." But there are many ways to define acceptable risk-taking, and that must be seriously addressed by Congress in terms of outlawing practices that involve blatant conflicts of interest and the willful gaming of regulations in order to gain unfair advantage.

A central problem that underlies deterrent strategies is that despite some high profile cases, the government has trivialized criminal fraud to the point that it is routinely dealt with at the lowest offense levels, and when larger cases are discovered they are more likely to be pursued civilly and not criminally. We can look at a key example in the current crisis. The FBI publicly announced in 2004 that there was likely to be "an epidemic of mortgage fraud," yet Attorney General Michael Mukasey declined to create a task force to investigate the roots of the subprime debacle, while likening the problem to "'white-collar street-crime' that could best be handled by individual United States attorneys' offices." The lack of government response after the alarm had been sounded by federal agents stands in direct contrast to the government's response to the savings and loan crisis; *a financial disaster that was approximately one-thirtieth the size of the one we are currently experiencing.*

Current laws likely fail to deter satisfactorily because white-collar offenders are aware of the absence of vigorous enforcement. The central issue here is *proactive policing.* With most traditional crimes, the fact that an offense has occurred is readily apparent; with most corporate crimes, the effect is not readily visible. Once the offense becomes known, however, apprehending suspects of corporate crime is almost always easier than apprehending those involved in traditional crime. When a house is burglarized or a car is stolen it is often difficult and costly for police to find the thief. If it is discovered that a company engaged in bribery to secure a defense contract, there is no need for police to set up roadblocks or print "Wanted" posters to find the corporate suspect. Unless, of course, the white-collar malefactor packages his ill-gotten gains and heads for a country with which the United States does not have a satisfactory extradition treaty.

Some scholars believe that we do not need "more" regulation; rather, we need "smarter" regulation. Simply applying harsher laws to corporations and individuals, they argue, will only produce a subculture of resistance within the corporate community "wherein methods of legal resistance and counterattack are incorporated into industry socialization." Regulation works best when it is a "benign big gun"—that is, when regulators can speak softly but carry big sticks in the form of substantial potential criminal penalties. . . .

A hierarchical structure of corporate sanctions also has been proposed, in which the first response to misconduct consists of advice, warnings, and persuasion; then escalates to harsher responses culminating in what is termed "corporate capital punishment" or the dissolution of the offending company. The goal of this model is compliance which is understood within a dynamic enforcement routine where enforcers try to get commitment from corporations to comply with the law and can back up their negotiations with credible threats about the dangers they face if they choose to go down the path of non-compliance. The strength of such a system is that it works at multiple levels and holds all the actors involved—executive directors, accountants, brokers, legal advisers, and sloppy regulators—accountable for criminal misconduct.

Besides considering harsher penalties, Congress needs to seriously consider having *chief criminologists and fraud experts as central officers of regulatory agencies*. A fraud analysis should be conducted before any new regulatory legislation is enacted so that we can avoid

---

DID YOU KNOW?

A Proposal for Executive Transparency

Joseph T. Wells, onetime FBI agent and the founder and former chairman of the Association of Certified Fraud Examiners, an organization of 60,000 members headquartered in Austin, Texas, has offered a control strategy to combat corporate crime that he labels *executive transparency*. Wells argues for a law requiring corporate executives to open up their personal bank accounts to scrutiny by auditors and regulators. The rationale is that in many of the high-profile corporate fraud cases, the crime is not discovered until after the money has been spent, often for wildly luxurious and frivolous things. Or, at times, the money is transferred to an overseas bank with stringent secrecy laws or deposited in the name of a relative or friend. Wells cites the huge "loans" Bernie Ebbers of the failed WorldCom gave to himself from the company treasury so that he could buy hundreds of thousands of acres of timberland and the biggest cattle ranch in British Columbia, Canada, as well as a hockey team. The profligate Rigas family used Adelphia funds as their private bank, paying out the money for, among other things, the construction of their own golf course. There were the millions of dollars embezzled by Mickey Monus to finance his personal basketball league; and the grotesque self-indulgence of Dennis Kozlowski of Tyco, among whose notorious purchases was a $15,000 umbrella stand and a $6,000 shower curtain. Wells points out that major corporate fraud cases almost always begin at the top:

> To head off the financial rape of public corporations, I would suggest a law that requires selected company insiders to furnish their individual financial statements and tax returns to independent auditors. They should also sign an agreement allowing access to their private banking information. The data should be available in cases where suspicions arise.

Wells notes that in the four decades that he has spent investigating and auditing fraudsters, he's seen bank presidents making less than six figures in salary who have deposited millions into their checking accounts. Politicians whose crooked bribe takings he unraveled, Wells notes, put the money into a checking account. "What I've never seen," he points out, "is a crooked executive who took the loot and buried it in the desert in the middle of the night."

repeating mistakes of the past which included ignoring both the potential for widespread fraud that acted as an accelerant for rapidly expanding economic bubbles, and the creation of "criminogenic environments" where conflicts of interest and regulatory loopholes allowed opportunities for fraud to flourish with impunity.

Source: Henry N. Pontell, Testimony before the Senate Subcommittee on Crime and Drugs, *Wall Street Fraud and Fiduciary Responsibilities: Can Jail Time Serve as an Adequate Deterrent for Willful Violations?* Senate Judiciary Committee, May 4, 2010.

The Financial Reform Law of 2010

- *Document:* After high-powered jockeying among the leaders of the political parties and the expenditures of vast sums of money by lobbyists, on May 20, 2010, by a vote of 59 to 39, the U.S. Senate passed the most extensive rewriting of the laws governing financial markets in almost three-quarters of a century. The vote was almost totally along party lines. Only four Republicans voted for the measure and two Democrats opposed it. In a statement on the White House lawn, President Barack Obama hailed the accomplishment.
- *Date:* May 20, 2010.
- *Where:* The Rose Garden of the White House.
- *Significance:* The President's remarks conveyed his view of the importance of what the Congress and his administration had achieved and sought to put into context the economic values that the reforms sought to uphold in this controversial landmark legislation.

DOCUMENT 13.3

The White House
Office of the Press Secretary

For Immediate Release   May 20, 2010
Remarks by the President on Wall Street Reform
Rose Garden
4:33 PM: EDT

THE PRESIDENT: Good afternoon, everybody. I want to say a few words on financial reform in the Senate today.

I've said many times that the recession we are emerging from was primarily caused by a lack of responsibility and accountability from Wall Street to Washington. It's part of the reason our economy nearly collapsed. It's what led to countless home foreclosures, the failure of community banks and small businesses, and a cascade of job losses that left millions of Americans out of work. And it's why I made passage of Wall Street reforms one of my top priorities as President—so that a crisis like this does not happen again.

Over the last year, the financial industry has repeatedly tried to end the reform with hordes of lobbyists and millions of dollars in ads. And when they couldn't kill it they tried to water it down with special interest loopholes and carve-outs aimed at undermining real change.

Today, I think it's fair to say that these efforts have failed. Today, Democrats and a handful of Republicans in the Senate have voted to break the filibuster and allow a final debate and vote on financial reform—reform that will protect consumers, protect our economy, and hold Wall Street accountable . . . I want to thank every American who kept the pressure on Washington to change a system that worked better for the banks on Wall Street than it did for families on Main Street . . .

Our goal is not to punish the banks, but to protect the larger economy and the American people from the kind of upheavals that we've had in the past few years . . .

Because of Wall Street reform, we'll soon have in place the strongest consumer protections in history. If you ever apply for a credit card, a student loan, or a mortgage, you know the feeling of signing your name to pages of barely understandable fine print. It's a big step for most families, but one that's often filled with unnecessary confusion and apprehension. As a result, many Americans are simply duped into higher fees and loans they just can't afford by companies that know exactly what they are doing.

Those days will soon end. The bill will crack down on predatory practices and unscrupulous mortgage lenders. It will enforce the new credit card laws we passed barring unfair rate hikes. And it will ensure that every American receives a free credit score if they are denied a loan or insurance because of the score . . .

[T]he American people will never again be asked to foot the bill for Wall Street's mistakes. There will be no more taxpayer-funded bailouts—period. If a large financial institution should ever fail, we will have the tools to wind it down without endangering the broad economy. And there will be new rules to prevent financial institutions from becoming "too big to fail" in the first place, so that we don't have another AIG.

Because of reform, the kinds of backroom deals that helped trigger the financial crisis will finally be brought to the light of day. And from now on, shareholders will have greater say on the pay of CEOs and other executives, so that they can reward success instead of failure, and help change the perverse incentives that encouraged so much reckless risk-taking in the first place . . .

And the reform I sign will not stifle the power of the free market—it will simply bring predictable, responsible, sensible rules into the marketplace. Unless your business model is based on bilking your customers and skirting the law, you should have nothing to fear from this legislation . . .

Thanks very much, everybody.

Source: Barack Obama, Remarks by the President on Wall Street Reform, May 20, 2010.

ANALYSIS

For people focusing on white-collar crime and interested in postmortems about its role in the economic collapse, the president's message, typically, is upbeat and future oriented—indicating what will be different. Noteworthy, for instance, is his use in the fourth from the final paragraph of the term "mistakes" for what went on in the boardrooms and on the trading floors of Wall Street firms. Mistakes are unfortunate and usually can be excused: crimes are quite another matter.

Summarizing the history of the reform effort, John Cassidy, the economics specialist for the *New Yorker*, wrote: "As welcome as the reform bill may be no one should think that it alone will prevent further meltdowns. It took twenty-five years of misguided economic theorizing and legislation, along with insufficient regulation, to create an outlaw financial sector. Rehabilitating it will be a mighty, multiyear effort."

The reform bill—or "rewrite," as some preferred to call the measure—was a printed document of some 1,500 pages. The pair of Democrats who voted against it did so because they thought it was not tough enough; the Republican bloc faulted the statute on the grounds that it, to their mind, did not definitively foreclose the possibility of future bailouts and that it imposed altogether too much regulatory interference with the operation of financial markets. For the winning side, Majority Leader Harry Reid proclaimed when the bill was passed by the Senate: "Simply, the American people were saying, 'you've got to protect us,' and we didn't back down from that. When this bill becomes law the joy ride on Wall Street will come to a screeching halt."

These were some of the major stipulations in the finance bill as summarized in the *Wall Street Journal*. The newspaper marked the advent of the reform bill with the headline: "Wall Street Braces for Seismic Changes." The report itself indicated that some persons were predicting that the new bill would cost investment companies 20 percent of their current income. Others disagreed, saying that the bill had enough loopholes that ever-shrewd Wall Street moguls would figure out ways to get around it. If not, some suggested they would likely take the derivative trading business, the major financial activity undercut by the new regulations, overseas. Here are some of the major ingredients of the measure:

1. It established a new council of regulators to evaluate risk with the goal of preventing companies from becoming too big to be allowed to fail, and would halt the creation of financial bubbles that might burst and leave chaos in their wake.
2. It created a consumer protection agency within the Federal Reserve charged with formulating new rules for mortgage lending and the issuance of credit cards.

3. It empowered the Federal Reserve to supervise the largest financial companies to ensure that the government comes to understand the risks being taken that could harm the broader community.

4. It allowed the government in extreme cases to seize and liquidate a failing company in a manner that would prevent taxpayers from future bailouts.

5. It provided regulators with new powers to oversee the derivatives market, increasing transparency by having most contracts traded through third parties instead of only between banks and their customers. Defaults on derivatives, which are contracts that allow people to make financial bets, had contributed significantly to the economic meltdown. Derivatives allow companies to hedge risks. If, for instance, soaring fuel prices have the potential to bankrupt an airline, it can buy a derivative that pays off if fuel prices jump.

6. The bill seeks to upgrade the performance of credit-rating companies whose misjudgment of the value and risk of mortgage securities produced disastrous results. Greater leeway is afforded bond holders to sue raters such as Standard and Poor's. In addition, rather than have a bond issuer choose what organization will rate the bond, thereby creating a conflict of interest, an investor-led board overseen by the SEC will make the rating assignment.

For consumers, the bill limited penalties for prepayments of mortgages, prohibited real estate agents from receiving higher fees for steering customers to loans with higher interest rates, and made it more likely that businesses will offer discounts to customers who pay with cash rather than by credit card. Before passage of the measure, credit card companies would not deal with outlets that offered discounts for cash payments. Visa and Master Card, which control about 80 percent of credit card transactions, charge as much as 3 percent of the purchase price to the seller and return 80 percent of that to the banks as an incentive to issue more cards. In 2009, businesses paid nearly $20 billion to credit card companies.

FURTHER READINGS

Baker, Dean. (2009). *Plunder and Blunder: The Rise and Fall of the Bubble Economy*. Sausalito, CA: PoliPointPress.

Cooper, George. (2008). *The Origin of Financial Crises: Central Banks, Credit Bubbles and the Efficient Market Fallacy*. New York: Vintage.

Krugman, Paul R. (2009). *The Return of Depression Economics and the Crisis of 2008*. New York: Norton.

Posner, Richard A. (2009). *A Failure of Capitalism: The Crisis of '08 and the Descent into Depression*. Cambridge, MA: Harvard University Press.

Shiller, Robert J. (2008). *The Subprime Solution: How Today's Global Financial Crisis Happened and What To Do About It*. Princeton, NJ: Princeton University Press.

Zandi, Mark M. (2009). *Financial Shock: A 360 Degree Look at the Subprime Mortgage Implosion, and How to Avoid the Next Financial Crisis*. Upper Saddle River, NJ: FT Press.

SELECTED RESOURCES: BIBLIOGRAPHY

REFERENCE WORKS

Specialized Encyclopedias

Gerber, Jurg, and Eric L. Jensen, with Jiletta L. Kubena, eds. *Encyclopedia of White-Collar Crime*. Westport, CT: Greenwood Press, 2007.

Salinger, Lawrence M., gen. ed. *Encyclopedia of White Collar & Corporate Crime*, 2 vols. Thousand Oaks, CA: Sage, 2005.

Wells, Joseph, ed. *Encyclopedia of Fraud*. Austin, TX: Obsidian, 2002.

Bibliographies

Duncan, J. T. Skip, and Marc Caplan, comps. *White-Collar Crime: A Selected Bibliography*. Edited by Marjorie Kravitz. Washington, DC: U.S. Department of Justice, National Institute of Justice, 1980.

Liebl, Hildegard, and Karlhans Liebl. *International Bibliography of Economic Crime*. Pfaffenweiller, Germany: Centaurus-Verlagsgesellschaft, 1985.

Tompkins, Dorothy Louise Campbell Culver, comp. *White Collar Crime: A Bibliography*. Berkeley: Institute of Governmental Studies, University of California, 1967.

U.S. Department of Justice, National Institute of Justice. *Topical Bibliography: White-Collar Crime*. Rockville, MD: National Institute of Justice/NCJRS Reference Department, 1987.

Books

Albanese, Jay S., ed. *Combating Piracy: Intellectual Property Theft and Fraud*. New Brunswick, NJ: Transaction, 2007.

Albanese, Jay S., ed. *White-Collar Crime in America*. Englewood Cliffs, NJ: Prentice Hall, 1995.

Bazley, Tom. *Investigating White Collar Crime.* Upper Saddle River, NJ: Pearson Prentice Hall, 2008.

Benson, Michael L., and Francis T. Cullen. *Combating Corporate Crime: Local Prosecutors at Work.* Boston: Northeastern University Press, 1998.

Benson, Michael L., and Sally S. Simpson. *White-Collar Crime: An Opportunity Perspective.* New York: Routledge, 2009.

Berger, Ronald J. *White-Collar Crime: The Abuse of Corporate and Government Powers.* Boulder, CO: Rienner, 2011.

Blumberg, Paul. *The Predatory Society: Deception in the American Marketplace.* New York: Oxford University Press, l989.

Brightman, Hank J., with Lindsey Howard. *Today's White-Collar Crime: Legal, Investigative, and Theoretical Perspectives.* New York: Routledge, 2009.

Calavita, Kitty, et al. *Big Money Crime: Fraud and Politics in the Savings and Loan Crisis.* Berkeley: University of California Press, 1997.

Chamber of Commerce of the United States. *White Collar Crime: Everyone's Problem, Everyone's Loss.* Washington, DC: Chamber of Commerce of the Unites States, 1978.

Clinard, Marshall B. *Corporate Corruption: The Abuse of Power.* New York: Praeger, 1990.

Clinard, Marshall B. *Corporate Ethics and Crime: The Role of Middle Management.* Beverly Hills, CA: Sage, 1983.

Clinard, Marshall B., and Peter C. Yeager. *Corporate Crime.* 1980. Reprinted with a new introduction by Marshall B. Clinard. New Brunswick, NJ: Transaction, 2006.

Coleman, James W. *The Criminal Elite: Understanding White-Collar Crime.* 6th ed. New York: Worth, 2006.

Conklin, John E. *"Illegal But Not Criminal": Business Crime in America.* Englewood Cliffs, NJ: Prentice Hall, 1977.

Croall, Hazel. *White Collar Crime: Criminal Justice and Criminology.* Philadelphia: Open University Press, 1992.

Dodge, Mary. *Women and White Collar Crime.* Upper Saddle River, NJ: Prentice Hall, 2009.

Ederhertz, Herbert. *The Nature, Impact and Prosecution of White-Collar Crime.* Washington, DC: U.S. Department of Justice, 1970.

Ermann, M. David, and Richard J. Lundman, eds. *Corporate and Governmental Deviance: Problems of Organizational Behavior in Contemporary Society.* 6th ed. New York: Holt, Rinehart and Winston, 2002.

Frank, Nancy and Michael Lombness. *Controlling Corporate Illegality: The Regulatory Justice System.* Cincinnati, OH: Anderson, 1988.

Friedrichs, David O. *Trusted Criminals: White Collar Crime in Contemporary Society.* 4th ed. Belmont, CA: Cengage Wadsworth, 2010.

Geis, Gilbert L. *On White-Collar Crime.* Lexington, MA: Lexington Books, 1982.

Geis, Gilbert L. *White-Collar and Corporate Crime.* Upper Saddle River, NJ: Pearson Prentice Hall, 2007.

Geis, Gilbert L., ed., *White-Collar Criminal: The Offender in Business and the Professions.* 1968. Reprint, New Brunswick, NJ: Aldine Transaction, 2006.

Geis, Gilbert L., et al., *White-Collar Crime: Classic and Contemporary Views.* 3rd ed. New York: Free Press, 1995.

Geis, Gilbert L., and Ezra Stotland, eds. *White Collar Crime: Theory and Research.* Beverly Hills, CA: Sage, 1980.

Glasbeek, Harry. *Wealth by Stealth: Corporate Crime, Corporate Law, and Perversion of Democracy.* Toronto, Ontario: Between the Lines, 2006.

Green, Stuart P. *Lying, Cheating, and Stealing: A Moral Theory of White-Collar Crime.* Oxford, UK, and New York: Oxford University Press, 2006.

Hinterseer, Kris. *Criminal Finance: The Political Economy of Money-Laundering in a Comparative Legal Context.* The Hague, and Boston: Kluwer Law International 2002.

Kim, Michael, and Jonathan D. Cogan. *White Collar Crime: Debtor-Creditor Fraud.* Eagan, MN: Thomson/West, 2009.

Laufer, William S. *Corporate Bodies and Guilty Minds: The Failure of Corporate Criminal Liability.* Chicago: University of Chicago Press, 2006.

Laufer, William, et al. *Debating Corporate Crime.* Cincinnati: Anderson, 2006

Leap, Terry L. *Dishonest Dollars: The Dynamics of White-Collar Crime.* Ithaca, NY: ILR Press/Cornell University Press, 2007.

Levi, Michael, ed. *Fraud: Organization, Motivation, and Control,* 2 vols. Aldershot, Hampshire, UK, and Brookfield, VT: Ashgate, 1999.

Mann, Kenneth. *Defending White-Collar Crime: A Portrait of Attorneys at Work.* New Haven, CT: Yale University Press, 1985.

Nelken, David, ed. *White-Collar Crime.* Aldershot, Hampshire, UK, and Brookfield, VT: Dartmouth, 1994.

O'Sullivan, Julie, ed. *Federal White-Collar Crime: Cases and Materials.* 4th ed. St. Paul, MN: Thomson/West, 2009.

Pearce, Frank, and Laureen Snider, eds. *Corporate Crime: Contemporary Debates.* Toronto: University of Toronto Press, 1995.

Podgor, Ellen, and Jerold H. Israel. *White Collar Crime in a Nutshell.* 4th ed. St. Paul, MN: Thomson/West, 2009.

Pontell, Henry, and Gilbert L. Geis, eds. *International Handbook of White-Collar and Corporate Crime.* New York: Springer, 2007.

Potter, Gary W., ed. *Controversies in White-Collar Crime.* Cincinnati, OH: Anderson Publishers, 2002.

Poveda, Tony G. *Rethinking White-Collar Crime.* Westport, CT: Praeger, 1992.

Punch, Maurice. *Dirty Business: Exploring Corporate Misconduct: Analysis and Cases.* London: Sage, 1996.

Reiss, Albert J., Jr., and Albert Biderman. *Date Sources on White-Collar Law-Breaking.* Washington, DC: National Institute of Justice, U.S. Department of Justice, 1980.

Rosoff, Stephen, et al. *Profit without Honor: White-Collar Crime and the Looting of America.* 5th ed. Upper Saddle River, NJ: Prentice Hall, 2010.

Savelsberg, Joachim J., with Peter Brühl. *Constructing White Collar Crime: Rationalities, Communication, Power.* Philadelphia: University of Pennsylvania Press, 1994.

Schlegel, Kip, and David Weisburd, eds. *White-Collar Crime Reconsidered.* Boston: Northeastern University Press, 1992.

Simpson, Sally S. *Corporate Crime, Law, and Social Control.* New York: Cambridge University Press, 2002.

Simpson, Sally S., and Carole Gibbs. *Corporate Crime.* Aldershot, Hampshire, UK, and Burlington, VT: Ashgate, 2007.

Simpson, Sally S., and David Weisburd. *The Criminology of White-Collar Crime.* New York: Springer, 2009.

Smith, Geoff, et al. *Studying Fraud as White Collar Crime.* New York: Palgrave/Macmillan, 2010.

Sutherland, Edwin H. *White Collar Crime: The Uncut Version.* New Haven, CT: Yale University Press, 1983. With an introduction by Gilbert Geis and Colin Goff.

Vaughan, Diane. *Controlling Unlawful Organizational Behavior: Social Structure and Corporate Misconduct.* Chicago: University of Chicago Press, 1987.

Weisburd, David, et al. *Crimes of the Middle Classes: White-Collar Offenders in the Criminal Courts.* New Haven, CT: Yale University Press, 1991.

Weisburd, David, et al. *White-Collar Crime and Criminal Careers.* Cambridge, UK, and New York: Cambridge University Press, 2001.

Wells, Joseph T. *Occupational Fraud and Abuse: How to Prevent and Detect Asset Misappropriation, Corruption, and Fraudulent Statements.* Austin, TX: Obsidian, 1997.

Wheeler, Stanton, et al. *Sitting in Judgment: The Sentencing of White-Collar Criminals.* New Haven, CT: Yale University Press, 1988.

Wisenberg, Solomon L. *White Collar Crime: Securities Fraud.* Eagan, MN: Thomson/West, 2009.

Zagaris, Bruce. *International White-Collar Crime: Cases and Materials.* Cambridge, UK, and New York: Cambridge University Press, 2010.

INTERNET SOURCES

General

Corporate Crime Reporter

http://www.corporatecrimereporter.com

Resources include a newswire and sample reports. Online materials are highlights drawn from the weekly print newsletter, available by subscription.

Center for Corporate Policy

http://www.corporatepolicy.org/issues/crimedata.htm

Nonprofit public-interest organization promoting corporate accountability. Website offers in-depth coverage of its initiatives on corporate crime and abuse, corporations and the Constitution, executive compensation, and corporate concentration.

Federal Bureau of Investigation

http://www.fbi.gov/about-us/investigate/white_collar/whitecollarcrime

Includes basic information about white-collar crime as well as a list of cases and case histories; fraud prevention overview and information about how to report fraud; common and ongoing scams; major threats; programs within the FBI's WCC unit; a list of wanted criminals.

Internet Crime Complaint Center

http://www.ic3.gov/default.aspx

A partnership among the Federal Bureau of Investigation (FBI), the National White Collar Crime Center (NW3C), and the Bureau of Justice Assistance (BJA). The center receives, develops, and refers criminal complaints of cyber crime. Provides an easy-to-use central reporting mechanism that alerts authorities to suspected criminal or civil violations. For law enforcement and regulatory agencies at the federal, state, and local level.

National White Collar Crime Center

http://www.nw3c.org/

> The nonprofit National White Collar Crime Center (NW3C) provides training, investigative support, and research to entities involved in the prevention, investigation, and prosecution of economic and high-tech crime. Membership consists of law enforcement agencies from all 50 states and four continents.

Blogs

White Collar Crime Prof Blog

http://lawprofessors.typepad.com/whitecollarcrime_blog/

> Edited and maintained by Professor Ellen Podgor of Stetson University College of Law, an attorney, and a research associate from Stetson University. Updated daily with links to news stories, academic articles, and notices of upcoming conferences. Part of the Law Professors Blog Network.

White Collar Crime News

http://whitecollarcrimenews.com

> News stories and opinion. Blog maintained by New Jersey attorney Jef Henninger, who specializes in fraud and other white-collar crimes.

SPECIFIC ISSUES AND TOPICS

Insurance Fraud

Coalition Against Insurance Fraud

http://www.insurancefraud.org/

FBI—Insurance Fraud

http://www.fbi.gov/stats-servicespublications/insurance-fraud

Insurance Fraud Bureau of Massachusetts

http://www.ifb.org/Content Pages/Public/\Default.aspx

International Association of Special Investigation Units

http://www.iasiu.com/

National Insurance Crime Bureau

https://www.nicb.org/

Internet Fraud

Firstgov.gov—Internet Fraud

http://www.usa.gov/Citizen/Topics/Internet_Fraud.shtml

Internet Crime Complaint Center

http://www.ic3.gov

Internet Fraud Watch

http://www.fraud.org/internet/intset.htm

Organized Crime

Dr. Frank Schmalleger's Cybrary—White-Collar and Organized Crime

http://talkjustice.com/links.asp?453053959

Nathanson Centre—Organized Crime and Corruption

http://nathanson.osgoode.yorku.ca/default.htm

Project America—Organized Crime

http:www.project.org/info.php?recordID=164

Securities and Investment Fraud

Financial Crimes Enforcement Network

http://www.fincen.gov/

North American Securities Administrators Association

http://www.nasaa.org

Statistics

FBI—Uniform Crime Reports

http://www.fbi.gov/ucr/ucr.htm

National Archive of Criminal Justice Data

http://www.icpsr.umich.edu/NACJD

SEARCH—National Clearinghouse for Criminal Justice

http://www.search.org

U.S. Bureau of the Census

http://www.census.gov

U.S. Bureau of Justice Statistics

http://www.ojp.usdoj.gov/bjs

INDEX

About the Author

GILBERT GEIS is an emeritus professor in the Department of Criminology, Law, and Society, University of California–Irvine. He is the former president of the Association of Certified Fraud Examiners, an organization of 60,000 members headquartered in Austin, Texas, and recipient of the Edwin H. Suthelrand Award for outstanding research from the American Society of Criminology.